D1605602

Afro-Atlantic Catholics

AFRO-ATLANTIC CATHOLICS

America's First Black Christians

JEROEN DEWULF

University of Notre Dame Press

Notre Dame, Indiana

Library of Congress Control Number: 2022935747

ISBN: 978-0-268-20280-4 (Hardback)
ISBN: 978-0-268-20282-8 (WebPDF)
ISBN: 978-0-268-20279-8 (Epub)

CONTENTS

Acknowledgments   vii

Introduction   1

ONE   Portugal   13

TWO   Africa   35

THREE   The Americas   89

FOUR   The Catholic Roots of African American Christianity   161

Conclusion   207

Notes   211

Bibliography   255

Index   311

ACKNOWLEDGMENTS

This book grew from a number of research projects on the early history of Black performance traditions in the Americas. Starting in 2013 with a project on Pinkster in New York, followed in 2017 with a study of the New Orleans Mardi Gras Indians and in 2018 of the Caribbean calenda, I had come to realize that brotherhoods are a key concept in understanding the cultural and social behavior of Black communities during the era of slavery. This sparked my interest in the importance of brotherhoods to the development of Catholicism in Africa and the way these mutual-aid and burial societies shaped Black Christian identity formation in the Americas.

This research would not have been possible without generous grants provided by the Andrew W. Mellon Foundation, the Luso-American Development Foundation (FLAD), the National Library of Portugal (BNP), the UC Berkeley Committee of Research, and the UC Berkeley Center for Portuguese Studies. Equally important was the financial and moral support that came with the Richard O. Collins Award in African Studies, the Independent Publishers' Gold Medal Award, and the Louisiana Historical Association President's Memorial Award, as well as the New Netherland Institute's Hendricks Award and Clague and Carol Van Slyke Prize for earlier research projects that built the foundations for this book.

I am especially grateful to Robin Derby for allowing me to discuss my research on Black Christian identity formation in the Americas at the 2018 "New Directions in the Study of Black Atlantic Religions" conference at UCLA, to Afe Adogame for his invitation to the 2017 "African Christians and the Reformations" conference at the Princeton Theological

Seminary, and to Cécile Fromont for inviting me to present my work at the 2015 symposium "Afro-Christian Festivals of the Americas" at Yale University. I would also like to thank the Núcleo de Apoio à Pesquisa Brasil-África at the University of São Paulo, in particular Marina de Mello e Souza, for providing me with an opportunity to discuss my research with a select group of Brazilian experts, and to José da Silva Horta and Paulo Fontes who allowed me to do the same in Portugal, at the Centro de História da Universidade de Lisboa and the Centro de Estudos de História Religiosa–UCP respectively.

At my university, I would like to thank the librarians Steve Mendoza, Liladhar R. Pendse, Jeremy Ott, and Claude Potts for their assistance in locating rare materials; my colleagues Larry Hyman and Michel Laguerre for their help with the analysis of a number of sources; and the graduate students Seth Meyer, Adam Nunes, Lauren Dooley, and Derek O'Leary for proofreading earlier versions of the manuscript. My gratitude also goes to Patricia Quaghebeur, for her help in my research of the archives of Jean Cuvelier at the KADOC Documentation and Research Center at the Catholic University of Leuven, to Hein Vanhee for sharing his knowledge on Kongo's Afro-Catholic heritage preserved at Belgium's Royal Museum for Central Africa, to Mark Ponte from the Mauritshuis research project on Dutch Brazil for sharing archival findings on the Black community in seventeenth-century Amsterdam, and to Koen Bostoen from the Kongo-King Research Group at Ghent University for his assistance with sources from Kikongo. Thiago C. Sapede, Michael Douma, Julie van den Hout, Leão Lopes, Inocência Mata, Jürgen Lang, Tjerk Hagemeijer, Ernst van den Boogaart, Carlos Almeida, Ana Lívia Agostinho, Gerhard Seibert, Jean Nsondé, Felix Kaputu, Raissa Ngoma, Afonso João Miguel, and Fernando Mbiavanga provided linguistic information and research materials. My gratitude also goes to my mentor, the eminent historian Luís A. de Oliveira Ramos, as well as Ana Luísa Ramos, Luís Amaral, Adélio Abreu, Hugo Dores, Luís Miguel Carolino, Salwa Castelo-Branco, Jorge Fonseca, Didier Lahon, and Franciscus van der Poel for their assistance with my research on popular Catholicism and confraternities in early modern Portugal. I would also like to express my gratitude to D. Ryan Gray for allowing the reproduction of his photographed image for the book cover.

Portions of this book have previously appeared in chapters 4 and 5 of my book *The Pinkster King and the King of Kongo: The Forgotten History of*

America's Dutch-Owned Slaves (Jackson: University of Mississippi Press, 2017) and chapters 4, 5, and 6 of *From the Kingdom of Kongo to Congo Square: Kongo Dances and the Origins of the Mardi Gras Indians* (Lafayette: University of Louisiana at Lafayette Press, 2017) as well as in the following articles: "Flying Back to Africa or Flying to Heaven? Competing Visions of Afterlife in the Lowcountry and Caribbean Slave Societies," *Religion and American Culture: A Journal of Interpretation* 31, no. 2 (2021): 222–61; "Rethinking the Historical Development of Caribbean Performance Culture from an Afro-Iberian Perspective: The Case of Jankunu," *New West Indian Guide* (2021): 1–31; "Iberian Linguistic Elements among the Black Population in New Netherland (1614–1664)," *Journal of Pidgin and Creole Languages* 34, no. 1 (2019): 49–82; "From Papiamentu to Afro-Catholic Brotherhoods: An Interdisciplinary Analysis of Iberian Elements in Curaçaoan Popular Culture," *Studies in Latin American Popular Culture* 36 (2018): 69–94; "From the Calendas to the Calenda: On the Afro-Iberian Substratum in Black Performance Culture in the Americas," *Journal of American Folklore* 131, no. 519 (Winter 2018): 3–29; "Black Brotherhoods in North America: Afro-Iberian and West-Central African Influences," *African Studies Quarterly* 15, no. 3 (June 2015): 19–38; "Emulating a Portuguese Model: The Slave Policy of the West India Company and the Dutch Reformed Church in Dutch Brazil (1630–1654) and New Netherland (1614–1664) in Comparative Perspective," *Journal of Early American History* 4 (2014): 3–36; and "Pinkster: An Atlantic Creole Festival in a Dutch-American Context," *Journal of American Folklore* 126, no. 501 (2013): 245–71. I thank the publishers for their license to republish parts of these publications in revised form in this book.

All translations in the book are my own unless otherwise indicated.

Introduction

In August 1733, Jacobus van Cortlandt placed a runaway advertisement in the *New-York Gazette* in an attempt to recover a "very black" and "tall lusty fellow" called Andrew Saxon. The latter had been working as a carpenter and cooper, either at the brewery the Van Cortlandts owned or at their wheat plantation in the Bronx, where today's Van Cortlandt Park is. His advertisement used the standardized language of the time, specifying certain physical characteristics of the runaway—Saxon walked "lamish with his left leg" and had a stiff left thumb "by a wound he had in his hand formerly"—language skills—he spoke "very good English"—stolen objects—Saxon took a broadax and other instruments with him—and clothing—he wore a pair of breeches and an old coat—but then the staunchly Protestant Van Cortlandt made a surprising reference to the fact that Saxon "professeth himself to be a Roman Catholic" and that "the shirts he had with him and on his back are marked with a cross on the left breast."[1]

By marking his shirts with a cross, Saxon clearly did not make a secret of his faith. Van Cortlandt's confidence that he would continue to wear these shirts as an escapee shows that it was a meaningful aspect of Saxon's identity. This zeal is all the more remarkable considering the profoundly anti-Catholic sentiment in a state where, only a decade later, rumors of a "popish plot" would lead to the execution of thirty Black and four (Irish) White people.[2]

While his origin is unknown, it is tempting to relate Saxon to so-called Spanish Negroes, Spanish-speaking Black or Mestizo soldiers who had been captured during battles and were subsequently enslaved. Those involved in the 1741 New York Plot proudly identified as Catholic. Significantly, all "Spanish Negroes" arrested in the course of the investigation insisted on being identified in court by their Iberian Catholic baptismal names—not as "Powlis" or "Tony," but as Pablo Ventura Angel and Antonio de St. Bendito. After one of them, Wan de Sylva (Juan da Silva), had been sentenced to death, he made a point of kissing a crucifix on the day of his execution.[3] As the *New-York Weekly Journal* confirmed, da Silva "died steadfastly in the Roman Catholick profession."[4]

It is also possible that Saxon was one of the many enslaved people who had been taken to New York from Caribbean islands such as Jamaica, Antigua, or Barbados. Despite being under English colonial rule, there is evidence that some of the enslaved on these islands identified as Catholic. For instance, when the French Catholic priest Antoine Biet visited Barbados (in disguise) in 1654, he met with a group of Africans, all "very good Catholics," who told him that they "were extremely sorrowed to see themselves sold as slaves in an island of heretics." He concluded that "if some of them received a tinge of the Catholic Religion among the Portuguese, they preserve it the best they can, doing their prayers and worshipping God in their hearts."[5] Saxon may also have come to New York via Curaçao. When Manhattan was still part of the Dutch colony of New Netherland, there had been close relations with this Caribbean island that served as a depot in a network of Dutch Atlantic slave trading operations. Even after the Dutch surrender to the English in 1664, New York families with Dutch roots, such as the Van Cortlandts, tended to maintain good relations with Curaçao. There, too, we find early signs of Catholicism among the enslaved. In 1660, for instance, the Dutch Reformed Church in Amsterdam received a letter from Curaçao, warning that "papists . . . who sometimes arrived here" were baptizing the children of the enslaved.[6] Catholic priests from nearby Venezuela did, in fact, regularly come to Curaçao to baptize newborn children of the enslaved. As a result, the island developed into a religiously segregated society; whereas the enslaved population was Catholic, the slaveholding elite was either Dutch Reformed or Jewish. The fact that enslaved people lived in a colony ruled by Protestants is, thus, no reason to assume that they had had no exposure to Catholicism.

However, Saxon may also have been brought to New York directly from Africa. The Van Cortlandts were closely related to the Philipse family, which since the 1680s had been involved in the transatlantic slave trade. Although Frederick Philipse focused mainly on the Madagascar Trade, he also brought to New York a number of enslaved people from Kongo, a region in Africa with a Catholic history dating back to the fifteenth century.[7] That Saxon may have had Kongolese roots is revealed by the fact that his shirts were marked with a cross. The use of shirts with an embroidered cross was prevalent among Catholics in the Kongo region, where it was a prerogative of those who had been granted knighthood in the Order of Christ.[8] In 1798 the Capuchin Raimondo da Dicomano confirmed that only knights of the Order of Christ enjoyed "the privilege to put lots of crosses made with pieces of cloth in several colors on their capes."[9] As the Portuguese explorer Alfredo de Sarmento observed in 1856, however, this once highly prestigious distinction had become so common that he had the impression that "all or almost all inhabitants . . . are knights in the Order of Christ." They were all wearing "the cross of the order made with pieces of cloth in several colors" or "shave their head and leave only a small plug of hair, which they style in the form of a perfect cross."[10]

If Saxon had, indeed, been knighted in the Order of Christ while living in Central Africa, it implies that he would have made an oath to a Catholic priest, with his right hand placed on the Bible. The priest would then have touched his shoulder three times with a sword, whereupon he would have sworn on the Holy Gospels "to defend our king [and] the Holy Catholic and Apostolic Church, to honor only one God, to assist all priests who come to the Kingdom of Kongo, and to persecute all idols and witchcraft."[11] While we can only speculate whether Saxon became such a "soldier of Christ," it would certainly explain his zeal and Van Cortlandt's surprise about an enslaved man who, in eighteenth-century New York, proudly "professeth himself to be a Roman Catholic."

Saxon's story becomes even more intriguing if we connect him to the city's earliest Black community, or "charter generation," at the time when New York City was still called New Amsterdam. There, not just a handful of individuals, but virtually the *entire* Black population originated from parts of Africa with a historically strong Portuguese influence: the Cape Verde islands, the island of São Tomé, Kongo, and, in particular, Angola.[12] The same predominance of people with roots in the broader Kongo region also characterized the charter generation in South Carolina.[13] If we turn westward to Louisiana, we find that, after the French king Louis XV granted all of the Louisiana territory west of the Mississippi to his cousin Charles III of Spain in 1762, the majority of enslaved Africans brought to the region had roots in Kongo. As Gwendolyn Midlo Hall confirms, "shortly after the Spanish took over, it became heavily Kongo in New Orleans."[14]

This implies that some of the main centers of African American identity formation in the United States share a history to which Africans originating from regions influenced by Portuguese and Catholic culture contributed substantially. It would, naturally, be naïve to assume that all enslaved Africans from those regions professed Catholicism with the same zeal as Saxon. Many, especially those originating from peripheral areas to the north and west of the Kongo kingdom, may have had little or no exposure to Catholicism, and, even among those who originated from the kingdom's heartland, many may have rejected the faith introduced by the Portuguese in the late fifteenth century. It would, nevertheless, be equally naïve to assume that their presence left no marks whatsoever and that African American religious history can be told accurately without taking into consideration the profound influence of Iberian Catholicism in the Atlantic realm, especially during the first two centuries of the transatlantic slave trade.

Large numbers of the earliest sixteenth-century enslaved inhabitants in the Americas had previously lived in the Iberian Peninsula or in heavily Iberianized African societies, such as those of the Cape Verde islands and São Tomé.[15] From the late sixteenth until the mid-seventeenth century, Luanda was the dominant source of America-bound Africans, which Linda M. Heywood and John K. Thornton aptly labeled "the Angolan wave" in the history of the transatlantic slave trade.[16] Considering the Portuguese influence in the Kongo/Angola region, there can be no doubt that many of these enslaved Africans shared familiarity with the Afro-Iberian customs previously introduced by the charter generations. As Joseph Miller has argued, upon their arrival in the Americas, these Central Africans came to live in intimate contact "with predecessors who had arrived in small numbers from backgrounds in slavery in late medieval Iberia";

"particularly those coming through Kongo channels, must have had a useful familiarity with Portuguese Christianity and used it to find places for themselves without relying on the more 'African' aspects of their origins."[17]

In his seminal 1996 article on "Atlantic creoles," Ira Berlin was among the first to emphasize the importance of the charter generations in the history of African American identity formation. Since these earliest enslaved communities often originated from coastal areas, where they had acquired a broad experience of the Atlantic world, they were fundamentally different, he claims, from those rooted in areas further toward the interior of Africa who were brought to America in later centuries. Hence, his decision to label those first generations as "Atlantic creoles."[18] While there is much to criticize about Berlin's article, in particular his controversial use of the concept "creole," his approach was of great importance in drawing scholarly attention to the impact of cross-cultural contacts between Africans and Europeans along the west coast of Africa in the early modern era. Following Berlin, scholars increasingly came to perceive the entire Atlantic basin as an intercultural zone, marked by intra- and extra-African cultural mixtures to which not only Arab Islamic, but also European Christian—predominantly Iberian Catholic—cultural elements contributed substantially. In fact, Berlin acknowledged that no other European nation shaped intercultural contacts between Europeans and Africans in the early modern period more strongly than Portugal. He specified that the multilingual identity of Atlantic creoles "weighted strongly toward Portuguese" and that their religious identity was "usually Catholic."[19]

However, Berlin ended his article on a pessimistic note, pointing out that the gradual transformation of mainland North America from "societies-with-slaves" into "slave societies" submerged the charter generations' descendants "in a régime in which African descent was equated with slavery" and that, as a result of this, "Atlantic creoles were overwhelmed by the power of the plantation order."[20] Unlike Berlin, I do not believe that the importance of charter generations should be reduced to a fascinating though ultimately inconsequential chapter in the history of America's Black culture and identity. Although I agree with Berlin that slave societies in America and the origins of enslaved Africans changed dramatically in the course of the eighteenth century, I do not consider these changes enough reason to assume that North America represents an exception compared to other parts of the Americas, where scholarly research has demonstrated a continuous influence of the foundations led by charter generations. As Sidney Mintz and Richard Price pointed out in *The Birth of African-American Culture* (1965), the earliest generations of enslaved Africans often had a major influence on how Black identity in the region was to evolve. They insisted that the "beginnings of African-American cultures must date from the earliest interactions of the enslaved men and women."[21]

Another important source of inspiration to this book was Thornton's articles "The Development of an African Catholic Church in the Kingdom of Kongo" (1984) and "On the Trail of Voodoo: African Christianity in Africa and the Americas" (1988), which he later expanded into the monograph *Africa and Africans in the Making of the Atlantic World* (1992). In his groundbreaking research, Thornton argued that "the conversion of Africans actually began in Africa" and that this acknowledgment is of crucial importance in understanding the history of Black Christianity. Although "only a limited number of slaves were Christians before their arrival in the New World," the impact of "African Christians was much greater than their numbers." For this reason, "we should consider the conversion of Africans as a continuous process, commencing in Africa and carrying over to the New World."[22]

While Thornton's studies mainly associate traces of African Catholicism in the Americas with Kongo, historical sources reveal that people who became Christian in other parts of Africa with a strong Portuguese influence, such as the Cape Verde islands or São Tomé, lived their Catholic faith in similar ways. They did so in spite of the geographical distance between them and the enormous differences in their respective indigenous cultures, traditions, and cosmologies. This convinced me that the development of Black Christianity in the Americas cannot be properly understood if started in Africa; rather, it should be seen as a process that began in late-medieval Portugal.

Speaking of Portuguese influence in Africa in the early modern era implies that all cultural or social elements were subject to religion. More than any other identity marker, religion was the key concept in Iberian society to distinguish between good and evil, friend and foe. The religion the Portuguese exported to Africa was a militant form of Catholicism, shaped by centuries of war. Not by accident, the caravels that brought Christianity to Africa featured the emblem of the Military Order of Christ on their sails. The Portuguese overseas expansion was a continuation of the *reconquista*, marked by the ambition to find new resources and new allies in the ongoing struggle against the Islamic Empire.

Equally important, however, is the realization that the Portuguese introduced Christianity in Africa before the foundation of the Society of Jesus and the Counter-Reformation. Part of the reason why Portuguese religious influence in Africa has often been underestimated or misunderstood is that scholars have tended to look at it from a post-Tridentine perspective, ignoring that the borders between traditional beliefs and Christianity were still blurred in early modern Iberia. As George Brooks has rightly argued, at that time in history Portuguese and Africans "shared similar beliefs concerning the causes and cures of disease, and in the efficacy of amulets."[23] Early modern Portuguese Catholicism was not only a recognizable religion to Africans, but also allowed the creation of what Cécile Fromont has labeled "spaces of correlation" where African and European thoughts and rituals met and mutually influenced each other, leading to the development of African variants of Catholicism, so typical for the syncretic processes and cross-cultural contacts that characterized the early modern Atlantic world.[24]

Fromont's concept also helps to avoid the pitfall of Eurocentrism. Studies on the globalization of Iberian cultural elements have a long history of sustaining the myth that Spain and Portugal have a glorious colonial history, devoid of oppression and racism. António Brásio, for instance, whose fifteen-volume anthology *Monumenta missionária Africana* (1952–1988) represents an indispensable tool in understanding the historical Portuguese influence in Africa, wrote in the year before the 1974 Carnation Revolution that "whenever he had the privilege of touching a piece of soil that belonged to Portugal's Empire," he felt growing deeply inside him "an inexplicable feeling of intense historical awareness about the greatness, glory, and pride of being Portuguese."[25] Such rhetoric was actively encouraged during the Portuguese dictatorship in an attempt to legitimize the nation's colonial wars in Africa. What it failed to acknowledge was that the globalization of Iberian elements had been anything but the expression of a humanitarian form of colonialism. Rather, this process took place under extremely hostile circumstances, marked by violence, exploitation, and enslavement, for which none other than these Iberian powers bore responsibility. The adoption of Iberian cultural elements by Africans, as such, should be understood not as a sign of friendship, but rather as a conviction that siding with the powerful created new opportunities, increased one's prestige, and made one less vulnerable in a world where only the strongest survived.

Moreover, the African adoption of Iberian elements necessarily implied a process of reinterpretation and reinvention, whereby Catholicism came to be adjusted to local customs and subsequently acquired new meanings. The focus of this study will, therefore, not be on the transmission process of Iberian religious elements as such, but on the new variant(s) that developed out of them. Building on Fromont's conviction that the dissemination of Catholicism in the Kongo region "had an impact well beyond the confines of the central African kingdom where it emerged" since "it traveled to the American continent" and, thus, had an influence that "resonated across the early modern Atlantic," I decided to adopt the term *Afro-Atlantic Catholics* in reference to those Africans who in early modern times embraced Iberian Catholicism, yet adjusted and reinterpreted in accordance with their traditional beliefs and traditions.[26]

This book intends to tell their history: how their Catholic identity was formed in Africa and further developed in the Americas, how they expressed their faith, and what remains of their legacy in North America. Combining the analysis of historical sources with data from anthropological and linguistic studies, I will pay particular attention to "popular" or "folk" Catholicism, with a focus on rituals (baptism, marriage, burial), saint devotion (prayers, cures, ex-votos, vows), social structures (brotherhoods, confraternities), and procession culture. The reason is that Afro-Atlantic Catholics largely lived their faith at the margins of society. Theirs is a Catholic history that was never fully recognized as such. The Church failed to understand their songs and dances as genuine expressions of Christian faith and has a long history of rejecting Afro-Catholic rituals as noise, immorality, and superstitious attempts to corrupt Catholicism with indigenous African elements.

Due to the paucity of sources, any study dealing with African American cultural and religious identity formation is speculative to a certain degree. This is no different in this book. In order to deal with this challenge, I made use of a comparative methodology, placing North America in a broader Atlantic context and comparing North American sources about social, cultural, and religious practices among members of enslaved communities to sources from Africa, Latin America, and the Caribbean. I did so in the conviction that early Black identity formation in North America followed an Atlantic pattern. By questioning the traditional assumption that Black culture developed in fundamentally different ways in the predominantly Protestant North as compared to the predominantly Catholic South of the Americas, I also felt required to correct an Anglo-Saxon bias in the dominant narrative on the development of African American religious history.

This book is divided into four chapters. Since the Portuguese introduced Catholicism in Africa before the Council of Trent (1545–1563), it begins with an overview of the main characteristics of late-medieval Catholicism in Portugal. In this chapter I also pay attention to the policy of the Portuguese authorities with regard to enslaved Africans and to the importance of confraternities in understanding the singularities of Black Iberian Catholicism.

In the second chapter I argue that the pattern thus set in Lisbon was to a large degree followed on the Atlantic islands of Cape Verde and São Tomé, yet with the difference that Portuguese settlers constituted only a small minority of the population. I, therefore, study the development of Catholicism in a broader social and racial context, with a focus on the influential role of Luso-Africans in spreading their own interpretations of Portuguese cultural, social, and religious customs on the islands and along the nearby African coastal areas. I then shift my attention to Kongo, where a different situation existed in the sense that Catholicism was introduced in a nation controlled by Africans who shared a common language, culture, and set of beliefs. I reject claims that Catholicism in Kongo only reached upper classes and had little effect on indigenous customs. Rather, I argue that the variant of Catholicism that developed in Kongo became a crucial element of Kongolese identity.

The third chapter presents an analysis of how African variants of Catholicism transited to the Americas in the context of the transatlantic slave trade. I do so with a focus on the sixteenth century, when the vast majority of Black people came directly from the Iberian Peninsula or via the Portuguese-controlled Atlantic islands; and the late sixteenth to mid-seventeenth century, when the region of Kongo-Angola was the dominant source of America-bound Africans. I show how these enslaved Africans brought a variety of Afro-Iberian elements with them to the Americas and how brotherhoods, in particular, became key institutions in the dissemination and transmission of these elements in Black communities.

While such claims have previously been made about Iberian slave societies, where confraternities flourished with the approval or, at least, the connivance of the Catholic authorities, I demonstrate that church institutions were not always necessary for Africans and their descendants to build mutual-aid societies modeled upon Iberian brotherhoods and that similar fraternal societies also existed in territories under English, French, Dutch, and Danish colonial rule.

The book's final chapter deals specifically with North America and investigates the long-term influence of Afro-Atlantic Catholics on the development of both African American fraternal traditions and evangelical churches. It calls for a revision of the traditional narrative by beginning the history of African American Christianity with a focus on Afro-Atlantic Catholic members in America's seventeenth-century charter generations and argues that the social structures of mutual support established by the latter had a profound impact on the way African American communities would later organize the earliest Baptist and Methodist congregations. It claims that the genesis of Black evangelical churches should not be reduced to a mixture of White Protestant and indigenous African elements. Rather, it highlights the importance of a third source of influence, namely that of fraternal practices rooted in ancient Afro-Atlantic Catholic traditions.

In the classic study *The Catholic Church and the American Negro* (1928), John Gillard's pioneering analysis of Black Christianity from a Catholic perspective paralleled some of the theories presented in this book with regard to the importance of social support in the form of brotherhoods. For instance, when trying to explain the popularity of Baptist churches in the Black community, Gillard pointed out that, there, "the church is the center of social life and intercourse," whereas "it cannot be said that there is anything in the Catholic Church as such which favors the demands of the Negro for a social religion." Gillard, of course, was well aware of the historical importance of confraternities in the Catholic Church but realized that such organizations had long lost their splendor. Despite this sharp insight into a fundamental aspect of Black Christianity, Gillard failed to understand the reasons behind this desire for a "social religion" and lost himself in painful speculations about the "nature" of Black people.[27]

In *The History of Black Catholics in the United States* (1990), Cyprian Davis distanced himself from such speculations but followed Gillard in pointing out the crucial importance of confraternities for the understanding of what he called "Afro-Latin spirituality."[28] Davis was also aware that "the black confraternities are an aspect of black Catholicism that needs further study" and expressed confidence that "more extensive research in this area of black Catholicism will no doubt reveal much more about lay initiative than was formerly known."[29] The same can be said with regard to Black Protestantism, where John Giggie observed in 2011 that the "explicit intersections between fraternal orders and religion [have] been left largely unexplored."[30]

This study not only confirms these statements but also goes beyond them by arguing that the importance of confraternities for the development of Black Christianity should be understood as a process that began in the fifteenth century on the Iberian Peninsula and the African Atlantic islands. This focus on Black brotherhoods will allow me to demonstrate how elements of Iberian Catholicism came to affect the daily lives of people in Africa and how Afro-Atlantic Catholics introduced their own interpretations of them in the Americas, where they were to influence Black religious, social, and, cultural identity formation in the centuries to come.

CHAPTER ONE

Portugal

When the Portuguese diplomat António Pinto da França visited the Indonesian island of Flores in the 1960s, he decided to reach out to the Catholic community in the town of Larantuka. To his surprise, he found out that people there were still saying their prayers in Portuguese. They did so almost four hundred years after the first Portuguese had settled on the island and taken local wives. The fact that Catholicism had thrived in this Eurasian community in the absence of priests intrigued the Portuguese diplomat. Upon further research, he identified the key institution responsible for the remarkable attachment of the population of Larantuka to the Catholic religion: the confraternity of the Rosary Queen, locally known as the Reinha Rosari. Due to the absence of priests, the Catholic community of Larantuka had organized itself in a brotherhood in which Portuguese Catholic rituals had been transmitted over generations, so that, four hundred years after their introduction, the *irmam* (brothers) would still stage processions on Christmas and Good Friday, wearing the traditional *opas* (sleeveless capes) and carrying an *andor* (litter) displaying a Portuguese statue of Our Lady of the Rosary.[1]

While relics of the Portuguese maritime expansion can be found all over the globe, they are often no longer recognized as such. Few people today are aware that the Hawaiian ukulele is derived from the Portuguese *cavaquinho*, that the Indian curry dish vindaloo was inspired by the Portuguese marinade technique *vinha d'alhos*, or that Japanese tempura is based on a Portuguese fritter-cooking technique for vegetables that replaced meat during the quarterly ember days (*quatuor tempora*).

That originally Portuguese elements, when reinterpreted by others, could over time look foreign to even the Portuguese themselves is revealed in the report João Vieira de Andrade sent to the Portuguese King José I in 1762 with a list of concerns about "errors against the Catholic Church" in Santiago. At that time, Santiago was little more than a forgotten island in the Cape Verde archipelago off the coast of Northwest Africa. In the early sixteenth century, however, it had been the hub of a Portuguese trading network that connected sub-Saharan Africa, Europe, and the Americas. The Portuguese auditor was particularly concerned about the mutual-aid and burial societies in Santiago, known as *reinados* (kingdoms). "In all neighborhoods of the island," he wrote, "women and men are elected to serve as kings and queens, who every Sunday and holiday stage parades with their drums and flutes in order to collect money," and, in the evening, "abuse with food and drink and commit the sin of gluttony." Each year, they "have a Mass organized at their kingdom, where they are crowned by the local priest, and in their houses, they build an altar, where they worship." These "most ridiculous exercises," Andrade argued, were "claimed to be Catholic," which he believed to be a lie since these "scandalous abuses, crimes, and transgressions" were undoubtedly "heathenish African customs." Andrade was either not aware or not willing to recognize that many of the practices he deemed "scandalous in the eyes of God" happened to be of Portuguese origin.[2] Their history went back to the early modern era, when a confraternity of Our Lady of the Rosary had been established in Santiago.[3] What Andrade complained about was, in fact, a Cape Verdean variant of the very same organization that Pinto da França later encountered in Indonesia.

While it is well known that Portugal, in the context of its overseas expansion, contributed greatly to making Christianity into a global religion, the crucial role of lay organizations in the dissemination of the religion in Asia, Africa, and the Americas has received surprisingly little scholarly attention. As Francisco Bethencourt confirms, however, the formation of confraternities was "one of the principal processes of transferring European structures to other regions of the world."[4]

Known interchangeably as *irmandades* or *fraternidades*, as derived from the Latin word for brother (*germanus* or *frater*, respectively), these brotherhoods or confraternities were highly influential organizations in late-medieval Portuguese society. Their foundations were laid before the beginning of the Council of Trent (1545) and the foundation of the Society of Jesus (1540), at a time when a large gap existed between the way ecclesiastical authorities envisioned Christianity and how it was understood by the people. It was also a time when the role of the priest was centered upon, and often limited to, performing sacraments. In that era, brotherhoods flourished. It was there that Christians effectively formed a congregation, honored traditions, practiced rituals, and provided solidarity to their brothers and sisters, both living and deceased.

Yet, in the eyes of Church reformers, these organizations were nothing but centers of superstition, gluttony, and corruption that, with their focus on rituals and saint devotion, exemplified everything they abhorred about medieval Christianity. While confraternities, in the aftermath of the Reformation, disappeared in Protestant nations, they remained important in Catholic societies. The emphasis the Tridentine Church placed on the visual aspects of faith, most notably in its procession culture, initially even increased their prestige. However, the reorganization of the Church in the aftermath of Trent limited the leeway to adjust Christianity to one's own reality, and subsequent efforts to bring lay initiatives in line with doctrine had a stifling effect on brotherhoods.[5]

While this evolution fundamentally changed the nature of Catholicism in Europe, the traditional role and prestige of confraternities remained virtually unchallenged in overseas territories with a historically strong Portuguese influence. It would, therefore, be wrong to explain Andrade's unfamiliarity with certain practices "claimed to be Catholic" by the local population in Santiago with reference to indigenous African influences only. We also need to associate them with late-medieval Portuguese customs that had once flourished in confraternities but, in the aftermath of Trent, gradually disappeared in Portuguese society. In fact, the Cape Verdean practices that shocked Andrade would have been perfectly recognizable to fifteenth-century Portuguese.

This conclusion is not unique to the Cape Verde islands. A parallel could be drawn to Portugal's largest colony, Brazil. As Thomas Bruneau writes, "The religion that came from Portugal was not that of the Tridentine reforms"; instead, "it was an earlier model, almost medieval in character."[6] In his classic study on the history of Catholicism in Brazil, Eduardo Hoornaert confirms an "absence of the Tridentine spirit" in the way the vast majority of Brazilians used to live their faith and argues that their Catholicism "was born under the sign of the brotherhoods or confraternities," lay organizations that constituted "a medieval form of Catholicism" and expressed "a popular desire to build community and to resist elitist attempts to be molded into an anonymous mass." The communities that developed in the context of brotherhoods, he claims, "developed as an attempt to safeguard human dignity against the catastrophic consequences of the introduction of the colonial system" and offered the poorest of the poor "as their only, final, dignity a coffin and a decent funeral." The importance of brotherhoods in Brazilian society came under pressure, however, when, in the course of the eighteenth century, Church authorities began to push forward an agenda shaped by a Tridentine understanding of Catholicism. "The more the Brazilian Church became a Roman Church," Hoornaert writes, "the more the brotherhoods lost influence."[7]

This acknowledgment of the importance of confraternities to the development of Christianity in parts of the world with a historically strong Portuguese influence requires a closer look at religious life in late-medieval Portugal. This is all the more important considering that the country had by that time already a relatively large Black community that organized itself in confraternities.

CONFRATERNITIES IN LATE-MEDIEVAL PORTUGAL

Understanding how people in late-medieval Portuguese society lived their lives as Christians represents a challenge because the available sources privilege the view of ecclesiastic authorities rather than what António de Oliveira Marques described as the "complex fusion of beliefs and practices" of the people, "in theory baptized with Christianity but in practice quite remote from it."[8] This assessment by Portugal's eminent historian is problematic as it reiterates the elite's conviction that it has the sole authority to define what and how Christianity is supposed to be. While there can be doubts as to whether certain popular practices corresponded to Church doctrine, no one will dispute that medieval Portuguese considered themselves proudly, even militantly, Christian.

Although they developed at the margins of the Church, lay interpretations of Christianity were, as Oliveira Marques himself indicates, "complex" in nature, which contradicts his decision to reduce them to "superstitious practices" and, subsequently, assume ignorance while claiming that "a great number of Christians grew up with only a scant knowledge of the most elementary precepts of their faith."[9] Considering, for instance, that the use of (pieces of) sacramental bread as an amulet of protection against evil forces was commonly perceived as an expression of Christian faith, it is questionable to categorize this as "superstition."[10] In fact, village priests sometimes encouraged such behavior in the assumption that it could only strengthen people's adherence to the sacraments. By the same token, Oliveira Marques is undoubtedly right in explaining that the "medieval church was not intended to be the place of worship only," since "dances were held [and] short religious dramas and mystery plays [performed]," during which time "people ate, drank . . . spoke loud, argued, and laughed." It is questionable, however, to interpret this as signs that "the man in the Middle Ages did not respect the church as does the modern Christian."[11] To medieval Iberian standards, none of this implied a lack of respect. On the contrary, singing, playing music, and dancing on specific days of the year was perceived as the duty of a good Christian and, thus, not fundamentally different from practices such as praying or fasting.[12] For instance, when their town was infested with grasshoppers, the people of Lousã organized a procession in honor of the Virgin, in which "everybody danced full of joy and jumped in praise of Our Lady, certain in their hearts that they had given her the highest grace."[13] Saints such as Saint Gonçalo, who cured fertility problems, explicitly required dancing, and people did so inside the church, in front of the altar. It was, after all, through music and dance that this saint had lured prostitutes away from their sinful behavior.[14] Not by accident, thus, did the thirteenth-century minstrel João Zorro become known by the phrase "Bailemos, agora, por Deus" (let us dance now, in the name of God).[15] It is true that, long before Trent, Church authorities already opposed such practices. In 1477, for instance, the bishop of Braga attempted to eradicate dancing during Corpus Christi celebrations with the argument that "this is what the heathen do for their dead and dirty idols" and "does not belong in the house of our Lord where everything is clean and holy."[16] It is, however, only in the aftermath of the Council of Trent that such practices were systematically combated.

The importance of music and dance in a late-medieval Iberian context needs to be understood in connection to ex-votos, in the Catholic tradition of expressing gratitude for the fulfillment of a vow. This practice of vowing is essentially a contractual relationship with a saint in the conviction that prayers alone are insufficient to obtain a saint's grace and that the latter requires the fulfillment of a promise. While this could involve a virtually endless range of activities, a common form of "payment" was to honor a saint by participating in the organization and execution of his or her feast, which typically involved some type of performance. There was a firm belief that not honoring one's vows or only doing so halfheartedly could have disastrous consequences, not just for oneself but also for one's relatives, friends, or community. Saints in medieval Portuguese society were attributed human characteristics and were believed to be capable of both good and evil. If they were satisfied with one's dedication, they could be counted upon to provide deliverance. However, saints could be moody, jealous, and vengeful. The still commonly used Portuguese proverb "Santo de casa não faz milagre" (the saint of the house does not make miracles) illustrates a concern in identifying the right saint for the right problem. To know precisely what dance to perform, prayer to recite, song to sing, or sacrifice to make in order to please a specific saint was a complex matter. This was all the more the case if one hadn't given the saint in question adequate attention in the past. In extreme cases, people would promise their own death by offering the saint a *mortalha* (burial shroud) and make a pilgrimage in a coffin that simulated one's funeral procession. By the same token, people who felt that a saint had let them down in spite of adequate dedication would not hesitate to express their anger by shouting insults at or even "punishing" that saint's statue.[17]

All of this does not mean that Oliveira Marques is wrong in identifying the continuous influence of pre-Christian, "pagan" beliefs in late-medieval Portuguese society. As everywhere else in Europe, the form of Christianity that developed in Portugal recycled older beliefs and traditions, some of which had roots dating back to the era of the Moors or even to Roman times.[18] Oliveira Marques mentions, for instance, a royal charter of 1385 listing "grave sins which in this city of Lisbon have been practiced since very ancient times" that included not only references to the use of "fetishes," the casting of an "evil eye," and the making of "cabalistic figures," but also to "the singing of *janeiras*-songs and the pouring of whitewash on doors in honor of Janus."[19]

Attempts by Church authorities to combat such traditions inevitably met with what Nicholas Griffiths has called "popular religious skepticism."[20] Religion is, after all, a social construct. Even if imposed from the top, it is lived by the people, who, as Carlos Rodrigues Brandão has argued, "re-translate" doctrine.[21] Unlike what is often assumed, this process of "re-translation" does not develop haphazardly, without any coordination or leadership. In their own way, lay interpretations of Christian doctrine constitute a logical system. In this respect, brotherhoods were of vital importance. It was there that doctrine was adjusted to people's own experiences and that the teachings and symbols of the Church were given life.

Confraternities were a typical phenomenon of late-medieval Portuguese society. They developed in response to growing urbanization in the late twelfth century, when increasing numbers of people moved to cities. The network provided by a brotherhood served as a replacement for the family connections people had left behind in the village. Thus, it was not by accident that confraternity members addressed each other as "brothers" and "sisters." New members had to pledge allegiance to the brotherhood's statutes or *compromissos*. The latter stipulated the election procedure for the *cabido* (board), which typically included a *mordomo* (chief administrator), *juíz* (judge), *escrivão* (secretary), *tesoureiro* (treasurer), and *andador* (convener). Members paid dues that, together with other sources of income such as alms and legates, were kept in an *arca* (safe box) that, in order to avoid theft, could often only be opened with several keys that were distributed among the board members. Brotherhoods promoted a variety of lay initiatives that fostered the development of rituals that centered on saint devotion, the honoring of the dead, the celebration of liturgical feasts, and charity work.[22]

The latter included an annual *bodo aos pobres* (banquet for the poor) that used to take place inside the church. By the late Middle Ages, however, this tradition came under pressure. In 1477 the bishop of Braga made it clear that "*bodos* should not be organized in church, because God does not appreciate excessive eating, drinking, and all profanities caused by this."[23]

Around that same time, the Crown and Church began to shift charity work to a new network of confraternities under their own control, the Santa Casas de Misericórdia (Holy Houses of Our Lady of Mercy).[24] By the early sixteenth century, King Manuel I went as far as prohibiting brotherhoods from organizing their traditional *bodos*, with the exception of "those dedicated to the Holy Spirit that are organized on the feast of Pentecost."[25] Not by accident, the latter holiday was closely associated with the Misericórdias.

After the Misericórdias assumed control over charity work, the devotional aspect of brotherhoods increased in importance. Each confraternity promoted the devotion of its respective *padroeiro* (patron saint). Members gathered on a weekly basis for prayer sessions known as *ladainhas*, hour-long recitations in call-and-response form. For these the rosary was an indispensable item, since its beads helped to count the devotional repetitions of the Ave Maria, Our Father, and Gloria Patri. In addition to the reciting of prayers, brotherhoods excelled in the singing of *loas* (veneration songs). At the occasion of the patron saint's holiday, they staged a procession that typically included a band, a member carrying the brotherhood's banner, and the board members, wearing their *opas*, some carrying the *andor* with the patron's statue.

The devotional aspect of confraternities also attended to the souls of deceased members. While it would go too far to speak of a cult of the dead, brotherhoods dedicated exceptional attention to funerals. Membership represented a form of death insurance, in the sense that the dutiful payment of fees guaranteed a decent funeral, burial space, and coffin, as well as spiritual attention after one's passing. This dedication to the souls of the deceased coincided with the dissemination of the doctrine of the purgatory, established in the Councils of Lyon (1274) and Florence (1439), as an intermediary place between hell and heaven for those who died in God's grace but were insufficiently purified to achieve eternal salvation. People believed that Christians would only in exceptional cases go straight to hell or heaven and that through manifestations of devotion, penance, and charity, the living could influence the redemption of the souls in purgatory. By assuming these tasks, brotherhoods functioned as intermediaries between the living and the dead.[26]

Because people feared that passing away without confession and viaticum resulted in a tormented soul, there was a great concern to receive the last rites from a priest. Once a person had passed away, the brotherhood ensured that a coffin was provided, the *círios* (wax candles) were lit, and all necessary rituals involving the vigil of the corpse were honored, including the seven or eight days of mourning, during which time friends and relatives joined family members in prayers to commend the dead's soul to God.[27]

In the context of brotherhoods, certain medieval funeral practices continued into the early modern era. For instance, while black gradually imposed itself as the color of mourning by the end of the Middle Ages, some continued to wear white clothing during funerals. Although a royal charter of 1385 had prohibited excessive crying and "tearing and plucking of one's hair in despair over the dead," the presence of *pranteadeiras* or *carpideiras*, professional female mourners, also continued.[28] During his trip to Portugal in the 1460s, the Bohemian nobleman Zdeněk Lev of Rožmitál observed that during funeral processions, women would "cry aloud and tear out their hair and claw their cheeks below the eyes until they bleed and call in other women, whom they pay, to cry and claw with them."[29] Such extreme expressions of sadness during vigils and funerals alternated, however, with joyful moments involving eating and drinking, the playing of music, singing, and dancing.[30] A medieval source from the town of Leiria reveals how members of a local brotherhood preceded a funeral procession while "playing music and dancing," and even at the funeral of King Manuel I in 1521, dancing was part of the program. Dancing was also common at the funerals of children because it was believed that, due to their innocence, they had become a present for the Virgin Mary in the form of little angels.[31]

Besides the annual commemoration of the dead on All Saints' Day and All Souls' Day, brotherhoods typically gathered after the first week, first month, and first year of a member's death. In addition, they organized prayer sessions or *saímentos* (processions with intercessory prayers) for the souls of deceased members. Another task was the completion of vows that had remained unfulfilled in case of a sudden death. It was believed that as long as such a promise remained unfulfilled, the deceased's soul remained "in pain" and, therefore, kept haunting the living. The presence of spirits of the dead in the world of the living is the topic of many Portuguese legends, most notably those of the Santas Companhas (Holy Companies) or Procissões dos Defuntos (Processions of the Dead), nightly processions of tormented souls wandering around in white, hooded cloaks. The latter may have developed out of (authentic) brotherhood processions, mostly at night, to the house of a dying member. They also recall a tradition known as the *encomenda(ção) das almas* (entrustment of the souls), nightly processions with calls for prayers for the souls in purgatory that typically took place during Lent.[32]

This mixing of sacred and profane elements also characterized festive traditions in late-medieval Portuguese society, including Christmas, the Holy Week, Pentecost, Corpus Christi, and the summer festivities in honor of Saints Anthony (June 13), John the Baptist (June 24), and Peter (June 29). As is revealed by their epithets *santos brincalhões* (playful saints), *santos bailadores* (dancing saints), or *santos brejeiros* (impish saints), veneration of the latter was accompanied by extensive merrymaking. The qualification "impish" applied, in particular, to Saint Anthony. The extreme popularity of this Lisbon-born saint dates back to the late Middle Ages, when António was, by far, the most popular name for males in Portugal.[33] As the saint of the soldiers, Anthony was frequently invoked as the protector of defensive structures. He was also venerated for his assistance in recovering lost items. The latter was interpreted broadly, from women praying to Saint Anthony in the hope of bringing an unfaithful husband back home to slaveholders hoping to retrieve an escapee. Since Saint Anthony died on the thirteenth (of June), it was believed that he conceded up to thirteen graces, which also corresponded to the thirteen days of prayer (*trezenas*) leading up to his holiday. More than any other saint, Anthony was believed to be standing close to the people and to be willing to turn a blind eye to the occasional human misstep.[34] Hence also came the tradition of putting pressure on the saint's statue until he fulfilled one's wish. As an example, we could refer to the Italian Capuchin Dionigi Carli, who in his seventeenth-century diary observed how Portuguese mariners "took the statue of Saint Anthony and attached it to one of the masts," then kneeled and said, "Saint Anthony, you who come from our land, will stay there until you give us fair winds to continue our journey."[35]

In spite of Saint Anthony's popularity, it was Saint John the Baptist who typically enjoyed the most boisterous celebrations, with processions and street animation, bonfires that were jumped over, holy baths, and a plethora of rituals and oracles in the realm of love. Since he was Christ's godfather, people assumed that the former owed Saint John obedience, which provided an opportunity to cross moral boundaries during the festivities in his honor. In 1699, for instance, the Franciscan François de Tours noted how, during Saint John celebrations in Braga, a group of masqueraded people entered church with guitars and drums to dance in front of the Holy Sacrament.[36]

An intriguing aspect of late-medieval Portuguese festive traditions in the context of brotherhoods was the emphasis on royal attributes and noble titles. The formation of *impérios* (empires), which involved the election, coronation, honoring, and parading of a "monarch" and his "court," was a popular phenomenon. While these honorific titles could have a satirical character in the context of charivari, such as during the festivities of Saint Stephen on the day after Christmas or the parading and burning of an effigy of Judas Iscariot on Holy Saturday, some groups did, in all seriousness, elect and parade their "emperors," "kings," or "queens" with procedures that imitated authentic coronation ceremonies and involved the blessing of a priest. This was particularly the case during Pentecost celebrations, known as the Festas do Divino Espírito Santo (Feasts of the Divine Holy Spirit). The latter traditionally began on Easter Sunday, when the "empires" paraded through town in a cortege. These parades continued every Sunday until the arrival of Pentecost, when the group's "emperor" offered his crown to God on the church altar. The priest would thereupon crown a new "emperor," whose election was followed by a lavish *bodo*.[37] Research revealed that the Feast of the Divine Holy Spirit was the most celebrated performance on Portuguese ships during the nation's overseas expansion.[38] Historian Jaime Cortesão even argued that Portugal's maritime expansion as a whole was perceived as a "national Pentecost," a desire to create a global Empire of the Holy Spirit.[39]

By the late fourteenth century, the importance of Pentecost as a public event came to be rivaled by Corpus Christi. Corpo de Deus, as the holiday is known in Portugal, was characterized by a spectacular procession that required participation of the entire Christian community. It was typically opened by a float featuring Lucifer and/or a *serpa* (dragon), swarmed with young men dressed as devils, who, covered with little bells and carrying whips, sticks, or inflated bladders, cleared the way. During a visit to Lisbon in 1582, the Spanish King Philip II compared this scene to "an apocalyptic vision," similar to those "in the paintings of Hieronymus Bosch."[40] Behind them, giant puppets paraded along with representatives of brotherhoods and guilds, each with their respective banner, king, or emperor, and each performing a choreographed scene, such as a Moorish dance, a "gipsy dance," a dance of "savages," or a sword dance. Meanwhile, floats presented biblical scenes in *tableaux vivants* that could have an almost carnivalesque character. For example, the float representing the "seven mortal sins" typically included a "fornication dance." The "serious" part of the procession consisted of the religious and military orders and ended with the ecclesiastical authorities escorting the monstrance with the Eucharistic Host, the Corpus Christi or "body of Christ."[41]

Another festive tradition of great importance was the performance of *autos sacramentais*, including the dramatic performance of a battle between good/civilized/Christian and evil/primitive/heathen forces. One such play, typically performed around Christmas, was the *pastoral*. It told the story of a group of shepherds who follow the star of Bethlehem, only to be interrupted by the troops of Herod, Lucifer, or other enemies of Christ, leading to a battle and an intervention by the archangel Michael and his angelic soldiers. A variant was the *reisado,* about the biblical Magi on their way to the infant Christ. In the context of the peninsular wars, yet another variant of this eternal struggle between good and evil developed, known as *Mouros e Cristãos* (Moors and Christians). In this mock war performance inspired by Carolingian mythology, the Moors initially seem to obtain victory but are eventually defeated and forced to bow down in order to be baptized.

Such public performances offered brotherhoods opportunities for fundraising, with members carrying baskets for donations; some of them were stilt walkers, a creative solution to the fact that wealthier families preferred to watch street entertainments from their balconies. More important than financial gains, however, was the opportunity that participation in and attachment to these performances provided to make vows and fulfill one's duty to a saint.[42]

In addition to the major festivals, late-medieval Portuguese society counted innumerable *romarias* or *arraiais*, group pilgrimages to specific shrines that, besides (extreme) acts of devotion, such as the carrying of heavy crosses or stones, also involved the playing of music, singing, dancing, drinking, and merrymaking. Much of this devotion was dedicated to the Virgin Mary. Although Marian devotion was an ancient tradition, it experienced tremendous growth in the fourteenth and fifteenth centuries when hundreds of hermitages, chapels, and churches were dedicated to

Our Lady. Inherent to this devotion was the importance of the Holy Rosary and the cult of the Seven Sorrows. The Virgin was worshipped in an almost endless variety of invocations, from the Nossa Senhora das Febres, who assists those suffering from fevers, to the Nossa Senhora do Ó, who assists pregnant women; the Nossa Senhora da Boa Viagem, who assists those who are traveling; and the Nossa Senhora da Boa Morte, who assists those in their final hours.[43]

In the next section we will explore another characteristic of popular religious culture in late-medieval Portuguese society: the participation of people of African origin.

BLACK CONFRATERNITIES

Slavery was mainly an urban phenomenon in Portugal, and no city had more enslaved Africans than Lisbon.[44] In the mid-sixteenth century, Cristóvão Rodrigues de Oliveira estimated that one in every ten people in the nation's capital was enslaved.[45] Other parts of the country—especially in the south—also had large concentrations of enslaved Africans. Until the late sixteenth century, most Black people in Portugal had roots in the Cape Verde islands or the coastal areas comprising present-day Senegal to Sierra Leone. In later decades, the majority of enslaved Africans arriving in Lisbon originated from Central Africa.[46]

In 1513 King Manuel I expressed concern about Africans who, after their arrival in Portugal, passed away without having been baptized. Whereas Christianized Africans tended to be buried like other Christians, unbaptized ones were "not well buried on the places where they are thrown and remain partly uncovered or entirely above the ground without anything covering them so that the dogs eat them."[47] The king's desire to baptize all Africans upon arrival in Lisbon received the support of Pope Leo X in the bull *Eximiae devotionis*. To enforce this rule, the Crown informed slaveholders that Africans who had not been baptized within six months of arrival would be confiscated. In 1515 the Vatican also allowed the baptism of enslaved Africans on board ships.[48]

Church authorities were well aware that such baptisms remained meaningless without catechization. Liam Brockey's research revealed that Jesuits in sixteenth-century Portugal used "enticements such as the flag-waving processions and new regimes of indulgences that required only basic knowledge of doctrine" to lure enslaved groups to take part in doctrine classes.[49] A revealing source is Telles's chronicle on the Society of Jesus that explains how, in 1587, the Jesuit reformer Ignácio Martins decided to reach out to the Black community in Lisbon, arguing that they "were all Christians," yet had "a great necessity of Christian doctrine." Telles's reference to baptized Africans as those who had been "whitened with the water of the holy baptism" shows the importance of Christianization in the Iberian process of becoming a *ladino*, an assimilated and therefore privileged Black person. According to Telles, Martins approached this community "in a soft way" by proposing a dialogue with "the leaders of all the nations," of which "there were twenty." His use of the term *nação* (nation) reflects a Portuguese policy of dividing enslaved Africans into groups based on their origin, ethnicity, and language. Martins's decision to reach out to the leaders of these nations indicates not only that the authorities recognized these groups as organized unities, but also that their leaders were considered legitimate spokespersons. From Telles's source, we learn that these leaders pointed out two difficulties with regard to regular classes in Catholic doctrine. The first was that "during the week they are unable to attend, because they need to work for their masters." The second related to the fact that "on Sundays and holidays . . . every nation gathers in its own neighborhood, where they relax from a week of work by enjoying their feasts and dances." Ultimately, all agreed that, henceforth, "every Sunday, five nations would come to doctrine classes," which meant one class per month. To initiate this new policy, "over a thousand blacks" came in "procession to the church of the *Hospital del-Rei*," Lisbon's All Saints Royal Hospital. This massive mobilization confirms how well the Black community in Lisbon was organized. It also shows that, in spite of the alleged lack of doctrine, its members were at least familiar with the basics of Catholic procession culture. Interesting is also Telles's observation that "Master Ignácio preached from the pulpit and spoke to them in their own way and almost in their own language so that they would better understand him," which suggests that he addressed them in a pidginized form of Portuguese. After they were "asked if they were satisfied with what he proposed," they "all answered with great joy" and staged a "celebration according to their custom." Telles ended his report with the observation that Black people in Lisbon "continued for many years to come to doctrine classes."[50] Martins's Sunday catechism classes are confirmed by the Jesuit Simão Cardoso, who specified that, after hearing his lessons, members of Lisbon's Black community followed him in procession through the streets, "dressed in white cloaks, and holding red staffs in their hands with such solemnity and gravity that they appear the officials of some reformed republic." They did so according to their nation, each of which had a banner, granted to their "elected kings" by the Jesuits.[51]

Research by Jorge Fonseca confirms that an average of 9.5 percent of the Black population in early modern Lisbon received chrism, which confirms a significant attachment to religious life.[52] This attachment cannot be explained with reference to one monthly doctrine class only and requires a closer look at the involvement of Black people in Portuguese confraternal culture.

The first known reference to Black members of a Portuguese confraternity dates to 1484.[53] This is relatively late compared to Spain, where earlier references were found in cities such as Seville, Barcelona, and Valencia.[54] In the history of Black confraternal culture in Portugal, the Lisbon brotherhood of Our Lady of the Rosary plays a key role. It was established in the fifteenth century at the church of the monastery of the Dominicans.[55]

This location is no coincidence. The history of the rosary brotherhoods started with the Dominican Alanus de Rupe, who founded the Confraternity of the Psalter of the Glorious Virgin Mary around 1470. Alanus used a model of monastic spirituality, which he adapted for a broad audience, in order to promote a more devout lifestyle. Other Dominicans followed his example, most famously Jakob Sprenger, dean of the Faculty of Theology at the University of Cologne. In his role as inquisitor, Sprenger considered the confraternity a useful instrument to combat pre-Christian traditions related to ancestor worship. He dedicated considerable attention to fraternal solidarity between the dead and the living and opened the brotherhood to the poorest of the poor without regard to ethnicity, gender, or social status, stating that "in our brotherhood no one will be kept out, no matter how poor he may be; but rather the poorer he is, the more disdained and despised, the more acceptable, beloved and precious will he be in this brotherhood."[56] Not only its welcoming attitude but also the opportunity to substitute prayers for dues made this brotherhood attractive to the poor. The rosary brotherhood became known for its weekly recitations, often collective, of the holy rosary. This devotion to the rosary acquired even greater popularity after the Christian victory over the Turks in the Battle of Lepanto on October 7, 1571. Since this victory was attributed to an intervention by the Virgin of the Rosary, the rosary holiday came to be fixed on the first Sunday of October.[57]

It is doubtful that the popularity of the rosary brotherhood among Black people in Lisbon relates, as is sometimes suggested, to "magic forces" of the rosary beads that proved attractive to Africans.[58] A more credible explanation is that they did not have any other choice, for brotherhoods tended to be restrictive in the selection of their members.[59] The sixteenth-century *Livro do Rosário de Nossa Senhora* explicitly mentioned that "other confraternities usually only admit people of standing. But the confraternity of the rosary welcomes people of all standing, whether they are male, female, tall, short, poor, rich, old, young, free, or enslaved."[60]

The Lisbon brotherhood of Our Lady of the Rosary enjoyed great prestige within the Black community due to its privilege, conceded by the monarchy, to defend people against slaveholders in court and to force the latter to grant manumission as soon as the fraternity was able to pay the required amount for the freedom of a faithful member. Paradoxically, its main source of income was a percentage of the royal tax that every ship arriving from Africa had to pay. People who acquired their freedom in such a way became *escravos indiretos* (indirect slaves) of the brotherhood until the loan provided for their release was paid back. Leading members of the rosary confraternity considered themselves the legitimate spokespersons for the interests of their community and were accepted as such by the Crown, which considered the brotherhood a useful channel through which it could regulate problems relating to the Black community.[61]

Like all brotherhoods, the Lisbon confraternity of Our Lady of the Rosary was a complex and heterogeneous organization with a broad range of interests among its White and Black members. It also underwent considerable changes in the course of its existence. Due to racially motivated disputes and accusations of improper behavior during feasts, the Black community separated itself and applied for its own charter as Irmandade de Nossa Senhora do Rosário dos Homens Pretos (Brotherhood of Our Lady of the Rosary of the Black Men), which it received in 1565. Its statutes did not differ much from those of White brotherhoods; members were expected to gather on a weekly basis for a joint prayer of the com-

plete rosary, to go every Sunday to Mass with song and candles in honor
of the Virgin of the Rosary, to organize a procession on the holiday of the
Virgin of the Rosary, to use that day to elect leadership positions, to celebrate All Saints' Day, to participate at funerals of deceased members and
their wives, to provide aid to sick and poor members, to assume the latter's
funeral costs, to keep the funds in a safe box that could only be opened
with the keys of the brotherhood's judge, administrator, and registrar, to
ensure that the latter wore their white capes on holidays, and to take care
of the brotherhood's chapel in church. It also stipulated that the treasurer
had to be a White person and that enslaved Black members, as well as
Moors, Mulattoes, and "Indians" (people with roots in the East Indies)
remained excluded from leadership positions.[62]

During the dynastic crisis of 1580, the Lisbon Brotherhood of Our
Lady of the Rosary of the Black Men responded enthusiastically to the
appeal by Pedro da Silva Manuel, nicknamed *o Negro*, to join forces with
António, prior of Crato, in his military campaign opposing the crowning
of King Philip II of Spain as the new king of Portugal. As ambassador of
the king of Ndongo (in Angola) and a knight in the Order of Santiago,
Silva Manuel was a highly prestigious African residing in Portugal. At its
seat in the Dominican monastery, the rosary brotherhood built an entirely
Black military unit of up to three thousand men in response to António's
promise to grant manumission to anyone willing to enlist, even if against
the will of his owner. The humiliating defeat of the prior of Crato and
subsequent accession to power of Philip naturally had consequences: Silva
Manuel was exiled to North Africa, while the rosary brotherhood lost several of its liberties and was expelled from the monastery.[63] In 1588 the
Dominican Order suspended the Black rosary brotherhood altogether,
only to reinstate a new, biracial one under White leadership. It took over
half a century, until 1646, for a new rosary brotherhood to be established
for the Black community in Lisbon, albeit without the privileges it had
once enjoyed.[64]

By that time, Lisbon already counted several other Black brotherhoods,
one of which was dedicated to Our Lady of Guadalupe at the church of
the monastery of the Franciscans, one dedicated to Jesus Maria Joseph at the
monastery of the Carmelites, and one dedicated to Saint Benedict in the
church of the monastery of Saint Anne. Most Black brotherhoods in other
Portuguese cities were dedicated to the Virgin of the Rosary.[65]

Under the impulse of the Franciscans, the Black Saint Benedict began to rival the latter's popularity in the seventeenth century, not only in Portugal but also in its overseas possessions. His popularity was such that, in seventeenth-century Angola, some believed that Saint Benedict's mother was Angolan. Saint Anthony also enjoyed great popularity among members of the Black community, as did the Black Franciscan Antonio da Noto, also known as Antonio of Caltagirone, who had been enslaved in Sicily and took his baptismal name in honor of the Portuguese saint.[66]

An interesting characteristic of Black brotherhoods was the use of Iberian aristocratic titles for leadership positions.[67] The 1565 charter of the Lisbon Brotherhood of Our Lady of the Rosary of the Black Men, for instance, called for election of a "prince, king, duke, count, marquis, cardinal, and any other dignity."[68] These titles did not relate to Africans of noble birth, nor should they be misunderstood as a form of parody or role reversal in the tradition of the Roman Saturnalia. Rather, these were common honorific titles in late-medieval Portuguese society. Although we know little about their precise meaning, brotherhood kings and nobles undoubtedly enjoyed great prestige within the Black community. Not by accident, the king, traditionally the first person to be elected, held the power to decide on even votes and had the authority to expel members.[69]

There are no indications that slaveholders opposed affiliation to brotherhoods. On the contrary, several sources show that they rendered support. A seventeenth-century document from the town of Vila Viçosa, for instance, reveals that the king of a local Black brotherhood, an enslaved person, worked at the ducal palace and had the privilege, granted to him by the duke, to annually invite "all members [of his brotherhood] for a grandiose banquet in the palace, to which lots of slaves came, males and females, who worked in the palace and in the village, all of them dressed nicely for the gala, with golden necklaces."[70] On the island of Faial in the Azores, we also find a reference to an election ceremony for a Black brotherhood king that was followed by a banquet offered by the owner of the elected man.[71]

Although these brotherhoods were all called "Black," they were required to have a White treasurer, had to submit their statutes for approval to the (White) city authorities, and their leaders were expected to function as community representatives vis-à-vis the authorities. As such, Black brotherhoods stood in a tradition that had started in fifteenth-century

Spain, when the monarchy appointed a member of the Black community as *alcalde de los Negros* (mayor of the Black people).[72] This has prompted certain scholars to consider these kings *reis de fumaça* (mock kings), who, as Mário de Andrade claimed, were "useful instruments in the hands of the slaveholders."[73]

It should be stressed, however, that these organizations were not forced upon the Black community. The desire to create a confraternity came from within the community itself. This is not surprising, considering that brotherhoods strengthened Black solidarity, provided a mutual-aid system in order to care for the needy, and secured a minimum of social mobility that, in exceptional cases, could lead to manumission. Moreover, brotherhoods provided support in handling disputes with slaveholders and functioned as a means of cultural affirmation, as they provided members with a chance to have their own chapels, to participate in processions with their own performances, and to make sure that members received an honorable funeral and burial place.[74]

There are some astonishing examples of Black brotherhoods using their influence to challenge abuses. In the 1680s, representatives from Spain, Portugal, and Brazil jointly supported an intervention spearheaded by Capuchins at the Propaganda Fide to condemn the enslavement of Christianized Africans. They did so by sending Lourenço da Silva de Mendonça, a Mulatto who claimed to be a descendant of the king of Kongo, as procurator to the Holy Office in Rome in order to plea for the excommunication of those responsible for the enslavement of African Christians.[75] In March 1684, the Propaganda Fide reacted to this plea by informing the nuncios of Portugal and Spain that "new and urgent appeals on the part of the Negroes of the Indies . . . have caused no little bitterness to His Holiness," and made it clear that "this involves a disgraceful offence against Catholic liberty, condemning to perpetual slavery not only those who are bought and sold, but also the sons and daughters who are born to them, although they have been made Christians," and — in vain — urged the nuncios to urge the Spanish and Portuguese Crown to issue orders that would prohibit the enslavement of Catholic Africans.[76] Another case is that of the free Black man Pascoal Dias, who in the late seventeenth century traveled to the Vatican at the request of a Black brotherhood from Salvador, in Brazil, to protest against the miserable living conditions of enslaved Christians there.[77]

The custom of electing "kings" may have had a particular appeal to Africans from the Kongo kingdom, where similar election procedures existed for the selection of monarchs and where, since the assumption to power of King Afonso I (c. 1456–1542/43), Iberian aristocratic titles— the same as those used in the brotherhoods—had been adopted by the local elite.[78] Although few in number, there are some references to African elements in Black brotherhood performances in Portugal. For instance, certain brotherhoods restricted membership to Africans of a specific "nation," mainly that of Kongo or Angola.[79] When, in 1588, Don Juan de Borja decided to donate his collection of relics to the Lisbon church of São Roque, the Jesuits staged a parade that was followed by the city's Black community. Simão Cardoso's eyewitness account reveals that they "brought an image of Our Lady beneath a canopy accompanied by many banners of their nations with a very good choir of singers and with some games and dances in their fashion." This was followed, the next day, by procession of the city's *gente parda* (Mulattoes), whose brotherhood carried an image of Saint Anthony to São Roque.[80]

An unauthored report from 1730 mentioned that a Black brotherhood of Our Lady of the Rosary in Lisbon was composed of Angolans and described how its members used to celebrate their patron saint with a religious service—inside the Church of Our Savior—that involved the playing of African music with "marimbas, frame drums, flutes, and berimbaus." After the service, they staged a parade in the Alfama neighborhood and performed an Angolan dance.[81] In the 1770s, the French diplomat Pierre Dezoteux witnessed another African dance in Lisbon and noted that it was common to see Black groups "carrying relics or little images of Christ with them that they try to sell everywhere. They are normally accompanied by a band playing drums, guitars, and trumpets and they sometimes dance the *fofa* in front of these objects of public veneration."[82] We could also mention a reference to a Black brotherhood procession in honor of Nossa Senhora das Neves (Saint Mary of the Snows) in August 1633, when members, some in native African dress, paraded and danced through the streets of Lisbon to the sound of castanets, drums, flutes, and other instruments. Some of the men represented warriors with bows and arrows, whereas the women carried baskets with ex-votos for the Virgin. Upon arrival at the Church of Saint Francis, they paraded two or three times around it before entering the church to leave the offerings, hear

Mass, and leave at the sound of African music.[83] African dance also characterized the 1731 Corpus Christi celebrations in Braga, where a float "pulled by two lions" featured "a Black king and queen," accompanied by "six male and four female dancers, two puppets, and a band, composed of musicians from the same nation," who sang, "See how the whites are amazed by the music and dance of the blacks, all the blacks, my Lord, who are your vassals, they dance, sing, play music, and jump as a gift to you."[84] These sources indicate that Black brotherhood celebrations followed a Portuguese pattern, yet with undeniably African characteristics in their clothing, music, dance, and songs.[85]

Different from their White counterparts, Black brotherhoods held on much longer to a performance pattern rooted in late-medieval lay Christianity. However, the social acceptance of such customs gradually declined, so that, by the early seventeenth century, the bishop of the Algarve prohibited "the *batuque* (drum) that blacks played [in the town of Lagos] during the Feast of the Rosary," and the city authorities of Beja prohibited the African dances of the Black brotherhood because they had caused "disorder."[86]

A racist bias in the implementation of such interventions cannot be denied. Foreign visitors in particular decried what in their view represented scandalously impious behavior. The Swiss David-François de Merveilleux, for instance, warned his readers in 1723 that "while the Portuguese enjoy watching blacks dancing, a foreigner should avoid being present at their celebrations. There are always things contrary to good manners going on that may lead to debauchery."[87] Fiercer in his rejection was the anonymous English author of *Sketches of Portuguese Life* (1826), who described how a "deputation of the brotherhood of Nossa Senhora d'Atalaya" consisting of "Lisbon Negroes" initiated the festivities with a "mass, which is followed by a sermon," but "no sooner are these ceremonials over, then a scene of debauchery follows," including "the lascivious and even frantic *landun*, danced by a negro and negress, whose very gestures and looks would to more delicate people serve only to create the utmost sensations of disgust."[88] Revealing is also the reaction by Marie Bonaparte-Wyse, known as Princess Rattazzi, when she witnessed the Black trumpeters of the Court of Saint George at the 1879 Corpus Christi procession in Lisbon. She spoke of a "group of ugly clothed blacks, with the pompous title of Musicians of Saint George, whose divine symphonies are made to plunge the refined dilettantes from Dahomey and Mozambique into sweet extasy! Poor Saint George!"[89]

We can only speculate why Black people, more than any other group in Portuguese society, remained so attached to brotherhoods and their ancient performance traditions. The fact that these performances included African music and dance may have played a role. Moreover, this marginalized community continued to face racism and discrimination. The conviction that the only ones you could really trust were members of your own community undoubtedly motivated membership in an organization that secured mutual aid, social affirmation, group consciousness, and other forms of solidarity. The fact that confraternities had been a crucial institution in obtaining liberty from slavery can only have strengthened their prestige in the Black community. One could also speculate about a religious motive, in the sense that brotherhoods gave their members more leeway to live their Christian faith in a way that appealed to them.

As the following chapter will demonstrate, however, the foundations of the Christian church in the western part of Africa were laid in the late Middle Ages, and the reforms decided at the Council of Trent made much less of an impact on the way Christianity was lived in Africa than in Europe. African Christians were, as such, familiar with a form of Christianity that, in accordance with a pre-Tridentine tradition, intimately related the expression of faith to dance, music, song, community building, mutual aid, and solidarity. This implies that brotherhoods, much more than the Church itself, allowed the Black community to live its Christian faith in ways similar to how it was lived in Africa. It was thanks to brotherhoods that Christianity could, genuinely, be their religion.

CHAPTER TWO

Africa

Studies of Black Catholicism in North America have long ignored the existence of Africans who already identified as Christian *before* their enslavement. When speaking about the seventeenth-century Dutch colony in Manhattan, for instance, Robert Emmett Curran assumed that "Catholics themselves were virtually a non-presence."[1] Original documents about New Netherland reveal, however, that virtually the entire African population had Iberian Catholic baptismal names, or what was known in Portuguese as a *nome de igreja* (church name). This was, for instance, the case of Francisco van Capo Verde and Anna van Capoverde, whose surnames indicate that they originated from the Cape Verde islands; Christoffel Santome and Maria Santomee, whose names point to the island of São Tomé; or Susanna Congo and Manuel Congo, who had surnames that refer to the Kingdom of Kongo.[2] Most enslaved Africans in Dutch Manhattan had surnames referring to Angola, where the main center of seventeenth-century slave trading operations was located: Luanda. What these surnames have in common is that they can all be traced back to parts of Africa with a historically strong Portuguese influence. This raises a number of questions: How strong was the Portuguese religious influence in Africa? What importance did Catholic baptismal names have for these Africans? How familiar was the earliest generation of enslaved Africans in Manhattan with the Portuguese language, culture, and religion? And how likely is it that they considered themselves Christian?

Since the names of the Manhattan charter generation were typically Iberian, it would be wrong to assume that they had been imposed by their (Protestant) Dutch enslavers. It would also be wrong to think that the Dutch pressured them to identify with European rather than indigenous African names. As Thornton explains, "Christian names were deep-rooted in Central Africa prior to the Atlantic slave trade."[3] That the identification with an Iberian name was their own choice can be demonstrated with reference to the seventeenth-century Dutch Cape colony, where some of the enslaved population originated from parts of Africa with a strong Portuguese influence while others came from regions where this influence was insignificant. While the latter identified themselves with indigenous African names, the former used Iberian names.[4]

This shows that the use of an Iberian, Catholic name by enslaved Africans from Cape Verde, São Tomé, Kongo, and Angola in New Netherland must have been a voluntary decision, perhaps even a matter of pride. We could, in this respect, again refer to the Dutch colony in South Africa. When the French Jesuit Guy Tachard visited the Cape Colony in the late seventeenth century and reached out to the enslaved population, some of them allegedly "fell on their knees and kissed our hands. They pulled chaplets and medals out of their bosoms to show they were Catholics, they wept and smote their breast."[5] In 1668, the Capuchin missionary Michelangelo Guattini had a similar experience in Pernambuco, Brazil, where he was approached by a "black woman, who kneeled, and clapped her hands upon her breast and on the ground." When he inquired what the woman meant by these motions, a Portuguese bystander answered, "Father, this black lady comes from Kongo, where she was baptized by a Capuchin; and being informed that you are going there to baptize, she is happy, and expresses her joy to you."[6] A third example comes from Portugal, where, upon his arrival at the port of Lisbon in 1682, Guattini's counterpart Girolamo Merolla da Sorrento was offered assistance by a "black native from Kongo," who helped him "without asking for any compensation," arguing that "we, the Kongolese, owe Italian Capuchins a lot."[7]

Scholars have traditionally been skeptical about such expressions of Catholic zeal among enslaved Africans, especially in the case of sources where a bias can be presupposed. The traditional assumption, after all, is that the baptism of Africans by priests at Portuguese slave entrepôts or onboard their ships remained a meaningless ritual. If we take the Cape Verde islands and Upper Guinea as examples, this assumption can easily be sustained with historical sources. In Fernão Guerreiro's early seventeenth-century report to the Society of Jesus we read that enslaved Africans waiting to be shipped to the Americas used to be baptized "in groups of 300, 400, 700," and since slave traders were in a hurry to sell them, they did "not provide opportunities to these unfortunates to be catechized or instructed in the faith that would at least make them understand why they received baptism."[8] Francisco de Moura, the former governor of Cape Verde, even argued in 1620 that many of the Africans who passed through these islands on their way to the Americas were not baptized at all and when "some of them died along the way, not only their lives were lost, but also their souls."[9]

While dedicating himself to the Christianization of newly arrived Africans in early seventeenth-century Cartagena, Colombia, the Jesuit Alonso de Sandoval quoted in his treatise several captains of slave ships arriving from the Portuguese stronghold of Cacheu, in Upper Guinea, who confirmed that Africans there were "baptized without any instruction" and that the priest "does not ask for the slaves' consent" because "they have no idea what the holy baptism means."[10] Attempts by Jesuits to change this pattern and to ensure that all enslaved Africans were properly baptized and catechized before being shipped to the Americas proved impossible to enforce. Slave traders systematically boycotted such attempts with the argument that it was too costly, too complicated due the linguistic diversity of the enslaved, and also too dangerous since keeping large numbers of people in confined places for weeks would increase the risk of uprisings. In addition, traders argued that these men and women were to be sent to Catholic nations, where they would be Christianized anyway.[11]

Jesuits must also have been aware that contraband flourished in Upper Guinea and that enslaved Africans sold and shipped to the Americas through such channels were not baptized. During his mission in Sierra Leone in the 1660s, for instance, the Jesuit André de Faro witnessed an attempt by Portuguese or Luso-African traders to sell a group of people to an English captain. Upon realizing that a priest was watching them, they canceled the deal, aware that they risked "the penalty of excommunication" for "selling blacks to the English or to other heretics."[12]

It would, however, be wrong to assume that these baptisms only caused confusion and fear among enslaved Africans because none of them knew what was going on. While the overall results of Catholic missionary work in sixteenth- and seventeenth-century Upper Guinea may have been meager, the Portuguese cultural and linguistic influence in the region was considerable, even among those who rejected Christianity.[13] This should caution against spontaneously assuming total ignorance about Christianity. Significantly, a letter from the Jesuit Sebastián Goméz dating to 1614 informs that, when a priest boarded a slave ship in Cacheu and asked whether anyone wanted to be baptized, "some of them on the ship shout[ed] 'yes, yes.'"[14] This source reveals not only that some, perhaps out of opportunistic reasons, volunteered to be baptized, but also that they understood what was asked. As Thornton has argued, it is likely that Africans "had a greater knowledge of Christianity before embarkation as a result of missionary endeavors and the proselytization of Christian merchants and other settlers than has usually been acknowledged."[15]

It should also be added that the Portuguese Crown took its Christianizing mission in Africa seriously. These missions are to be understood in connection to the *padroado*, the patronage over the administration of the Church in overseas territories, which Portuguese monarchs possessed as Grand Masters of the Order of Christ. This patronage has a history that goes back to the crusades and the establishment of the Order of Christ in Portugal in 1319. Since the monarchy understood its overseas expansion as a continuation of the *reconquista* in the name of the Order of Christ, it requested from the Vatican the right of *padroado* for all territories outside of Europe where it introduced Christianity. This request was confirmed in successive Papal bulls and briefs, most importantly *Dum Diversas* in 1452, *Romanus Pontifex* of 1454, and *Inter caetera* of 1456. Starting with King Manuel I in 1495, Portuguese monarchs inherited the *padroado* with their ascension to the throne. As Grand Masters of the order, they had the right to control missionary activities, which, in practice, gave them the ability to instrumentalize the Church in order to serve Portugal's commercial and political interests.[16]

The Crown had, thus, every reason not to put the *padroado* in jeopardy by neglecting its missionary obligations. In the awareness that the expansion of the Church in Africa required native experts, King João II invested heavily in the formation of African interpreters and priests in late fifteenth-century Portugal.[17] When the German humanist Hieronymus Münzer visited Lisbon in 1494, he noted that dozens of young Africans were being trained in Latin and theology at the monastery of Saint Eloi, with the goal of spreading the faith in their homelands. Münzer was so impressed by what he had seen that he thought it was "likely that in the course of time, the greater part of Ethiopia [Africa] will be converted to Christianity."[18]

While Münzer's comment was more wishful thinking than a realistic assessment of the situation, there are good reasons to question Albert Raboteau's claim in his classic study *Slave Religion* (1978) that the expansion of Christianity along the west coast of African only took off when "Christianized slaves began to return from Europe and America to Africa in the late eighteenth century" and that everything before that had "very little success."[19] Regardless of how one wishes to define "little success," the fact is that Portuguese missionary endeavors did have an important impact in Africa and that, as David Wheat confirms, some of the enslaved Africans brought to the Americas through Portuguese channels were "plainly familiar with Portuguese religious culture before disembarking in the Americas."[20]

For evidence of this, we could point again to Sandoval, who made a rigorous analysis of the validity of the baptisms Africans had received before their arrival in Cartagena. While most of them "need to be examined thoroughly in order to find out whether they had become Christians," he argued, others "have been baptized as infants and do not need to be examined."[21]

There can, in fact, be no doubt that a significant number of the enslaved Africans arriving in the Americas from regions with a historically strong Portuguese influence identified as Catholic. Equally important, however, is the acknowledgment that their understanding of what it meant to be Catholic differed from European standards, especially those of the post-Tridentine Church. The following sections will focus on the Portuguese religious influence in Africa, not as a study of the institutional organization of the Church, but, rather, as an attempt to understand how this influence shaped the way Africans lived (and live) their Christian faith.

THE CAPE VERDE ISLANDS

It was in Santiago that the dreadful story of the African transatlantic slave trade began. Much of what was originally tested on this largest island of the Cape Verde archipelago would later be exported across the Atlantic and shape slaveholding societies all over the Americas. The Portuguese colonization of Santiago started in the 1460s. Unlike the Azores and Madeira, where mainly Portuguese and other European immigrants settled, the distance to and dry climate of Cape Verde made European settlement difficult. The earliest settlers were mainly banished men and *cristãos novos* (New Christians), forcefully converted Jews. In order to stimulate immigration, the Crown granted settlers a number of exceptional liberties, including the freedom to engage in trade along the coast of Upper Guinea, roughly the area from present-day Senegal to Sierra Leone. Santiago thereupon developed into a slave trading center that connected West Africa, the Iberian Peninsula and, later, the Americas. On the island itself, settlers also relied heavily on the work of enslaved Africans. By 1582 the latter formed 87 percent of the population in Santiago.[22]

The Portuguese authorities were well aware that the whip alone was insufficient to keep control over the quickly growing African population and dealt with this challenge by establishing a hierarchy within the Black community that, in exceptional cases, could lead to freedom. Being Black in Santiago was, thus, not tantamount to being enslaved. The rise in hierarchy went hand in hand with the display of acts of loyalty to the authorities, as well as the adoption of Portuguese identity markers, most notably the Portuguese language and religion. This process became known as *ladinização*, whereby a newly arrived African, known as *boçal* (or *bozal*, in Spanish) was first made "human" by being baptized and then, gradually, moved up to a quarter, half, and, ultimately, full *ladino* status.[23]

On an island where White women were virtually absent, this system naturally privileged the offspring of Portuguese men and Black women. Soon, Santiago had a Black and Mulatto elite known as *brancos da terra* (Cape Verdean Whites) or *nobreza da terra* (Cape Verdean nobles).[24] In as early as 1533 we have evidence of a free Mulatto man obtaining civil rights equal to those of the White community, and in 1598 a Cape Verdean with a Portuguese father and a Mulatto mother was knighted in the Order of Christ.[25] This Black and Mulatto elite increasingly assumed positions of leadership. When John Barrow visited Santiago while on his way to Asia in 1792, he observed that "the clergy were people of color, and some of them perfectly black. The officers of justice, of the customs, and other departments in the civil and military services, the troops, the peasantry, and the traders, were all blacks," yet "most of them aspire to the honor of Portuguese extraction."[26]

As the Cape Verdean historian Daniel Pereira argued, "to a certain degree, Cape Verde colonized itself."[27] The Black elite was, in fact, very conscious that they were the driving force behind the colonization of the islands. To their frustration, however, positions at the very top of society remained firmly in the hands of *reinóis*, White men sent over from Portugal. In a 1546 letter of complaint to the Crown, the island's Black elite argued that it was in the interest of Portugal to open up such positions to locals, considering that they were the only ones capable of keeping the enslaved population under control. Frustrations over the privileged position of *reinóis* also contributed to the fact that the Black elite adopted Portuguese identity markers but never completely assimilated. Significantly, they spoke the Portuguese language not as it was spoken in the Lusitanian motherland, but rather a creolized form of it that became the lingua franca of the islands.[28]

Frequent contact between Cape Verde and the nearby mainland contributed to the dissemination of this creole language along the coastline of continental Africa. From there, countless enslaved Africans were brought to Santiago and subsequently shipped to the Iberian Peninsula and, starting around 1520, the Americas. The booming slave trade also encouraged Portuguese and free Cape Verdeans to establish themselves on the African continent and build networks that reached far into the interior. The Portuguese authorities distrusted these *lançados* or *tangomaos*, in spite of their crucial role as middlemen, not only because many of them were New Christians, but also because they adjusted themselves to an African lifestyle and did not hesitate to do business with European rivals or even with (Muslim) traders from Northern Africa.[29]

The Portuguese presence on the African continent grew in importance when, around 1588, the Crown decided to establish a permanent settlement in the port town of Cacheu, in present-day Guinea-Bissau. Increasingly, traders began to buy enslaved Africans in Cacheu and sail directly to the Americas without passing through Santiago. The subsequent economic decline of the island was only accelerated by attacks led by French, English, and Dutch privateers. Once a key player in the transatlantic slave trade, Santiago gradually became a forgotten corner of the Portuguese colonial empire.[30]

In consequence of this isolation, the island has not received the scholarly attention it deserves for its pioneering role in Africa's religious history. It was, after all, in Santiago that many of the captive Africans had their first encounter with Christianity. It was also there that, in the context of the Portuguese policy of *ladinização*, enslaved Africans came to perceive a Christian baptism as a crucial first step on a path to better living conditions and possibly freedom.

In his treatise on slavery, Sandoval identified enslaved Africans arriving in Cartagena from Cape Verde and Cacheu as being of three different groups: 1) *bozales*, enslaved Africans coming directly from Cacheu; 2) *ladinos*, enslaved people who had been born in continental Africa and had adjusted during their stay in Cape Verde to a Luso-African lifestyle; and 3) *naturales* (natives), enslaved people who had been born and raised in Cape Verde. Sandoval explained that those of the first two groups "need to be examined thoroughly in order to find out whether they had become Christians," whereas those of the third group "have been baptized as infants and do not need to be examined."[31] Members of the latter two groups are of particular importance to the history of Christianity because they introduced the singular variant of Catholicism that had developed in Cape Verde to the Americas.

Unfortunately, Sandoval gave no indication as to the size of each group. There can be no doubt, however, that the overwhelming majority belonged to the first group. As Frederick Bowser's research in early colonial Peru revealed, slave purchasers often preferred *bozales* because *ladinos* "were considered too knowing of Iberian ways to be easily disciplined."[32] In 1526 King Charles V even determined that "from here forward in time no one can or will carry the said Negros *ladinos* from these our kingdoms nor from other parts if they are not *bozales*, because such *bozales* are those that serve, peacefully and obediently."[33] In spite of this import restriction, there continued to be a demand for *ladinos* (and *naturales*) on the slave market because their familiarity with Iberian culture and language made them the preferred choice for specific tasks, such as that of overseer or housekeeper. Slave traders themselves had an interest in this group because their price was generally higher. In 1569 the English merchant William Fowler explained that "if a negro be a *Bossale* that is to say ignorant of the Spanishe or Portugale tonge then he or she is commonly soulde for 400 and 450 pesos. But if the Negro can speake anye of the foresaide languages any thinge indifferentlye (which is called *Ladinos*) then the same Negro is commonlye soulde for 500 and 600 pesos."[34] The number of *ladinos* and *naturales* shipped to the Americas also fluctuated in accordance with local conditions. For instance, long periods of drought or failed harvests often caused slaveholders in Cape Verde to sell part of their experienced captive workforce.[35] Equally important is Toby Green's observation that "the slavers on these ships were often Luso-Africans, with Portuguese fathers and African mothers."[36]

As a reflection of Santiago's key role in Portugal's missionary ambitions, it was elevated to bishopric in 1533. However, its first bishop never bothered to set foot on the island, and in later decades, absentia remained a problem.[37] In 1603, for instance, the Crown had to send an order to the appointed bishop to finally "join the faithful he was responsible for since he had been absent for almost ten years without proper justification."[38]

The Church in Cape Verde also faced a problem of credibility. It did not, in any form, oppose slavery. On the contrary, leading Church members were personally involved in the slave trade, as were religious orders. Moreover, the Christianization of the Black population in Santiago was not a matter of choice. Although both the Crown and the Vatican prohibited forced conversions, there was simply no escape to baptism and Christianization for all those unable to flee and lead the risky life of a fugitive.[39]

That Christianity nevertheless managed to establish strong roots in the Cape Verde archipelago was primarily the result of local clergy and lay catechists. Paraphrasing Pereira, one could argue that, to a certain degree, Cape Verde Christianized itself. Since 1518, a papal brief had authorized the royal chaplain in Lisbon to ordain Africans who were considered apt for priesthood upon the condition that they return to their homelands. Soon, the majority of priests in Santiago originated from the island itself.[40] During his visit to Santiago in 1652, the famous Portuguese Jesuit António Vieira met with "clergy and canons, who were as black as jet," but "so serious, so authoritative, so learned, such great musicians, so discrete and so upright that they may be envied by those in our own cathedrals at home."[41]

Attempts by the Society of Jesus to establish a seminary in order to further increase the number of priests and professionalize their education failed, however.[42] In consequence, Santiago suffered from a chronic short-age of priests, particularly outside of urban centers. Only once a year, typi-cally during Lent, priests would visit communities in rural areas, baptize the newborn, hear confessions, and depart. Data from 1582 show that all of the 5,700 enslaved people living in Santiago's capital Ribeira Grande were listed as being *de confissão* ("confessing Christians"), the Portuguese equivalent of catechized. In (Vila da) Praia (de Santa Maria), the island's second city, only 800 of the 1,000 enslaved Africans were catechized, whereas this number declined to 3,000 of the 5,000 enslaved people in rural parts of Santiago. Elsewhere in Cape Verde, these numbers were even lower. Still by the mid-seventeenth century, several of the archipelago's smaller islands didn't have a single priest in residence.[43]

Due to the absence of clergymen, Portuguese slaveholders ended up having a strong influence on the way Africans were introduced to Catholi-cism. Their inclusion in holiday celebrations, processions, and saint venera-tions induced, in its own way, a process of Christianization, albeit very different from what Jesuits had in mind.[44] As Susana Costa has argued, the type of Catholicism that came to be embraced by the Black population in Santiago was deeply influenced by "the late-medieval religious experience and cultural baggage brought to the island by the first settlers."[45] As examples of this "baggage" we could cite the case of a Portuguese settler who arrived on the island in 1513 with a statue of Saint Anthony in the conviction that it "would help him against the evil air" or the decision by concerned settlers in 1542 to react to a mysterious throat disease with the building of a chapel in honor of Saint Blaise, which "pleased Our Lord, who made the island healthy again." The late-medieval character of reli-gious celebrations is reflected in the concern of Church authorities over the "great abuses" that took place on the feast day of Saint John in 1592 and in the long list of attractions prepared for the 1604 Corpus Christi celebration, including "dances, revelry, mock war fights, St. James on his horse, a dragon, trumpets, and shawms."[46]

Even more than slaveholders, Black laypeople (enslaved and free) in-fluenced this Christianization process. In the awareness that, especially in rural areas, their capacity was limited to an annual visit at best, priests es-tablished a network of laypeople, whom they introduced to the basics of Catholic doctrine and trained in certain rituals, such as prayer sessions, hymns, funeral customs, and processions. "Even in the most isolated places, where there were no priests and no church," Júlio Monteiro writes, "There was always someone who knew about the rituals, and whose help could be solicited by the people."[47] As an example, we could mention the case of Seis Cento Lobos, a Black man whom the Dutch merchant Hendrik Haecxs met in 1646 on the island of Maio, and who "due to the absence of a pope served as priest, in which function he was also respected by the governor."[48]

These lay catechists, known as *mestres* (masters), enjoyed great moral authority in the community. They ensured that people said the right prayers, prepared on time for the upcoming holidays, and executed rituals in accordance with (their understanding of) Catholic doctrine. They also advised community members on how to best protect the newborn or what to do when someone was in agony. Since Jesuit attempts to establish a seminary in Santiago failed and the shortage of clergy continued, the prestige of the *mestres* remained virtually unchallenged in rural areas until the mid-twentieth century.[49]

It is possible, as George Brooks has suggested, that *mestres* thrived in Cape Verde because the late-medieval form of Portuguese Catholicism they adopted had much in common with indigenous African beliefs, which encouraged "mutual accommodation, acceptance, and syncretism of religious beliefs and practices."[50] Nineteenth-century European visitors who assessed the state of religion on the islands tended, in fact, to complain about a lack of orthodoxy. In 1818, for instance, Manuel Lucas de Senna argued that "while everyone is Catholic, people do not observe the religion they profess, unless in their own way, like pagans."[51] Twenty years later, José Chelmicki and Francisco Varnhagen wrote that a general "lack of education" had resulted in a type of Catholicism whereby "the sign of the cross and the word of God, Jesus, and Our Lady" had been mixed with "superstitious rituals from Guinea."[52]

A well-known example of such a syncretic Cape Verdean tradition is *guarda cabeça* (protecting the head), a ritual to protect newborns against the "evil eye" in the seven days leading up to baptism and involves both Catholic prayers and the use of indigenous amulets.[53] We could also mention the *esteira* or *txoru*. One of the oldest references to this funeral practice is João Vieira de Andrade's letter from 1762 to the Portuguese monarch about "errors against the Catholic Church" in Santiago. Andrade defined the *esteira* as a "heathenish African custom," whereby people gather with "a hellish noise" in the house of a recently deceased person, speak to the corpse, and make requests "to transmit messages [to other deceased] by putting letters in the coffin" and then, for several days in a row, "abuse with food and drink and commit the sin of gluttony."[54] Some fifty years later, Senna confirmed the practice of "sending recommendations to those in heaven" during the eight days of mourning that followed someone's death, which not only involved an "act of devotion to the soul but also to the stomach of these false devouts" because they eat and drink so much during these days "that, at the end, they all become drunk" and their devotion degenerates into "pleasantries, laughter . . . screaming and dancing."[55] In a similar vein, the nineteenth-century Portuguese folklorist Teófilo Braga argued that "the house of the *esteira* becomes a *rendez-vous* place, whereby it is not uncommon that boys and girls take advantage of the prayer nights to court each other."[56]

According to the Cape Verdean folklorist Félix Monteiro, such denigrating comments reflect not only a disrespect for but also a lack of understanding of the island's Afro-Catholic heritage. He highlights, for instance, that the faithful in Santiago share a firm belief that "saints hate sadness." According to popular belief, he explains, saints consider grief over a loss "a form of censorship to their superior decisions," which, if not handled appropriately, "can cause their ire." Hence the necessity to please the saints by regularly *cortar o nojo* (breaking the sadness) during funerals with dance, laughter, and joy.[57]

The alternation between sad and joyful moments has, to this day, remained a characteristic of *esteiras*. Since historical sources provide only a limited understanding of this tradition, it is worth adding data from anthropological research. It reveals that the tradition typically starts with the announcement of someone's death with *salvas de tristeza* (salutes of sadness) by drum players or conch shell blowers, which is followed by moments of crying and screaming, known as *pranto*, that include comments about both the virtues and flaws of the deceased. The following day, the corpse is removed from the house and carried in procession to the cemetery, which involves singing and dancing to the music of the accompanying band. After the burial is completed, people plant a shrub or leave pots, cups, or bottles of water on or near the gravestone in the conviction that the deceased's soul remains thirsty and likes shade. Families are also expected to observe seven (for ordinary family members) or eight (for heads of family) days of mourning, known as *nojo*. Every evening, family members and friends then gather for novenas, prayer sessions starting with the *acto de contrição* (mea culpa), followed by the recitation and singing in call-and-response form of the rosary and ending with a prayer dedicated to the alms in purgatory. The days of mourning end with a *véspera*, a prayer session that follows the pattern of a novena but concludes at sunrise with a procession around the house to complement the transition of the deceased's soul to the "spirit of light." If the deceased did not die a natural death, this ritual involves the catching of the soul in order to keep it from torturing the living. The latter occurs with a series of Catholic prayers, followed by the actual "catching" of the soul with a white cloth. This *véspera* can be understood as a "second funeral"; whereas the first one involved the deceased's corpse, the second funeral applies to the soul.[58]

People repeat a novena for the soul of the deceased one month and one year after the person's death. From then on, the deceased is commemorated annually on All Souls' Day, typically with a nightly prayer session known as *staçon*. In the 1830s, Joaquim Lopes de Lima witnessed such a *staçon* when "at midnight on the night of November 1 (eve of All Souls' Day) families pray in chorus at the closed doors of churches for the souls of their deceased."[59]

These gatherings to pray for the souls of a deceased highlight the important social dimension of Catholicism in Santiago. In this respect, we should stress the role of confraternities that functioned both as networks of mutual aid and as burial societies by covering the funeral costs of members in good standing, avoiding a shameful burial without a decent coffin. As early as in 1495, Ribeira Grande had a church for the Black confraternity, dedicated to Our Lady of the Rosary.[60] By 1612 Santiago's capital counted five confraternities, two of which were dedicated to the Black population: the Irmandade da Nossa Senhora do Rosário (Our Lady of the Rosary) and the Irmandade da Santa Cruz (Holy Cross).[61] These two oldest and most prestigious brotherhoods served as models for a vast network of mutual-aid and burial societies that developed on the Cape Verde islands. Similar to how these organizations had once served as a replacement for the loss of family networks by those who moved from rural to urban parts of Portugal, it was in the context of brotherhoods that enslaved Africans found aid, comfort, and solidarity. Moreover, confraternities provided members enough leeway to reinterpret Portuguese traditions by infusing indigenous elements and thereby stimulated the development of a new, Cape Verdean group conscience.[62]

In his 1762 letter about "errors against the Catholic Church," Andrade provided insight into the functioning of Black brotherhoods, also known as *reinados* (kingdoms) because they were led by a "king." He explained that "in all neighborhoods of the island women and men are elected to serve as kings and queens, who then every Sunday and holiday stage parades with their drums and flutes in order to collect money." At the end of such parades, "they abuse with food and drink and commit the sin of gluttony." Every year, he continued, they "have a Mass organized at their kingdom, where they are crowned by a local priest, and in their house, they build an altar, where they worship." Although these rituals were "claimed to be Catholic" by the local population, Andrade advocated for the prohibition of these "scandalous abuses, crimes and transgressions." In 1764 another Portuguese administrator, João Gomes Ferreira, also complained about the "scandalous abuses, crimes, and transgressions by the so-called kingdoms or rosary fraternities," who "during the Holy Week from Maundy Thursday until the Sunday of Easter go around, asking for alms in the name of Our Lady of the Rosary" and in "their churches organize vigils," where "they eat, drink, and sleep" and pretend that all of this is done "out of devotion to the saints."[63]

According to the nineteenth-century historian Christiano José de Senna Barcellos, brotherhoods in Santiago used to have not only their own rules and regulations, but also a court of justice and even a type of army. This may explain why, in 1723, the Crown ordered the governor of Cape Verde to prohibit the customary marches on the holidays of Saint James and Saint John by the "armies of free and enslaved blacks, with their own governors, lieutenant-generals, colonels, sergeants, captains of infantry, and subordinates."[64] Apparently this intervention had little effect; in 1772 the colonial authorities again prohibited the *reinados'* public rituals, which they deemed "scandalous in the eyes of God."[65]

It seems, in fact, that brotherhoods didn't let themselves be intimidated by prohibitions. Braga's late nineteenth-century description of a Cape Verdean *reinado* shows that its members continued to organize saint celebrations in ways highly similar to those described by Andrade a century earlier. According to the Portuguese folklorist, these festivities were announced by "men blowing a conch shell," whereupon girls dressed in flowers began to collect donations. Then, an election took place, "where it was determined who would play the role of the white people and who would act as the slaves of the saint." The elected candidates thereupon made "a sort of chapel, with a small altar, decorated with silk scarfs in a variety of colors and panels of the saint, where they place the statue of the saint" and have it flanked by "two girls with a rod in their hands, imitating cherubs." From there, they went in procession to Mass; the queen, identified by her crown, rode "a donkey" and was "guided by two masked men called *carrascos*" (executioners). Several women accompanied the queen and, waving white flags, "danced to drum music." Then came the king, who "was riding a horse and wearing a hat similar to those of the disciples of Loyala." After Mass they organized a banquet. For the following day, they had "invited the best singers of the land for a litany." According to Braga, they "continued these celebrations for three or four weeks."[66]

Black brotherhoods, today known as *tabancas* (villages), continue to play an important role in Santiago. Anthropological research shows that they are typically led by a "king," a "governor," and a "queen," who are elected by the members. *Tabancas* also have a "court" that is assisted by a councilor, judge, jester, executioner, a number of soldiers, court ladies or *filhas-do-santo* (daughters of the saint), and even *catibos* (slaves). Although they still organize funeral marches for deceased members and help each other with specific tasks, *tabancas* are mainly associated with the annual celebration of the society's patron saint. These celebrations follow a late-medieval pattern, consisting of a "theft" of the saint's banner (usually a white flag with a cross), which, after a search known as *buscâ santo* (search for the saint), is recovered. The "executioner," wearing an indigenous African mask with horns, then arrests the "thieves," whereupon the "king of the celebration" agrees to "buy" the saint, which implies that he covers the costs of the feast. The triumphal recovery of the society's banner takes the *tabanca* on a joyful parade through the streets with musicians playing drums and blowing conch shells, followed by a singing and dancing crowd and, finally, the king and queen, who are guarded by uniformed "soldiers." These "soldiers" not only protect their monarchs but also guard the "chapel" where the recovered banner and ex-votos for the saint are kept. Stories about rivalries and violence between *tabancas* indicate that these "soldiers" may have had a real function in the past. Once the banner is hoisted, the festivities can start. These involve entertainment and also prayer sessions and songs in call-and-response form, using a mixture of Latin, archaic Portuguese, and Cape Verdean creole.[67]

Traces of ancient brotherhood traditions can still be observed in the annual Holy Cross festivities, which involve the ritual hoisting of the brotherhood's banner, the praying of a novena, and a nightly procession with torches followed by dances and songs accompanied by *batuque* drum music. Similar in nature are the celebrations in honor of Saint John that combine Mass and prayer sessions with dances and the jumping over bonfires. On the island of Fogo, saints are honored with *bandeiras* or flag celebrations that, as in medieval times, involve jousts. Until the early twentieth century, the standard bearers entered church on horseback and, as if Trent had never happened, displayed tricks of horsemanship in front of the altar before the priest blessed the brotherhood's banner.[68]

As the local folklorists José Semedo and Maria Turano have shown, *tabancas* display several indigenous African features, yet preserve a structure and modus operandi that correspond to medieval Portuguese customs.[69] In spite of their Portuguese, Catholic roots, however, these brotherhood traditions found their strongest opponents in the colonial and ecclesiastical authorities. In 1941, the latter made a joint effort to initiate a "civilization campaign" in rural parts of Santiago, spearheaded by newly arrived missionaries of the Congregation of the Holy Spirit. This led to a clash between the local Luso-African variant of Catholicism and the Congregation's post-Tridentine understanding of what Catholicism was supposed to be. The Spiritans' aggressive approach met with fierce resistance by rural Cape Verdeans. Known as the *rebelados* (rebels), they decried the missionaries as henchmen of the devil, eager to lure people away from true Catholicism. As proof they pointed out that these missionaries prayed the Our Father and Salve Regina "with the wrong words," that they didn't honor the saints "in the proper way," and that they distributed rosaries containing metal, which, in view of the fact that metal nails had caused the death of the Savior, could only mean that they were in cahoots with Satan. Their resistance was broken only after the colonial authorities exiled the most vocal *mestres* to other islands.[70]

UPPER GUINEA

In 1488, an early attempt by Portuguese missionaries to establish a Christian community in Senegambia by converting the Jolof prince Bu(u)mi Jeléen (or Bemoiom) failed.[71] Even so, subsequent missions continued to invest in a top-down approach. This policy reflected a practical necessity, since missions required permission by local rulers, but also the hope that the successful baptizing of African nobles would initiate mass conversions. To stress the point that the acceptance of baptism sealed an alliance with Portugal, missionaries typically dressed a ruler on the day of his baptism "in the Portuguese way" and "in keeping with his rank." Once baptism was completed, "guns were fired."[72] This strategy rarely bore fruit; either the baptized rulers returned to traditional practices themselves, or their successors refused to follow the new faith.[73]

Meanwhile, bottom-up initiatives were also in motion. As José da Silva Horta rightly pointed out, the Christianization of Upper Guinea primarily occurred in an "informal way," whereby each Portuguese or Luso-African person in the region acted as a potential missionary.[74] Over the course of the sixteenth century, a number of Luso-African creole communities had developed in and around Portuguese trading posts, known as *praças* (squares). In 1594, for instance, André Álvares d'Almada observed that in Upper Guinea "there are many [Africans] who speak our Portuguese language and dress like us" and that some privileged African trading partners of the Portuguese had converted to Christianity.[75] Not unlike those who had converted to Islam, members of these Christian communities, known as Kristons, lived segregated from other Africans, and some acquired literacy. Although they remained attached to certain indigenous African beliefs and customs, they tended to look down upon other Africans and identified themselves as Christian.[76]

Much of the information about Kriston communities comes from European explorers and Jesuit, Capuchin, and Franciscan missions in the region.[77] In 1623 the English merchant Richard Jobson observed that "howbeit they have amongst them, neither Church, nor Frier, nor any other religious order," Kristons "use . . . with a kinde of an affectionate zeale, the name of Christians."[78] Nicolas Villault, Sieur de Bellefond, noted during a visit to the coast of West Africa in 1667 that "several had converted" as a result of "their frequent interaction with the Portuguese."[79] In the 1680s, Michel Jajolet de la Courbe characterized these Luso-Africans as people who speak a "jargon that resembles somewhat Portuguese" and "bear the names of saints." They wear "a large chaplet around their neck [and] a hat, a shirt, and breeches like the Europeans," and "although they are black, they nevertheless claim to be white, by which they mean that they are Christians, just like white people." However, "when they are with other black people, they perform *rakat*, and when they are with whites, they take their rosary and pray like them." Indeed, "those who are Christian go to Mass but afterwards sacrifice to their idols or engage in other pagan ceremonies."[80] Such a flexible religious mindset was also observed by the Cape Verdean merchant André Donelha in his account from 1625, in which he described a meeting with "a black Mandinga youth, named Gaspar Vaz," who dressed like a Muslim but claimed that he did "not believe in the Law of Mohammed" and even "abhor[red] it." He then "took off his smock, beneath which he wore a doublet and shirt in our fashion, and from around his neck drew out a rosary of Our Lady," claiming that he commended himself on a daily basis "to God and the Virgin Our Lady by means of this rosary."[81]

Kriston communities did not disappear after the bulk of the transatlantic slave trade shifted further south, to the Bay of Guinea and Central Africa, nor did the growing English and French influence in the region lead to the swift disappearance of their Luso-African identity.[82] When French Capuchins arrived in 1635 in the coastal area of today's Senegal, they reported on villages such as Rufisque and Portudal, where "almost all the blacks spoke Portuguese" and where Catholicism was vibrant in spite of the absence of priests.[83] In 1701 the French Dominican Godefroy Loyer met in Rufisque with "people, whom locals call Portuguese" and who "have remained Christian," in sign of which "they wear a large rosary and recite among themselves some prayers in Portuguese, baptize their children themselves, and instruct them in the little they know about the mysteries of our religion." While they had neither "chapels" nor "priests," they tried "in this way, to preserve as much as they can of the Christian faith." Loyer also "examined some about the Mysteries of our religion and they satisfied me fairly well." He was particularly pleased about what he learned "about the way in which they baptize their children," because "they acquitted themselves very well of it."[84]

When visiting the Gambia in 1726, William Smith argued that Kristons were "still pretty numerous up in the inland country." According to this employee of the Royal African Company, they had "very imperfect ideas of Christianity," yet nevertheless insisted on "distinguish[ing] themselves from the pagans, &c. by wearing a little crucifix about their necks."[85] Their self-segregation was also noted by Francis Moore, who, in 1738, wrote that they "reckon themselves still as well as if they were actually

White, and nothing angers them more than to call them Negroes, that being a term they use only for slaves."[86] As Christoph Kohl has argued, Luso-African communities in Guinea-Bissau to this day "stress their historical roles as brokers for the Portuguese, emphasizing their part-European genealogies, urban residence, and Christian beliefs and often, in doing so, drawing a boundary between them and the 'uncivilized' (religiously and socially) rural population."[87]

Over the course of the seventeenth century, a number of churches and chapels were erected in *praças* that had their own priest or vicar. The oldest and most prestigious one was the church of Cacheu, dedicated to Our Lady of Victory.[88] Other churches and chapels in the region were dedicated to Our Lady of the Rosary (in Geba), Our Lady of the Candles (in Bissau), Our Lady of Light (in Ziguinchor), Our Lady Mediatrix of All Graces (in Farim), and Saint Anthony, a saint who Francisco de Lemos Coelho in 1669 claimed to "enjoy great devotion," not only by the Portuguese residing in Guinea "but also by the natives."[89] Kristons who lived outside of these urban centers had to content themselves with the occasional visit of a priest. Around 1607, English explorers in Sierra Leone observed that a "fryer with 2 more" lived in the region, who "doe keepe heer aboute Sierra Leona amongst the Portingalls to say masse, also to procure some of the black people to become Christians." Some of the locals, they claimed, "are by Portugall Priests and Jesuits made Christians, and have a Chapell, wherein are written in a table, suche dayes as they are to observe holy." They singled out a certain Lucas Fernandes, who "had lived at St. Iagoe [Santiago] in former time [and] was turnid Christian." He could "argue well of his faith, onely hee is ledd by the delusions of the fryars according to the popish religion."[90]

Typically during Lent, a priest—known among Kristons as *visitador* (visitor)—would come from Santiago or one of the *praças* to baptize newborns and hear confessions.[91] Moore confirmed that, in the Gambia, "they christen and marry by the help of a priest sent yearly over thither from S. Jago," whereas John Matthews observed in Sierra Leone that those who "profess the Roman Catholic religion" were visited "once or twice a year by a priest from the Portuguese settlement at Bassou [Bissau]." According to Matthews, Kristons were "merely nominal Christians. Their religion principally consists in repeating a Pater Noster, or an Ave Maria, and in wearing a large string of beads round their neck, with a cross, or crucifix, suspended."[92]

Portuguese Church authorities tended to share this disdain. Since the Christianization of Africans in Upper Guinea had followed a path that deviated from the Catholic standard, they referred to them as mere *cristões por ceremónia* (ceremonial Christians).[93] Yet, when the French Abbé Demanet, chaplain of Gorée, visited Kristons in the Gambia in 1764, he was impressed to meet a community of "scrupulous observers of the faith" in spite of the fact that they had not seen a single priest in over twenty years.[94]

The fact that Kristons had remained attached to their religion in spite of the absence of a clergy indicates that these communities had largely taken Christianization into their own hands. Similar to what had happened in Santiago, they did so by creating mutual-aid and burial societies modeled upon Iberian brotherhoods. Thanks to the support of wealthy merchants, confraternities — known as *manjuandadis* — were highly prestigious organizations in Kriston communities, and their "kings" and "queens" functioned as mediators with the colonial authorities.[95] Historian João Barreto defined these brotherhoods as "a form of miniature parliaments, with members elected by the people, who assumed the right to administer justice, adopt laws, and discuss orders received from the authorities."[96]

A distinctive feature of Kriston brotherhood culture was *folgar*, the celebration of Catholic holidays according to a Portuguese model.[97] As early as in the 1560s, there are references to the performance of *autos sacramentais* in the settlement of Buguendo on the Cacheu River.[98] In 1610 the Jesuit Manuel Álvares participated at an Easter celebration in a church at the Sierra Leone peninsula port of Porto do Salvador that involved a grandiose procession with "all the instruments, musicians, singers, and feasts that one could find in that part of the world."[99]

Not unlike in late-medieval Portugal, many of these brotherhood rituals related to the souls of the deceased. In May 1858, the Portuguese officer Januário Correia de Almeida complained during his stay in Bissau about nightly assemblies on All Souls' Day, which involved "sung litanies" alternating with drum music, dance, and laughter.[100] Another officer, Henrique Augusto Dias de Carvalho, provided a more detailed description of these rituals in the late nineteenth century. On the eve of All Saints' Day, he claims, "they all unite in front of the church, and from there they proceed with torches in procession through the streets, mixing Ave Marias with indigenous songs," while wearing "fantastic costumes, as if it was carnival." These celebrations involved "acts of debauchery" and ended, the following day, with a banquet and the praying of "Ave-Marias for the souls of all the deceased." When Carvalho asked why they celebrated All Souls' Day in such a way, people answered that "it was because of the catechization of the first missionaries."[101] As Brooks rightly observed, Carvalho's decision to reach out to the ecclesiastic authorities with a request to "put an end to this expression of contempt for our religion" is not devoid of irony, considering that the Afro-Catholic ritual he witnessed had undeniably Portuguese roots.[102]

SÃO TOMÉ AND LOWER GUINEA

Soon after colonizing the Cape Verde islands, the Portuguese Crown initiated the colonization of a number of islands in the Gulf of Guinea: Fernando Po (today's Bioko), Príncipe, São Tomé, and Annobón. The initial focus was on São Tomé. According to an anonymous sixteenth-century pilot, the relationship between Portuguese men and African women was "an accepted practice" on the island "because the Negro population is both intelligent and rich, and they bring up their daughters in our way of life, both as regards custom and dress."[103] Similar to what had happened in Santiago, this practice resulted in a hierarchical society that included a Black, predominantly Mulatto, elite, known as Tomistas.[104]

São Tomé's tropical climate offered better opportunities for the cultivation of lucrative crops than Cape Verde. The introduction of sugarcane required intense labor, which made Portuguese settlers and their multiracial offspring aggressive players in the African slave markets. By the mid-sixteenth century, however, the Portuguese shifted the bulk of the sugarcane production to Brazil; Tomistas reacted by transforming the island into an entrepôt for Brazil-bound enslaved people.[105]

According to Sandoval, the three groups of Africans he identified for Cape Verde—*bozales*, *ladinos*, and *naturales*—"also applies to São Tomé," which shows that, not unlike those coming from Santiago, shipments of enslaved Africans from São Tomé also included Christians. Moreover, the "language of São Tomé," which Sandoval defined as a "corrupted version of Portuguese," was allegedly understood by many Africans from the Gulf of Guinea.[106] This dissemination of Portuguese cultural influences in Lower Guinea resulted not only from direct connections with São Tomé but also from a series of fortresses erected along the African coastline, the most important of which were Fort São Jorge da Mina, also known as El-mina Castle, built in 1482; Fort Santo António in Axim (1515); and Fort São Sebastião in Shama (1520).[107]

From these fortresses, missions regularly departed in the hope of converting local leaders. King João II was confident that "with the bait offered by the worldly goods . . . they might receive those of the Faith through our doctrine."[108] After several failed attempts, Diogo D'Alvarenga excitedly reported to the Crown that "Sasaxy, the king of Afuto," had "received the water of baptism and was converted to the faith of Our Lord, and then with him six knights, all the principal persons of the place became Christians, including two wives of the king and one son." In 1513 Afonso Caldeira informed the Crown that the "king of Futo [Fetu] says he wishes to be a Christian and also that all his land should become Christian, I should see that he be made a Christian and also his wives" and, in 1516, the Portuguese monarch learned in a letter from Duarte Pires that "the king of Benin gave his son and some of his noblemen so that they might become Christians and also he ordered a church to be built in Benin, they made them Christians straightaway and also they are teaching them to read."[109] While such missions initially seemed promising, they rarely had a lasting effect.

Nevertheless, Augusto de Castilho still witnessed in the late nineteenth century how French priests in Porto Novo, Benin, used "local interpreters who repeated the entire prayer, in loud voice and phrase by phrase, in Portuguese."[110] Elements of Portuguese Catholicism also ended up influencing indigenous rituals, as is revealed by Henry Lewis Ward-Price, who during his service as colonial administrator in Benin in the early twentieth century observed that the royal Aruosa cult included "a brass crucifix" that the Oba of Benin every morning would press "to his forehead" while praying "for the Oni of life . . . and all the other Yoruba kings. This had for long been the custom, he said, whether the Oba was a Christian or not."[111]

Portuguese Catholic influence was particularly strong in the small Kingdom of Warri, in the Niger Delta, where the local ruler converted in the 1560s and was succeeded by a son he had sent to study in Portugal and who returned with a Portuguese wife.[112] According to the Dutch scholar Olfert Dapper (who based himself on the writings of Samuel Blommaert), the latter had a "mulatto son," who "dresses like the Portuguese, always wearing a sword at this side." Dapper also described "a church" in seven-teenth-century Warri with "an altar, a crucifix, statues of Mary and the Apostles." Locals "come into this church with the rosary constantly in their hands, just as proper Portuguese do" and "recite it together with other popish prayers."[113] In the late eighteenth century, John Adams observed how the ruler of Warri still used to dress "in the European style," with clothes "of Portuguese fabric" that "at a former period [had] been worn by some noble peer or knight." Upon entering the palace, he found "several emblems of the Catholic religion, consisting of crucifixes, mutilated saints, [and] a large wooden cross." Upon inquiring about their origin, Adams was told that "several black Portuguese missionaries had been at Warré, many years since." Although a "large wooden cross . . . was remaining in a very perfect state," Adams claimed that locals "trouble themselves very little about religion of any kind."[114] However, the British naval officer John King still witnessed a "large Christmas procession" with "people carrying crucifixes and some other symbols of Christianity" when visiting Warri in 1820.[115]

Meanwhile, several Luso-African communities had developed in or near the Portuguese fortresses as a result of relationships between Portuguese traders and local women. In his report about the Gold Coast from 1602, the Dutch merchant Pieter de Marees observed that it would be wrong to assume that none of the Africans in the region were familiar with Christianity. "Many of those who can speak Portuguese," he wrote, "are starting to . . . acquire some knowledge of God's word." In fact, "Blacks who live with the Portuguese can tell a lot about God and his commandments. I met some who could tell a lot about the birth of Christ, the Last Supper, his bitter passion, death, and resurrection, and other points related to our Christian religion." He had "a good friend," who "had lived with a monk in Castle Elmina" and "was able to read and write Portuguese very well and was quite well versed in the Scriptures." When the Dutch would bring up "certain points against the Catholic faith," he would "argue against those by pointing to passages in the Gospel and the Apostolic Letters."[116] Later that century, Jean Barbot confirmed that "the natives of Mina are all either blacks or mulattoes. Of the latter, there are about two hundred families, and they are baptized and call themselves Portuguese." According to this French Protestant, their Catholic faith was "mixed with much pagan superstition."[117]

Elmina was conquered in 1637 by the Dutch, who banned all Catholic priests. Nevertheless, Jacobus Capitein, a Dutch Reformed minister of African birth, reported in 1743 that the majority of African Christians in the region were Catholic.[118] In his 1855 Dutch translation of Brodie Cruickshank's *Eighteen Years on the Gold Coast of Africa* (1853), D. P. H. J. Weijtingh referred to Portuguese baptismal fonts in Elmina and nearby Eguafu that were considered "holy objects" by locals and to the lighting of wax candles for the dead, a custom he related to "ancestors of families who had been Christianized by the Portuguese."[119] As late as in the 1870s, when Father Louis Charles Gommenginger was asked by the Propaganda Fide to explore the best place to start a Catholic mission in the Gold Coast, he recommended Elmina because people there "still retained some Catholic traditions from Portuguese times," despite the fact that no Catholic priests had operated in the region for over two centuries.[120] When this Elmina mission started in the 1880s, Auguste Moreau and Eugène Murat confirmed that locals still held "old worn statues" from "Portuguese times" in their houses. They also mentioned the existence of a temple, Ntona Buw (Anthony's Temple) and its associated fraternity, known as the Santonafo or Antonifo (the people of Saint Anthony), whose members, dressed in knee-length distinctive gowns, used to carry a Portuguese statue of the saint in procession through town in order to call for rain. Annually, this statue was ceremoniously washed until, one day, it fell apart and the broken pieces were collected at Ntona Buw. Out of the belief that the water used to wash the statue acquired magic force, a ritual that mixed Catholic and indigenous elements developed. Known as Kotobun Kese, it consisted of a nightly parade during which salutes were fired and water was sprinkled all over town to scare off evil spirits. An annual procession also continued from Ntona Buw to the ancient Portuguese fortress and back, led by a person carrying an iron cross fastened to a long pole, including a prayer session for the *Yankufion Embahina* (Servants of God) buried outside the castle walls. Moreover, newly established Elmina chiefs were required to visit Ntona Buw as part of their enthronement, after which they were carried on a palanquin in procession through town.

Moreau and Murat also reported that another mutual-aid and burial society, the Santa Mariafo (the people of Saint Mary), existed in Elmina. The members of this brotherhood possessed a statue of the Virgin Mary and went about the village every Friday dressed in long white gowns, carrying candles, and chanting the Portuguese words "Santa Maria." Whenever one of the members of this fraternity died, the body was laid out, three burning candles were placed around it, a small cross was placed on the person's breast, and the statue of the Virgin was set on a table nearby with a burning candle on either side of it. There was also a dish of water at hand, with a small branch lying in it that was used to sprinkle the corpse. Members of the Santa Mariafo believed that the soul of the departed ascended into heaven, and they also presented the parents of a newborn, seven days after birth, with a crucifix in a special ceremony with a lighted candle.[121]

The Christianization of the Black population in São Tomé itself started in the fifteenth century. By 1494 African priests trained in Lisbon had been sent to the island, which, in 1533, became a diocese, elevating the fifteenth-century Church of Santa Maria to the category of cathedral. When visiting the island in the 1660s, Nicolas Villault claimed that it was "larger and more beautiful" than the Church of Saint-Merri in Paris. The French merchant witnessed a "procession on the first day of the Rogation days" and claimed that the entire Black population of São Tomé "was Christian." He highlighted the presence of "black priests" and was impressed by the "black altar servers," who "sang as well as those in France."[122]

As had happened in Santiago, however, successive ecclesiastics designated to serve as bishop never came or died from tropical diseases shortly after their arrival.[123] Attempts to establish a seminary on the island were inconsistent and ultimately failed, which increased concerns among Church authorities that the gospel was being preached on the island by "people without any knowledge," whose sermons spread "thousands of absurdities."[124] Complaints about "superstitions and indigenous abuses among the blacks, both natives and newly arrived ones" even reached the Lisbon Inquisition in 1623.[125] Such concerns were echoed by Barbot when visiting the nearby island of Príncipe in the late seventeenth century. After witnessing a procession "at night by the light of many lamps which they lit on the balconies of their houses" and a church service led by "Moorish priests," the Huguenot wrote that it was "enough to make anyone weep to see the expressions of superstition that they inculcate in these peoples. The whole of their religious worship is confined to a blind faith in rosaries, paternosters, and the miracles of Saint Anthony."[126] The same Protestant bias characterized the late seventeenth-century observations by Willem Bosman about the island of Annobón. This Dutch merchant referred to the inhabitants as "half Christians, although they bear the name of full ones; because if only they could say a Pater Noster and an Ave Maria, confess to the popish priest, and bring some offerings with them, they pass for good Christians." He also met with two Capuchins, who "invited us to come and see their two churches, which we did, and found them clean and in good state, large enough for four times the number of inhabitants of the island."[127]

As in Santiago, the influence of the Black and Mulatto elite on the islands also reflected itself in the prestige of confraternities. In 1526 the Crown authorized the confraternity of Our Lady of the Rosary to purchase the freedom of any enslaved person, male or female, who had proven to be a loyal member, even if against the will of the owner. Annually, its members celebrated the patron saint with "animated festivities" that lasted two weeks, the first of which was for the brotherhood's free members and the second for members who were still enslaved.[128]

That their Catholic traditions had, over time, deviated considerably from post-Tridentine European standards is reflected in Francesco da Monteleone's complaints about the island's rosary brotherhood. According to this seventeenth-century Italian Capuchin, the latter formed the greatest obstacle to his priestly work in São Tomé. He accused the rosary brotherhood of "thousands of insults against God," including the organization of feasts that attracted "dishonest public women" and degenerated in "revelry, dancing, and dishonest, crapulent touching."[129]

The influence of brotherhoods remained strong after the islands entered an economic decline following the mid-sixteenth-century decision by the Crown to send enslaved Africans directly to Brazil from Angola.[130] The Church also lost interest, and, in 1677, ecclesiastical authority over São Tomé and the nearby islands transferred to the archdiocese of Salvador, in Brazil. In 1778 Fernando Po and Annobón became Spanish territory. When visiting the latter island in the mid-nineteenth century, the Portuguese explorer Francisco Travassos Valdez identified nine churches and noted that the population was Catholic but that "their religious ideas are very peculiar, inasmuch as, though they are anxious that White priests should administer to them the sacraments, they are unwilling to allow them to exercise any authority." For this reason, Valdez observed, "it is now nearly a century since a single curate could be obtained for any of these churches."[131]

The Catholic congregations in São Tomé and Príncipe, the two islands that remained under Portuguese rule, continued to function in semi-isolation until the nineteenth century, when the coffee and cacao boom reignited Portugal's interest in the islands. The reestablishment of the archdiocese in 1884 brought the Church back under Portuguese control. In response to attempts to bring local Catholicism in line with European standards, the ancient brotherhoods became sanctuaries of religious resistance. People's attachment to the brotherhoods grew even stronger after the arrival of immigrant workers. Following abolition in 1836, the people of São Tomé and Príncipe refused to do any further manual work, whereupon the colonial authorities imported fieldworkers from other Portuguese colonies in Africa. In order to distinguish themselves from these African immigrants, the natives turned to their *lumandadgis* (brotherhoods) as unique cultural identity markers to which newcomers had no access.[132]

Meanwhile, the Portuguese ecclesiastical authorities tried to wipe out the "plays and highly indecent profanities, supported by the devil" during the annual "rosary celebrations."[133] A governmental document from 1812 complained about "the more than two thousand feasts that are celebrated every year [by] brotherhoods, [whose leaders] are elected [and organize] numerous processions," whereas "not more than six people show up for our church services." It also lashed out against "the canons" of the island, for being "devoid of virtue and among the most ignorant ones in the universe."[134] In 1836, Raimundo da Cunha Matos reported that "a lot of confraternities and poor brotherhoods" still existed on the islands and that their "feasts of the Rosary" were among the most splendid ones, although "the degree of profanation and irreverence during the feast of the Rosary has declined in comparison to what it used to be in the past."[135]

Much of the islands' popular culture can be traced back to the mixture of pre-Tridentine Portuguese Catholic traditions and indigenous African elements that once thrived in brotherhoods. This is, most notably, the case with funeral rituals that have characteristics similar to those in Santiago, including processions accompanied by music bands, mourning rituals known as *nojo* that alternate moments of extreme sadness with joy, and the celebration of a "second burial" for the deceased's soul, called *fissu*.[136]

In his late nineteenth-century ethnographic study, José de Almada Negreiros pointed out that brotherhoods also organized "Kongo dances."[137] The earliest extensive description of such a dance, known as *Dança Congo*, can be found in the context of a nineteenth-century *auto sacramental* in honor of Our Lady of Peñafrancia that tells the story of Captain Kongo, who, with the help of soldiers and angels, defeats the dragon.[138] Kongo dances are still performed on the islands on major Catholic holidays. They are more of a pantomime than a dance and can last up to six hours. These dances have characteristics in common with other folkloric performances on the islands that relate to Portuguese chivalric culture. While in São Tomé, groups annually perform the *Tragedy of the Marquis of Mantua and the Emperor Charlemagne*, locally known as the *Tchiloli*, the island of Príncipe hosts a mock fight between Moors and Christians in its *Auto de Floripes*. Participation at these performances used to be considered a form of ex-voto to a saint, locally known as *paga devê* (to pay back what you owe). According to Gerhard Seibert, these traditions recall "performances dedicated to the King of Congo in Brazil, Colombia, and Panama. Such performances, called *congos* or *congadas*, constitute an integral part of the festivals of religious brotherhoods."[139]

KONGO

The earliest contacts between Portugal and Kongo date back to 1483, when the explorer Diogo Cão and his crew arrived at the mouth of the Congo River, where they met with local rulers and took some Kongolese with them to Portugal. Upon their return in 1485, these Kongolese brought not only numerous gifts, including a banner with the cross of the Order of Christ, but also a new religion. Impressed by what they had to say about their stay in Portugal, the *manikongo* Nzinga a Nkuwu decided to send a number of diplomats to Lisbon, where they stayed in a monastery, learned about Christianity, and were baptized. In 1491 these diplomats returned with a Portuguese committee that included a number of priests, who first baptized the ruler of the province of Soyo and, later, Nzinga a Nkuwu, who was given the baptismal name João, the same as the Portuguese king. Several nobles were also baptized, as was the *manikongo*'s oldest son, Mvemba a Nzinga, who received the name Afonso. The delegation also brought masons, blacksmiths, and carpenters, who started building a church. During those early days of Kongo's Christianization, a revelation occurred when two Kongolese nobles allegedly dreamed simultaneously about a beautiful woman encouraging them to embrace Christianity. The following day, one of them discovered a stone in the form of a cross. Portuguese missionaries reacted enthusiastically to this revelation and brought the stone in procession into the newly built church.[140]

While his father soon abandoned Christianity, allegedly over a dispute about monogamy, Afonso took his conversion seriously. He surrounded himself with Portuguese priests, teachers, and diplomats, to whom he reached out for military support when the question of succession came up. In 1506 Afonso defeated his half brother in the battle of Mbanza Kongo. As the new "king" of Kongo, Afonso I related his victory to a miraculous intervention by the Virgin Mary and Saint James the Greater. In an account of the battle he sent to Portugal, Afonso explained that Saint James, wearing a scarlet cape and riding a white horse, had appeared under the sky leading an army of knights under a white Constantine cross. It is likely that Afonso's vision, which was to become the foundation story of his kingdom, was inspired by Portuguese missionaries. Following the fierce battle for control over the Iberian Peninsula, Saint James the Greater (also known as Saint James the Apostle), had come to enjoy great popularity among Christian Iberians. Afonso's vision paralleled the intervention of Saint James in the (legendary) battle of Clavijo in 844 that had rendered a crucial victory to the Christian troops over the Moors in their struggle for control over the Iberian Peninsula. It was this myth, constructed in the twelfth century, that had led to the adoption of James as patron saint of the army under the name Santiago Matamoros (Saint James the Moor-Slayer). One may even suspect that, by the day of the prince's baptism, missionaries had deliberately established a connection to Saint James. By baptizing him with the name Afonso, they connected the young man to Afonso Henriques, Portugal's first king, who had defeated the Moors in the battle of Ourique in 1139, also thanks to an alleged intervention by Saint James the Greater.[141]

In a letter to the lords of his kingdom in 1512, quoted by the sixteenth-century Portuguese historian Damião de Góis, Afonso wrote that "the weapons that [the king of Portugal] has sent us symbolize the cross that we have seen in the sky, together with Saint James the Apostle and the other saints, who have battled with us, and who, with the help of the Lord, made us victorious." It continued, "God Almighty, our Lord, had ordered his angels to give these very same weapons to the first king of

Portugal when he was fighting numerous Moorish kings, enemies of the holy faith, on the day when he gave him the victory and defeated the Moors."[142] Following Afonso's victory over his half brother, James was adopted as patron saint of the Kongo kingdom. His symbol, the sea scallop, and the swords of his knights featured on the kingdom's coat of arms, and July 25 became the kingdom's official holiday. On Saint James's Day, nobles from all the provinces were expected to come to the capital, Mbanza Kongo, to pay taxes, where they were greeted with spectacular *ku-sanga* war dances, which the Portuguese called *sanga(mento)s*.[143]

Afonso used his privileged partnership with Portugal to reorganize the kingdom in order to foster unity and loyalty to himself. He adopted Portuguese as the kingdom's language of diplomacy and sent numerous young Kongolese, including some of his nephews, cousins, and even his own son Henrique, to Portugal to be trained for leading positions. The latter was ordained in Lisbon and later consecrated suffragan bishop of Utica by Pope Leo X. In 1521 Henrique returned to Kongo to assist his father in developing the new Church, but his subsequent work is unknown.[144]

At Afonso's request, the Portuguese kings Manuel I and João III sent additional teachers and clergymen to Kongo, including the royal chaplain Rui d'Aguiar, who, in an enthusiastic letter to the Portuguese king, called Afonso "an angel who the Lord sent to this kingdom" and who "knows more than us about the prophets, the gospel of Our Lord Jesus Christ, the lives of the saints and so many other things about our holy Church." Aguiar also wrote that Afonso "punishes those who worship idols and burns those idols" and that he "has schools where they teach our holy faith," including "schools for girls."[145] In fact, not only did Afonso acquire literacy himself, he also established a large-scale Portuguese educational program by gathering "four hundred young men and boys," ordering "the building of great walls with many thorns on top so they could not jump over it and flee," and "entrusted the fathers with teaching them."[146] This allowed Afonso to gradually replace foreign teachers with Kongolese ones and send out graduates to teach the new religion in the different provinces of his kingdom.[147]

Afonso's policy to disseminate the new religion in Kongo went hand in hand with a struggle against "pagan" enemies who represented a threat to his power. As a sign that a new era had arrived, those who had been fighting on the side of his half brother and repented were forced to clean the floor of the church before being baptized.[148] Afonso also made the provocative decision to cut down the trees surrounding the royal cemetery, "where in the past kings were buried, in accordance with their ancient idolatry." On that sacred site he built a church, dedicated to Our Lady of Victory, and erected a towering cross at the heart of the kingdom's capital.[149] In 1514 Afonso asked his Portuguese counterpart to also send him "cannons and guns" because he intended to "burn down a large house of idols" and feared that, in retaliation, his enemies could launch "a war and kill us."[150]

The Kongolese elite quickly realized that the display of Catholic zeal could strengthen their influence in the new regime. They did so by establishing churches, chapels, and schools, erecting giant crosses in their principal towns, celebrating Catholic holidays, ordering Catholic artifacts, and stimulating church attendance. They themselves adopted Portuguese clothing styles, music, court etiquette, and symbols of royalism.[151] When the Dutch merchant Pieter van den Broecke visited the Kongolese province of Soyo in 1608, he identified "eight or ten schools just like in Portugal, because all the children need to learn Portuguese. Everyone goes the whole day with a book in hand and with a rosary."[152] During his time in Soyo between 1611 and 1613, Samuel Brun, a Swiss barber-surgeon in Dutch service, confirmed that people "speak the Portuguese language quite well" and that they had "teachers."[153] Another Dutch merchant, Ferdinand van Capelle, reported in 1642 that Kongo was "full of wooden crosses, before which people bowed devoutly" and that every noble had "his own church at his village with a wooden cross."[154]

Meanwhile, Afonso also used Catholicism as a tool of international diplomacy by requesting a Bull of Crusade from the Vatican, so that his expansionist policies could be justified as an attempt to spread the "true faith." In 1512 he sent a mission, led by his cousin and including his son Henrique, to the Vatican. A second mission in 1535 failed to reach Rome. Afonso's eagerness to establish direct links with the Vatican could be interpreted as a first attempt to be less dependent on the Portuguese. Following the death of Bishop Henrique, the Portuguese Crown had placed Kongo under the jurisdiction of the newly created diocese of São Tomé. This decision coincided with growing tensions between Portugal and Kongo over the control of the slave trade, where Afonso's monopoly was challenged by Tomistas and increasing numbers of freeborn Kongolese were stolen away.[155]

Even after the relationship with Portugal had soured, subsequent Kongolese kings continued to position themselves in the lineage of Afonso, using his coat of arms and Portuguese-style symbols of royalty such as the crown, sword, cape, scepter, and, above all, religion to legitimate their claim to the throne. Following the model set by Afonso, a Catholic priest had to officiate the coronation of newly elected kings. This, however, made Kongolese rulers dependent on the goodwill of Portugal that did not hesitate to (mis)use its *padroado* in order to interfere in local affairs. Kongolese frustration over this interference is reflected in the decision by King Diogo I to allow Jesuits to establish a seminary in the kingdom's capital in 1548, only to expel them seven years later when they tried to enforce the authority of the bishop of São Tomé over the Church in Kongo. With this bold decision, Diogo made it clear that he only accepted a Church that was under his control. Very much against the will of the Portuguese, subsequent Kongolese kings also assumed the right to knight loyal supporters in the Order of Christ.[156]

In the 1570s, King Álvaro I of Kongo faced a major threat, likely caused by an invasion of foreign African warriors. In exchange for military assistance, he allowed Portugal to establish a stronghold in Luanda. From this small island in the southern edge of the kingdom, Portugal gradually expanded the territory under its control—known as Angola—and developed its own slave trading networks.[157]

In spite of the tensions between Kongolese rulers and those who had brought them Christianity, the former did not abandon the new faith. Yet they wished to liberate themselves from the Portuguese *padroado*. With skillful diplomacy, Álvaro I convinced the Vatican to create a separate diocese for Central Africa in the late sixteenth century, with the seat in the kingdom's capital, now renamed São Salvador. Implemented in 1596, the diocese failed to achieve its purpose because Portugal successfully insisted on its right to appoint the bishop for the new seat. In response to this, Kongolese rulers again turned to regular orders and welcomed the Jesuits back in 1619. Meanwhile, they continued efforts to win sympathies at the Vatican in 1608 by sending a delegation led by the Kongolese diplomat António Manuel, who died upon arrival and is memorialized with a bust at the Saint Mary Major sanctuary. These diplomatic efforts, supported by influential European allies such as Juan Baptist Vives, undoubtedly contributed to the decision by Pope Gregory XV to create the Propaganda

Fide in 1622. The fact that the Roman Curia now became responsible for missionary work dealt the deathblow to the *padroado*. Portugal reacted in 1624 by boldly moving the de facto seat of the Central African diocese from the Kongolese capital to its own stronghold in Luanda. Under pressure of the Vatican, however, it could not avoid the sending of new priests, mostly Italians, of the Order of Friars Minor Capuchin to Kongo.[158]

Considering not only the religious but also the political importance to the Kongolese monarchy of the Capuchins, whose blessing was crucial for the consecration of newly elected kings, it is not surprising that these priests were also employed in diplomatic missions. Shortly after their arrival in 1645, King Garcia II selected two of them as ambassadors to represent Kongo at the Vatican and in the Netherlands.[159]

The latter was important because, by the early seventeenth century, the Dutch had appeared as a new force in Central Africa. Between 1641 and 1648 they managed, with Kongolese support, to occupy Luanda and (temporarily) take over control of the transatlantic slave trade. In spite of his political alliance with the Calvinist Dutch, King Garcia's decision to send a Capuchin as his ambassador to The Hague shows that he was not considering conversion to Protestantism.[160] In a letter to Johan Maurits, the ruler of Dutch Brazil, from May 1642, Garcia refused to accept Protestant proselytism in his kingdom, arguing, "I practice the true Catholic faith."[161] When the Dutch minister Nicolaus Ketel gave him a Calvinist book in Portuguese translation, he allegedly reacted by ordering a fire to be lit, and "in the presence of everybody, including the Dutch, he fervently exhorted all the people to stay firm and stable in the Catholic faith, and then impetuously threw the book into the fire."[162]

Because of the importance of the Capuchin mission to the Kongolese monarchs, the latter backed the missionaries in their efforts to combat "superstition" and destroy "heathenish" objects. More than earlier missionaries, Capuchins ventured into peripheral parts of the kingdom and even beyond its borders, which regularly caused conflicts. The Flemish Capuchin Adriaan Willems, better known as Joris (or George) van Geel, was killed by an infuriated crowd in 1652 when he attempted to burn objects of indigenous worship. King Garcia reacted to this murder by enslaving the entire population of the village, some two hundred people, and sending them to Brazil.[163]

Meanwhile, the Portuguese managed to retake Luanda from the Dutch. With the financial support of plantation owners in need of enslaved workers, an army led by Salvador Correia de Sá departed from Rio de Janeiro and successfully recaptured the city in 1649. The fight for Luanda, which for a long time remained a mere footnote in world history, has only recently been acknowledged as the largest military campaign organized by inhabitants of the New World on the other side of the Atlantic before John Joseph Pershing sent his Expeditionary Forces to France in 1918. After expelling their Dutch competitors, the Portuguese prepared for a decisive battle against the king of Kongo. In 1665, with the assistance of African warrior bands known as *imbangala*, they defeated the Kongolese army, beheaded King António I, and sealed his head in one of the walls of the Church of Our Lady of Nazareth in Luanda.[164]

From that moment, the once mighty Kongo kingdom dissolved into a civil war, the region of Soyo split away from the kingdom, and countless Kongolese were caught up in battles and sold to the Americas. Portugal attempted to take advantage of the situation, but, in 1670, its troops suffered a major defeat against the Soyo army, backed by the Dutch, in the Battle of Kitombo, which forced them to retreat to Luanda. The Portuguese defeat did not put an end to the civil war, and the kingdom further disintegrated. In 1678 São Salvador was ransacked and abandoned by the population. When the Capuchin Luca da Caltanissetta entered the former capital in the 1690s, he saw that "all the churches had been dismantled," and "while the cathedral was still standing, the roots of trees had cracked its walls."[165]

By the early eighteenth century, relative calm returned to Kongo. During all these years the Capuchin mission continued, albeit with declining numbers.[166] By the 1750s, there was but one left, Cherubino da Savona, who kept sending positive reports from Soyo, where "the inhabitants are almost all Christians" and the prince is a "good Christian," who "can read and write in Portuguese."[167] A French mission to the region northwest of the Congo River in the 1760s failed to obtain results but did reveal the presence of Catholic communities who had migrated there from Soyo. "Although they had no pastors to lead them, they self-organized themselves," Liévin-Bonaventure Proyart wrote, "and gathered on Sundays to chant the hymns and canticles in honor of the true God."[168] In 1770 another French priest specified that "the population of Kongo has no priests, no access to sacraments or baptisms," but, in spite of this, it "celebrates the holy days with chants, hymns, processions, and sermons, preached to the people by its own leaders."[169]

After the last Capuchin had left, Kongo still maintained its political autonomy and priests occasionally came over from Luanda to bless its newly elected kings. In 1779, a Portuguese mission arrived in Luanda and four of its members, including a Black priest from Brazil, traveled to Kongo.[170] In his report, the Franciscan Rafael Castelo de Vide expressed surprise that, in places where not a single priest had come in over two decades, one could "hear at night and in the early morning prayers to the Virgin." He also noted that it was customary for people to sing the Ave Maria in Kikongo when traveling. In Mapinda he was welcomed with "joyful dances called *sangamentos*, which are military exercises" that offered "protection against demons," which was "badly needed," people claimed, since "priests had been kept from coming to the kingdom."[171] Castelo de Vide's plans to revive the Catholic splendor in the region failed, however.

Nevertheless, missionaries kept coming. In 1814 the Capuchin Luigi-Maria d'Assisi traveled from Luanda to São Salvador, baptizing hundreds of children along the way, blessing dozens of garments of knights in the Order of Christ, and crowning King Garcia V of Kongo. The latter sent to Luanda one of his sons, who, after being ordained, returned and served as a priest in São Salvador until 1836.[172] In 1844 the Angolan priest Francisco das Necessidades claimed to have found an eighteenth-century Kongolese document entitled "Memoir of How Our Christianity Came from Portugal" during his mission in São Salvador. It referred to the arrival of the Portuguese and the stone marker they left on the Congo riverbank, the first baptism of a Kongo king, the reign of King Afonso and the Order of Christ, as well as the glories of the bishops of Kongo and their connections to Rome.[173] In 1855 King Henrique III approached the authorities in Luanda with the request to send a new priest to Kongo and expressed concern about the fact that "all Christians are required to go to confession at least once a year because otherwise they go to hell." He excused himself for having "nothing to offer" in exchange "because nowadays slaves are no longer in demand."[174]

Portugal did, eventually, reestablish a Catholic mission in São Salvador in the late nineteenth century. It did so in response to the founding of a British Baptist mission that, according to Father António Barroso, had provocatively used stones of the ancient cathedral to build a Protestant church.[175] In 1914 Portugal formally abolished the Kongolese monarchy and subsequently incorporated the kingdom's few remaining territories into its colony Angola.[176]

Looking back in time, there can be no doubt that the arrival of Christianity made a major impact in the region. The Spanish Carmelite Diego de Santissimo Sacramento, for instance, was positively surprised about the state of religion he encountered in Kongo in the 1580s, claiming that he "did not find anyone who was apostate from the faith or returned totally to idolatry" and that "it was a point of honor to be Christian and they know well the error in which they sin. I only found that they go for reasons of illness to their fetishers and priest of idols, and these are very cautious and do it secretly."[177] By the time the Capuchins arrived in 1645, Kongo had thirteen parishes, each with a curate, and every provincial capital had a church. Its capital had a cathedral with an organ, choir, and bell tour, five additional churches, and a Santa Casa de Misericórdia with its own confraternity.[178] In 1631 Bishop Francisco de Soveral reported that, on Sundays and holidays, the churches in São Salvador were too small for the large crowds, so services had to be held on the central square.[179] While Christianity undoubtedly stood stronger in urban centers, "even in remote regions far from the established parishes and missionary convents, and even outside the territories controlled by the kingdom," Fromont writes, "crowds of men and women could experience memorable, if few, Christian rituals and see or own modest Christian images." Christianity, she claims, "was part of the world of many Central Africans."[180] The new religion also became an identity marker. As Thornton has argued, "Christianity set true Kongolese aside from their neighbors, and in their view made them superior to the 'heathens,' even those to the north and east who spoke dialects of the same Kikongo language."[181]

The remarkable expansion of and attachment to Christianity in Kongo was primarily the result from the decision by King Afonso and his successors to embrace and promote the new faith. Their ambition was not to copy the faith of the Portuguese but to develop a Kongolese variant of Christianity under their own control. In order to build a Kongolese Church, they found important allies in Bras Correa, a Spaniard who had come to Kongo as a young man, learned to speak Kikongo fluently and, in 1601, was ordained a priest by the first bishop of São Salvador, as well as in Manuel Roboredo, a Kongolese priest, ordained in 1637, whose parents were a Portuguese nobleman and a sister of the Kongolese king Álvaro V.[182]

Even more important was the role of lay catechists. Whenever Europeans went on a mission, they worked alongside Kongolese interpreters, catechists, and churchwardens and, in practice, very much depended on them.[183] As we have seen, Afonso had from the beginning of his reign been eager to develop such a local intelligentsia. By 1514, he started to send recently graduated *mestres* (*maestri* in Italian) out into provinces of his kingdom to spread the new faith, and this policy was continued by his successors. The *mestres* worked alongside the *muleke* ("boys"), who assisted them with practical matters. The latter were a special category of enslaved people who worked for the Church and were known in Portuguese as *escravos da igreja* (slaves of the church).[184] Similar to what we have seen in Santiago and São Tomé, the *mestres* were instrumental in spreading and consolidating the new faith. In 1561 Father Sebasitão de Couto reported from the province of Bamba that there were several churches "built according to the fashion of the country," where "graduates of the chapel of King Diogo teach the Christian doctrine, precepts, and rules."[185] The *mestres* must have been quite numerous. In 1760 the Capuchin Rosario dal Parco estimated that there were about six thousand Kongolese nobles and that almost all of them had several *mestres*.[186] Around the same time, Cherubino da Savona confirmed that "almost all nobles have several *mestres* who speak the Portuguese language and teach the catechism." This way, "when the missionaries arrive in their land, they find people there who have already been initiated in the mysteries of our holy faith so he can right away start confessions and marriages."[187]

The Kongolese nobility also relied on brotherhoods to strengthen its control over the development of Christianity. A letter from the Kongolese ambassador in Lisbon reveals that no fewer than six confraternities existed in São Salvador by 1595—those of Our Lady of the Rosary, the Holy Sacrament, Saint Mary, the Immaculate Conception, the Holy Spirit, and Saint Anthony—whose members gathered daily to celebrate "Masses for the souls of the dead people."[188] According to the Jesuit António Franco, people who joined a confraternity were expected to proselytize and took an oath that they would "teach the Christian doctrine to uncultured and ignorant men, especially to the members of their own household."[189] Membership was initially the privilege of the kingdom's elite and therefore conferred great prestige. Those admitted to a confraternity enjoyed royal protection and could in theory not be sold into slavery.[190]

Starting in the early seventeenth century, King Álvaro II and his successors stimulated the creation of confraternities all over Kongo.[191] Capuchins also contributed to the dissemination of sodalities in Kongo as a way to spread the new faith and to "purify" Kongolese Catholicism by eradicating certain indigenous traditions that they perceived as superstitions.[192] The importance of confraternities to the Capuchins' missionary strategy is apparent in the case of Van Geel, who carried several prewritten documents with the text "Rules of the brotherhood of . . . founded at the Church of . . ." with him when he started his mission in 1651.[193] In his report on late seventeenth-century Soyo, the Capuchin Giuseppe Maria da Busseto pointed out that the prestige of the confraternity dedicated to Saint Francis was such that "all the counts are elected from among the members of this congregation."[194] According to Franco, people who joined a confraternity were expected to proselytize and took an oath that they would "teach the Christian doctrine to uncultured and ignorant men, especially to the members of their own household.[195] It was, thus, not without reason that Caltanissetta imposed a rule in 1701 that whenever a Capuchin priest embarked on a mission into the interior, he had to be accompanied by "a nobleman, who is member of a confraternity."[196]

The Spanish Capuchin António de Teruel reported in the mid-seventeenth century that he had "established schools for the education of children and several confraternities" in Mbata that were "modeled upon those in São Salvador."[197] In 1693 Caltanissetta confirmed that, in Mbata, there were "confraternities for men, for women, and for youngsters."[198] The Capuchin Bernardo da Gallo reported in 1710 that there were four confraternities in Bamba (those of the Holy Trinity, Our Lady of Carmel, Saint Francis, and Saint Anthony), whose members came to church every evening and held a procession every first Sunday of the month. On Monday, Wednesday, and Friday evenings, they "used the discipline," some of them "with iron, so that they bled." Gallo also provided a detailed description of the rosary confraternity he established in Bengo "in order to educate them and to make sure they maintained devout and saintly exercises." The people of Bengo apparently showed great interest in joining the brotherhood and attended the rosary prayer sessions, processions, and Masses "with order and devotion." Several of them made "a short white vest, in the manner of the Portuguese, to assist Mass and participate in processions."[199]

The decision by people in Bengo to spontaneously make *opas* reveals how familiar they were with Portuguese fraternal traditions. The same can be observed in Dionigi Carli's report about Bamba, where he, at night, witnessed how "a group of people sang, but in a melancholic fashion that scared me," while "carrying heavy logs of wood" for "penance." When he asked the reason for this, people answered that it was done "because it was a Friday in March," which "surprised" Carli, who apparently was unfamiliar with the Portuguese tradition of staging nightly processions for the souls in purgatory during Lent. He then opened the doors to the church, but, before entering, they "stopped, kneeled during a quarter of an hour, while singing in their language the Salve Regina with very sad voices." Inside the church, the two hundred men "used the discipline with leather-thongs and bark of trees" and finished their flagellation with the singing of *loas* to the Madonna.[200]

In his 1674 report about the state of the Church in Soyo, Busseto wrote enthusiastically about church attendance, in particular on Christmas Eve and All Souls' Day, when "the crowd is such that our church is too small for the multitude and we are obliged to use the church square instead that, in spite of its size, doesn't provide enough space for everyone to attend."[201] One decade later, the Capuchin Andrea da Pavia noted that, every third Sunday of the month, a procession in honor of Our Lady of the Rosary was held in Soyo's capital, Pinda. On Corpus Christi he witnessed how cannons and muskets were brought to the church square, where there was "a large pathway that leads to a type of theater . . . in the middle of which a magnificent altar is made." When these preparations were concluded, "children initiate the procession, carrying the cross, then the congregationists follow in due order, then the members of the confraternity of the holy sacrament with their red capes, then the lay priests wearing their surplices, then comes the canopy carried by six of the most noble men of the county." Following "a great number of people playing musical instruments," the prince "walks behind the holy sacrament and wears clothing decorated with gold, silver, and jewels."[202]

Impressed by the level of concern people had for the souls of the deceased, Pavia decided to establish a new confraternity, dedicated to the recommendation of the souls. To this purpose, he built a chapel with human bones. "No one," he wrote, would ever pass in front of the chapel "without praying an Ave Maria for the poor souls."[203] Kongolese concern over the souls in purgatory is also reflected in the decision by King Álvaro VI to build a church dedicated to Saint Michael Archangel, the redeemer of purified souls, in the mid-seventeenth century.[204] Moreover, it was a customary practice in Kongo to pay *mestres* alms with the request to hold special services for the souls of the deceased and to place a cup, mug, jar, or bottle on their graves.[205]

In spite of similarities to the way Catholicism evolved in Santiago and São Tomé, it should be stressed that, in Kongo, local elites held tight control over the work of *mestres* and brotherhoods. Another difference from the Atlantic islands is that, in Kongo, the new faith was transmitted not in (a creolized form of) Portuguese, but in the local Kikongo language. Translating the words spoken by missionaries into Kikongo was a complex endeavor. In the mid-seventeenth century, the Capuchin Bonaventura de Alessano considered translation to be one of the "many intolerable crosses we must bear here" because "we depend on the mouths of others" and Teruel observed that, during confessions, "people would say their sins directly to the interpreter instead of the confessor, because they think that the latter is not able to understand their weaknesses well and doesn't understand their sins because he is a foreigner."[206] Another revealing source is an anonymous manuscript, dating back to the early eighteenth century, that explains how preaching typically involved the assistance of two or three interpreters, whereby one interpreted directly while the other(s) whispered missing sections in the former's ear. It warned missionaries "to be attentive because of the disloyalty of some of the *mestres*, who, for their own convenience, may say the opposite of what the priest first said" and are so eager "to receive alms from penitents" that they sometimes bring "penitents to missionaries without first hearing their confession and then told them an invented confession." To remedy such problems, the author suggested that missionaries "should learn the language of the country well enough in order to be able to discover similar cases of deception."[207]

As early as 1556 we find references to the use of bilingual materials for missionary purposes, and it is likely that Cornélio Gomes, a Jesuit born in Kongo of Portuguese parents, used Kikongo in his catechism from 1557. In 1624 the Jesuit Mateus Cardoso published a Kikongo translation of a Portuguese catechism, made with the assistance of *mestres*. The most famous work of translation was the Latin-Spanish-Kikongo dictionary produced in the mid-seventeenth century by two Spanish Capuchins in cooperation with Roboredo. While copies of this dictionary have been preserved, the seven religious books in Kikongo, including one about the feast days for the Virgin and a prayer book for confraternities, which Teruel requested the printing of in 1662, have been lost.[208]

The use of Kikongo implied that doctrine had to be translated with words and expressions rooted in pre-Christian traditions, such as *Nzambi*, meaning ancestor or deity, for God; *moyo*, meaning the immortal part of a person, for soul; or *nganga*, spiritual healer, for priest. That this had consequences for the way the new faith, its belief system, and its rituals came to be understood in Kongo can be illustrated with reference to baptism. Since priests at that time used not only water but also a grain of salt to baptize newborns, "to be baptized" was translated in Kikongo as *curia mungua*, meaning "to eat salt." Considering that salt had traditionally been served in Kongolese culture as protection against evil spirits, this translation strengthened the popular belief that baptism was a ritual that protected against witchcraft.[209]

Such forms of cultural reinterpretation also affected Christian objects that were decorated with Kongolese motifs and made into *min'kisi*, magic objects that protected against evil forces. Writing about Kongo in the seventeenth century, the Capuchin Giovanni Cavazzi admitted that the Kongolese had not completely abandoned "heathenish practices" in the burial of their dead and the commemoration of ancestors on All Souls' Day. Since it was "impossible to reform this corruption," he suggested showing some flexibility with regard to customs "that did not prejudice the essentials of the [Catholic] religion."[210] As Raimondo da Dicomano's late eighteenth-century diary shows, the Kongolese resisted attempts by missionaries to impose their orthodoxy. "They are so convinced of their own ideas and so attached to their own customs, that it has become impossible to guide them away from this," he wrote, and "when one explains them . . . a truthful idea about the Holy Mysteries or about the precepts of God and the Church, they do not pay attention and often respond that these are their customs and the way things are done in Kongo and that the priest is still new to the region and not well informed."[211] As Heywood and Thornton have argued, the Kongolese "did recognize and accept the principal rituals and symbols of Christianity. They identified with the cross, religious paintings, priestly garb and paraphernalia, and other blessed objects as a part of their own religious lives," however, they "did not adopt outright these Christian elements, for many people retained many of their older beliefs within the forms of Catholic rites, worship, and devotion."[212]

How this ancient belief system looked is difficult to say, since we have little knowledge of the sixteenth-century indigenous belief system and cosmology. Based on information about practices that missionaries rejected as superstition, Thornton outlined some widely held pre-Christian beliefs of the Kongo region, such as the power of spiritual beings from the Other World or of spirits of deceased ancestors and wicked people against whom protection was required, in the form of charms.[213] Wyatt Mac-Gaffey added the results of his own anthropological research in the region to these historical sources, which led him to conclude that Kongolese cosmology is likely to have had a religious structure composed of four categories of otherworldly beings: the souls of ancestors, territorial deities, lesser spirits that can be captured in charms, and harmful spirits that wander around.[214] MacGaffey distanced himself from the controversial studies about Kongolese cosmology by the self-taught Kongolese scholar Fu-Kiau kia Bunseki and criticized the work of historian Anne Hilton and art historian Robert Farris Thompson, who popularized Fu-Kiau's theory of the "Kongo cosmogram," as studies "characterized more by [their] romantic appeal than by historical or ethnographic verisimilitude."[215]

While much of what has been written about Kongo's ancient belief system remains speculative, there can be no doubt that Christianity in Kongo coexisted and/or syncretized with indigenous beliefs, traditions, and customs. Research by Silva Horta into inquisition inquiries between 1596 and 1598 revealed that, in the marketplace of the provincial capital of Mbata, there were tents selling crucifixes, images, and even bones of saints next to attributes of indigenous health practices and animistic beliefs.[216] This coexistence of Catholic and indigenous elements was of great concern to Capuchins. Caltanissetta observed with horror that "some men and women told his interpreter that it was wrong to be an enemy of the sorcerers and to burn their idols." They also told him that "they couldn't abandon the customs of their country and, as Christians, first turned to God to cure this illness, but, since that hadn't worked, they turned to the sorcerers in order to obtain the healing from the devil who is honored in their idols."[217]

An even greater concern to missionaries was the development of hybrid phenomena such as the one observed the by Girolamo Merolla da Sorrento when entering a church in Noki, on the Congo River, in the late seventeenth century. To the dismay of the Italian Capuchin, Christian symbols had been mixed with those of the indigenous Kadiabemba religion and, instead of an altar, he found "a big tomb or heap of sand with an animal horn stuck in it."[218] Missionaries were also worried about the influence of secret societies known as *impasi* (singl. *kimpasi*). Although it is not known whether some of their beliefs and practices, such as the symbolic death and resurrection ritual for novices or the use of the symbol of the cross, already existed before Christianity was introduced in the region, there can be no doubt that, as Fromont has observed, certain of "Kimpasi's rituals and symbolism . . . echoed and even emulated those of the church."[219] In the 1660s the Capuchin Girolamo de Montesarchio was deeply upset when he learned that "members of the society had at the entry of their meeting place a large portico with the holy sign of the cross painted in different colors." To his frustration, he had to admit that "no leader, how great he may be, had power over them."[220] Another hybrid phenomenon that became a serious threat to the Catholic Church in Kongo was Dona Beatrice Kimpa Vita's early eighteenth-century Saint Anthony Movement.[221] According to Gallo, the movement of this "false St. Anthony" claimed that Jesus had been born in Kongo and that Saint Anthony, whom Kimpa Vita venerated as a God with a "Salve Antoniana" prayer, was to establish a new kingdom in São Salvador. At Gallo's recommendation, King Pedro IV ordered Kimpa Vita to be burned as a heretic in 1706.[222]

Such hybrid phenomena strengthened hardliners in their conviction that previous generations of missionaries had been too relaxed about orthodoxy. The Jesuit Baltezar Barreira, for instance, claimed in 1592 that Kongo had "a very weak Christianity" because "people were baptized by stupid priests who do not teach them any doctrine."[223] In the early eighteenth century, the Capuchin Lorenzo da Lucca even argued that Kongo had always remained a pagan society.[224] Not surprisingly, Protestants shared this conviction. Dapper, for instance, claimed in 1668 that Kongolese Christianity was merely "a sham," since "many who call themselves Christians don't act like that, except when white people are present because then it is in their interest to pretend to be Christian."[225] Peter Mortamer, the commander of Luanda during the city's brief Dutch occupation, reduced Kongolese Christianity to a number of "superstitions they have learned from the Portuguese" and spoke with disdain of people carrying "chaplets around their necks and constantly muttering prayers without understanding anything."[226]

Such a tendency to dispraise the unique variant of Catholicism that had developed in Kongo only grew stronger in later centuries, especially among Protestants. In 1860 Charles Thomas wrote that "the Romanism taught" in Kongo was "a barbarized Christianity [that] pursued the erroneous policy of attracting the savages by compromising with the native religion."[227] Precisely because "Christianity worked hand in hand with *nkissism*," Richard Dennett argued in the 1880s, the answer to the question what harvest the Portuguese were reaping after four hundred years of missionary work in Kongo "is none."[228] Their conversion, Robert Hamill Nassau claimed in the early twentieth century, "caused no jar to . . . old beliefs, nor change in its practice, except that the new fetish was worshipped in a cathedral and before a bedizened altar."[229]

The debate over the nature of Kongolese Catholicism continues today. Thornton argues that "Christianity conquered Kongo peacefully—but at the cost of adapting itself to the 'conquered' people's conception of religion and cosmology" and sees parallels to China and India, where rites developed that combined Christianity with local Confucianist and Hinduist elements. He adds that, even in isolated parts of the kingdom, "visiting Jesuits only occasionally mentioned the presence of 'fetishes' and then only in the context of the inhabitants of the far eastern provinces. Otherwise, they seemed to believe that Kongo's shortcomings were those not of a newly converted people but of the normal sins of disrespect of the clergy."[230]

According to MacGaffey, however, Kongolese Christianity ignored several themes that are central to Roman Catholicism, such as the idea of the Original Sin, the idea of God as Creator *ex nihilo*, and the Immaculate Conception. Subsequently, he characterized the European-Kongolese religious interaction as "dialogues of the deaf."[231] In view of the fact that Christianity in Kongo adapted itself to the indigenous conception of religion and cosmology, several scholars have argued that Kongolese Catholicism was only Catholic in name and hardly affected existing indigenous beliefs.[232] One could argue against such skeptical voices that there are plenty of examples to be found of Kongolese who proudly identified as Catholic and that the one institution with authority to decide over Catholic orthodoxy, the Vatican, recognized Kongo as a Catholic nation. This is not to say that these scholars are necessarily wrong in their skepticism. As the case of the Kimpa Vita illustrates, there are, indeed, examples to be found of syncretic cults that grew out of a mixture of indigenous beliefs and Catholicism. Moreover, there is no reason to believe that everyone in Kongo embraced the new faith, nor that those who did embrace Christianity subsequently rejected all traditional beliefs and customs. Sources reveal that, for many Kongolese, both could coexist perfectly well and that people moved from one to the other according to necessity. However, this was not necessarily different in Portugal, where pre-Christian beliefs, customs, and rituals also had a profound influence on the way people lived out their Christian faith. As Adrian Hastings has argued, "the Catholicism of fifteenth- and sixteenth-century Portugal or Spain had far more in common with African religion than might be imagined," since "the popular Christianity of late medieval Europe had absorbed into itself a great deal of the pre-Christian religion."[233] Although it was not at all uncommon in Portugal that people in agony or fear turned to non-Christian rituals for solace or protection, none of this has been used by scholars to question their Christian identity.

The complexity of Kongolese Catholicism should caution us not to give in to generalizations. The impact of the new religion was undoubtedly stronger in the region surrounding the capital, São Salvador, and the coastal region between Luanda and Pinda, where over a third of the kingdom's population lived, than in peripheral areas.[234] In 1710 Gallo confirmed that "the Kongolese and, in particular, those in São Salvador, embrace entirely and with love our holy faith. They have a true knowledge of it and became good Christians." They "learn from each other the Christian prayers, the symbols of the faith and the mysteries, the best they can," regularly attend Mass, and "love the exercises and spiritual discourses." They "honor the main feasts of the year, with the greatest possible pomp," they "love to wear lots of medals, crucifixes, rosaries, and chaplets," they "are very devoted to the souls of the purgatory" and, "on All Souls' Day, they spend the night praying the rosary, singing litanies and then give lots of alms." Had Catholicism only superficially affected indigenous beliefs and customs, it is unlikely that Gallo would have written this. He acknowledged, however, that "in the provinces," where "the peasants were baptized in great numbers," people "never acquired true knowledge of our holy religion" because they "never abandoned their pagan customs."[235]

The fact that we continue to find references to Catholic elements in Kongo long after the last missionaries had left is another indication that the new faith made a deeper impact in the region than some have suggested.[236] In the 1850s, for instance, Sarmento witnessed people staging nightly processions in the region of Bamba with "prayers to the Most Holy

Virgin," while carrying "large crosses" and wearing "crucifixes around their necks." They venerated, in particular, "St. Francis, St. Anthony, and the Holy Virgin, whom they called mother of God and of Kongo."[237] When, in 1816, the British officer James Hingston Tuckey explored the region of Soyo, he met with communities known as the *gente da igreja* (people of the church), whom he characterized as "Christians after the Portuguese fashion." Among them, Tuckey identified a *mestre*, who was "qualified to lead his fellow Negroes into the path of salvation, as appeared from a diploma with which he was furnished. This man and another of the Christians had been taught to write their own names and that of Saint Antonio, and could also read the Romish litany in Latin." All of them "were loaded with crucifixes, and satchels containing the pretended relics of saints."[238]

When Antoine-Marie-Hippolyte Carrie, a missionary of the Congregation of the Holy Spirit, explored the same region in the 1870s, he was welcomed by king "Dom João," who was wearing a "brigadier hat with a golden cockade, a loin cloth in brilliant colors, and a black frock." Accompanied by an interpreter, Carrie was taken to the Chapel of Saint Anthony, where he met with the "people of the church," some of whom "fulfill the functions of a priest." Upon entering the chapel, he saw a chandelier, a crucifix, and statues of Saint Anthony and the Virgin Mary. When Carrie asked them to say their prayers, they "all kneeled religiously on the ground, put their hands together and . . . a black man, representing the priest, kneeled on the footboard of the altar . . . , made the sign of the cross and . . . then recited prayers." People concluded each prayer with the words "Amen, Jesus!" When the prayers had ended, attendants took little bells from the altar and the *mestre* began to sing the canticles "in the local language, but mixed with lots of Portuguese and Italian words." Carrie referred to this community as "people who were still Christians, at least from the outside."[239]

A decade later, the German explorer Max Buchner met with a similar, perhaps even the same, Afro-Catholic congregation in Soyo. He described an approaching procession, with bell music and the screaming of sixty warriors, who guarded their leader, known as the Kukulu, dressed like an admiral, with a sword, a suit with golden epaulets, and a feathered hat. Someone then handed the Kukulu "a silver cross of about one meter length that in the past may have served as the tip of a banner." After kissing and waving a banner, he "blessed the crowd, just like Catholic priests use to do." People kneeled and beat their breasts with their fingers, while some of the younger ones acted like ministrants and sounded the bells.

Buchner was then asked to spend a bottle of liquor, whereupon the Kukulu was handed a chalice, to which he said a short prayer, blessed it, filled it with liquor, and held it upward. People once again kneeled and beat their breasts, while others rang the bells. Thereupon, the Kukulu drank the liquor. The German ethnographer assumed that what he had just seen were "the final, caricaturesque relics of a form of Christianity that over a hundred years ago had existed here" and had but little respect for the scene, calling it "a gruesome farce" and "scornful disgrace."[240]

When the Baptist Mission arrived in São Salvador in 1879, William Holman Bentley observed that "some old people . . . called themselves *minkwìkizi*, 'believers', in some of whom there seemed to have lingered some faint glimmerings of such light as had been brought in the old times," which expressed itself in the sprinkling of water during funerals, the marking of crosses, and the preservation of "a large crucifix" and "some images of saints," that, "if the rains were insufficient . . . were sometimes brought out and carried round the town." He concluded, however, that Kongo had degenerated into "a heathen land" and that "king and people were wholly given to fetishism and all the superstitions and cruelties of the Dark Continent."[241]

That nineteenth-century Europeans sometimes overlooked elements rooted in Kongo's century-old Catholic history can be illustrated by the carrying of large statues of saints in processions. When the German ethnographer Adolf Bastian visited São Salvador in the 1850s, he met a man who proudly showed him his "diploma of knight in the Order of Christ," authenticated with the "red seal of the Kingdom of Kongo," and pointed him to three "men-size wooden figures of Capuchins," which the people of Salvador used to "carry in procession, with music and song, around the ruins of the former churches." When exploring the Kongo region for King Leopold II in the 1880s, the Belgian Charles Callewaert observed a highly similar man-sized wooden figure, but without further investigation classified it as a "fetish."[242]

ANGOLA

As the de facto seat of the diocese for Central Africa in 1624, (São Paulo da Assunção de) Luanda served as the center of Portuguese missionary activities in the region of Ndongo, the ruler of which was called *Ngola*, which gave origin to the Portuguese term *Angola*. Unlike in Kongo, missions in this region accompanied Portuguese military expansion. As a result, Christianity tended to be perceived as a foreign religion that was either imposed by force or embraced for strategic and political reasons.[243] As Thornton and Heywood confirm, "although Ndongo formally adopted Christianity, the people never embraced the religion to the same degree that those of Kongo did."[244] A revealing case is that of Queen Njinga of Ndongo and Matamba, who converted, abandoned, and returned to Christianity in accordance with the political circumstances and available allies in the region. Soon after the local confraternity of Our Lady of the Rosary had laid Njinga to rest in 1663, the Capuchin mission in Matamba came to an end.[245]

Jesuits in particular favored a missionary policy whereby they, and not local elites, would be in control. This approach may have been influenced by a negative experience in the 1560s, when the ruler of Ndongo had initially welcomed a Jesuit mission but later changed his mind and imprisoned the missionaries. One of them, Francisco de Gouveia, was kept prisoner until his death in 1575. In one of his letters, Gouveia complained bitterly that "it seems almost impossible to achieve anything with these people if they are not governed by the King of Portugal." While his disappointment was undoubtedly influenced by personal circumstances, it also reflected a broader disappointment in Jesuit circles about the results obtained in Kongo. In fact, Gouveia added in his letter that "not even those of Kongo can be called good Christians."[246]

Not by accident, thus, did sixteenth-century Portuguese missionaries argue that "the conquest of these lands had to be extended to its alms" and that "baptisms would not be granted in the same liberal way" as in Kongo because, first, "all idolatry and abuses had to be destroyed."[247] A revealing example of this aggressive approach can be found in the report by the Jesuit Pedro Tavares, who during a trip along the river Bengo in the 1630s, entered a village where he observed the statue of an "idol," which he started to destroy with a knife. Upon seeing "the surprised and angry faces of . . . lots of locals, carrying bows and arrows," he told them that "I was their master" and that "if one of them would dare to shoot an arrow at me, the Portuguese would come to fight them."[248]

Unlike on the Atlantic islands, however, the Portuguese influence in the region was too weak for a missionary policy that used (a creolized form of) Portuguese. Similar to what had happened in Kongo, thus, missionary work in Angola had to take place in indigenous languages, mainly Kimbundu and Umbundu.[249] The dependence of missionaries on the assistance of local interpreters can be illustrated with Manuel Ribeiro's strategy in the interior of Angola in the 1670s, where he would visit a village, teach doctrine for a number of hours that was translated by one of his *mulekes*, and then move on to the next village, leaving a native catechist behind to follow up his work with the local population. If, upon his return to the village, he was satisfied with the results obtained by his catechist, he would proceed with the baptism of the population.[250] While this procedure confirms a tighter control by Jesuits, it still shows how dependent they were on locals and how the process of Christianization, if successful at all, occurred through indigenous channels.

Meanwhile, Catholic influences also disseminated in the interior of Angola and along the coastline in the context of Luso-African trading communities, known as *pombeiros, ambaquistas, filhos da terra* (sons of the land), or *pretos calçados* (shoe-wearing Blacks).[251] According to the nineteenth-century Portuguese historian Elias Corrêa, these Africans had Portuguese baptismal names and felt "honored to be regarded as whites."[252] As Beatrix Heintze explains, however, their attempt to emulate Portuguese culture and to be treated as *mindele* (Whites) was often cause for ridicule among the Portuguese.[253] Despite this disdainful treatment, Buchner noted in the late nineteenth century that Luso-Africans themselves tended to look down upon other Africans, "whom they condescendingly called gentiles," and "proudly designat[ed] themselves as subjects of His Majesty."[254]

Buchner also reported that many people in the interior of Angola used to wear crucifixes around their necks, which they called *santos* (saints), and that new, Afro-Catholic legends developed in the region, most notably in the city of Muxima, with its "huge church and miraculous Madonna statue, to which infertile African women go on a pilgrimage" and where locals claimed that "after someone had brought with him a statue of the miraculous Saint Joseph of Massangano and left it with the Madonna overnight, a small new statue of Saint Joseph was discovered there the following day, which now decorates the chapel of Dondo."[255]

Not unlike in Kongo, several brotherhoods were created in Angola, even in places as far into the interior as Massangano or Cambambe, where Luso-African communities thrived. As seat of the diocese, Luanda had an abundance of churches, with their respective brotherhoods, including those of Saint John, Saint Francis, Our Lady of Nazareth, Our Lady of the Cape, and Saint Amarus. The most prestigious brotherhood for the city's Black population was that of Our Lady of the Rosary.[256] António de Oliveira de Cadornega witnessed a rosary celebration in seventeenth-century Luanda that attracted "over 20,000 people, the majority of them slaves but also free blacks."[257]

As Roquinaldo Ferreira has argued, "Christianity was only one dimension of the multilayered religious fabric of Luanda."[258] The tradition to "paint . . . their entire face or sometimes only the forehead . . . with a type of powder [that] looked like it was clay" during processions in Lent reveals, in fact, how strongly Catholic rituals were influenced by indigenous customs.[259] Church authorities were especially concerned about the *banganga* (healers) and *entambes*, wake services that, similar to those in Cape Verde, consisted of eight days of mourning during which people gathered, prayed, danced, and organized processions for the soul of the deceased.[260] Corrêa characterized these practices as an "abominable superstitions."[261]

We could also refer to the music, songs, and dances performed by members of the rosary brotherhood in the processions they held on the first Sunday of the month. Disgusted by what he had seen, Corrêa disparagingly referred to them as "celebrations without religion."[262] In his harsh judgment, the nineteenth-century historian ignored the city's long tradition of staging processions with music, which had started with his own ancestors. The Portuguese had, in fact, celebrated the foundation of the city in 1575 with a "solemn procession" that included "noble and well-armed men" who marched "to the sound of innumerous trumpets."[263]

The anonymous description of the celebrations following the canonization of the Jesuit Francis Xavier in 1620 provides further insight in the development of a Luso-African festive culture in Luanda. The celebrations started with the making of "a banner and a portrait of the saint." Then came a procession in honor of Saint Francis Xavier, where "in front one could see three giants . . . followed by Creoles from São Tomé, who performed their dances . . . and amongst them was their king, before whom they gave speeches, according to their custom." Then the city's brotherhoods followed: "The confraternity of Saint Lucia, of the Holy Mary Magdalene, of the Holy Body (Corposant), of Saint Joseph, of the Souls of Purgatory, of Saint Anthony, of Our Lady of the Rosary, of Our Lady of the Conception, and of the Most Holy Sacrament, all with their respective pennants." Then one would see a ship "that represented how the saint traveled to India. . . . Behind the ship one could see a swordfight that was as well performed as the best one can see in Portugal." Then a theatrical play was performed, "whereby the Kingdom of Kongo welcomed the saint." On the eighth and final day of the celebrations, a mock war performance was organized, featuring "a scene from the life of St. Francisco Xavier about the time when he was preaching in Malacca and prophesized that the Portuguese would obtain a victory against those from Ache, which involved a great spectacle of war."[264] Traces of this ancient Luso-African procession culture continued to live in local carnival parades. Until the ruling Marxist MPLA regime decided to "decolonize" the annual carnival parade in the city of Luanda, it used to feature a "Kongo king," a "queen Jinga," and men dressed with Portuguese "armors and helms who recall legendary epic personalities from medieval history."[265]

CONCLUSION

The complexities of the Christianization process in parts of Africa with a historically strong Portuguese influence can be illustrated by referencing the Battle of Kitombo in 1670. Convinced that they had been victorious in this battle thanks to a miraculous intervention by Saint Luke, the rulers of the Kongolese region of Soyo decided to establish a new national holiday dedicated to this Catholic saint. They did so after their army had administered a humiliating defeat to the Portuguese, members of the same nation that had once brought them Christianity.[266] While it may seem counterintuitive to think that Africans would have voluntarily and genuinely converted to the religion of the same nation that initiated the transatlantic slave trade and used Christianity as part of an aggressive policy of oppression and exploitation, the occurrences surrounding the Battle of Kitombo illustrate that it would be wrong to assume that the adoption of the new faith was tantamount to sympathies with Portugal or submission to its policies.

In fact, the complexities of the historical Portuguese presence in Africa cannot be understood if analyzed from a narrowly postcolonial perspective. Although the context in which Portugal brought Christianity to Africa was not devoid of conflict, violence, oppression, abuse, and acts of extreme cruelty, it should be stressed that it took place at a time when the continent was still firmly in the hands of Africans. As Sylvester Johnson confirms, "The royal court of the Kongo Kingdom decided to adopt Christianity . . . out of its own motivations . . . and not under any compulsion of European colonialism."[267] As an illustration of these complexities, we could refer to the letter King Pedro II of Kongo sent to King Philip IV of Spain (who then ruled over Portugal as Philip III) in 1622, complaining that several members of the Kongolese aristocracy had been enslaved and sold to Brazil. The request by the Kongolese king to return some eighty nobles was honored by his Iberian counterpart, and at least some of them made it back to Africa.[268] It shows that Portuguese achievements in early modern Africa depended on alliances with local rulers and, therefore, required a pragmatic attitude. Even on the Atlantic islands that were under their own control, native Portuguese constituted only a fraction of the population, which forced them into constant compromise with the local Black elites.

These specific circumstances allowed, and to a certain degree even stimulated, lay initiatives in the development of Christianity in Africa. This was not exceptional for the time. We should not forget that the king of Kongo converted to Christianity before Columbus started his first voyage to America. In fact, the Portuguese mission in Africa even anticipated the Council of Trent and the foundation of the Society of Jesus at a time when European Christianity, especially in a peripheral place such as Portugal, was still profoundly medieval in nature. When the Portuguese began to preach in Africa, it was common practice in the Lusitanian motherland for girls to rub their genitals against the tomb of Saint Gonçalo to increase their fertility, and for people to laugh and shout at actors performing devils in stage performances inside the churches. More importantly, it was a time when the Church and its priests lacked the power to impose a rigorous doctrine and when laypeople, organized in confraternities, had considerable leeway in determining how they lived their lives as Christians.

There are, thus, good reasons to question William Randles's distinction between two phases in the missionary history of Kongo, one under the sign of Saint James and the other under the sign of Saint Anthony, and his characterization of the first one as "aggressive and intransigent."[269] Independent of the fact that Saint Anthony was already prominently part of the earliest phase of Christianization in Kongo, Randles's assessment of this phase ignores that, in the aftermath of Trent, missionaries brought to

Africa a much more orthodox understanding of what Christianity was supposed to be and displayed a much more intransigent attitude vis-à-vis lay initiatives.

By the time this new phase started, however, the foundations of Christianity in Cape Verde, São Tomé, and Kongo had already been firmly established and, unlike in Europe, the limitations of the clergy in both numbers and authority did not allow the imposition of a post-Tridentine model. As a result, African Christianity remained engrained in a pre-Tridentine mindset. As Hastings confirms, attempts to impose "a post-Tridentine model . . . simply did not work in Africa."[270]

There can be no doubt that, because of this, indigenous cosmologies, beliefs, and rituals profoundly influenced the development of Christianity in parts of Africa with a historically strong Portuguese influence. However, it would be wrong to reduce the singularities of African Catholicism to indigenous influences only. Historical sources reveal an abundance of parallels to the customs, rituals, and traditions that characterized late-medieval Portuguese society. These parallels are not unique to the heavily Iberianized societies on the Atlantic islands, where the Black community consisted of people with a broad variety of indigenous African backgrounds who forcefully adopted a Portuguese pidgin for intercommunication, but, to a large degree, they also apply to Christian communities on the African mainland that were not enslaved and did not live under Portuguese rule. In spite of the geographical distance and ethnic differences between Black Christians in, for instance, the Cape Verde islands and Kongo, we observe remarkable similarities in the way they organized themselves in confraternities, buried their dead, prayed for the souls of their ancestors, made vows to saints, used rosaries as protection, and paraded with music and dance in processions.

Naturally, the fact that virtually all sources on the development of Catholicism in Africa originate from European missionaries or administrators may have enhanced this perception. After all, these men wrote about what they were familiar with and tended to reject the unknown as witchcraft, magic, superstition, idolatry, or what the Portuguese called *feitiçaria*. Had these sources been written by African Christians themselves, they would likely have focused more strongly on elements rooted in the respective indigenous traditions they were familiar with. Thus, it may well be that, deep down, indigenous beliefs and cosmologies determined more strongly how African communities lived their Christian faith and that the differences between the forms of Catholicism that developed in Cape Verde and in Kongo were more profound than suggested in this chapter.

Even if this were the case, the fact that these Christianized African communities shared a number of Luso-African structural elements is of high importance in the context of the transatlantic slave trade, in which people were snatched away from familiar surroundings and forced to readjust to a new life in a profoundly intimidating environment. As Joseph Miller has observed, enslaved Africans from parts of Africa with a strong Portuguese influence came, upon arrival in the Americas, in contact "with predecessors who had arrived in small numbers from backgrounds in slavery in late medieval Iberia," and "particularly those coming through Kongo channels, must have had a useful familiarity with Portuguese Christianity and used it to find places for themselves without relying on the more 'African' aspects of their origins."[271]

Not by accident, Miller placed the term *African* in quotation marks. It is, in fact, questionable whether seventeenth-century people from Kongo or other parts of Africa with a historically strong Portuguese presence considered Iberian elements that had been introduced in the fifteenth century "un-African." As Thornton suggested, "a Kongo peasant living in the mid-eighteenth century might have been unaware that knowledge about some of the beings he worshiped—as the Virgin Mary, so often invoked in times of danger or emergency—actually originated outside his country."[272] For many Kongolese, rosaries, vows, and confraternities were a natural part of the religious culture they had grown up with. As Herman Bennett confirms, Catholicism in Kongo had "transformed into an indigenous phenomenon."[273] As the next chapter will show, the observation that the Kongolese perceived Christian elements as part of their own African culture is of crucial importance to understand the further development of Black Christianity in the Americas.

CHAPTER THREE

The Americas

In Lope de Rueda's sixteenth-century comedy *Los engañados* (The Fooled), the African character Guiomar is asked why she no longer wants to become a nun. Guiomar answers, with a heavy Afro-Portuguese accent, that her family already has a "very religious cousin," who is a "nun, prioress, abbess, over there in my country, the land of the honorable *Manicongo*."[1] This passage shows how there used to be a widespread awareness in the Iberian world that Kongo was a Catholic kingdom. Over time, this awareness disappeared, at least among White people. Hence the surprise of the Cuban anthropologist Lydia Cabrera when one of the elderly Black people she interviewed in the 1930s told her that, back in the day, there used to be a confraternity "of the Portuguese Kongos" in Cuba, who had a "saint" they called *gangasímba*—a likely corruption of the Kikongo term *nganga a Nzambi*, meaning priest (of God)—to which another person added that "Jesus Christ, in ancient times, went to Kongo . . . and there were churches over there and a lot of Christian Kongolese."[2]

This answer reveals that, even in the early twentieth century, some members of Cuba's Black community preserved a recollection of the Catholic

Kongo kingdom. They themselves may have been descendants of one of the many thousands of enslaved Kongolese shipped to the Americas. "The conquered become the slaves of the conquerors," Merolla da Sorrento wrote in his diary about the ongoing wars in seventeenth-century Kongo, adding with horror, "This happens also with Christians."[3]

The religious identity of enslaved Kongolese in the Americas received little scholarly attention. Research on African religious influences traditionally focused on indigenous religions and, as Stephen Selka pointed out with regard to Brazil, often departed from the "questionable presumption that Catholicism is somehow epiphenomenal in Afro-Brazilian religious life."[4] Signs of Catholic devotion among the enslaved, such as a certain Manuel in eighteenth-century Bahia who, on the deck of his cabin, had built "an altar, with a statue of Christ, and another one of Our Lady of the Rosary, and other saints, where, every day, he sang the rosary together with his wife and children" tended to be perceived as a ruse to gain favors or a smokescreen behind which Black people secretly continued to practice their "truly African," indigenous rituals.[5]

In 2005 the Brazilian historian Marina de Mello e Souza proposed a radical change in perspective by highlighting that to many enslaved Africans in the Americas, in particular those from Kongo, "Catholicism represented a link to their native Africa."[6] This chapter further explores the fate of Afro-Atlantic Catholics in the Americas from the perspective suggested by Souza. It starts in Latin America and, from there, continues to the Caribbean and North America.

AFRO-ATLANTIC CATHOLICS IN LATIN AMERICA

As established in the Portuguese *padroado* and the Spanish *patronato*, the Iberian Crowns were responsible for the Christianization of all people in their American colonies. Afro-Atlantic Catholics played an important role in this. In seventeenth-century Cartagena, for instance, the Jesuits Alonso de Sandoval and Pedro Claver divided newly arrived Africans into groups of ten, separated according to gender and ethnicity, and assigned each group to a Black catechist. The latter spoke their language and prepared them for baptism. On the day of their baptism, the group members sat in a circle around the altar, where they received an Iberian baptismal name and a medal with the face of Christ or the Virgin Mary engraved on it. Many of their catechists were Afro-Atlantic Catholics. One of Claver's assistants, for instance, was Manuel de Capo Verde, a *ladino* from the Cape Verde islands. Another one, José Monzolo, had been baptized in Kongo. The Kimbundu-speaking Ignacio Angola declared that he was already Christian before his arrival in Cartagena and that, together with Alonso Angola, he was taken there on purpose to serve as an interpreter for the Jesuit school.[7]

In theory, the catechization of newly arrived Africans had to be continued by the slaveholder with the assistance of a local priest or chaplain.[8] The Jesuit Cristovão de Gouveia, who in 1583 came to evaluate the Christianization process in Brazil, determined that priests had to visit plantations annually and list the enslaved inhabitants who had been baptized, gotten married, or made confession. He also insisted on the importance of catechization.[9]

Especially in rural areas, the latter represented a challenge. According to the seventeenth-century Jesuit Giorgio Benci, all priests did when visiting plantations was ask enslaved people "if they knew their prayers and Ten Commandments"; "when they see that they know them," he continued, "or rather, that they know how to pray (because many of them pray without knowing what they pray), they immediately give them the sacraments without caring about doctrine."[10] His contemporary Giovanni Antonio Andreoni shared these concerns. He claimed that baptized Africans often "do not know who their creator is, what they have to believe, what law they should follow, how to entrust themselves to God, why Christians go to Church, why we worship the consecrated host, what to tell the priest when they kneel and speak to him in his ear, whether they have a soul and where it goes after they die," but he concluded that priests and slaveholders rather than the enslaved individuals were to blame for this ignorance.[11]

Gouveia seems to have been aware of the limitations in what priests could achieve because he encouraged both slaveholders and priests to stimulate Catholic lay initiatives within the enslaved community.[12] This was not an extraordinary suggestion. Upon arrival in the Americas, Africans were generally trained for their work on the plantation by an experienced member of the enslaved population.[13] To extend this policy to catechization was the natural thing to do. As the British explorer William Bennet Stevenson observed in Lima, Peru, slaveholders were, in principle, responsible for the catechization of the enslaved, yet they typically assigned this task to "some of the oldest and most steady of the slaves."[14]

Afro-Atlantic Catholics were an obvious choice for this task, which convinced Thornton that "the impact of African Christians was much greater than their numbers."[15] It is, indeed, tempting to assume that the privileged position of Afro-Atlantic Catholics as mediators between the world of the enslaved and the world of the enslaver allowed and even stimulated the dissemination of beliefs and rituals rooted in African Catholic traditions.

It would, however, be wrong to perceive African Catholicism as a religion that fostered accommodation. Sources indicate that Afro-Atlantic Catholics frequently operated autonomously or even developed into a force of opposition against the colonial authorities. In 1764, for instance, Pedro, an enslaved African "of the Kongo nation," was arrested in Brazil and investigated by the Portuguese Inquisition after being accused of conducting religious services outside of the control of Church authorities in a "synagogue." Pedro defended himself by stating that all he had been doing was "teaching Christian doctrine" to recently arrived Africans, including "ten women and one man from the Mina nation."[16]

We could also point to the prominent role of Afro-Atlantic Catholics in Maroon societies. If all enslaved Africans had perceived Catholicism as a religion of oppression, one would assume that those who were able to escape immediately liberated themselves from all Christian elements and returned to exclusively indigenous African religious practices. While such cases undoubtedly existed, there are also plenty of examples of Maroon communities that remained attached to certain Catholic traditions and established their own congregations under Afro-Atlantic Catholic spiritual leadership.

In his report from 1581, the Franciscan friar Pedro de Aguado characterized Miguel, the founder of a *palenque* (Maroon settlement) in Venezuela, as "a *ladino* black who spoke Spanish fluently" and explains that, after having been proclaimed "king," Miguel "nominated one of his followers to be bishop," who then "immediately built a church to congregate his filthy sheep." Aguado also spoke in detail about another sixteenth-century *palenque,* built by a certain Bayano in Panama, that included a man "whom all the others recognized as their prelate and whom they honored with the title of bishop." This man "baptized, catechized, and preached in a superstitious and heretic way." He also "performed ceremonies which they called celebrating or saying Mass." After their village had been captured by the Spanish, Aguado noted that the runaways were given an opportunity "to return to the Catholic faith." They refused and, even on the day of their execution, insisted that "their backward and vain ceremonies were a real religion." The community's "bishop" even claimed that "he would rather be killed immediately, because after he and his followers had died, he planned to take revenge" by "going to his homeland in the form of a spirit and to return with copies of people who would help him to completely destroy and devastate the city."

When we look more closely at how this community celebrated its religion, we detect an abundance of Catholic elements. According to Aguado, the "bishop" wore "a shirt of a Negress and on top of it a carmine tunic" during church services and "prepared a sort of altar, located in a sanctuary," on top of which "they had placed a pitcher with wine and a large [loaf of] bread." The bishop then "sang something in his language to which those in attendance responded," whereupon "they all ate the bread and drank the wine." Then the bishop also preached, and, during his sermons, "persuaded his listeners to conserve with obstinacy their liberty, to defend with their weapons in hand the village and the land they occupied and possessed, and to support their king." When he performed baptisms, "lots of Negros and Negresses gathered as godfathers and godmothers and together they walked with the baby to the sanctuary." There, "they drank wine, danced, and sang together with their bishop," who then "took a pitcher with water, and poured the water over the baby," whereupon all those in attendance "began to dance and sing and drink again." Unfortunately, Aguado mentioned but failed to explain other ceremonies practiced in this community, dismissing them as "vain and ridiculous."[17]

While his bias makes it difficult to characterize this religion, Aguado's description seems to point more toward a form of Catholicism influenced by indigenous African beliefs and rituals than the opposite. What becomes clear, however, is that these runaways may have perceived the Catholic Church as oppressive, but not so the Catholic religion. Other examples lead to similar conclusions. When, for instance, Spanish soldiers attacked a Maroon settlement near Lake Maracaibo, Venezuela, in 1585, they found one runaway who "walked around in a surplice and bonnet and said mass and baptized the children who were born."[18] Francisco de la

Cueva Maldonado, Archbishop of Santo Domingo, reported in 1662 about a Maroon community in the mountains of Ocoa where people had erected a church and held Mass with their own communion wafers. They had crosses in front of their houses and prayed the Our Father and Ave Maria, yet also "committed errors of idolatry."[19] The leaders of the seventeenth-century *palenque* Matudere, located near Cartagena, Colombia, came in search of a Catholic priest whom they took to their settlement in order to perform the sacraments. According to Father Zapata, people in Matudere "lived in Christianity, knew the prayers, sustained the church, and prayed the rosary." The founder of Matudere, Domingo, had Angolan roots.[20] A similar case has been observed in Veracruz, Mexico, where a certain Yanga ruled a *palenque*. Yanga, who belonged to the West African Brame/Bran people of today's Guinea-Bissau, had, because of his advanced age, delegated all military responsibilities to an Angolan man who used the Iberian baptismal name Francisco. When Spanish soldiers attacked their village in 1609, Yanga sought rescue in "the small church they had built," where he and his people "held lighted candles in their hands" and kneeled "in front of the altar," where they "kept saying their prayers during the battle." Since the Spanish were not able to defeat them, both parties started negotiations, which allowed Yanga's community to preserve its autonomy on the condition that new runaways would henceforth be returned to the authorities. Yanga also secured the promise that his settlement, now rebaptized San Lorenzo de los Negros, would regularly receive a priest to serve its religious needs.[21]

Seventeenth-century Portuguese and Dutch sources about the largest Maroon settlement recorded in history, that of Palmares in Brazil, reveal that its "king," Zumbi, did not allow the presence of "fetishists," and that there was a chapel with images of "the Christ-child, St. Blaise, and Our Lady of the Conception."[22] The Dutch explorer Johan Nieuhof reported that people in Palmares "more or less maintain the religion of the Portuguese" and had "their own priests and judges."[23] A Portuguese source from 1678 confirms that "They selected one of the most *ladino* members of their community, whom they venerate as their priest and who baptizes and marries them."[24] Palmares was a cause for debate within the Church. While some advocated for the sending of a chaplain to cater to the spiritual needs of its inhabitants, the influential Jesuit António Vieira vigorously opposed this with the argument that enslaved people who ran away committed a mortal sin. Sending them a chaplain was, in Vieira's view, tantamount to legitimizing rebellion. Consequently, he defended an intensification of the military campaign that eventually led to the destruction of Palmares in 1694.[25]

Outside of Maroon communities, traces of African Catholicism are mainly to be found in the context of Black brotherhoods.

BLACK BROTHERHOODS

Church authorities in Iberian colonies stimulated the establishment of mutual-aid and burial societies for the enslaved population. In his late sixteenth-century report on Brazil, Gouveia explicitly encouraged slaveholders and priests to allow enslaved people to form confraternities.[26] A Jesuit source in Lima from 1540 confirms this, describing it as part of a strategy "to bring order to their lives and customs, teaching them how to live in a Christian manner."[27] In 1552 the Jesuit António Pires wrote about "a rosary brotherhood" in Olinda, Brazil, that was composed of "local slaves and slaves from Guinea [Africa]." While members of the Portuguese confraternity "were unable to maintain order and were talking all the time" during processions, the Africans "walked with such order and such concert, one behind the other, with the hands in the air, shouting, 'Ora pro nobis,'" that they offered "a great example of devotion to the white population."[28]

Brotherhoods also served a practical need by assuming responsibility for funerals.[29] According to Sandoval, Africans depended on the brotherhoods of their respective "nations" to bury them. These societies were of vital importance, he noted, because without them, corpses would be left unburied, "thrown in the rubbish dump, where they will be eaten by dogs."[30] Sandoval's use of the term *nation* suggests that the division of newly arrived Africans into ethnic groups to facilitate their catechization continued in the context of brotherhoods.

In the 1540s, the Italian conquistador Girolamo Benzoni had observed in Hispaniola that "each nation recognizes its own king or governor, which keeps the tribes separate" and, as examples of such "nations," mentioned the "Quinei" (Guineans), "Manicongri" (Kongolese), "Gialopi" (Wolof), "Zapi" (Sape), and "Berbesi" (Serer people).[31] The same occurred with regard to leadership positions that had developed in these "nations"; in Cuba we find a 1568 reference to enslaved Africans who "called themselves queens and kings and organized gatherings."[32]

That a misinterpretation of this custom could have disastrous consequences can be illustrated with a case from Mexico City, where plans by the confraternity of Our Lady of Mercy to elect a king and queen as well as dukes, marquises, and counts in 1611 were (mis)understood as a plot, which led to the execution of its leaders and the prohibition of all Afro-Mexican brotherhoods.[33] However, as Joan Cameron Bristol pointed out, "in the 1620s the crown sent an ordinance regulating confraternities of blacks and mulattoes in Mexico City, suggesting that even if they had been dissolved after 1612 they were reformed again quickly."[34] Black brotherhoods could, in fact, continue to operate in seventeenth-century Mexico and other Iberian colonies, albeit under the scrutiny of the authorities.[35]

To Afro-Atlantic Catholics, confraternities were not a new phenomenon. As Heywood has argued, "Many Kongos and not a few Angolans . . . would have been familiar with the brotherhoods in Luanda, Soyo, and Kongo, and the central role they played in the creole society of Kongo, Angola, and São Tomé."[36] These transatlantic parallels are also visible in the choice of patron saints. Similar to what we observed in Iberia and Africa, a surprisingly high number of Black brotherhoods in Latin America were dedicated to Our Lady of the Rosary. Lucilene Reginaldo's research on eighteenth-century Bahia, for instance, revealed that no fewer than seventeen of the twenty-six confraternities of the Black population were rosary brotherhoods.[37]

Familiarity with this institution gave Afro-Atlantic Catholics an advantage over other groups in negotiating concessions with the authorities. When, in 1683, the rosary brotherhood in Olinda petitioned the king of Portugal for permission to purchase the freedom of enslaved members, they received authorization to do so, "following the example set by the brothers of the Rosary in São Tomé and Lisbon."[38] Another example is the letter from a rosary brotherhood in the Brazilian city of Salvador to Queen Maria of Portugal, dating back to 1786, with a plea to reconsider the prohibition of "masks, dances in the idiom of Angola with their related instruments, canticles, and praises," because the latter were "still in use in many Christianized lands."[39] Illustrative of how these transatlantic connections facilitated the integration of Afro-Atlantic Catholics into Latin American society is the decision by the prestigious seventeenth-century confraternity of

Our Lady of Mercy in Sabará, Brazil, to adjust its restrictive membership rules. While, in the past, only Black people born in Brazil or Portugal could become members, they decided to make an exception for "natives of São Tomé" because the *ladinos* from that island were "similar to us."[40]

Historical documents frequently refer to brotherhood "kings" of the "Kongo nation." A fascinating source is the 1791 report Joseph Rossi y Rubí published under the pseudonym Hesperióphylo in the *Mercurio Peruano* on Lima's confraternity of Our Lady of the Rosary and its "rey de los Congos" (Kongo king). When visiting its headquarters, Rossi y Rubí observed that "all the walls . . . were painted with figures representing their original kings, with their battles and their jubilations." "Whenever one of the members of the brotherhood dies," Rossi y Rubí continued, "the tribe gets together to wake the dead body and everyone contributes to cover the costs of the burial and the purchase of drinks for the funeral." He also explained that, during Lima's annual Corpus Christi procession, one would see the "brotherhood's king," who, "protected from the sun by an umbrella," held "his scepter in the one hand and a cane in the other." Young members of the Kongo brotherhood would "disguise themselves as devils" or "as feathered men," while others "represented monsters." Those accompanying the brotherhood's king and queen would "carry weapons such as bows, arrows, clubs, and shields" and make "gruesome gestures as if they were about to attack their enemies." These performances confused the Peruvian author, who thought that their outfit was "better suited for a type of masking feast at a carnival" than for a religious procession, and he considered their belligerent gestures "indecent in an ecclesiastic context." Rossi y Rubí was relieved, however, that the authorities had at least "prohibited the blacks to carry with them firearms and to shoot them in the air during the procession as they used to do in the past."[41]

Kongo brotherhoods also thrived in Cuba, where the most prestigious one, the Congo Reales, reserved membership for those with roots in the heartland of the Kongo kingdom. It was known for its impressive regalia, high-quality musical performances, and its many *diablitos* (devil pranksters) at the traditional Epiphany festivities, Corpus Christi processions, and *fiestas de mamarrachos* (June festivals).[42] During a trip to Cuba in the 1850s, the Swedish writer Frederika Bremer visited their headquarters, where she saw "a sun with a human face" painted on the wall and "several Christian symbols and pictures."[43] In the 1870s, Walter Goodman observed a *comparsa* (festive parade) of "Congo Negroes" in Santiago de Cuba that was "headed by a brace of blacks, who carry banners" and who were followed by "a battalion of colonels, generals, and field-marshals, in gold-braided coats and gilded cocked-hats." "These are not ordinary masqueraders," the English painter explained, "but grave subjects of his somber majesty King Congo, the . . . lawfully appointed sovereign of the coloured community."[44]

During his stay in Pernambuco from 1809 to 1815, Henry Koster observed "the yearly festival of our Lady of the Rosary, which was directed by negroes; and at this period is chosen the King of the Congo nation." According to the English coffee-grower, "The Congo negroes are permitted to elect a king and queen from among the individuals of their own nation, the personages who are fixed upon may either actually be slaves or they may be manumitted." These sovereigns "exercise a species of mock jurisdiction over their subjects which is much laughed at by the whites; but their chief power and superiority over their countrymen is shown on the day of the festival." Standing in the doorway of his house, Koster witnessed "a number of male and female negroes, habited in cotton dresses of colours and of white, with flags flying and drums beating" and "discovered among them the king and queen, and the secretary of state. Each of the former wore upon their heads a crown, which was partly covered with gilt paper." Koster also explained that the expenses of the church service were to be provided for by members of the Black community and that "there stood in the body of the church a small table, at which sat the treasurer of this black fraternity and some other officers, and upon it stood a box to receive the money."[45]

A revealing example of the prestige these kings enjoyed in Brazil is the complaint made in 1711 by Father Leonardo de Azevedo Castro to the governor of Minas Gerais about Black brotherhoods in the region expecting people to move out of the way and remove their hats whenever approached by their king, to give him the best seat in church, and even to allow him to free brothers from jail. "The blacks recognize the reelected king as a true king," Castro wrote, "they hold him as an oracle, render him obedience, and treat him as their king also outside the functions of the church."[46] This prestige is confirmed by Rossini Lima, whose research revealed that the Kongo king of the rosary brotherhood in Atibaia was known as "king of the kings," and not a single other brotherhood king would have dared to start a parade before showing his respects.[47] Elizabeth

Kiddy observed similar procedures in documents from eighteenth-century Pernambuco, where other African nations were only allowed to create brotherhoods after obtaining approval of the king of the Kongo nation.[48]

There are strong indications that the election rituals of these brotherhood kings were modeled upon authentic king election ceremonies. The Cuban ethnographer Fernando Ortiz Fernández claimed already in the 1920s that the election of brotherhood kings "seems to mimic the process for electing kings in the Kongo kingdom."[49] His contemporary Cabrera also suspected that the Congo Reales brotherhood was modeled upon "the true Kongo de Totila . . . the same Kongo with the king and queen, a court, vassals, and all order and respect," with the term *Totila* being derived from the Kikongo *Kongo dia Ntotela* (Kongolese from the heartland of the kingdom). One of Cabrera's interviewees explained that "it was always the brotherhood of the Congo Reales that initiated the procession [on Epiphany], followed by the other brotherhoods."[50]

In the 1930s, the Brazilian anthropologist Arthur Ramos argued that "Congo dances or *cucumbis* [are] a survival of coronations of African monarchs in their original land."[51] Around the same time, Mário de Andrade claimed that brotherhood king elections in Brazil were "derived from the customary dances in Congo to celebrate the proclamation of a new king," that "the dramatic elements in Congo dances were directly influenced by choreographed mock war scenes from Congo," and that the colors blue (for Christians) and red (for pagans) could be traced back to "the coat of arms of the King of Kongo."[52] After comparing descriptions and drawings of king election festivals of the Kongolese nation in Brazil to sources from Kongo, Fromont confirmed in 2013 that the insignia and ceremonials relating to King Afonso I of Kongo must have served as a model for these brotherhoods. "The comparison," she claimed, "holds true across all descriptions."[53]

In fact, when the English geographer Richard Burton, who had previously explored the Kongo region, visited Brazil and witnessed a parade of a Kongo brotherhood in the mid-1860s, he immediately recognized parallels to what he had seen during his stay in Central Africa. According to Burton, the members of the Brazilian brotherhood were "dressed, as they fondly imagined, after the style of the Agua-Rosada House, descended from the great *Manikongo* and hereditary lords of Congo land. . . . All were armed with sword and shield, except the king, who, in sign of dignity, carried his scepter."[54]

The recurrent references to weapons, soldiers, and mock war scenes in descriptions of king elections and parades recall the *sanga(mento)* war dances that used to honor kings in Kongo, which strengthens the assumption that enslaved Kongolese built on their African heritage in organizing brotherhoods. It could also explain why the Kongo community, in particular, became attached to Catholic religious dramas involving king parades and battle scenes, such as the dramatic play *Moors and Christians.* Variants of this originally Iberian performance tradition still thrive in Brazil under the name *congadas.* Its dancers, called *soldados* (soldiers), typically use swords, cudgels, or sticks and have rosaries draped around their upper bodies. The drama uses the same basic structure—a parade, meeting of the enemies, heated discussion, mock fight, and bowing of the defeated group to receive baptism—as *Moors and Christians,* yet those performing the role of Christians are led by the king of Kongo.[55] As José Rivair Macedo confirms, in *congadas* "the ritual of Moors & Christians has been mixed with traditionally Kongolese king election rituals."[56]

Congadas also exist in Panama. As Judith Bettelheim has shown, this performance developed out of "a form of Christianity, particular to areas of West-Central Africa [that] arrived in the Americas along with the slave trade" and reflects "a particular Christianity that the Central Africans themselves practiced."[57] According to Ronald Smith, the *congada* groups in Panama continue to operate in an ancient brotherhood tradition and "maintain a communal sense of society throughout the year."[58] Their performance is a mimetic dance theater that takes place before the beginning of Lent and includes a queen, king, and prince, devils, angels, and the *Capitán de Congo.* The latter commands a group of "soldiers," who darken their faces with charcoal and use strands of (rosary) beads around the necks. The performers are accompanied by a band that has a *revellín* (song leader) and *segundas* (chorus), composed of women, who sing in Spanish but occasionally use Kikongo words and phrases. Their enactment of the eternal fight between good and evil, angels and devils, Christians and heathens ends with the capturing of the "devils." Once captured, each "devil" chooses a godparent, whereupon he is baptized by a *padre Congo.*[59]

It is important to stress that the mixture of elements rooted in Iberian and Central African traditions was initiated in Africa. We know that Kongolese added European musical instruments, weapons, and insignia to their *sangamentos.* For instance, in the mid-seventeenth century, Giovanni

Francesco Romano observed that the Kongolese played "several musical instruments" during *sangamentos*, including "indigenous drums and European drums that were imported from Portugal and the Netherlands."[60] Merolla da Sorrento even witnessed a *sangamento* at "the Festival of St. James the Apostle" in Soyo that had two parts: one "according to the style of the country" in which the king used "a bow and arrows," followed by a second one in which the king wore "a chain, a cross of gold . . . and a small scarlet overcoat, embroidered with gold thread" and used as his weapon a "harquebus."[61] Both the cross and the red cape are likely allusions to iconography of Saint James and recall the mythical foundation story of the Catholic kingdom of Kongo under Afonso I.[62]

All of this strengthens Souza's theory that even in the case of members of Black brotherhoods wearing "European clothing" and celebrating "a Catholic saint," we "discern the direct link to . . . an African past that was already infused with European elements . . . since the beginning of the sixteenth century."[63] This assumption requires a closer look at the types of religious rituals celebrated in the context of Black brotherhoods.

AFRO-ATLANTIC CATHOLIC RITUALS

While I do not disagree with George Reid Andrews that "African worshippers [in Latin America] were receptive to Christianity, but insisted on retaining African gods and rites as well" and that "the *cabildos* [brotherhoods] were the setting within which these gods were worshipped and preserved," it is important to complement this information with the acknowledgment that a considerable percentage of the enslaved population in Latin America had already embraced Catholicism in Africa. In their brotherhoods, the latter retained not indigenous African gods and rites, but rather a Christian god and saints, whom they worshipped with Afro-Catholic rites.[64]

In the 1930s, Ramos was among the first to suggest that the devotion to Our Lady of the Rosary among Black people in Brazil may have "come directly from Kongo."[65] Later, in the 1970s, Hoornaert spoke about rosary devotion as a "pastoral bridge between Africa and Brazil."[66] More recently, this idea was explored by Ronaldo Vainfas, who concluded that "African Catholicism, as it existed in Kongo and Angola, influenced the way

Catholicism developed within the black community in Brazil, with its brotherhoods of Our Lady of the Rosary and its celebrations at the occasion of the coronation of black kings."[67]

An important source for understanding the legacy of Afro-Atlantic Catholics in Latin America is Andreoni's report from early eighteenth-century Brazil. This Italian Jesuit had an open mind about giving enslaved people enough leeway to preserve some African traditions in their brotherhoods. He informed plantation owners that it would be unwise "to completely deny them their celebrations, which is the only joy they have." Doing this would "turn them sad and melancholic." He also recommended that slaveholders "not be surprised when they in all innocence elect their own kings, and sing and dance for a couple of hours in the afternoon after having celebrated Our Lady of the Rosary and Saint Benedict in the morning" and suggested that they give them "some type of reward."[68]

In his pragmatic approach, Andreoni reduced the afternoon singing and dancing to elements of joy and separated them from the "serious" saint devotion that took place in the morning. What he, and many others after him, failed to understand is that, in an African Catholic tradition, this set of performances formed a unity. This unity is still visible today in the *velación*, also known as *noche de vela, velada, velorio de santo, belén de santo*, or *arrullo*, prayer sessions that relate to vows. They are typically led by a *mestre* or *rezador(a)* or *rezandero/a*, a layperson who is knowledgeable in Catholic rites and traditions.[69]

It is in the context of saint veneration that we find some of the clearest traces of Afro-Atlantic Catholic influences in Latin America. Besides the well-known devotion to Our Lady of the Rosary and Saint Benedict, Stanley Stein's analysis of interviews with formerly enslaved people in Vassouras, Brazil, revealed that Saint Anthony was the "preferred saint of all slaves" and that it was common practice to put pressure on this saint until certain graces were obtained. According to Stein, "St. Anthony frequently held in his left arm a small black child who sat upon a peg or nail from which he could be easily removed" and "if a slave wished to obtain a request, he removed the child while promising to return it only after the request was performed."[70] Traces of an African form of Saint Anthony veneration can also be found in the annual feast in honor of the Portuguese saint in Quibra Hacha, Cuba, which involves the ritual washing and dressing of Saint Anthony's statue, followed by a procession and a musical performance in gratitude for the fulfillment of vows. According to Mercedes Lay Bravo, this celebration can be traced back to Portuguese influence among "the peoples of the ancient Kingdom of Kongo," which explains why "St. Anthony came to be adopted by the majority of brotherhoods of the Kongo nation, including the one from Quibra Hacha."[71] While doing research among descendants of Maroons in the Dominican Republic, Milagros Ricourt identified similar practices in honor of Saint Anthony, including the singing of veneration songs, the holding of religious services known as *hora santa* [holy hour], the staging of processions with flags of the saint, the erection of crosses of the saint, the playing of specific *palo* drum rhythms in his honor, and the custom of dressing in brown, "Saint Anthony's color."[72]

The importance of Saint John also needs to be highlighted. Pavia observed a "great celebration with fires and other demonstrations" on Saint John's Eve in seventeenth-century Kongo. While he did not explain what type of demonstrations he saw, the Italian Capuchin added that he had spoken about these festivities "with priests in Brazil, who confirmed that people over there celebrated Saint John in the same way."[73] Saint John celebrations in Brazil typically involved bonfires that people jump over or walk through barefoot as well as collective bathing, including that of the saint('s statue), and lay baptisms to protect newborns against evil forces. Although they occurred in the absence of a priest, the latter were a serious ritual performed in the presence of godparents, whereby the lay baptizer marked a cross with water on the child's forehead and thereupon—in a tradition that recalls baptismal rituals in Kongo—placed a grain of salt in the infant's mouth.[74] Similar traditions, known as *echar agua*, have been observed in Venezuela. In the Barlovento region, Saint John is known as *San Juan Guaricongo*, *San Juan Congo*, or *San Juan Congolé* and celebrated with nightly *velorios* that involve prayers and dances as *promesas* in gratitude for the saint's interventions. Festivities end with a sad song to the saint, known as *malembe*, the Kikongo word for quiet, sad.[75]

Traces of African Catholicism can also be found in Black funeral procedures that alternate expressions of sadness with joy and give considerable attention to the souls of the deceased in order to obtain a *buena muerte/boa morte*, a "good death." Confraternities dedicated to the Blessed Souls of Purgatory used to stage "viaticum processions" with a band of musicians to the house of a dying person so that even the agony of death acquired a festive character. This festive element was particularly visible in practices known as *mampulorios*, *baquinés*, or *baquinís*, wake and burial procedures for children, who, because of their innocence, were believed to have become angels.[76]

One of the best-known brotherhoods in contemporary Latin American society is the Cofradía de los Congos del Espíritu Santo (Confraternity of the Kongos of the Holy Spirit) from Villa Mella, in the Dominican Republic. This Kongo brotherhood is dedicated to the Holy Spirit and has its major annual celebration on Pentecost. On this holiday, the king and other brotherhood dignitaries parade in procession through town. Besides Masses and communal dinners, the festivities include *velaciones*, consisting of *loas* (veneration songs), *salves* (Salve Regina prayers), and group recitals of the mysteries of the rosary that are accompanied by drum music, hand clapping, dancing, and singing in call-and-response form. The latter include frequent references to Kongolese culture. Their funeral songs, for instance, are known as *nbembo*, as derived from the Kikongo term *mbembo* (dirge).[77]

We could also point to Brazil, where one of the thanksgiving songs of the *folias/companhias de reis*, who reenact the journey of the Magi to the infant Christ, has a syncopated melodic structure that is known as the *Reis de Congo* (Kongo kings).[78] Michael Iyanaga's research on Black Catholic communities in Bahia confirms how, to this day, prayer sessions for saints involve music and dance. He describes, for instance, how a novena is typically sung in call-and-response form by the participants, who subsequently perform samba dances as ex-votos to saints. When asked why they sing and dance, participants gave answers similar to that recorded by Félix Monteiro in the Cape Verde islands, namely that saints hate sadness and like to be venerated with joy. These Afro-Brazilian communities perceive dancing as an obligatory part of proper saint devotion. They do so in the conviction that saints want humans to be joyful and perceive expressions of sadness as a form of human disapproval of divine decisions.[79]

Outsiders often failed to understand such Afro-Atlantic Catholic expressions of faith and profound trust in God's almightiness, even in people's darkest hours. They tended to misunderstand the drum music and dances as attempts to smuggle indigenous African elements into serious Catholic prayer sessions that, in the eyes of ignorant skeptics, only proved that the catechization of Africans never went beyond a thin veneer. Such rituals were often (mis)interpreted as forms of Black resistance to Catholicism. While they could be characterized as resistance to the orthodoxy of the Church, it should be stressed that they were never intended as opposition to Catholicism as such. On the contrary, these songs and dances are, at their core, genuine expressions of (Afro-)Catholic faith.

In their eagerness to impose post-Tridentine standards in the Americas, Church authorities reacted to such customs with censorship and prohibitions. As Hoornaert has argued, the "more the Church in Brazil became a Roman Church, the more brotherhoods lost power."[80] Not just in Brazil, but all over Latin America, Afro-Catholic traditions came under increasing pressure in the course of the eighteenth century.[81] In Venezuela, for instance, Bishop Mariano Martí prohibited *velorios* "under penalty of excommunication" and compared the dances that used to accompany these prayer sessions to circles "in the middle of which stands the devil."[82]

Following abolition, brotherhoods gradually acquired a social stigma within the Black middle class, where these societies came to be associated with poverty and backwardness. Black people who were slightly better off began to look down upon the once highly respected brotherhoods as an embarrassing reminder of an era they wished to forget.[83] One of Nancy Pérez Rodríguez's informants in Havana still remembered how, by the end of the nineteenth century, the king of the local Kongo brotherhood "became sad and depressed because nobody would pay attention to him any longer when he would go out on the streets on festive days."[84]

Nevertheless, the continent's rich Afro-Catholic performance culture had a long-lasting influence on Latin American performance traditions. This legacy is most visible in the context of carnival. Once brotherhoods were no longer allowed to consecrate their kings in church and were expelled from religious processions, the Afro-Catholic procession culture that for centuries had been cultivated around Christmas, Epiphany, Corpus Christi, and Pentecost celebrations shifted toward carnival. Due to commercialization, with prizes for those who best adapted their performances to new, "civilized" standards, traditions rooted in African expressions of Catholic faith gradually adapted to the taste of the elites and tourists. What survives today in the famous carnival parades of Rio de Janeiro, Barranquilla, and other Latin American cities is therefore only a shadow of what these performances once were.[85]

In rural areas, some brotherhoods continue to elect their kings and queens in a traditional fashion. Although the Catholic Church has since adopted a more tolerant attitude and these societies have received ample public recognition — the Kongo brotherhood of Villa Mella was even proclaimed a UNESCO Masterpiece of the Heritage of Humanity in 2001 — the explosive growth of Pentecostal churches in Latin America makes their future uncertain. While these new churches are very effective in combining religious services with mutual aid and, in this way, take over many of the social functions formerly provided for by brotherhoods, those who join them do so at the price of abandoning their Afro-Atlantic Catholic traditions.

Skeptics of the impact of Afro-Atlantic Catholics on the development of Black Christianity in the Americas may be inclined to question the African roots of these traditions. If we limit ourselves to a Latin American context, refuting this skepticism with factual evidence represents a challenge. Since its roots go back to Portuguese Catholicism, it is difficult to distinguish Afro-Atlantic Catholic elements from those that enslaved Africans only adopted after their arrival in the Americas. This is different, however, if we leave Latin America and explore societies outside of the Iberian realm.

AFRO-ATLANTIC CATHOLICS IN THE CARIBBEAN

Curaçao

In 1634 the small Antillean island of Curaçao was seized from the Spanish by the Dutch West India Company (WIC), which soon after also occupied the neighboring islands of Aruba and Bonaire. While the new rulers spoke Dutch, the Black population adopted an Afro-Iberian creole called Papiamentu as its lingua franca. The origin of this Iberian-based language — the name of which is derived from the Portuguese *papear* (to chat) — is intriguing considering that the Dutch, following their conquest, expelled the Spanish population of the island, as well as most of the Indigenous inhabitants.

Unfortunately, few historical data are available about Curaçao's earliest Black community. After the first WIC went bankrupt in 1674, many of its documents were lost. While substantial documentation of slave trading operations of the second WIC, established in 1675, exists, these data do not provide information on the Africans who arrived in Curaçao in earlier decades. One way to deal with the paucity of primary sources is by using a comparative methodology. Naturally, the observation that a similar practice existed in more than one place does not automatically imply that the origin and historical development of one corresponds to that of the other. Yet, as results obtained by linguists who have used a comparative methodology in their analysis of Papiamentu show, such an approach can add new perspectives that stimulate further research.

A case in point is Bart Jacobs's groundbreaking study *Origins of a Creole* (2012), which revealed an abundance of parallels between Papiamentu and the Portuguese-based creoles spoken on the Cape Verde islands as well as in Guinea-Bissau and the Casamance region (in Senegal), which led him to conclude that Curaçao's charter generation must have predominantly originated from Upper Guinea and communicated in a Portuguese-based creole. Considering that, after 1677, Africans arriving in Curaçao came almost exclusively from Kwa- and Bantu-speaking areas in Africa, Jacobs is convinced that the "very first [Africans] to populate the island" were crucial in the "formation of Papiamentu."[86]

While there exist dozens of other studies on the island's creole language, Curaçao's religious history has received far less scholarly attention. This is surprising considering that the island is exceptional not only because its Black population developed a language different from that of the Dutch colonizers, but also because they had different religions. While slaveholders in Curaçao were either Dutch Reformed Christians or Sephardic Jews, the enslaved community was Catholic. Given that Jacobs's study is considered the most authoritative work on the genesis of Papiamentu, his findings call for a deeper analysis of parallels between Black religious traditions in Curaçao and parts of Africa with a historically strong Portuguese influence, in particular the Cape Verde islands. This requires, first, a closer look at the (few) available historical data about Curaçao's African population during the earliest decades of Dutch rule.

Following the Dutch conquest in 1634, the approximately thirty-two Spanish residents, including the island's only priest, were deported from Curaçao to nearby Venezuela. Approximately five hundred Indigenous people were removed as well, while some seventy-five of them were kept as forced laborers. There are no references to enslaved Africans at the time of the Dutch conquest.[87] Curaçao's first Dutch director, Johan van Walbeeck, suggested developing the island with the help of "blacks from Angola." The WIC board of directors thereupon stipulated that all enslaved people captured by Dutch privateers operating in the Caribbean had to be taken to Curaçao.[88] These were probably small numbers. Data from 1643 show that, by that time, only about forty enslaved Africans lived on the island.[89] According to Morris Goodman, the Portuguese reconquest of Dutch Brazil in the mid-seventeenth century may have resulted in an influx of enslaved people brought to Curaçao by Dutch and Jewish settlers who fled Brazil.[90] The only available evidence, however, is that Abraham Drago brought the Angolan man Juan Pinto to Curaçao and Isaac Serano brought his "mulatto servant."[91] Another indication that claims of a massive influx of enslaved people from Dutch Brazil to Curaçao are probably unfounded is Matthias Beck's complaint in 1655 to Petrus Stuyvesant, his superior in New Netherland, that, of all the enslaved living in Curaçao, "no more than twenty . . . are able to do heavy labor."[92]

This does not mean that the Portuguese reconquest of Dutch Brazil had no consequences for Curaçao. In order to secure a steady stream of workers for the sugarcane plantations in its Brazilian colony, the WIC had conquered several Portuguese slave trading posts in Africa. Now that Brazil was lost, the Dutch ventured into new markets in order to make their remaining holdings along the African coast profitable. Ironically, the company that had originally been created to fight the Spanish now became the main supplier of enslaved Africans to Spanish plantation owners. In the context of this new policy, Curaçao acquired strategic importance as an entrepôt of the Dutch slave trade. Starting around 1656, thousands of enslaved Africans arrived on the island, where they were sold to the Spanish and other Europeans in the region.[93]

It is unclear what criteria the Dutch used to decide which Africans they wanted to keep in Curaçao and which were to be sold. Inhabitants of the island were not allowed to buy healthy people for private service until 1674, which indicates that many of those who remained were probably *manquerons,* enslaved people whose physical condition did not allow hard labor and were therefore difficult to sell.[94] In 1659, for instance, Beck referred to the arrival of "twenty-eight Cape Verdean slaves," who due to their condition and age were "almost worthless."[95] The total number of those who remained on the island must, initially, have remained small. Significantly, Beck informed Stuyvesant in 1659 that he was unable to send him "any of the old Company Negroes as requested," because "twelve of them are occupied at Bonayra [Bonaire]" and, therefore, "there are not enough [enslaved people] here to carry out the necessary duties for the Company."[96]

The only explicit reference to the ethnic origin of Curaçao's charter generation comes from a letter by Beck, sent to Stuyvesant in 1660, about the arrival of two Spanish captains from Cádiz eager to fill their ships with enslaved Africans at a time when none were available. In order to not disappoint these customers, Beck requested "both from the freemen as well as from the Company's servants that they loan the Company as many Negroes as possible from their plantations with the promise that they shall be compensated with good Negroes in their place from the first Company Negroes who arrive." He identified the sixty-two people he was able to gather "with great difficulty from the Company as well as private parties" as "Cape Verdean blacks."[97]

If we now shift our attention to religion, it is important to note that, in 1660, Michiel Zyperius informed the classis—the Reformed Church's administrative body—that "Papists . . . who sometimes arrived there" were baptizing Black and Indigenous children in Curaçao.[98] Despite the anti-Catholic bias in seventeenth-century Dutch Reformed circles, the authorities did not take measures to prevent priests from coming to the island.[99] The apparent lack of concern should be seen in the context of Dutch attempts to obtain the *asiento*, a license from the Spanish crown to trade in enslaved Africans. Equally important was the geographical proximity of the Spanish-controlled mainland and the fact that the Spanish authorities issued several provisions promising liberty to enslaved people who fled on the pretext of embracing Catholicism, which culminated in the 1750 royal decree determining that "black slaves of both sexes who come from English and Dutch colonies to seek refuge (whether in times of peace or of war) in my domains to embrace our Holy Catholic Faith shall be free."[100] The desertion of enslaved Africans to Spanish territory for religious reasons was not a chimera. As late as 1773, the Apostolic Prefect reported that Black people from Curaçao had been fleeing to Tierra Firme on the pretense that, in Spanish territory, they could freely practice their Catholic faith.[101] It seems, thus, that the Dutch tolerance of Catholic priests in Curaçao was not a matter of neglect but, rather, a conscious decision resulting from the awareness that preventing the enslaved from having their children baptized would only increase escape attempts.

Since Curaçao technically still belonged to the Diocese of Coro in Venezuela, the bishop of Caracas formally authorized two priests in 1677 to travel clandestinely to the island with a portable altar to perform sacraments. During this first officially sanctioned visit by Catholic clergy since the Dutch conquest of the island, the priests baptized some 320 people, the vast majority of whom were of African descent. Research by Linda Rupert revealed that only twenty of the African mothers—less than 10 percent—had not yet been baptized, which suggests that most "already had been Christian before they left West Central Africa."[102]

We do not know what missionary strategy itinerant priests from Tierra Firme used before the establishment of a permanent Jesuit presence on the island in the early eighteenth century. Considering that they had to operate in a semiclandestine way, could only stay for a short period of time, and were limited in number, it seems unlikely that they would have been able to reach the entire enslaved population on their own. This makes one wonder how the dissemination of Catholicism in the island's Black community could have been so successful. A possible explanation is assistance by lay catechists from within the Black community.

Beck's reference in 1659 to *manquerons* from Cape Verde and, in 1660, to sixty-two Cape Verdeans residing on the island not only renders credibility to Jacobs's claim that Curaçao's charter generation predominantly consisted of Africans with roots in Cape Verde/Upper Guinea who communicated in a Portuguese-based creole, but also suggests that at least some of them were Afro-Atlantic Catholics. This raises the question whether the dissemination of Catholicism may have followed a similar pattern in Curaçao as in Upper Guinea, where priests sporadically visited communities to baptize the newborn and to train catechists, who then provided religious assistance to communities that self-organized themselves in confraternities.

Rupert confirmed that, by the mid-eighteenth century, "Several religious brotherhoods (*cofradías*) in Coro had direct ties to similar societies in Curaçao" and "one such society in Coro, the *Cofradía del Carmen*, even sent a delegation to collect alms from their brothers on the island."[103] This assumption can be strengthened by referencing a number of Black cultural traditions on the island that correspond to Afro-Iberian fraternity practices. There are, for instance, clear parallels between parades of brotherhood kings in Cuba and those of crowned Epiphany kings in Bonaire.[104] Another example is the apparently incongruous comment by the free Black community of Curaçao that they, rather than the free Mulattoes, should march first in the 1740 parade because "they had kings of their race, which the mulattoes did not have."[105] Such discussions were common in Latin America, where Mulattoes were often excluded from confraternities formed by African nations and forced to form their own societies, which were not allowed to have "kings."[106]

Several other traditions of Curaçao's Black community, such as the announcement of someone's death by blowing a horn, the honoring of the deceased with eight days of mourning (known as *ocho dia*), the hourlong praying of novenas and singing of *dumve* (corrupted versions of Gregorian prayer songs) under the guidance of a sacristan or *resadó* (lead singer), the chasing of the spirit of the deceased out of the house at the end of the *ocho dia*, the singing of Ave Maria prayers during the mourning of an *angelito* (innocent child turned angel), the use of rosaries as charms (especially during Lent, when the evil spirits or *zumbis* are strongest), the celebration of Saint John with bonfires, and the bathing of the saint's statue on Saint John's Eve all correspond to customs that, in parts of Africa with a historically strong Portuguese influence and in Latin America, typically flourished in the context of brotherhoods.[107]

Salt was also used during baptismal rituals in Curaçao, and, similar to what was observed in Kongo, served as a form of protection against evil spirits in the days leading up to a newborn's baptism, when the latter *ta jora bautismo* (cries because it has not yet been baptized). Also intriguing is the popularity of Saint Anthony, locally known as Lele Toni, which recalls how this saint was known in Kongo, namely as (N)toni.[108] As in Portugal, Africa, and Latin America, Saint Anthony enjoyed a dubious reputation in Curaçao as womanizer and *santu di paranda* (party saint), whose veneration typically involved *tambú* music and dances. It was even considered improper for unmarried women to have a statue of Saint Anthony at home. People also would put pressure on Saint Anthony to fulfill a wish by temporarily turning his statue's face against the wall, blindfolding it, placing it in the tropical sun or upside down in water, removing the infant Christ, or even removing the saint's own head.[109]

We also find parallels between the Iberian tradition of beating and burning an effigy of Judas and the Curaçaon practice of *Bati Húda* (beating Judas).[110] The earliest reference to it in Curaçao dates to 1682, when the crew of a Spanish ship hoisted an effigy dressed as the island's rabbi with the intention of making its head explode.[111] Well into the twentieth century, this tradition maintained an anti-Semitic character in Curaçaon society, which could be associated with an Iberian tradition of anti-Semitism that pervaded sixteenth-century Cape Verdean society.[112]

The Dominican Paul Brenneker, a pioneer in the study of Curaçaon folklore, also pointed to the importance of Afro-Catholic burial societies, known as *sociedads di caha* (coffin societies) or *seters*, referring to the candle-holders that these societies provided for the *ocho dia*. "Every neighborhood has one," he explained, "and people are often members of more than one." Every month people paid a fee because these societies were "considered a basic necessity in order to avoid a poor-people's-funeral." Like brother-hoods, these societies had their own banners and names referring to a Catholic patron saint, such as San Pedro, La Birgen Nos Mama, San Hosé, or Santa Lucia. They assisted families in organizing *ocho dia* rituals by providing not only candles and candleholders, but also a coffin, extra chairs, and liquor for the male visitors, who, after paying respect to the deceased, were expected to *laba man* (wash their hands), a euphemism for drinking a shot of brandy.[113]

The important role of *sociedads di caha* in Curaçaoan society may also help us to understand Han Jordaan's observation that there was consider-able resistance within the Catholic Black population to organizing the burial of newcomers from Africa who passed away before being baptized and, thus, never contributed to any of the Catholic burial societies.[114] Not unlike Kristons in Upper Guinea, Black Catholics in Curaçao considered unbaptized Africans inferior. Significantly, they used to refer to the latter with the slur *bouriques* (asses), a corruption of the Spanish *bozales*, and called the burial place for unbaptized people the *chiké*, the "pigsty."[115]

There are, thus, strong indications that Afro-Atlantic Catholic cus-toms did indeed influence the development of social and religious tradi-tions among Curaçao's Black population. The parallels with the Cape Verde islands and Upper Guinea also suggest that at least some of these traditions may have been introduced by members of Curaçao's charter generation. While it is impossible to sustain this assumption with seven-teenth-century documentary evidence, Brenneker's observation that the catechization of people in rural parts of Curaçao had historically occurred through Black laypersons known as *sacristans*, which he translated as "a type of catechists," does point in this direction.[116] Armando Lampe also referred to Black laypeople teaching newcomers from Africa the catechism and the rosary prayer. He highlighted that laypeople performed baptisms and concluded that, in Curaçao, "the oppressed" (i.e., the enslaved) have been "evangelized by the oppressed."[117]

We could here briefly return to the topic of language. As was pointed out before, Papiamentu probably derived from the Afro-Portuguese creole spoken by the Cape Verdean/Upper Guinean charter generation. By the late 1670s, however, enslaved Africans arriving in Curaçao came almost exclusively from Kwa- and Bantu-speaking areas. References to no fewer than forty-one different African "nations" in Father Gambier's 1755 baptismal book confirm that the ethnic origin of the Black community had diversified tremendously by the mid-eighteenth century.[118] The survival of Papiamentu as lingua franca indicates that some mechanism must have allowed the preservation of crucial elements of the charter generation's cultural identity, including language, at a time when the ethnic composition of the island's Black community changed dramatically. No other institution could have better taken care of this task than brotherhoods. It is not difficult to imagine how the repetitive nature of prayer sessions, where the words of the *rezador* are repeated over and over again, formed authentic teaching sessions for newly arrived Africans. We could, in this respect, refer to parallels between Papiamentu and Papia Kristang, a creole of Portuguese origin that is spoken in Southeast Asia. Alan Baxter's research of Papia Kristang confirmed that brotherhoods played a key role in community formation and the preservation of identity markers, including language, long after Portuguese rule in the region had ended. "That religion itself was quite important is clearly suggested by the word *kristáng*," Baxter wrote, and "the role of the fraternity of the *irmáng di greza* (brothers of the Church) in providing an element of cultural continuity was significant."[119] Considering these parallels, it is probably no coincidence that a variant of the very same creole that laid the basis for Papiamentu is known as *Kriston* in Casamance and Guinea-Bissau.[120]

All of this suggests that the situation that existed in Curaçao may have been similar to what we identified in Upper Guinea, where Afro-Catholic communities incorporated brotherhoods that received sporadic support, mainly at the level of sacraments, by priests. While we do not have documentary evidence of lay catechists and confraternities among Curaçao's charter generation, this theory does provide a credible explanation for the development and persistence of a strong Afro-Catholic identity under adverse circumstances.

That the Dutch authorities, in spite of their tolerant policy vis-à-vis Spanish priests operating on the island, remained distrustful of Catholic influence is reflected in the comment by Governor Jean Rodier in 1780 that in the event of a Spanish attack, he would not be able to count on the island's free Black and Mulatto communities because they were all "blind Roman Catholics."[121] The latter's attachment to Catholicism was an enigma to the Reformed Church in Amsterdam, which, in 1741, asked its pastor, Wigboldus Rasvelt, to launch an investigation. In his response, Rasvelt pointed to his predecessors, who had refused to accept enslaved people as members of the Reformed Church, and to slaveholders who did not allow Protestant evangelization out of concern that the children of enslaved people, once baptized, could no longer be sold. They did not have such concerns with regard to Catholic baptisms. Rasvelt concluded that, in his opinion, Protestant Christianity was unfit for Black people, who "ex nativitate et quasi ex natura" are "inclined to Catholicism" because it is a religion where people "who don't understand anything about the Christian faith and, at very most, mumble some prayers, though without knowledge or attention, can still bear the name of Christians."[122]

Over time, the religious customs of Curaçao's Black population also became a matter of concern to the island's Catholic authorities. When, in the course of the eighteenth century, Church officials tried to impose a post-Tridentine form of Catholicism in Curaçao, they clashed with the Black community, which was eager to preserve its own Afro-Catholic traditions. In 1759 tensions were such that the Black population threatened to leave the Catholic Church and establish its own church.[123] These tensions were further exacerbated following the elevation of Curaçao to an apostolic prefecture in 1823. In their eagerness to "civilize" Curaçaoan Catholicism, Church authorities went so far as to exclude people from the congregation for playing *tambú* music in honor of Saint Anthony and honoring *ocho dia* funeral traditions. The population resisted, as captured in the words of a popular song: "Ta un kachó mi tabatin / tende kon m'a yam'é? / M'a mara un sinta na sua garganta / dunele nòmber di kongrenis" (I used to have a dog / do you know how I called her? I put a leash around her neck / and called her congregation).[124]

While the religious history of this tiny Antillean island may seem like a unique case that is of little importance to the rest of the Caribbean and, for that matter, to the history of Black Christianity as a whole, one could also argue the opposite. If we return once again to language, we find that what makes Curaçao unique in the eyes of linguists is not that its seventeenth-century charter generation spoke a Portuguese-based creole, but rather that they successfully passed their language on to later generations.[125] This would imply that not just in Curaçao, but also in other parts of the Caribbean, charter generations included people who communicated in an Afro-Portuguese creole and identified as Catholics. One such place may have been Suriname.

Suriname

The settlement of the second Anglo-Dutch War with the Treaty of Breda (1677) determined that Suriname, the central part of the Guianas, was to become a Dutch colony, while the English would keep New Netherland, now renamed New York. Unlike in Curaçao, the Dutch authorities did not allow Catholic priests to operate in Suriname. At the request of one of his Catholic trading partners in Amsterdam, however, the new governor, Cornelis van Aerssen van Sommelsdijck, brought two Franciscans with him in 1683 and, one year later, welcomed two more. Three of them passed away quickly, and after the fourth returned to the Dutch Republic in 1686, the mission was not renewed.[126]

Since the 1683 mission had failed and the Dutch Reformed Church focused almost exclusively on Dutch settlers in the colony, it is generally assumed that Christian proselytizing among the enslaved population in Suriname started in 1735, with the arrival of the Renewed Unity of the Brethren, commonly called the Moravian Church. However, seventeenth-century sources include an abundance of references to enslaved Africans with Iberian Catholic baptismal names such as Lucretia, Victoria, Diana, Thomas, Gabriel, Francisque, Matteus, Christina, and Congo Maria.[127] This was recognized by the seventeenth-century Dutch explorer Adriaan van Berkel, who claimed that enslaved Africans in the Guianas did "not have any religion at all, notwithstanding that several among them are baptized."[128] In spite of significant Portuguese lexical influence, the creole that developed as the lingua franca of the Surinamese Black community was largely based on English, the language of the first slaveholders. In fact, the charter generation was more diverse in Suriname than in Curaçao and people from parts of Africa with a historically strong Portuguese influence had much less of an impact on the development of Surinamese Black culture than on that of the Dutch Antillean islands.

Nevertheless, an intriguing reference to the presence of Afro-Atlantic Catholics in Suriname can be found in Coronie, a district where plantations were not established until the early nineteenth century. During his mission to Coronie in the 1820s, Father Paulus Wennekers discovered "a number of Portuguese slaves," who "carried a small cross on their chest" and walked "for several hours in order to attend the church service."[129] It was also in Coronie that an enslaved man called Colin had attempted to organize an uprising in 1817. Investigations revealed that Colin had been influenced by Christianity and that, for instance, he referred to meetings as "having church." While this Christian influence has traditionally been explained through references to Moravian missionary work, the fact that "King Colin" was addressed by his followers as *tata*, the Kikongo term for "father," indicates that these Christian influences may also have been of Kongolese origin. One does not exclude the other, however, since Moravian missionaries may have built on earlier Afro-Atlantic Catholic elements.[130] An interesting place to further explore this theory is the Danish Virgin Islands.

Danish Virgin Islands

After a failed attempt by the Dutch WIC to establish a plantation colony on Saint Thomas in the 1650s, this island was resettled by the Danish in the early 1670s. Shortly after, the Danes also occupied Saint John. In 1733 they purchased Saint Croix from the French. Similar to what happened in Curaçao, Catholic priests from nearby Puerto Rico occasionally visited these islands to perform baptisms among members of the Black community. This practice was tolerated by the Danish authorities, probably to limit attempts by the enslaved to flee to Puerto Rico "in search of the Catholic religion," as Governor Estivan Bravao de Rivero argued in 1716.[131]

The Moravian Mission in the Virgin Islands began in 1732. The islands are of particular importance to the history of the Brethren's Congregation because it was a formerly enslaved man from Saint Thomas, Anton Ulrich, who convinced the church's leaders to start a mission among the enslaved populations in the Americas. He famously did so with the observation that, in order to be successful, Moravian missionaries would have to live like the enslaved people they wished to convert.[132]

The Moravian missionary strategy in the Virgin Islands relied heavily on a network of Black helpers, called "fishermen." Following a Catholic model, these helpers were encouraged to approach newcomers, communicate with them in their native languages, and form small groups or "bands."[133] In the 1760s, the German missionary Christian Oldendorp admitted that "a lot, one could even say most, of the blessings occurred by blacks among each other. When one of them had learned something about the Savior, he passed it on to others on the plantation where he lived and invited others to join him in his blessing."[134]

Among these helpers was a woman named Shelly, who, before joining the Moravian congregation and changing her name to Rebecca, had been baptized by a Catholic priest.[135] She was not unique. Jon Sensbach's research revealed that at least twenty-five of the earliest Black converts to the Moravian Church had a Catholic background.[136] While Rebecca's commitment to Christian missionary work among the enslaved population is astonishing, Sensbach also noted that, long before her, Afro-Atlantic Catholics had engaged in similar proselytizing activities and that Moravian missionary workers "simply adopted many of these customs to fit their own message [in order to] incorporate Africans into the evangelical family."[137]

One of the earliest references to the presence of Afro-Atlantic Catholics on the islands comes from the Moravian missionary Friedrich Martin, who reported in 1738 on a conversation with "a Portuguese Negro who was baptized [in Kongo]."[138] Oldendorp later confirmed that "the majority of those who come from [Kongo] to the West Indies have knowledge of God and their Saviour." From conversations with one of them, Oldendorp learned that the Portuguese had brought "many blacks to the Catholic Church" in Kongo, especially "among those who live close to them," and that "most people in his land went to a Christian church and were baptized and married by a priest." The man also informed Oldendorp that the Kongolese "had priests of their own nation, who baptized people, organized Masses, could read, and had their own religious books." Those who did not live in urban areas "were also influenced by Christianity, albeit mixed with heathenish customs."[139]

Oldendorp further learned that an enslaved Kongolese man who used to live in Saint Thomas had "a religious book that white people could read." This man would "read from the book for men when it was new moon, and when it was full moon, the women could join as well." Oldendorp confirmed that most Kongolese he met were "Catholics and know something of the Christian faith. They call God *sambiampungo* and call on Mary. They believe that the soul is immortal." Their funeral rituals consisted of "sewing the corpse into a white sheet . . . placing it in a coffin, and carrying it in procession to a crypt. Those who had a bad life are not buried and receive neither a funeral sermon nor a procession." Oldendorp also explained that it was common "among blacks who came from Portuguese countries . . . particularly those from Kongo" to perform "a kind of baptism," characterized by "pouring water over the head of the baptized, placing some salt in his mouth, and praying to God in the Kongo language."[140]

While he added that this Afro-Catholic baptismal ritual "was not considered baptism by [Protestant] Christians," Oldendorp acknowledged that enslaved Kongolese engaged in Afro-Catholic missionary work. Similar to the way priests in Kongo examined "prisoners or those who were sent to the shore to be sold into slavery" in order to find out "their sins and, in particular, whether they ever had eaten human flesh" and, thereupon, "teach, absolve, and baptize them," certain Kongolese in Saint Thomas provided "a form of baptism to those *bozals* who desire this." Before the baptism could take place, however, "an adult *bozal* had to receive five to six lashes from the baptizer, for the sins he had committed in Africa." Oldendorp also clarified that "those *bozals*, who desire this, receive someone who assumes the role of father or mother for them." Once a newcomer was admitted to the Afro-Catholic community, "there is a Negro celebration" and baptismal fathers and mothers "adopt those whom they have baptized as their children and look after them as best they can, in particular, when they pass away, because then they provide them with a coffin and burial clothing." The person who originally baptized the deceased typically "sings at his grave and holds a short sermon" at burial ceremonies that "involve a lot of eating, mourning, and dancing."[141]

Oldendorp's observations, thus, seem to confirm what we suspected earlier about Curaçao, namely that Afro-Atlantic Catholics in the Americas took Christianization into their own hands and built their own societies. Significantly, Sensbach noted parallels between the Kongolese societies in the Virgin Islands and "black confraternities" in Latin America.[142] The fact that Afro-Catholic Kongolese catechists catered to the needs of newly arrived enslaved Africans and organized baptisms and funerals does, in fact, indicate that they operated in the context of a brotherhood and, as

Maureen Warner-Lewis suggested, used rituals that "may have derived from practices within the Catholic fraternity in Koongo [*sic*]."[143]

Despite all missionary efforts by the Moravian Church, the 1839 Von Scholten's Report revealed that the majority of Black people on the islands of Saint Croix and Saint Thomas identified as Catholic.[144] Albert Campbell's sociological study from the 1940s on the Black population of Saint Thomas also showed that lower-class people on the island still had what he called "semi-religious burying societies" with unmistakably Catholic names, such as "the St. Joseph's" and "the Mary and Joseph's."[145] While there is no evidence that, similar to Latin American brotherhoods, these societies also elected "kings," "queens" and other leadership positions with aristocratic titles, Thurlow Weed reported in 1845 from Saint Croix that "the slaves on each estate elect their queen and princess, with their king and prince, whose authority is supreme. These have their maids of honor, pages, &c." According to this New York publisher and politician, "The free colored people and house slaves form their parties, elect their kings, queens, &c., and dance in like manner" in the towns as well.[146] Even after the abolition of slavery in 1848, the Black population preserved a strong attachment to this tradition. In 1856, for instance, a local newspaper reported on the "absurd exhibition of mock royalty" by a king and queen, who were "richly attired in silk and satins."[147] In the twentieth century, after these islands had been purchased by the United States, people still recalled "kings and queens marching around the streets."[148]

Similar scenes have been reported in former British colonies in the Caribbean.

British West Indies

Occupied by the English in the 1620s, Barbados developed in the 1640s into a sugarcane plantation colony that depended heavily on enslaved labor. Unlike in Curaçao and the Virgin Islands, there was no Spanish-controlled territory in the immediate vicinity of Barbados. One Catholic priest who did visit the island (in disguise) is Antoine Biet. In 1654 this French priest estimated that about two thousand Catholics lived in Barbados; they were mainly Irish, but some were enslaved Africans. Biet met, for instance, with a group of six Africans, all "very good Catholics," who allegedly told him that they were "extremely sorrowed to see themselves sold as slaves on an island of heretics." He also observed that slaveholders didn't care about the religious instruction of the enslaved and limited themselves to "letting their children baptize in the house." While it is not clear what he meant by this, Biet added that "if some of them received a tinge of the Catholic religion among the Portuguese, they preserve it the best they can, doing their prayers and worshipping God in their hearts."[149]

The complaints about being sent to an "island of heretics" echo those of Capuchin missionaries in Kongo, who tried to use their prestige to prevent African Catholics from being sold to colonies ruled by Protestants. In the 1660s, the Propaganda Fide examined these concerns and sided with Capuchins in condemning the enslavement of Catholic Africans.[150] Upon realizing that this condemnation failed to achieve its goal, the Capuchins narrowed their focus to Protestant slave traders. In the 1680s, Merolla da Sorrento tried to convince the prince of Soyo to "at least exclude the heretics from dealing in this merchandize, especially the English, who take them to Barbados."[151] After the bishop of Luanda threatened those who sold African Catholics to Protestants with excommunication, the prince of Soyo wrote a letter to the pope in 1701, requesting an exception with the argument that only Protestant slave traders were willing to pay with the firearms he badly needed to defend his territory.[152] Lorenzo da Lucca reported that the prince was eventually excommunicated, received absolution, and then was excommunicated again after restarting business with the English, to which Lucca added, "It is not fair that people baptized in the Catholic Church are sold to enemies of their faith."[153]

The slave trader James Barbot confirmed that the prince of Soyo insisted that the men and women he intended to sell to the English "should be instructed in the Christian faith." For the Capuchins, however, verbal reassurances were not enough. They "started some difficulties," Barbot wrote, and alleged that "the English carried the slaves to Barbados, to the hereticks."[154] Similar concerns can be detected in a Spanish document from 1735, where we find a condemnation of the fact that shipments from English slavers operating in Central Africa included "several male and female slaves, of different ages, from the Kingdom of Kongo, all of them Christianized and baptized as children, some with a limited instruction in the basics of our Holy Faith, others very well catechized, ready to receive the sacraments of Our Holy Mother Church."[155]

Like in Curaçao, some of the earliest enslaved Africans in Barbados originated in Cape Verde. In 1645 John Winthrop recorded in his journal how a ship brought "wine, and sugar, and salt, and some tobacco" to New England, "which she had at Barbadoes, in exchange for Africanoes, which she carried from the Isle of Maio," the latter being an island in the Cape Verde archipelago.[156] In 1647 Thomas Modyford and Richard Ligon sailed from England to Barbados by way of "St. Jago, one of the Ilands of Cape Verd; where wee were to trade for Negros . . . which we were to sell at the Barbados."[157] Others originated from the region of Kongo/Angola. In 1646, for instance, the Dutch ship *Tamandaré* took to Barbados most of the 270 enslaved people who had recently arrived in Dutch Brazil from Luanda and then sold the remaining people in Manhattan.[158] In 1685 the Dutch New Yorker Frederick Philipse brought a group of 105 enslaved Africans from Soyo, in Kongo, to Barbados. He sold 96 of them on the island and took the remaining people, who had physical limitations that made them unsuitable for work on plantations, to Manhattan.[159]

The presence of enslaved Africans influenced by Portuguese culture is noted in Ligon's observation in 1657 that on James Draxes' plantation, one of the largest in Barbados, several enslaved Africans had been "bred up amongst the Portugalls." According to Ligon, these "Portugall Negros" had "some extraordinary qualities, which the others have not," such as "singing and fencing," both "at rapier and dagger."[160] Other evidence of the presence of Afro-Atlantic Catholics comes from the Barbados Council, where, in 1688, three African men were freed because they had been able to provide proof that they were "free borne and Christians." One year later, however, the council became worried about the fact that these three men "doe openly profess themselves Roman Catholick," and ordered them to be "sold or transported and sent off this island." David Barry Gaspar's research also revealed how in the early eighteenth century, an enslaved Black man called Francisco Delgaudo requested his freedom with the argument that he was "a Christian Negro and a subject of the King of Portugal" and how four "Portuguese mulattoes," who had been seized by privateers in Cape Verde, taken to the island of Saint Lucia, and bought by a man from Barbados, protested against their enslavement, claiming that they were "freemen, Christians, and subjects to the King of Portugal, and could not be sold as slaves."[161]

Jenny Shaw demonstrated that concerns over Black Catholics among the colonial authorities in Barbados often coincided with fears about the

Irish "seducing and drawing of[f] the Negroes and other slaves of this island" to the Catholic faith, "as well as other wicked attempts and designes
[that] might follow thereon." She also showed that, in 1689, the authorities in Saint Christopher (today's Saint Kitts) expressed concerns over the
fact that "many of the French, mulattoes . . . & Negroes" were "imbodyed
with the Irish."[162]

In fact, also in Saint Kitts and other English colonies in the Caribbean
can we find traces of Afro-Atlantic Catholics. In Antigua, where one of the
earliest and largest Afro-Protestant communities of the Caribbean would
develop in the 1780s, the investigations following the 1736 plot revealed
that several members of the earliest generations of enslaved Africans were
literate and had been "initiated into Christianity according to the Romish
Church."[163] Research conducted by John Catron into Moravian Church
records about Antigua revealed that the vast majority of African converts
originated from Kongo. He also encountered designations such as "Portu-
give" and "Portuguese Guinea," which led him to conclude that some
"had been exposed to Christian teaching before Protestant missionaries
came on the scene" and that the "chances that a substantial number of
Afro-Antiguans were Christians before they crossed the Atlantic are greater
than previous studies have found."[164]

Speaking about the earliest enslaved community in Jamaica, James
Phillippo confirmed in 1843 that "some of them were Papist." The Baptist
missionary also mentioned the existence on the island of Afro-Christian
communities, or what he called the "mysteriously blending together" of
"important truths and extravagant puerilities," allegedly established by
"some [Black people] who had been imported" from North America in
the immediate aftermath of the revolution and who had become their
"teachers and preachers." According to Phillippo, some members of the
Black community in Jamaica "pretended to read—to foretel future events;
to possess the gift of tongues; and to prophesy." They also "interpreted
what little they knew of the Scriptures literally" and, at certain seasons,
wandered "into the woods and most secluded parts of the country, in
search of the Saviour, professedly after the manner of John the Baptist in
the wilderness." Those who did so were organized in brotherhoods and
paid great attention to the viaticum because "when any of the fraternity
were confined to their beds by sickness, the minister, or father, as he was
usually called, anointed them with oil in imitation of the anointing of the

Saviour by Mary Magdalene, before his crucifixion." The usual method of its application was "by pouring it into the palm of the hand, and rubbing it on the head of the patient; the *tata*, or father, singing some ditty during the operation, being joined in loud chorus by all who assembled to witness the ceremony." Phillippo specified that "these infatuated men professed a firm belief in purgatory, and, like the Romish priests, pretended an acquaintance with the destinies of the deceased." Dreams and visions were so important to this community that "some supernatural revelations were regarded as indispensable to qualify for admission to the full privileges of their community." Furthermore, Phillippo explained, "the meetings of this fraternity were frequently prolonged through nearly half the night" and "the priests enjoined on their followers the duty of fasting one or two days in the week." They also encouraged a "weekly meeting at each others' houses, alternately, to drink 'hot water' out of white tea-cups . . . which they designated by the . . . epithet of 'breaking the peace.'" At these assemblies, they sang "the childish story of *the House that Jack Built*" and "things if possible still more absurd . . . while 'hallelujah' was repeated at the end of each verse in loud chorus." Also, their posture during prayers surprised him, since "they either stood with their arms extended, and their whole bodies as though transfixed against the wall or prostrated themselves upon the earth; and in this attitude they remained many hours at a time . . . uttering the most discordant sounds expressive of internal anguish and agonizing supplication." The fraternities also coordinated clandestine missionary activities, sending out disciples, who traveled "by night to avoid apprehension" and then "communicated their instructions from house to house." Phillippo added that "on public holidays, particularly those of Christmas . . . each of the African tribes upon the different estates formed itself into a distinct party, composed of men, women, and children. Each party had its King or Queen, who was distinguished by a mask of the most harlequin-like apparel." These groups then "paraded or gamboled in their respective neighborhoods, dancing to the rude music."[165]

It is true that some Christianized Black people from North America, most notably Moses Baker and George Liele, ended up in Jamaica during or immediately after the American War of Independence, where they led the foundations of the island's "Native Baptism" and also influenced the further development of a Black religious movement known as Mayalism).[166] However, the formation of brotherhoods with kings and queens, administration of the viaticum, and belief in purgatory are all typically Afro-Catholic features. This shows that the history of Myalism and of Black Christianity in Jamaica cannot be reduced to an indigenous African and/or Protestant narrative. It would, indeed, be wrong to ignore that the island had a Spanish colonial history that lasted until 1655, that after the English invasion some enslaved Africans from the Spanish era, known as "Spanish Negroes," ran away and formed Maroon communities, and that several of the enslaved Africans taken to Jamaica were Afro-Atlantic Catholics. Newspaper advertisements from the 1790s about runaways refer, for instance, to a "Negro woman with a crucifix necklace" and another one "speaking Portuguese."[167] Moreover, the communities described by Phillippo used the term *tata*, which is the Kikongo word for father.

It is interesting to note that these communities also integrated English cultural elements in their religious system, as in the cases of the nursery rhyme "This Is the House That Jack Built" and the habit of drinking hot water from teacups. The latter can be considered an early reference to a custom that became known in Jamaica (as well as in Barbados) as a "tea meeting," a social gathering of a Black mutual-aid society where alcohol was served, music was played, dances were performed, speeches were held, stick fighting was practiced, and kings and queens were elected.[168]

References to Kongolese people organized in mutual-aid associations have also been found in other formerly English colonies in the Caribbean. One such place is the Guianas, where James Rodway observed in his *History of British Guiana* (1893) that, just like in Latin America, enslaved Africans organized themselves in "nations," with their own kings and other court members, known as princes or dukes. He explained that "Negroes of every nation in a district . . . choose head-men or 'Kings,' under whom were several subaltern officers of the same nation." The duties of the "kings" were "to take care of the sick and purchase rice, sugar, &c., for them, to conduct the burials, and see that the corpse was properly enclosed in a cloth, and that the customary rites and dances were duly observed." Rodway made a specific reference to the Kongolese community when explaining that "an end was put to these 'Companies'—as they were called—among the Congoes, by a quarrel between them and their 'King,' who at a certain burial declared that he had no money, although the people believed he had enough for the purpose, as it was impossible that their contributions could all have been exhausted." In consequence, "the 'Company' was abolished, and on each estate they had since taken care of their own dead." Rodway continued that "from the confessions of the Congoes, it appeared they had a 'King,' Governor, General Drummer, and a Doctor or Lawyer."[169] In the late nineteenth century, the British missionary Lawrence Crookall also reported on a "small tribe of 'Congo Africans,'" who had probably come as indentured workers to British Guiana. One of them addressed Crookall as "Gorgonzambe," which he explained as "de African name for de minister . . . which mean God-doctor." The latter term undoubtedly derived from *nganga a Nzambi*, the Kikongo term for priest that literally translates as "doctor of God."[170]

In the late nineteenth century, George Northcroft highlighted in one of his studies that, on the Bahamas, Black communities had formed societies to "help their members when sick, and to bury them decently. Everybody tries to belong to a burial society." On certain holidays, he explained, these societies go "to worship at some church," while marching in full regalia to and from their "sacred edifice . . . headed, if possible, by a band."[171] During his stay in Nassau in 1886, Louis Diston Powles also noted that "every August," some of the Black people "elect a queen whose will is law on certain matters" and that "about Christmas time they seem to march about day and night with lanterns and bands of music."[172] Howard Johnson's study confirmed the importance of fraternal societies to the islands' Black community and argued that "an organization of that type, on a more informal basis, might have existed during the slavery era."[173] Rosanne Adderley later identified one of these societies as the "Congo Nr. 1 Society" that, in August 1888, sent a letter in the name of the "Natives of the Congo" to Leopold II, "King of the Belgians and King of the Congo Free State," with the request to allow them to return.[174]

References to Kongo can also be found in Trinidad, where the investigation of a plot in 1823 revealed that, among the Black population on the island, there were "many Societies . . . under the military designation of *regiment* . . . to be used on the occasion of dances on holy days to denote different parties, tribes or nations such as *Regiment Congo*."[175] In 1853 the *Port of Spain Gazette* reported on "Africans of the Congo nation, who have associated themselves together as 'the Congo society', and who have purchased certain premises in Charlotte street, known as the Congo yard" and "when any of the society die . . . the dead body is brought to this yard to be 'waked.'"[176] In 1889 the *New Era* characterized these societies as "secret brotherhoods, with rituals and symbols resembling . . . those of the Masonic fraternity."[177] In a letter from 1885, Father Marie Bertrand de Cothonay provided a detailed description of such a Black mutual-aid society in Saint-Dominic-Village, in the Carenage region, claiming that "almost all men are members of a fraternity dedicated to Saint Dominic that is half religious and half secular. They really celebrate their patron saint extensively. They have pennants, flags, musical instruments, firecrackers, and a nice piece of furniture to carry six blessed breads." During the procession, "the women recite the rosary, the men sing the litanies of the saints, and the children English canticles." After Mass, "the king of the society appears with his diadem of gilded paper" and "the queen . . . whose function it is to distribute the blessed bread." Their banquet takes place in a hut, which serves as "the palace of Their Majesties." According to Cothonay, the "king and queen are elected annually" and "there is also a governor." After learning that this tradition had once been suspended at the request of a parish priest, but then reinstated after the relations between this priest and the Black population had soured, Cothonay decided to "destroy the palace . . . and once and for all put an end to this diabolic celebration."[178] This early presence of Afro-Atlantic Catholics in Trinidad convinced Dianne Stewart that the Catholic saints in the local Orisa or Shango cults were not, as was long assumed, a smokescreen behind which devotees secretly worshipped (indigenous African) Yoruba gods, but rather a sign that the cults were built on earlier foundations established by the island's Afro-Atlantic Catholic charter generation. It made her conclude that "Afro-Catholics provided the ritual architecture that allowed Yoruba sacred traditions the necessary institutional space to manifest and blossom into a nationally recognized religion."[179]

The case of Trinidad is complex because the island had a long Spanish colonial history and was mainly developed by French planters and their enslaved workforce in the 1770s before it was conquered by the British in 1797. Several other Caribbean islands have similarly complex histories. Dominica, for instance, was a French colony until it was conquered by the British in 1761. Its chief justice Thomas Atwood observed in his *History of the Island of Dominica* (1791) that many among the island's Black population "profess the Christian religion, especially that of the Roman Catholicks, and some of them pay great attention thereto."[180]

The island of Saint Christopher passed between French and British rule several times until the latter imposed themselves in 1783 and renamed it Saint Kitts. In the late seventeenth century, the superior-general of the Jesuit mission to the French Antilles had complained that, following the English conquest of the island, "six thousand blacks, all Catholics . . . became the slaves of the English [who] do not baptize their slaves." Seeing themselves deprived of the sacraments, he claimed, they self-organized prayer services and baptisms and even "got married in the presence of their Catholic friends." Others "decided to flee [to] Guadaloupe," where they "could live as Christians."[181] While one might be skeptical about the veracity of these words, Father Jean Mongin had reported in a 1682 letter from Saint Christopher that "his church was full of blacks during catechism"; that, during Mass, he had to refuse entry to large numbers of Black people because "he could only offer place for up to about a hundred of them"; and that in the island's annual procession marched "about one thousand female blacks and the same amount of male blacks, four in four, singing their catechism while holding chaplets in their hands."[182]

This Catholic zeal surprised Sue Peabody, who pointed out that, before 1700, only few Africans on this island had originated from the Kongo region. As Peabody herself indicated, however, the earliest Africans to arrive on the island in the 1640s had all been "confiscated from Portuguese and Spanish ships."[183] Only much later, in the 1680s, did Father Mongin observe that the new Africans arriving on the island were ignorant of Christianity, "excepting several who come from Kongo."[184]

Peabody also found evidence in the work of Guillaume Moreau, Jesuit superior of the Guadeloupe mission from 1706 to 1710, about pressure the Afro-Catholic Black community placed on unbaptized newcomers from Africa. According to Moreau, Afro-Catholics "teach" these newcomers "the prayers . . . take them to church and to catechism, make them attend Mass, make them observe the ceremonies, and try to give them the most dedicated religion possible, often repeating to them that, having been brutes as they are, they have become children of God." It was, thus, enslaved Black people who "by dint of laying siege to them, telling them so by reason, by example, and by invitations, . . . persuade them to ask for baptism." Whenever these Black Catholics convinced newcomers to accept baptism, they took them to a priest, who then "puts them in the hand of one of the Negro catechists."[185] In other words, Black people not only pressured unbaptized newcomers to become Catholic, but also assumed responsibility for the catechization of those who decided to join the Catholic community.

Like Saint Christopher, the island of Saint Lucia passed between French and British hands several times until the British imposed their rule in 1803. In the 1950s, A. F. and D. Wells presented evidence that Black communities in socially disadvantaged neighborhoods on this island had societies with a "coffin fund," built up by means of regular periodical contributions, which provided for an "extra payment on the death of a member" in order to cover the costs of burial.[186] This was not a new phenomenon. References to Black mutual-aid societies have been found in Saint Lucia since as early as 1769. In 1844 Henry Breen reported extensively on two Black mutual-aid societies on the island, the Roses and the Marguerites. He explained that "each society has three kings and three queens, who are chosen by the suffrages of the members" and that "the first, or senior, king and queen only make their appearance on solemn occasions, such as the anniversary of their coronation or the *fête* of the patron saint of the society." While Breen argued that "the history of the Antilles is involved in such total obscurity in all that concerns the black population" and that, therefore, "it would be impossible at the present time to trace the origin of the Roses and Marguerites," the existence of a "patron saint" and references in their songs to "de Sainte Rose c'est la fête," "U sé sésé èvèk Set Wòz dé Lima" (You are a sister of Saint Rose of Lima), and "Sé Dié ki kwé-I, Lamagéwit, Sé pu la Rédempté" (It is God who created them, the Marguerites, it is for the Redeemer) point in the direction of ancient Afro-Catholic confraternities. Daniel Crowley's observation that "There are persistent legends about cloth-of-gold church vestments in the Immaculate Conception Cathedral in Castries which were contributed by one of the societies" only strengthens this theory.[187]

The many references to Afro-Catholic elements in former French colonies such as Saint Christopher and Saint Lucia call for a closer look at the French Antilles.

French Antilles

Although Capuchins based in Saint Christopher, the first French possession in the Caribbean, had opposed the enslavement of Catholic Africans in the 1640s, their expulsion from the island and replacement by other religious orders shifted the paradigm. Christianization was henceforth no longer an argument to oppose the slave trade but, rather, one to justify it. This becomes clear in the Code Noir from 1685, which stipulated that all enslaved Africans arriving in French colonies had to be baptized, catechized, and buried in consecrated soil.[188]

As in Latin America, French priests catering to the enslaved community typically employed Black catechists. As the Jesuit Jean Chrétien explained in 1718, upon the arrival of new Africans, "Black fathers [*Pères noirs*] come to see them and teach them how to make the cross" and, thanks to these catechists who spoke their language, the newcomers soon "learn that baptism gives them a sort of relief." While many slaveholders "had the good habit to assemble their slaves every morning and evening for the catechism and prayers," some neglected this duty. In those cases, priests would select a "black man who knew the prayers well" and make him into "chaplain of the sugar cane plantation." Once enslaved Africans were able to communicate in a French creole, Chrétien would personally "go to the field where they worked," "interrupt their work," and speak to them individually in order to "teach them the doctrine . . . and the prayers," but also to "console them in their trouble" and "listen to their complaints."[189]

Some of these Black catechists may have been Afro-Atlantic Catholics. The fact that Capuchins in Saint Christoffer complained about the enslavement of Catholic Africans is an indication of the early presence of Afro-Atlantic Catholics in the French Antilles. In the 1650s, the pastor Charles de Rochefort, who had traveled to the French Antilles in order to cater to the spiritual needs of Huguenots, observed that "some Negroes . . . punctually observe abstinence all the time of Lent, and all the other Fasting-days appointed by the Church, without any remission of their ordinary and continual labour."[190] It is doubtful that this Catholic zeal was exclusively the result of French missionary work.

In fact, the Jesuit Jacques Bouton referred in the 1640s to the presence on the island of Martinique of "blacks or Moors from the Cape Verde islands," who had "already been whitened with the water of the holy baptism." Although most had "an intolerable ignorance of the mysteries of our faith," he recognized that some "had been admitted to the holy communion."[191] The Dominican Jean-Baptiste Du Tertre explained in his seventeenth-century studies on the history of the French Antilles that the earliest enslaved people in the French Antilles were either brought there from Africa or had been "taken from the Spaniards along the coasts of

Brazil." He also mentioned the presence of Central Africans when commenting that "our planters rate Angola Negroes much higher than those of Cape Verde." According to Du Tertre, "All those who come from the Angolan coast are baptized, either by the Spanish . . . or by Christian priests of their own nation, because several among them confirmed to me that they have priests who do the same things like us." He also mentioned the case of Phillippe de Longvilliers de Poincy, the owner of some seven to eight hundred enslaved people who lived in a quarter in Saint Christopher that was known as "Angola city."[192] In 1659 the Dominican André Chevillard wrote that Angolans "are good Christians when they affectionately embrace the religion."[193] In the late seventeenth century another Dominican, Jean-Baptiste Labat, confirmed that many "blacks from Kongo and Angola" lived in the French Antilles and "secretly preserve all their superstitions and idolatrous cults, which they mix with Roman Catholic rituals." With reference to the syncretic variant of Catholicism that had developed in Kongo, Labat sighed, "Just imagine what type of Christianity they have over there!"[194]

Some Black Catholics also reached the French Antilles in consequence of the Portuguese reconquest of Dutch Brazil. Research by Franz Binder revealed how three privateers rescued Dutch settlers from the island of Itamaracá after the fall of Recife in 1654 and took them to "the Antilles." Upon arrival, the privateers "confiscated half of their slaves in compensation of their costs."[195] Du Tertre confirmed the arrival of hundreds of refugees from Dutch Brazil, accompanied by their enslaved workers, in Martinique and Guadaloupe in 1654. He added that the Dutch brought not only Black people but also Indigenous Brazilians to the islands and that when, in 1657, two Franciscan priests from the Azores found rescue in Martinique after being chased by Dutch privateers, "it was incredible to see the fruits they reaped among these enslaved Brazilians, who from all over the island came to see them . . . delighted that these priests spoke Portuguese with them since most of them spoke that language perfectly well." According to Du Tertre, Dutch privateers tended to sell anyone with a black skin color who happened to be onboard an Iberian ship they managed to capture, including free people. He mentioned the case of two free Black men, a deacon with two years of theological study and knowledge of Latin and a wealthy merchant, whom Dutch privateers had sold in Martinique in 1657 and who were released from bondage by the French authorities after an investigation had revealed that they were "subjects of the Portuguese king, ally of France."[196]

We also find references to Afro-Atlantic Catholics in Cayenne, the Guianas, where Father Biet observed in the 1650s how a Black man, before his execution, made "the sign of the cross and said in Portuguese 'al nombre de dios.'"[197] In 1687 the arrival of a shipment with three hundred enslaved people from Angola represented a challenge to Catholic missionaries in Cayenne because they were unable to find catechists. According to the Jesuit Jean de la Mouse, there were only "six or seven Angola Negroes" in the French colony at that time, who were "old" and had "forgotten or nearly forgotten the language of their country."[198] Some of these enslaved Africans from Angola were sold to the Rémire plantation, where their supervisor Jean Goupy des Marets made a detailed analysis of their ethnic backgrounds. His report reveals not only that these "Angolans" were in actuality all Kongolese, but also that they, together with the Cape Verdeans who lived on the plantation, identified themselves with their Portuguese baptismal names, whereas those from other parts of Africa used their indigenous names even after receiving a French baptismal name.[199]

In the 1770s the British administrator Edward Long claimed to have seen many enslaved Black people in the French Caribbean "with store of crosses, relicks, and consecrated amulets, to which they paid the most sincere veneration" and churches with "images of black saints," just like those of "the Portuguese at Madeira."[200] We also find references to Black brotherhoods. As early as the 1650s there are reports of the existence of a rosary confraternity in Martinique.[201] While the Jesuits tended to favor the establishment of confraternities for the Black population, the colonial authorities were critical and, in 1752, rejected such a proposal because of the "necessity to contain" the enslaved community.[202] In 1756, however, Black people did manage, with Jesuit support, to establish a confraternity under their own control in Martinique and, in 1802, built a chapel with a capstone inscribed "Built by Slaves." This convinced Peabody that there existed within the Black community a desire to develop "an autonomous black Catholic community," which reflected itself in "attempts to found black confraternities."[203] In fact, several other Black brotherhoods were established in later decades.[204]

As in Iberia, Africa, and Latin America, these brotherhoods were led by kings and queens and had masters of ceremony, generals, and treasurers.

Corpus Christi celebrations provided an opportunity for their members to take to the streets, dressed in the finest luxuries provided by their owners.[205] In 1758 the French governor of Martinique noted that on this holiday, several Black people "were richly dressed to represent the King, Queen, all the royal family, even grand officers of the crown" and that "in one of the parishes of the island, the priest of the blacks [*curé des Nègres*] had in the previous year introduced two blacks who imitated the King and Queen into the sanctuary." The governor expressed concern about the fact that the latter was escorted by Black people carrying weapons. "All they lacked," he wrote, "was a commander."[206]

In 1697 France and Spain settled their hostilities over Hispaniola by dividing the large island into an eastern part, known as Santo Domingo (today's Dominican Republic), and a western part, known as Saint-Domingue (today's Haiti). The latter was to become France's most important colony in the Caribbean. In the early eighteenth century, the Jesuit Pierre-François-Xavier de Charlevoix observed that many Africans in Saint-Domingue had roots in Kongo, but "although many of them are baptized," he claimed that "only very few of them have a slight tinge of our mysteries."[207] In his late eighteenth-century description of the island, the local scholar Médéric Moreau de Saint-Méry confirmed that "there are a lot of Kongolese here," who "have knowledge of Catholicism . . . which they obtained through the Portuguese." However, he referred to their version of Catholicism as "a rather monstrous mixture." Similar to what we observed in Curaçao, unbaptized newcomers, who, according to Moreau, were nicknamed *chevaux* (horses) by others, were "eager to get baptized . . . often without any preparation, and without any other concern than getting a godfather and godmother . . . and protecting themselves from the insults directed against the non-baptized."[208]

As Vincent Brown has suggested, Catholic Africans in Saint-Domingue may have "served as the key interpreters of missionary doctrine to other slaves."[209] In fact, as elsewhere in the Caribbean, there are indications of Afro-Catholic missionary work in this French colony. In 1761, for instance, the authorities in the province of Cap Français issued an ordinance warning that Black people had "constituted distinct congregations" that "often mixed holy elements of our religion with profane objects of an idolatrous cult." They gathered in churches, where they established their "own choir leaders, beadles, and church wardens" and then "catechize[d] and preach[ed]." Some of them even went "into the suburbs to catechize in the houses and dwellings without having authorization to do so."[210] Félix Carteau, a local merchant, confirmed that Black women "adopted" newly arrived Africans "as soon as they spoke a little French" and, after "catechizing them," became their "godmothers." Of all residents in the French colony, Black people were "the most attached community to the exterior aspect of the sacret cult." Although they "didn't like confessions," the "churches were packed" and they enjoyed "singing hymns and participated in large crowds at processions."[211]

Following the 1791 revolution and subsequent independence, the Catholic Church was expelled from what in 1804 was officially renamed Haiti. An observer of the events, Father Lecum, noted that "all the churches, except those of Port-au-Prince, Saint-Marc and Cayes, are burnt already; the three which remain will certainly be burnt also. All missionaries except five have died of illness or have been murdered." He added, however, that "in most parishes, blacks took pieces of holy ornaments and sacred vessels, and though they don't know how to read, they administered all the sacraments and even celebrated masses."[212] A reference to this can be found in John Candler's notes about his three-month stay in Haiti in 1841. The English abolitionist reported finding, in a remote village "which the parish priest, in his rounds but seldom visits," a "household altar dedicated to the Virgin, and strewed with crosses, where the poor devotees of the little settlement repair to pay their devotions" that included "a page or two of a missal or some Romish legend . . . placed in due order on a table before the crucifix."[213]

After a failed attempt in the 1840s, the Catholic Church officially returned to Haiti in the 1860s, spearheaded by missionaries of the Congregation of the Holy Spirit. Not surprisingly, their attempts to enforce a post-Tridentine form of Catholicism met with opposition from Afro-Catholic *prêts savanne*.[214] In his study on the Valley of Mirebelais from the 1930s, Melville Herskovits described how important these "bush priests" were to communities in setting up home altars, baptizing children, marrying people, organizing burials for the deceased (a first one for the corpse, followed by a second one for the soul), reciting novenas, and singing canticles (in broken Latin). He also highlighted their cooperation with the *hungans*, who performed Vodou rituals. Considering that the Catholic Church had been virtually absent on the island since the revolution, Herskovits's assumption that this "amalgamation" of indigenous African and Catholic elements resulted from the fact that "Negroes have continuously been subjected to the influence of Catholicism during the centuries that have passed" is questionable.[215]

The term *Vodou* derives from the Fon *vodu(n)* (god), the same word that was used by Domingo Morrás in his translation of the Christian God in the Fon catechism he prepared for the Capuchin mission to Allada in 1658.[216] Whereas scholars traditionally assumed that Vodou developed out of indigenous West African—predominantly Yoruba, Ewe, and Fon—religious practices that were later overlaid with a thin layer of (French) Catholic elements, recent scholarship has revealed that many of the Catholic elements in Vodou can be traced back to Kongolese Catholicism.[217] There is increasing evidence that the development of Vodou corresponds to what the Cuban ethnographer Ramiro Guerra labeled the "double syncretism" of Kongolese culture. What started as a Luso-Kongolese syncretism in Africa was followed by a second process of syncretization with other European and African cultures in Haiti.[218]

A clear example of Kongolese influence in Vodou is the devotion to Saint James the Greater, who is worshipped as Sen Jak, the deity of war. Parallels to the Kongo kingdom are particularly visible in the salutary ritual of the sequined *drapo* (flag) depicting the saint. This ritual involves a ceremony with a mock war dance executed by the *laplas* (swordmaster), which Patrick Polk characterized as "one of the most dazzling spectacles in Vodou," comparable to those relating to "the kingly banners of the *congadas*" in Brazil and "the courts of the Kingdom of Kongo."[219] The turning and wheeling with synchronized precision of the *laplas* does, in fact, echo Kongolese *sangamento* performances. As is confirmed by Donald Cosentino, the "feast of St. James in the Kingdom of Kongo" must have functioned as a "model for what Africans would reinvent in Haiti."[220]

It is also intriguing that the Portuguese brotherhood term *loa* (saint veneration song) corresponds to the Vodou term used in reference to spirits/gods.[221] As a Haitian informant once told the Swiss anthropologist Alfred Métraux, "one has to be Catholic in order to be able to serve the loas."[222] In fact, one of the oldest recorded *loas* prayers in a Vodou ceremony is "Santa Maria Gratia, Toni, rele Kongo. O Santa Marya, O Toni, rele Kongo" (Holy Mary of Grace, Saint Anthony, call on the Kongo. Oh Holy Mary, oh Saint Anthony, call on the Kongo). It not only makes an explicit reference to Kongo but also addresses Saint Anthony as "Toni," as in Kongo.[223]

In Haiti we also find numerous references to mutual-aid and burial societies modeled upon Afro-Catholic brotherhoods. Some of the earliest date back to the island's revolution. In September 1791 an anonymous French militiaman reported that "the Negroes celebrated two marriages in the church at L'Acul. On the occasion they assumed titles, and the titled blacks were treated with great respect, and the ceremony was performed in great pomp." A "Capuchin called Cajetan was retained among them," who "has been obliged to officiate. Their colors were consecrated and a king was elected. They have chosen one for each quarter."[224] In the North Province, where the rebellion started, one of the leaders, Makaya, respectfully referred to the king of Kongo as "master of all the blacks" and descendant of "one of the three Magi."[225] An anonymous report, dating back to 1785, from Haiti's North Province also mentions that Black people had their own "gathering places, kings, and queens," and paid "a subscription of several *portugaises* and burial fees" in order to ensure that after their death they would be buried with "large processions."[226]

When the French abolitionist Victor Schoelcher visited Haiti in 1840, he reported to have seen "companies" of Black people, each with "its own name, its own flag, and king."[227] William Seabrook witnessed similar companies, known as "Congo societies," in the 1920s, each with their own banners, kings, and queens.[228] Anthropological research in later decades revealed the existence of an abundance of secret societies that functioned as mutual-aid and burial organizations, led by emperors and queens, with their respective courts, flag-bearers, scouts, and "soldiers."[229]

These connections to Kongo also offer an alternative explanation to the monarchical ambitions of leaders in post-independence Haiti. A famous example is that of the insurgent leader Romaine Rivière, who claimed to be the Virgin Mary's godson, adopted the name Romaine-la-Prophétesse, and expressed a desire to become "king of Santo Domingo."[230] We could also mention Henri Christophe, who, after Jean-Jacques Dessalines's assassination in 1806, assumed the title of Henry I, King of Haiti, and established a Haitian nobility that consisted of princes, dukes, counts, barons, and knights. As pointed out by Laurent Dubois, "the institutional heart of Christophe's regime . . . was the European-style hereditary landed aristocracy, complete with heraldic crests and mottoes that he created to administer his kingdom."[231] While it is tempting to explain this phenomenon as a desire to emulate Napoleon, one should not ignore parallels to the Kongolese monarchy. In fact, already in the nineteenth century the German anthropologist Adolf Bastian pointed out that Haitian leaders used Iberian aristocratic titles similar to those of members of the Kongolese nobility, including that of "knight in the Order of Christ."[232]

As these examples demonstrate, it would be wrong to limit the search for Afro-Atlantic Catholic influences in the diaspora to Latin America. While there can be no doubt that the vast majority of enslaved Africans who originated from areas with a historically strong Portuguese influence were sent to Iberian colonies, many also ended up in Dutch, Danish, English, and French colonies in the Caribbean. Although the total number of enslaved Africans who identified as Catholic may have been small, the fact that they composed a substantial minority or, in some places, perhaps even the majority of the islands' charter generations allowed them to play a key role in Black social and religious identity formation. As the next section will demonstrate, this was no different in North America.

NORTH AMERICA

We started our section on the Caribbean with a reference to language in Curaçao. In her famous study on the history of Afro-Baptist churches in North America, *Trabelin' On* (1979), Mechal Sobel established a similar connection between language and religion. She did so by building on Joey Lee Dillard's linguistic research on the history of African American Vernacular English and his identification of three phases: one in which Black people spoke indigenous African languages, one in which they had developed an African American pidgin English, and a third one in which they spoke African American Vernacular English, or "black English," as Dillard called it in 1977. According to Sobel, the Christianization of North America's Black population followed a similar evolution.[233]

Sobel's decision to study the Christianization of North America's Black population in parallel to their use of the English language is problematic because it ignores other European languages, most notably French, and thereby unavoidably presents an Anglocentric perspective that privileges Protestant Christianity. Even if we decide to follow a traditional approach by studying the history of the United States with a focus on the original thirteen states, Sobel's study remains problematic because it ignores the importance of Iberian languages to the charter generations. Their use of a Portuguese/Spanish-based pidgin puts into question Sobel's decision to begin the history of Black Christianity in North America with English, Protestant missionary work. It shows that this history cannot be properly understood without acknowledging the importance of an Afro-Iberian/Catholic substratum. A good case study to illustrate this is Manhattan.

New Netherland

Ruled by the Dutch WIC from the 1620s until the English takeover in 1664, New Netherland had a relatively large Black community. In its final years Black people, both enslaved and free, made up about 6 to 8 percent of the population, while in its capital, New Amsterdam, on the island of Manhattan, this is estimated to have been between 10 and 17 percent.[234]

The first explicit reference to the presence of enslaved Africans in Manhattan dates back to 1628, when the Dutch Reformed Minister Jonas Michaëlius referred to "Angolan slave women" in one of his letters.[235] These women had probably been on Iberian vessels that were captured by privateers. In later decades, several dozen enslaved people arrived in New Netherland via Dutch Brazil and Curaçao. In 1664 the *Gideon* brought close to four hundred enslaved Africans from Curaçao to Manhattan, which roughly doubled the enslaved population in the Dutch colony. Only twelve days later, however, English forces conquered New Netherland.[236] In order to justify his decision to capitulate without resistance, director Petrus Stuyvesant claimed that the arrival of a large group of "half-starved Negroes and Negresses" had not left enough food supply to withstand an English siege, thus making enslaved Africans indirectly responsible for the Dutch loss of Manhattan.[237]

Virtually all members of Manhattan's charter generation used Iberian Catholic baptismal names. Some also had Iberian surnames such as Grande, Britto [Brito], Premier or Premero [Primeiro], and Albiecke [Albuquerque], which reveals that they were most likely *ladinos*. In several other cases, the person's origin was added to the first name, generally starting with the Dutch preposition *van* or Portuguese *de* (both meaning "from"). The following list provides an overview of documented names with indication of origin:

From Angola: Susanna van Angola/Susanna d'Angola; Samuel Angola/Samuel van Angola; Marie d'Angola/Marie van Angola/Maria de Angola/Maria Angola; Mayken van Angola/Maijken d'Angola; Isabel d'Angola; Emanuel van Angola/Emanuel de Angola; Lucie van Angelo/Lucie d'Angola/Lijcije van Angola; Cleijn Anthony van Angola; Jacob Anthony van Angola; Anthony Angola/Anthony van Angola; Catalina van Angola/Catharina van Angola; Laurens van Angola; Magdalena van Angola; Emanuel Gerrit de Rous, van Angola; Susanna Simons van Angola; Andries van Angola/Andries d'Angola; Pallas van Angola/Palassa van Angola; Lucretie d'Angola/Lucretia Albiecke, van Angola; Paulus van Angola/Paolo d'Angola/Paulo Angola; Jan van Angola; Christijn van Angola/Christina de Angola; Mattheus de Angola; Phizithiaen d'Angool; Francisco van Angola/Francisco d'Angola; Anna van Angola; Isabel Kisana, van Angola; Philippe Swartinne van Angola; Jan Francisco, j.m. van Angola [young man from Angola]; Maria Malaet, j.d. uijt Angola [young lady from Angola]; Domingo Angola/Dominicus van Angola; Antony Domingo Angola; Dorothea Angola; Gerasy Angola; Lovys Angola/Louis Angola; Swan van Angola; Assento Angola; Gratia Angola/Gracia d'Angola

From Kongo: Simon Congoy/Simon Congo; Emanuel Congo/Manuel Congo/Emanuel Congoij; Susanna Congoy; Anthonij de Chongo/Antony Congo

From Loango: Swan van Loange

From Guinea: Louis Guinea

From the Cape Verde islands: Francisco van Capo Verde; Anna van Capoverde

From São Tomé: Pieter St. Thome/Pieter Santome; Christoffel Crioell, van St. Thomas/Christoffel Santome; Maria Santomee

From Portugal: Anthony Fernando, Portugees/Anthony Ferdinand, j.m. van Cascalis [from Cascais], in Portugal/Anthony Portugies; Willem Antonys Portuguese; Pieter Portugies; Maria Portugies

From Spain: Emanuel van Spangien/Manuel de Spanje

From Latin America: Sebastiaen de Britto, van St. Domingo; Jan Augustinus, j.m. van Cartagena; Francisco Cartagena; Bastiaen from Pariba [Paraíba], Portuguese

From North America: Jan Virginia; Susanna van Nieuw Nederlant; Jan, van 't fort Orangien/Jan Fostranien

Unknown: Francienne Mandeere [Madeira?]; Mokinga[238]

Although these names represent only a fraction of the colony's enslaved population and may in some cases refer to more than one person, they leave no doubt that virtually all Black people in New Netherland originated from the Iberian Peninsula, Latin America, or parts of Africa with a historically strong Portuguese influence, in particular the region of Kongo/ Angola. This makes it likely that a large number of those composing Manhattan's charter generation shared familiarity with Iberian culture.

A court case from 1662 confirms that Resolveert Waldron, a Dutch settler, and an enslaved Black man called Mattheu "spoke Portuguese to each other."[239] The same Mattheu was also involved in another case in which he, together with a certain Swan [João/Juan] and Frans requested Waldron to be their interpreter in court.[240] Frans can be identified as Francisco, who was captured in 1652 by privateers on a Spanish ship that was on its way from Jamaica to Cuba; he was subsequently sold in New Amsterdam.[241] While it is not specified which language Waldron spoke in court, it is likely to have been Portuguese because he had previously lived in Dutch Brazil.[242] The fact that he spoke Portuguese may also explain why he was put in charge of a group of enslaved workers who had to "break stones and strengthen the ramparts of Fort [Amsterdam]."[243]

A similar case is that of Captain J(oh)an de Vries, who had served about ten years in Dutch Brazil before coming to New Netherland in 1645. He brought with him a Brazilian woman identified as *swartinne* (Black woman). The likelihood that De Vries spoke (some) Portuguese may account for his proximity to the Black population. He stood up in church as godfather to their children and leased land to several of them. He was particularly close to a free Black man called Bastiaen [Sebastián/

Sebastião], who had the Iberian surname de Britto. The added reference "van St. Domingo" shows that this man was born or had at least lived in a Spanish colony. Bastiaen is referred to as "Capt. van de Swarten" or "Captijn van de Negers" (captain of the blacks), which suggests that he was the leader of a Black militia. The establishment of such militias was common practice in Iberian colonies and was soon adopted by other European forces in the Americas. In New Netherland a group of Black people under Bastiaen's leadership assisted the Dutch authorities in maintaining order, hunting down enslaved Africans who ran away, and fighting Native Americans. Bastiaen's prestigious role as "captain" may explain why he was invited to be a baptismal witness for De Vries's mixed-race son Jan, whose mother was the abovementioned Brazilian woman.[244]

Another indication that at least some of the Black people brought to New Amsterdam may have been *ladinos* comes from Northampton, Virginia, where the charter generation included many Africans bought by Edmund Scarborough in New Amsterdam.[245] In 1667 a certain Fernando filed a lawsuit in Northampton, claiming that he was a Christian and presenting "severall papers in Portugell or some other language which the Court could not understand which he alleged were papers from severall Governors where hee had lived a freeman." Most likely these were *cartas de alforria*, letters in Portuguese that confirmed Fernando's manumission. However, nobody in Northampton had knowledge of Portuguese, and his request was rejected.[246]

The only recorded words of a Black person in New Netherland are unmistakably of Iberian origin. In 1655 Teunis Kraey bought a recently arrived Black woman of unknown origin. On their way home, she "fell to the ground" and, after shouting the word *ariba*, lifted herself up again. However, "10 to 12 paces farther on" she fell again, "with eyes turning around in her head and white on her mouth," as Kraey described it. Thereupon a carpenter came forward. When asked what ailed her, "the woman said *more! more!*, while pointing at her breast and legs," which the carpenter "rendered into Dutch saying, the negress is drunk." The woman died soon after.[247] The term *more* has nothing to do with being drunk, but is most likely the Portuguese third singular form of the verb *morrer* (to die), whereas *ariba* relates to the Spanish/Portuguese *arriba!* (up!) that may have been spoken by the woman to give herself the courage to stand up again. While hardly used in contemporary Portuguese, *(ar)riba* was common in seventeenth-century Portuguese and survives in Cape Verdean and Upper Guinean creoles.[248]

These examples show that it would be wrong to assume that English was the first European language that allowed people from different parts of Africa to communicate both among themselves and with Europeans in the original colonies. In Manhattan, it is likely that an Afro-Iberian pidgin initially served this function.[249] If we now turn to religion and apply this finding to Sobel's theory, we have to conclude that it is wrong to start the history of Black Christianity with English-speaking, Protestant missionary work. Rather, it is important to first explore the existence of an older, Afro-Iberian, Catholic substratum.

Contradicting Sobel's assumption that "at the outset of interreligious contact in North America, the African has a basic disrespect for white religion," historical documents reveal that there was a strong desire among members of the Black population in Manhattan to have their children baptized in the Dutch Reformed Church.[250] Although Dutch Calvinists had strict criteria about baptism, records show that the Reformed Church in New Amsterdam baptized at least fifty-six children of Black families.[251]

In 1618 the Synod of Dordt—the council of Reformed theologians that established the tenets of Calvinist orthodoxy—had introduced a specification regarding the children of enslaved people. In *De Ethnicorum Pueris Baptizandis*, it presented a reasoning based on Genesis 17:11–13, God's command to Abraham to circumcise all males in his household, including those who had been bought with money. Since circumcision was considered the equivalent of baptism, it was assumed that members of the Reformed Church were morally obliged to grant all children in their household access to baptism and to a Christian education.[252]

However, the Dutch Reformed baptismal practice was rooted in the concept of the Thousand-Generation Covenant, which limited baptism to children who had at least one ancestor within the last thousand generations who was a believer in Christ. Since the Reformed Church did not question the legitimacy of a Catholic baptism, the Covenant included children with a Catholic ancestor but excluded Jews, Muslims, and "pagans." Members of the latter group had to provide proof of a thorough understanding of Calvinist doctrine before their baptism or that of their children could be considered.[253]

In 1637, and in accordance with the covenant, the classis in Dutch Brazil had made a distinction between the children of baptized and un-baptized parents, claiming that those whose parents "had been baptized and profess Jesus Christ may and should be allowed for baptism," whereas *heidenkinderen* (children whose parents were "pagans") had to wait until their parents had been baptized or until they were old enough to provide proof that they understood the principles of Calvinist Christianity. In total, the Reformed Church accepted some six hundred Black children for baptism during the twenty-four years of Dutch Brazil's existence.[254]

In New Netherland, Reverend Everardus Bogardus followed the Bra-zilian example and accepted dozens of Black children for baptism during his time in office between 1633 and 1647. The fact that these children were baptized can serve as evidence that the Reformed Church in Man-hattan recognized the legitimacy of their parents' Catholic baptism and, ipso facto, acknowledged their Christian identity. Their baptismal wit-nesses were in most cases members of the Black community who had mar-ried in the Reformed Church, but Bogardus himself and other Europeans sometimes assumed this role. In 1641 the Reformed Church in New Am-sterdam reported that "the [Native] Americans come not yet to the right knowledge of God; but the Negroes, living among the colonists, come nearer thereto, and give better hope."[255]

As Leendert Joosse has argued, the interest of the Reformed Church in the Black community should not be reduced to "a matter of proselyti-zation." It also reflected a desire to exterminate "'popish' influences" in the colony.[256] In order to understand the Dutch Calvinist mindset of the time, it is important to realize that the Netherlands' overseas expansion started in the immediate aftermath of the uprising against (Catholic) Spanish rule. Anti-Iberian and anti-Catholic militancy had been of key impor-tance to the creation of the WIC in 1621. The illusion that Dutch Calvin-ists were the new Jews, a chosen people, whose mission it was to destroy Iberian dominance and transform the Americas from a predominantly Catholic into a Protestant continent, stimulated a flexible attitude in guid-ing toward "God's true Church" those who—from a Calvinist point of view—had been misguided by Iberian Catholics.[257]

It is not without reason that Reformed ministers who accepted Black children for baptism also insisted on the importance of schooling.[258] Their concern reveals a lack of trust in African parents who had been baptized as

Catholics and the fear that, even though they had married in the Reformed Church, they would be unable or unwilling to educate their children in accordance with Calvinist principles. Not by accident, these schools were supposed to teach children the Dutch language. This becomes evident if we add information from the Dutch Cape colony, where, in 1649, Governor-General Rijcklof van Goens explicitly warned Jan van Riebeeck to "take care that the Portuguese language is not introduced here, and prevent this in every possible way." In the memorial he prepared for his successor in 1662, Van Riebeeck proudly mentioned that all the enslaved people who had been baptized in the Reformed Church were starting to learn Dutch and were "not becoming acquainted with Portuguese."[259] In seventeenth-century Dutch Ceylon, the eagerness to "abolish the Portuguese language and to forever delete the memory of our enemies," was such that, in 1659, owners were ordered to "shave off all the hair of slaves and to prohibit them from wearing hats for as long as they are unable to speak the Dutch language."[260] These references confirm a strong anti-Iberian bias in seventeenth-century Dutch Reformed circles.

Following the loss of Dutch Brazil in 1654 and the adoption by the WIC of a new policy that mainly focused on selling enslaved Africans to the Spanish, the Reformed Church lost interest in missionary work and transformed itself from an all-embracing church into a church of the elected that placed greater emphasis on orthodoxy.[261] The case of Curaçao reflects this. In the early years of Dutch colonization, the Reformed Church still made an effort to convert Native Americans and enslaved Africans. In 1641 Pastor Jan Cornelis Backer informed the classis that, to his regret, little progress had been made because the Natives "were Catholic" and, in spite of all his efforts, remained stuck "to their blindness."[262] In 1650 the classis received better news when it learned that Reverend Charles de Rochefort had succeeded in baptizing "twelve adult persons, all blacks" in Curaçao after they "had been reasonably well instructed in the Christian doctrine."[263] Only ten years later, however, the classis reacted angrily to the news that Reverend Adrianus van Beaumont had baptized fifteen Native American children on the island. It rebuked the minister and reminded him that "no one, who is an adult, is [to be] admitted to baptism without previous confession of his faith. Accordingly, the adult Negroes and Indians must also be previously instructed and make confession of their faith before the Holy Baptism may be administered to them." The condition for baptism had switched, thus, from "reasonably well instructed" to a "confession of faith," which implied proof of a comprehension of the beliefs of the church, including the ability to answer all 129 questions in the Heidelberg catechism. Moreover, the classis added that "As long as the parents are actually heathens, although they were baptized in the gross (by wholesale, by papists), the children may not be baptized." With this stipulation, the classis indicated that even Catholic Africans—those who had been baptized "by papists"—were now to be treated as pagans, which implied that children could not be baptized until their parents had made a confession of faith. Van Beaumont apologized for his actions and referred to Dutch Brazil, where "baptismal practices had been very liberal," and then promised that he would henceforth adopt "a stricter policy."[264]

The adoption of stricter rules in Curaçao mirrored the situation in New Netherland, where the baptism of enslaved children had sharply decreased by the late 1650s. One of the few slaveholders in New Netherland who continued to care for the baptism of enslaved children was Director-General Stuyvesant. In 1664, when he learned that a group of enslaved children whom his wife Judith Bayard had prepared for baptism had been accidentally sent to Curaçao and probably sold to Spaniards, Stuyvesant ordered Vice Director Matthias Beck to do everything possible to return them, though in vain.[265] This case was exceptional. Dutch Reformed proselytizing efforts among the enslaved population came to a virtual standstill in the final years of New Netherland.

This change in policy coincided with increasing doubts among slaveholders about the long-term consequences of these baptisms. Different opinions had been expressed in Dordt, one of which was put forward by the Genevan theologian Giovanni Deodatus. Based on Leviticus 25:39–40, which stipulated that no Israelite could hold another Israelite in perpetual bondage, Deodatus had argued that "those baptized should enjoy equal right of liberty with all other Christians and that, concerning the danger of apostasy, they be safeguarded, as far as it can be done, by the prohibiting for the future of all selling and transferring of them to another. . . ."[266] The ellipsis at the end was crucial. If *another* meant "another pagan," it implied that these children could still be sold as long as their new owner was Christian. If it meant "another person," it implied that the baptized child could no longer be considered salable property. In his influential book *'T geestelijk roer van 't coopmansschip* (The Spiritual Rudder of the

Merchant's Ship, 1638), the Dutch Reformed minister Godefridus Udemans followed the latter interpretation and argued that slavery was justified for "heathens," but that as soon as people decided "to submit themselves to the lovely yoke of our Lord Jesus Christ, Christian love requires that they be discharged from the yoke of human slavery."[267] A similar argument had been made in 1627 by the classis of Amsterdam in a letter to representatives of the Dutch Reformed Church in Batavia, present-day Jakarta. In their response to the classis's request to ensure that, once Christianized, enslaved people would be manumitted, the former explained that it was "virtually impossible" to implement this directive because the liberation of enslaved people "cannot be enforced."[268]

The consequence of these uncertainties was that Dutch slaveholders in New Netherland began to obstruct the baptism of Black children. After the English conquest, most Dutch slaveholders who stayed in what had now become New York and New Jersey remained opposed to the baptism of enslaved people. In 1708, for instance, the Anglican missionary Elias Neau complained that he had not been able to catechize in New Jersey because "they are almost all Dutch there and . . . are afraid that their slaves may demand their freedom after baptism."[269]

As we will see next, similar concerns about the baptism of enslaved people also existed among English colonists in North America.

The English Colonies

The "20 and odd Negroes" whom settlers in Virginia bought from a Dutch privateer in August 1619 are considered the earliest enslaved Africans to arrive in the original British colonies. They had been on a Portuguese ship from Luanda that, on its way to Veracruz, Mexico, was captured by English and Dutch privateers.[270] Thornton considers it "quite possible [that] those slaves who ended up in Virginia instead of Vera Cruz had at least been introduced to the Christian faith."[271] In the years to come, privateers brought many more enslaved Africans to Virginia. In 1628, for instance, the *Fortune* captured "an Angola man with many Negroes," who were "bartered in Virginia for tobacco."[272] Between 1631 and 1639, English privateers alone captured at least sixteen Portuguese ships carrying a total of three thousand Africans.[273] Among the earliest recorded names of the enslaved in Virginia we find those of Congo and his wife Cossongo, [Do]mingo, Manuel, Couchaxello [Conceição], António a Negro, Isabel(la), Bashaw [Sebastião] Farnando/Ferdinando [Fernando], John Francisco, Susanna Grace, Francisco a Negro, Mary, Emanuel, Thomas Driggus/Drighouse/Rodriggus [Rodrigues], and Tony Longo [probably António Luango]. These names confirm that, similar to the Manhattan charter generation, many of the earliest enslaved Black people in Virginia used Iberian baptismal names and were probably familiar with Iberian culture.[274]

In a relatively short time, several members of the Virginia charter generation acquired freedom. Among them was António, known as Anthony, who took the surname Johnson of his former slaveholder after being manumitted, married a Black girl named Mary, and became a landowner himself. Their grandson later called the farm *Angola*.[275] As in New Netherland, members of the Virginia charter generation were eager to have their children baptized. In 1624, for instance, Anthony and Isabella took their child to Jamestown to be baptized in the Anglican Church.[276] As we can see in the case of Manuel, baptism could have an immediate effect on one's status. The latter had been sold as "a slave for-ever" but, after being baptized in 1644, it was decided that he only had to "serve as other Christian servants do."[277]

Soon, however, concerns over the baptism of enslaved people grew stronger. In 1667 the General Assembly felt the need to clarify that "the conferring of baptism doth not alter the condition of the person as to his bondage or freedome" and defined the term *slaves* as "imported servants who are not Christians." In 1682 it rephrased this definition as "servants . . . whose parentage and native country are not Christian," probably after realizing that many of the enslaved Africans arriving in Virginia had been baptized as Catholics.[278] The concerns over baptizing enslaved people remained, however, and not only Dutch but also English slaveholders began to oppose it.[279] In 1702 Franz Ludwig Michel, a Swiss visitor to Virginia, noted that "even if they desire to become Christians it is only rarely permitted" due to concerns that, if baptized, they would be "freed in accordance with the Mosaic law."[280] In 1730 John Usher wrote to the Society for the Propagation of the Gospel that, in Bristol, Rhode Island, he had "sundry negroes make application for baptism" but that he was "not permitted to comply with their request" because baptism was "being forbid by their masters."[281]

In the search for traces of Afro-Atlantic Catholics in the original colonies, Maryland is a distinctive case because of its early Catholic history and the presence of Jesuit plantations run by enslaved workers.[282] References to "Matthias Sousa, Molato" and "Francisco, a Molato" in a list of Jesuit indentures from 1638 confirms the presence of Black Catholics with an Afro-Iberian background in Jesuit service. The former is, in later sources, also mentioned as a free Black man who became an elected representative at a Maryland Assembly meeting in 1641.[283] While the Black population in Maryland remained small in the first half of the seventeenth century, this changed by the 1670s.[284] Among the newcomers were some from New Netherland. Shortly after the English conquest of Manhattan in 1664, Robert Carr informed Deputy Governor Richard Nicolls that he had "sent into Merryland some Neegars which did belong to the late Govenore [Stuyvesant] att his plantation."[285] We also learn about a certain Sarah Driggus [Rodrigues], who, together with a number of other Black men and women, petitioned the Somerset County court in 1688 to no longer tax them as enslaved people because they were freeborn.[286] In her research on racially mixed marriages in the seventeenth-century Chesapeake Bay, Martha Hodes found several references to Catholic marriages between members of the Irish and African communities. One of them was the "Negro Charles" who, in 1681, married the White servant Eleanor Butler, known as Irish Nell, in a wedding ceremony performed by a Catholic priest.[287] As James Sweet has argued, these marriages suggest that "Central Africans . . . used their prior knowledge of Christianity as a tool to integrate into the community of servants."[288]

The charter generations in New England also consisted mainly of Black people who had been captured on Iberian ships. In Winthrop's journal we read that, in 1638, "Mr. Peirce, in the Salem ship the *Desire*, returned from the West Indies," where he had "taken divers prizes from the Spaniard, and many Negroes."[289] Seventeenth- and early eighteenth-century sources from New England frequently mention enslaved people whose names suggest an Afro-Iberian connection, such as James Spaniard, Angola, Juan, [Do]mingo, John Whan or Juan, Anthony, Maria Negro, Bastian, and "a Negro boy named Jack, alias Emannuel," who was sold in Boston in 1705 after having been "taken from the Portuguese . . . and brought into this port."[290]

Most traces of Afro-Atlantic Catholics in North America have been found in the Carolinas. At least 60 percent of the enslaved Africans arriving in Charleston in the period between 1710 and 1740 originated from Kongo/Angola.[291] According to Thornton, the majority of them "were probably from Kongo" and were "proud of their Christian and Catholic heritage, which they believed made them a distinctive people."[292] Late seventeenth-century records from South Carolina contain, in fact, dozens of references to enslaved people with Iberian baptismal names such as Antonio [António], Mattheias [Mateus], Salvidore [Salvador], [Do]mingo, Maria, Francisco, Emanuel [Manuel], Isabel, and Jossee [José].[293] Their Catholic identity is confirmed in the anonymous "Account of the Negroe Insurrection in South Carolina" (1739)—which became known as the Stono Rebellion—that revealed how "amongst the Negroe slaves there are a people brought from the Kingdom of Angola in Africa, many of these speak Portugueze . . . and . . . profess the Roman Catholic religion." The same source continued that "some Angola Negroes assembled . . . and one who was called Jemmy was their Captain. . . . Several Negroes joined them, they calling out liberty, marched on with colours displayed, and two drums beating."[294] Considering their Afro-Atlantic Catholic identity, Mark Smith suggested that those involved in the Stono Rebellion may have deliberately linked the uprising to their veneration of the Virgin Mary.[295]

It is likely that those involved in the Stono Rebellion had the ambition to reach Saint Augustine, the Spanish border town in Florida. Similar to the situation in the Caribbean, enslaved people escaping from British territory could be granted freedom in Florida, provided they were Catholic or wished to convert.[296] Research by Jane Landers confirmed that several of those who managed to flee to Spanish Florida were, indeed, Kongolese and identified as Catholic. She mentioned the case of Miguel and Francisco, both from Kongo, who, upon arrival in Florida in 1744, were given a conditional baptism by Father Francisco Xavier Arturo because "each told the priest he had been baptized by a priest in his homeland and taught to pray in his own language." After Miguel was baptized, "he blessed himself in that unidentified language." In 1748 Father Arturo gave a conditional baptism to Miguel Domingo, another enslaved Kongolese who had fled from South Carolina and, upon arrival in Florida, declared that he had been baptized in Africa and taught how to say Catholic prayers in Kikongo. Landers's research also revealed that Black Catholicism flourished in the fortified frontier town of (Gracia Real de Santa Teresa de) Mose, largely inhabited by escapees from South Carolina, where the villagers would "fire celebratory gunshots and light extra candles" on Catholic holidays and built a chapel "that was larger than the Church in St. Augustine."[297]

When the British took over Florida in 1763, they guaranteed the liberty of the Catholic religion. In spite of this, virtually the entire Catholic population, including many Black people, moved to Cuba. By the time the second period of Spanish rule in Florida came to an end in 1821, the Black Catholic community had decreased substantially in size.[298] In spite of this, Gary McDonogh's research revealed that in early nineteenth-century Saint Augustine, "Protestant missionaries were beaten by Negro Catholics when they attempted to establish Baptist and Methodist congregations."[299] That Black Catholic zeal remained strong until at least the outbreak of the Civil War can also be illustrated by the observation of Thomas Higginson that one of the most popular songs of the first free Black regiment that fought against the Confederacy was "I want some valiant soldier here to help me bear the cross, O hail, Ma-ry, hail! To help me bear de cross. O hail, Ma-ry, hail!" Higginson recognized that "the 'Hail, Mary' might denote a Roman Catholic origin," which he explained with reference to the fact that he "had several men from St. Augustine who held in a dim way to that faith."[300]

The Spanish presence in North America extended far beyond Florida. In the spring of 1700, Native Americans informed the French explorer Jean-Baptiste Le Moyne de Bienville, on an expedition to the mouth of the Mississippi River, about "a Spanish settlement" in the region composed of "whites, mulattoes, and blacks." Le Moyne also refers to another village in the region, which Native Americans called Connessi, meaning "village of the blacks." There, "only Negroes with their families," who were "rather numerous," lived. The fact that the inhabitants of Connessi "did not welcome any white Spaniard; and when whites once came, the blacks drove them off without speaking to them" makes it likely that this was a Maroon community.[301] The Jesuit Paul du Ru, who explored the Mississippi from its mouth northward in 1700, confirmed that "quite a large group of Negroes and mulattoes, men and women, have deserted and are established in a separate district where they persist in their revolt."[302] This indicates that Afro-Catholic Black people may have been living in the Lower Mississippi Valley since at least the late seventeenth century. The following section will further explore traces of Afro-Atlantic Catholics in the region's Black Catholic community.

Louisiana

In the early years of French colonial rule in Louisiana, the enslaved population consisted mainly of Native Americans. Only a handful of enslaved Black people were brought there from the Caribbean. Starting in 1719, however, the number of enslaved Africans increased considerably. Records show that between 1719 and 1743 twenty-three ships brought some 4,000 enslaved people from Senegambia, some 1,750 from the Gulf of Benin, and some 300 from Cabinda, in Central Africa, to Louisiana. The fact that, in his 1734 account of Louisiana, Antoine-Simon Le Page du Pratz includes the "Congo and Angolan nations" in his list of largest African groups in the French colony suggests that the Central African community may by then have been larger than just those who had arrived on the ship from Cabinda.[303] In any case, their number increased further in 1758 when a British ship carrying some 120 enslaved people from Angola was captured and brought to Louisiana.[304]

In 1762 France granted all Louisiana territory west of the Mississippi to Spain. Under Spanish rule, the total number of enslaved people rose to at least twenty-four thousand. Research by Gwendolyn Midlo Hall revealed that many of the newcomers had roots the region of Kongo/Angola. "Shortly after the Spanish took over," she claimed, "it became heavily Kongo in New Orleans."[305] In 1800 Napoleon forced Spain to cede Louisiana and subsequently sold it to the United States. Soon after the Louisiana Purchase of 1803, the sugar and cotton boom transformed what had hitherto been a provincial outpost into a prosperous state. This further increased the demand for enslaved workers, who now arrived in the thousands from the original British colonies. These English-speaking Black people mainly settled uptown, with Canal Street/Rue du Canal serving as the point of division between their neighborhoods and those of downtown New Orleans, where mainly French-speaking Black people lived. Louisiana also experienced the arrival of large numbers of refugees from Saint-Domingue/Haiti in the aftermath of the 1791 uprising. Their total number is estimated between fifteen and twenty thousand, more or less equally distributed between White, free Black, and enslaved Black people. Many of them settled in New Orleans, doubling the city's population and increasing the percentage of nonwhites to over 60 percent. These newcomers had a tremendous impact on the city's Black culture.[306] As Paul

Lachance confirms, "several of the distinctive features of New Orleans slave culture . . . reflect the influence of slaves from the French Caribbean on their peers."[307]

Considering the strong Kongolese presence in Saint-Domingue, the refugees' arrival likely increased the number of Black people with roots in Kongo. Significantly, Louis Baudry des Lozières opted for the Kikongo language when, in 1803, he decided to make a list of words and expressions to facilitate the interaction of plantation owners with their enslaved workers. A study of inventories in Saint Charles Parish between 1780 and 1818 confirms that enslaved people identifying as "Congo" numbered almost triple the second-largest group, that of West African "Mandinga." Not by accident, thus, it was this African "nation" that gave its name to what became the main gathering place of New Orleans's enslaved population on Sunday afternoons: Congo Square/Place Congo.[308]

In accordance with the Code Noir, all enslaved people arriving in Louisiana under French rule had in theory to be baptized, catechized, and eventually buried in consecrated soil.[309] In a letter dating to 1725, the Capuchin Raphaël de Luxembourg admitted, however, that many of those who lived far from New Orleans remained "without baptism and without any knowledge of the true God."[310] While data on the Christianization process for the enslaved population in rural areas is scarce, all available evidence on church membership and godparenting in the city of New Orleans and in the Gulf ports of Mobile and Pensacola shows a strong attachment of the Black community to the Catholic faith. By the late eighteenth century, two-thirds of the children baptized at New Orleans's Saint Louis Cathedral had a Black mother.[311] In the early nineteenth century, John Watson wrote about New Orleans, "Visit the churches when you will, and the chief of the audience is formed of mulattresses and negresses." Around the same time, C. C. Robin noted that "women, Negroes, and officers of the governor's staff are almost the only people who go to church" and whereas "the funerals of white people are only attended by a few, those of colored people are attended by a great crowd."[312] About two decades later, the architect Benjamin Latrobe confirmed that the majority of congregants at Saint Louis Cathedral were Black women and that "the colored people" were "the most attached to their religion."[313] Black people were also enthusiastic participants in the city's procession culture. When, in the early nineteenth century, the New

Orleans Creole poet Mirtil-Ferdinand Liotau described, in his poem "Une Impression," the "great feast day" for his community, when "true happiness [was] shown in their eyes" and "all was forgotten on this occasion of joy," he was referring not to Mardi Gras but to the annual procession and festivities in honor of Saint Barbara.[314]

As in Latin America, Catholic missionaries in Louisiana relied heavily on Black catechists. In 1820, for instance, Michel Portier wrote enthusiastically about his Black *"jeunes gens"* who "teach the blacks to pray, they catechize, they instruct [and] promise to fight daily like valiant soldiers of Jesus Christ."[315] Some of these catechists may have had an Afro-Atlantic Catholic background. As Emily Clark and Virginia Gould pointed out, at least some of the enslaved may "not have been entirely unfamiliar with the . . . Roman Catholic [baptismal] ritual" before their arrival in Louisiana.[316] Considering that a large number of Black people in Louisiana had Kongolese roots, this assumption is legitimate.

The identification of Afro-Atlantic Catholics in this community is challenging because they used rituals that were often not recognized as Catholic by outsiders. In 1838 the British feminist Harriet Martineau went as far as to characterize the way enslaved Black people in Louisiana practiced Catholicism as "the most abject worship of things without meaning."[317] Although they expressed themselves in softer terms, later scholars shared this skepticism. To John Gillard, for instance, the ways in which Black people in Louisiana had been living their Catholic faith in former times was "primitive" and not worth of any scholarly attention. "To compare these colored Catholics with the colored Catholics of today," he wrote in 1941, "is to invite erroneous conclusions, for while quantitatively there may be a basis for comparison, qualitatively there is little or none."[318] Commenting on an eighteenth-century report from Saint-Domingue stating that the clergy's most important source of income was surplice fees "arising from Masses purchased by the blacks" for their souls, Thomas Ingersoll expressed few sympathies in his study on eighteenth-century New Orleans for those Black people who "gave in to this sentimental dead-end" and "lavished their pathetic savings on priests." He, rather, was convinced that "the majority . . . snorted or raged at all gods as cruel jokers" or "interpreted Christianity to fit the worldviews inherited from their African past."[319] According to Sobel, the influence of Catholicism on the development of Black Christianity in Louisiana was "minimal, notwithstanding the ostensible Catholicism of the practitioners."[320] Berlin also assumed that "if free people of color embraced Christianity and identified with the Catholic Church, there was little evidence of Jesus' presence in the quarter."[321]

In reality, Catholicism was very visible in the quarter. In order to see these expressions of Catholic faith, however, we need to follow Michael Pasquier's advice not to "focus exclusively on sacramental forms of Catholicism" and, instead, to "operate with a more flexible definition of Catholicism."[322] As an example, we could mention the "crowd of at least 200 Negroes" with "pitch black faces" that Latrobe in 1819 followed on their way to the cemetery. Of the women, "one half at least carried candles, & as the evening began to be dark, the effect was very striking, for all the women & many of the men were dressed in pure white." As soon as the priest arrived, "they began their chant, lazily enough, & continued it till they arrived at the grave." While the priest said his prayers, "a great crowd of women pressed close to the grave, making very loud lamentations" and a "very old African (Congo) negress" then "threw herself into the grave upon the coffin." When asking why she did that, Latrobe was told by a bystander that "cela est une manière" (that's how we do things).[323]

Judging by their clothing and behavior during the funeral witnessed by Latrobe, the women who accompanied the deceased were probably members of one of New Orleans's female burial societies, such as Les Dames Amies Sacrées, Les Dames aux Tignons, and Les Dames de la Poussinière. There are surprising parallels between their "*manières*" and the complaints made in 1623 by the Church authorities in Lima, Peru, about members of the Black confraternity of Our Lady of the Kings "throwing themselves on top of the deceased" during funerals, which they deemed a "pagan ritual," similar in nature to "the other pagan and evil rituals" that "take place during the six or eight days of mourning for the deceased" that "are barbarous and have little to do with Christianity."[324] While it may be tempting to interpret such funeral scenes as reflections of indigenous African customs, it should be noted that they correspond to Rožmitál's description of a Portuguese funeral scene in the 1460s. There too, the Bohemian nobleman noted that the "women come and throw themselves into the grave," only to be pulled out again by their "next friends."[325] Similar practices have been recorded on the Cape Verdean island of Santiago, where Félix Monteiro observed that *tabanca* burial societies followed the ancient Portuguese custom of wearing white as a color of mourning during funeral processions and, as Maria

Clara Saraiva added, frequently "try to throw themselves into the grave to be with the deceased."[326]

Latrobe also pointed out that Black Catholics in New Orleans made frequent vows to saints.[327] Here, too, we find remarkable parallels between Black practices in Louisiana and ancient Portuguese customs. Lyle Saxon's opening chapter in *Fabulous New Orleans* (1928), for instance, presents a unique perspective on the practice of making vows when narrating how he, in the company of the Black servant Robert, explored Mardi Gras and, when entering Robert's room, saw "walls covered with pictures of saints: Saint Lucy carrying her eyes on a plate, Saint Roch with his sores, followed by a collie that held a cake in its mouth; Saint Somebody Else being burned at the stake." To Saxon's surprise, Robert also "rescued" a "small statue of St. Joseph," which he had placed "upside down on the wash-stand, propped in this uncomfortable position between tooth mug and soap dish." He had done so to put pressure on the saint in order to help him get authorization to celebrate carnival. Now that he had been called to serve as a guide to the White boy, Robert "righted the outraged saint, and after placing him upon the altar beside the statue of the Virgin, he fell upon his knees and began to pray rapidly."[328] The popularity of this Catholic saint among members of New Orleans's Black Catholic population is also revealed in the rosary that was uncovered in 1984 during excavations at the St. Peter Street Cemetery (ca. 1725–1788) and had two medals attached to it, one depicting Saint Joseph.[329]

The latter was formerly believed to be representing Saint Anthony, since both saints are typically depicted holding the infant Christ in their arms. Saint Anthony also enjoyed considerable popularity among Black Catholics in New Orleans, and customs similar to the one described by Saxon have been observed in connection to this Portuguese saint. When interviewed as part of the Louisiana Writers' Project, Marie Dédé recalled that Marie Laveau, the famous "queen of Vodou," had "a big [statue of] St. Anthony" and that "she would turn him upside down on his head in her yard when she had 'work' to perform."[330] As we have seen, the decision to put pressure on a saint by "punishing" a statue is a phenomenon with a long tradition in Portuguese religious culture, in particular in relation to Saint Anthony. Punishing statues of Saint Anthony was also common practice among the enslaved in Brazil, as was the custom of saying prayers while balancing a plate with lighted candles on one's head, yet another practice that was observed at Laveau's Vodou services.[331]

Just how strong the Catholic influence on Laveau's ceremonies was can be seen in Oscar Felix's 1940 interview with Edmund Burke, according to whom Laveau's services on Saint John's Eve typically began "with Roman Catholic prayers," whereby "everybody would kneel before the alter and rap on the ground three times, one-two-three . . . in the name of the Father, Son, and Holy Ghost." After that "we would sing in Creole [and] the leader would begin with praise to St. John . . . just like a mass in a regular church." Following the prayers, people "would dance the 'Creole dance,'" and afterward, "everybody would bow down their knees . . . and say the 'Our Father.'"[332]

We find another parallel to Afro-Catholic traditions in an 1871 article in the *New Orleans Picayune* about a "Society for Waking the Dead" that had a "heathenish band" to "mourn anybody's dead friends for a pecuniary consideration." According to the newspaper, when "a Congo Negro" is dying, "the band proceeds to his house, a brother prays in a loud voice and the choir chants a doleful dirge. Then there is a pause for a few minutes, at the end of which all pray and shriek and howl together."[333] In reality, there was nothing "heathenish" about this society. It clearly parallels Black confraternities in Latin America that were dedicated to the souls in purgatory and known for organizing "viaticum processions" to the houses of dying people.[334]

It is remarkable that even an expert in local folklore such as Saxon failed to understand the strong Afro-Iberian influence on New Orleans's Black performance culture. In *Fabulous New Orleans* he described how "after traversing several squares we turned from Canal Street into another thoroughfare" and witnessed "many Negroes in costume who seemed to be holding a Mardi Gras all their own," including "men wearing purple elephants' heads of papier-mâché; huge donkey's heads. Sometimes two men would combine in order to represent a comical horse or a violet-colored cow. A man passed by on stilts . . . two men were dressed in black tights, painted with white to imitate skeletons."[335] Men walking with stilts, dressed as oxen, riding hobbyhorses, and wearing gigantic heads made of papier-mâché are all typically associated with Black street celebrations during Iberian Epiphany and Corpus Christi processions.[336] An interesting figure is the man imitating a skeleton, which survives in the Skull and Bones "gang" that performs during Mardi Gras today. Contrary to general assumptions, this is hardly a uniquely New Orleans tradition that was "invented" in the Tremé neighborhood in 1819.[337] This once highly serious tradition can be traced back to Iberian procession culture. After carnival entertainment had ended on Ash Wednesday, the first day of Lent used to host a—deadly serious—procession in Iberian societies.[338] In 1718 Le Gentil de la Barbinais described such a procession in Salvador da Bahia, Brazil, consisting of men dressed as skeletons accompanying a group of flagellants who reminded viewers that we all began as dust and that our bodies will return to dust until we are raised up by Christ.[339] Over time, this serious Ash Wednesday procession came under pressure from the expanding carnival festivities and was eventually canceled. The flagellants disappeared and, ironically, the tradition of dressing up like a skeleton became popular during carnival parades.[340]

Saxon also showed surprise that "two Negro nuns" decided to rent a "red devil costume" in preparation for Mardi Gras and haggled over the price, arguing that it was "for the church."[341] As we have seen, the presence of *diablitos*—little devils—was characteristic of Afro-Iberian brotherhoods' street performances on Catholic holidays.[342] That such old Iberian traditions had over time transited to carnival can be seen in James Creecy's *Scenes in the South*, whose description of the 1835 Mardi Gras parade in New Orleans shows that its major attraction was a "large nondescript car," drawn by horses "draped with fiery dragons, serpents with numerous heads, scorpions with many stinging tails," that was the "prison of his most satanic majesty, ignominiously and vulgarly chained securely— head, horns, tails, and all—blowing from his volcanic mouth, flames of fire and fumes of Sulphur" and surrounded "with his familiars imps of the most infernal appearance conceivable, 'cutting up' and playing antics."[343] This scene with Lucifer, a dragon, and devils is an almost exact copy of old Epiphany and Corpus Christi parades in the Iberian world.[344] Unaware of these Iberian origins, however, Saxon wrote that "to this day the renting of that red devil costume by the Negro nuns has remained an unsolved mystery in my mind."[345] This confession only shows how little Anglo-Americans like him understood of the city's Black culture.

It also cautions against reducing the history of Black Catholicism in Louisiana to French missionary work only. Several forms of Catholicism coexisted in colonial Louisiana, including one rooted in Afro-Iberian traditions that thrived at the margins of society. Following the Louisiana Purchase, however, all customs with visibly African elements came under pressure. Whereas Catholic slaveholders typically adopted a laissez-faire attitude vis-à-vis Black performances, their drum music and dances profoundly offended Anglo-American Protestant sensibilities.[346] In 1861 William Howard Russell observed a group of Black people who were "going off to a dance at the sugarhouse" on a Sunday and commented that "the planters who are not Catholics rarely give any such indulgences to their slaves."[347] Anglo-Americans were particularly concerned about the gatherings and dances on Congo Square. In 1822 William Paxton characterized the "Circus public square" as a place where "the Congo, and other negroes dance, carouse, and debauch" and characterized this practice as "a foolish custom that elicits the ridicule of most respectable persons." He, therefore, recommended that "they could be ordered to assemble at some place more distant from the houses."[348] When, in 1852, Anglo-Americans conquered the majority in the New Orleans city council, they passed Ordinance no. 3847 to regulate "the numerous assemblages of persons of color." An 1858 ordinance even required that all forms of Black Christian worship had henceforth to be conducted "under the supervision of a white minister" and that written permission from the mayor was required for any meeting held by people of African descent.[349]

The growing Anglo-American influence in the region coincided with the arrival of large numbers of German, Irish, and Italian immigrants who came to dominate the Catholic congregations in Louisiana.[350] This put further pressure on rituals with visibly African features. In the 1820s, Father Marcel Borella actively campaigned in New Orleans against Black dancing. One decade later, Archbishop Antoine Blanc went as far as to order priests not to offer benediction to any Black person who "shouted" or "danced" in church.[351]

Such campaigns only encouraged Black people to fulfill their spiritual and communal needs elsewhere, most notably in evangelical churches.[352] A revealing observation comes from Elizabeth Ross Hite, who was born into slavery on a plantation in Louisiana and later recalled, "We used to hide behind some bricks and hold church ourselves. You see, the Catholic preachers from France wouldn't let us shout, and the Lawd done said you gotta shout if you want to be saved."[353]

In the early twentieth century Louisiana also experienced the expansion of Spiritual churches that, although Pentecostal in nature, feature many Catholic elements. According to Reverend J. J. Johnson, "Spiritual people are almost like Catholics" because "we got almost the same doctrine.

We believe in the altars; we believe in the priestly robes; we believe in the saints and in the creed."[354] Michael Smith characterized these churches as an "almost medieval [form of] Catholicism" because they hold to a pre-Tridentine form of Christianity.[355]

In the context of Louisiana's societal transformations, Afro-Catholic rituals receded into Black social societies, where they were visible to outsiders only on particular days of the year, such as Saint John's Eve, Saint Joseph's Night, or Mardi Gras, classified by the *Daily Picayune* in 1874 as times "of unrestrained license for the Negroes."[356] It is revealing that the most iconic Black performance traditions in New Orleans—from the coconut-throwing Krewe of Zulu to the city's many second-line clubs to the Mardi Gras Indian "gangs"—all developed in the context of mutual-aid and burial societies.[357] Mesmerized by their spectacular street performances, outsiders have displayed a tendency to focus almost exclusively on these organizations' festive aspects. One of the few exceptions was Robert Tallant, who in the 1940s pointed out that groups such as the Mardi Gras Indians are "formally organized," that they hold meetings "at regular intervals throughout the year," that "members pay dues," and that they "hold elections."[358] Later research by David Elliott Draper confirmed that Mardi Gras Indian "gangs" provide financial aid to members and cover funeral expenses. To adult members, he claims, the social entertainment of the gang is "of secondary importance in comparison with the instrumental qualities of being a member of the mutual-aid association."[359]

Considering the long history of Black brotherhoods, it should not come as a surprise that we find several Catholic elements in these performance traditions.[360] For instance, Mardi Gras Indians not only perform on Fat Tuesday but also reappear in the middle of Lent. This corresponds to the ancient Catholic tradition of concluding the carnival season on Laetare Sunday, a day of relaxation in the middle of Lent. As the "feast of light," Laetare was traditionally celebrated with festive night processions with lanterns, similar to how Big Chief Donald Harrison Sr. recalled Saint Joseph's Night parades in his interview with Al Kennedy. Harrison also explained that "in times past, Mardi Gras Day began for some Mardi Gras Indians with a recitation of the 'Our Father' . . . in anything we did, we put God in it." The 1998 funeral of this legendary chief of the Guardians of the Flame took place in the St. Augustine Catholic church. Big Chief Donald Harrison Jr. of the Congo Nation—note the name—later honored his father by leading the Mardi Gras Indian procession past this iconic church of New Orleans' Black Catholic community.[361]

While the long-term influence of Afro-Atlantic Catholic elements may come as no surprise in a place such as New Orleans, with its century-old Catholic history, its connection to Cuba, its large population with Kongolese roots, and its proud attachment to street parades and music, the next chapter will show that there are good reasons to have a closer look at the impact of Afro-Atlantic Catholics on the development of Black social and religious culture on the East Coast as well.

CHAPTER FOUR

The Catholic Roots of African American Christianity

In 1733 the New York City authorities prohibited the enslaved population from placing a pall over the deceased's coffin in order to show respect for their dead.[1] Historian Erik Seeman interpreted their use of a pall as a sign that "people of African descent began to adopt some of the material trappings of Euro-American deathways" and that Christianity filled "a spiritual vacuum" for African Americans once "memories of Africa faded farther into the distance."[2]

Considering the origin of Manhattan's charter generation, one could also suggest a different interpretation of this prohibition. After all, the enslaved population in New Netherland originated from parts of Africa where European funeral customs had been adopted since the late fifteenth century. As an example, we could quote the description of the 1622 funeral for King Álvaro III of Kongo, which mentions how the corpse was taken in procession to the Chapel of Saint James, with "trumpeters and drummers," followed by "the flag of the Holy House of Mercy with its fraternity, the crosses of the confraternities, the clergy and dignitaries, and six nobles who carried a litter with the king being placed, with his weaponry, on a carpet and a velvet pillow, and covered with a cloak of the Order of Christ."[3] The decision by enslaved Black people in New York to show respect to their dead by placing a pall on their coffins might, thus, reflect something different from what Seeman suggested: not an African American imitation of Euro-American deathways, but rather a desire by the charter generation's descendants to keep honoring a Luso-African funeral ritual.

Studies have revealed that charter generations tended to have a profound impact on the development of Black cultural traditions in the Americas. Their long-term influence is explained by the fact that newcomers were typically trained by their peers before being put to work, which stimulated adjustment to the customs of earlier generations.[4] As Robin observed in early nineteenth-century Louisiana, newly arrived enslaved people were only "gradually accustomed to work" and were "distributed in small numbers among experienced slaves in order to dispose them better to acquire their habits."[5]

Berlin is, therefore, convinced that the influence of the charter generations "faded, but never quite disappeared, from mainland North America." With regard to religion, he made a distinction between the charter generations, whom he referred to as "Atlantic Creoles" or "cosmopolitans," and Africans who arrived in later decades, whom he characterized as "provincials, for whom the Atlantic was a strange, inhospitable place." Whereas the former "had demonstrated a willingness to incorporate Christianity into their system of belief," the latter "were loathe to accept the religion of their enslavers." Since "slaves viewed Christianity with all of the suspicion and hostility due the religion of the owning class," missionaries "attracted few slaves." Wherever they reached out to Black populations, they were met with "defiant opposition, if not contempt, of the mass of black people." Apart from a few individual cases, it was only after "a series of revivals along the James River in 1785" that "black men and especially black women came to Christianity in unprecedented numbers," drawn "by the hope of eternal grace or temporal equality."[6]

Berlin's conclusion raises the question of why the influence of charter generations "never quite disappeared," yet apparently failed to have any effect on religion. Speaking about the South Carolina Lowcountry, Annette Laing criticized Berlin's interpretation, arguing that "neither the quantity nor the quality of the American evidence supports the belief that most Africans . . . rejected . . . Christianity."[7] Moreover, as the cases of the Virgin Islands, Jamaica, and Saint Christopher reveal, Afro-Atlantic Catholics successfully engaged in missionary activities among unbaptized newcomers from Africa, which stands in contrast to Berlin's assumption that the latter all hated Christianity and saw it as "the religion of their enslavers."

All of this leads one to question whether Berlin may have underestimated the charter generations' long-term influence on the development of African American Christianity. It is, in this respect, important to repeat that one of the main reasons for recurrent misunderstandings about Black religious identity formation in North America is the assumption that enslaved Africans perceived Christianity as a foreign religion. While this may have been the case for the vast majority of them, there can be no doubt that, especially among the charter generations, many, if not most, were familiar with Catholicism. In fact, to Kongolese living in seventeenth-century Manhattan, certain indigenous rituals from West Africa may have been more foreign than rosaries, crucifixes or, for that matter, the use of a pall during funerals.

To determine the long-term religious influence of Afro-Atlantic Catholic members of North America's charter generations is a challenging task because it has depended on a large variety of factors, including the number and prestige of their descendants; the policy of the colonizing authorities, slaveholders, and churches; the nearby presence of Iberian territory; the origin and numbers of enslaved people who arrived in later decades; and the speed with which the charter generations' descendants were outnumbered by newcomers from other parts of Africa.

Further complicating factors are Catholic missionary work among the enslaved, by Ursuline nuns in Louisiana, for instance, or by Jesuits on their plantations in Maryland. When, in 1733, we find in New York a reference to the enslaved man Andrew Saxon, who "professeth himself to be a Roman Catholic," and in 1741 to Mary Jorga, characterized as a "free Portuguese-baptized Negress," or read that, in 1740, "a servant woman named Catherine Roach," who "can speak both Spanish and Portugueze, and is a Roman-Catholick" escaped from her owner in Philadelphia, and in the 1790s, Anthony Boston was granted freedom in Maryland after convincing the court that he was the descendant of "a yellow woman being a Portuguese," it is by no means certain that these references to

Catholic or Iberian elements in North America's Black population can be traced back to the charter generations. During the eighteenth century, newcomers from parts of Africa with a historically strong Portuguese influence kept arriving in North America. In 1721, for instance, "several Negro men from St. Jago [Santiago]" arrived in New England, where, in 1749, a ship brought another six enslaved Africans from that same Cape Verdean island, and in 1784 *The Virginia Gazette, or, The American Advertiser* wrote about a Portuguese-speaking man, also from Santiago, who was "fond of marches and Church music, particularly of that belonging to the Roman Catholic religion, which he professes."[8]

Moreover, some of the enslaved people who arrived in eighteenth-century North America from Caribbean islands identified as Catholic. When Cyprian Davis's research revealed that at least a third of the members of the late eighteenth-century Catholic fraternities established by the Sulpician mission in Baltimore were Black, their French names show that these Black Catholics had most likely come in the refugee wave from Saint-Domingue at the outset of the Haitian Revolution.[9]

We should also refer to the ongoing wars between Great Britain and Spain, during which dozens of Catholic Black, Mulatto, and Mestizo soldiers were captured and subsequently sold in British colonies. In a petition submitted to New York governor Robert Hunter in 1712, a group of these men complained that "they were free men, subjects to the King of Spain, but sold here as slaves." Hunter admitted that only "by reason of their colour which is swarthy, they were said to be slaves," and, though he "secretly pittyed their condition," he did not free them for "haveing no other evidence of w' they asserted then their own words."[10] It is, thus, not by accident that these "Spanish Negroes" had the reputation of being rebellious. A runaway advertisement from 1765 indicates that the Albany skipper Abraham Douw owned a "Spanish Negro man named Tom" who "pretends to be a free man" and escaped "in the company of a mulatto Spaniard belonging to Mr. Barent Ten Eyck."[11] No fewer than thirteen "Spanish Negroes" were involved in the 1741 plot in New York. In court, they insisted that they were free men who had been enslaved illegally and demanded to be identified by their proper names; not as "Powlis" or "Tony," but as Pablo Ventura Angel and Antonio de St. Bendito. Their Catholic identity is notable in the decision by Wan de Sylva [Juan da Silva] to pray and kiss a crucifix before his execution.[12]

The search for traces of Afro-Atlantic Catholic influences on African American identity formation is further complicated by concerns among slaveholders about Christianized Black people. As Edgar McManus explained, "many believed that heathenism justified slavery and that baptism or conversion would automatically free a slave."[13] Patricia Bonomi argued that, because of this attitude, "planters must have been tempted to deny that some incoming blacks might be Christians" and had an interest in downplaying all religious practices among the enslaved population as "heathenish, idolatrous, [and] pagan" superstitions that had absolutely nothing to do with Christianity.[14]

We should also take into consideration that African expressions of Catholic faith were different from what European settlers and their descendants understood as Catholicism. Not only was the form of Catholicism that enslaved Black people perceived as their own embedded in an African mindset and cosmology, but its rituals were also rooted in a mixture of indigenous African and pre-Tridentine Iberian traditions that, by the eighteenth century, looked foreign even to the native Portuguese.

In spite of all of this, the cases of Oldendorp, Phillippo, and others reveal that those who made an effort to approach the enslaved population had no difficulties in identifying Catholic features in their rituals. The reactions of these missionaries reveal, however, that African expressions of Catholic faith only reinforced Protestant biases against Catholicism. What Phillippo saw he described not as an African expression of Catholic faith, but rather as "extravagant puerilities" of a "religious system" that was "absurd, monstrous, and discordant."[15] These biases require us to be cautious in analyzing references to religious practices in early missionary reports about enslaved Black people. As an example, we could quote Reverend John Sharpe, who observed in 1712 that enslaved people in New York were "buried in the common by those of their country and complexion," who performed "heathenish rites . . . at the grave by their countrymen."[16] While it may be tempting to understand this statement as a reference to indigenous African rituals only, we should not forget that, at the time, descendants of the Manhattan charter generation still formed a sizable minority of New York's Black population.[17] It is, therefore, very possible that, besides indigenous African practices, Sharpe's "heathenish rites" included Afro-Atlantic Catholic rituals.

Moreover, only a small minority of the Black community in New Netherland joined the Dutch Reformed Church. Most of them did not.

The decision by the Reformed Church to adopt a much more restrictive policy by the 1650s gave the enslaved no alternative but to self-organize their funeral ceremonies. Since Afro-Atlantic Catholics had brought a form of Christianity to America that was characterized by making vows and a strong belief in purgatory, the Manhattan charter generation is likely to have felt a need to observe a set of rituals to redeem the souls of the deceased. The most logical response to this need was the formation of a brotherhood. Not surprisingly, thus, Graham Hodges's research into the organization of the New Netherland charter generation led him to conclude that the "association" they built in order to provide "a supportive model" resembled "the confraternities or brotherhoods found among Kongolese and Angolan blacks living in Brazil."[18]

Hodges's conclusion is legitimate. In the preceding chapters we explored countless examples that show how crucial brotherhoods were to Afro-Atlantic Catholics. If Afro-Atlantic Catholics had any long-term influence on Black social and religious identity formation in North America, these continuities are likely to be most visible in the context of mutual-aid societies, since these organizations are known to periodically take to the street with banners, music bands, and "soldiers" escorting their "kings." Even if the White community largely ignored the social activities of the Black population, these boisterous and colorful parades, if anything, must have attracted attention. This requires a closer look at African American parading traditions during the era of slavery.

BLACK MUTUAL-AID SOCIETIES IN NORTH AMERICA

Starting around the mid-eighteenth century and ending in the mid-nineteenth century, sources from Rhode Island, New Hampshire, and Connecticut refer to a practice known as "Negro Election Day." On these days, enslaved Black people elected their leaders, whom they called "governors" or "kings." In his *Annals of Salem* (1845–49), Joseph Felt explained that, on Election Day, Black people could be seen "attired in their best, with drums, banners, guns, and swords" and, having elected their leaders, "they adopted regulations as the circumstances of their association required."[19] Felt's use of the terms *regulations* and *association* indicates that these were not impromptu gatherings or forms of carnivalesque fun, but, rather, well-organized cooperative structures. The existence of such structures questions the assumption that enslaved Black people were "socially dead" people and gives credit to Melvin Wade's theory that, in New England, "black captive and white captor existed in a relationship of give-and-take that permitted enough autonomy for blacks to assert themselves in a culturally continuous and complex fashion."[20]

Other sources show that, during some of the Election Day parades, salutes were fired and elected kings were given a crown, sword, and other emblems of royalty.[21] One of them subsequently paraded through town "on one of his master's horses, adorned with plaited gear, his aides side *à la militaire*."[22] While the election points to a democratic process, there are also indications that there existed a hierarchy whereby those who served "a master of distinction" occupied leading positions.[23] Slaveholders did not attempt to prevent these forms of limited self-government. Rather, as Wilkins Updike has shown, they offered support, taking pride in clothing enslaved people with some of their finest luxuries on Election Days because "it was degrading to the reputation of the owner if his slave appeared in inferior apparel, or with less money than the slave of another master of equal wealth."[24] The reason that slaveholders supported this tradition may also relate to the fact that elected "kings" or "governors" were expected to take charge of misdemeanors among the enslaved population.[25] Orville Platt even mentions the existence of "a sort of police managed wholly by the slaves" and a Black "court" whose punishments had more of an effect since "people of their own rank and color had condemned them, and not their masters." As an example, William Piersen cites the case of an enslaved man called Prince Jackson who, upon being found guilty of stealing, was given twenty lashes by "King" Nero's deputy sheriff.[26]

For this reason, Lorenzo Greene characterized the existence of such a "Negro government" as a "subtle form of slave control."[27] It should be admitted, however, that these Black community leaders enjoyed considerable respect. In August 1786, for instance, the *Massachusetts Centinel* announced the death of "His Excellency Luke Belcher, late Governor of the Africans in this town. He was universally respected by every rank of citizen."[28] While there are also examples of White authorities harassing elected kings and governors, there can be no denial that slaveholders granted the enslaved considerable leeway on Election Day. In spite of the countless acts issued to prohibit enslaved people from carrying arms, multiple sources refer to the use of weaponry in Election Day parades. A 1758 source from Salem, Massachusetts, confirms how Black people "assembl[ed] together, beating drums, using powder, and having guns and swords."[29] Such practices seem to have had a long tradition. In 1680 the authorities in Virginia saw the need to prohibit "the frequent meeting of considerable numbers of Negroe slaves under pretense of feasts and burials" and the carrying of "staffe, gunn, sword or any other weapon."[30] Swords in particular were objects of importance to these elected Black community leaders. Significantly, Boston Nichols was buried in Hartford's South Congregational Church in 1810 with his sword laid across the coffin.[31]

This public display of weapons is remarkable not only because it ignored prohibitions, but also because these gatherings continued to take place after the bloody crackdown on the New York plot in 1741. Even in New York itself, the harsh punishments inflicted on the enslaved population did not deter Black people from engaging in similar practices. In spite of the fact that New York Colonial Laws prohibited enslaved people from using firearms of any sort except under the direction of their master, Judge Daniel Horsmanden reported in January 1742, only months after thirty Black people had been executed, that "particularly in Queens County, on Nassau alias Long Island," some of the enslaved had "formed themselves into a Company about Christmas last" and "had mustered and trained with the borrowed arms and accoutrements of their masters."[32]

Considering the parallels to what occurred in New England, there may have been a connection between this "formation of companies" and the election of slave "kings" in the state of New York. The latter typically occurred in the context of Pinkster celebrations. As Sterling Stuckey confirms, the "Election Day ceremony [served] much of the same function for blacks [in New England] that Pinkster served for New York blacks."[33] Just as Lynn had its King Pompey, South Kingstown its King Prince Robinson, and Portsmouth its King Nero Brewster, the town of Schaghticoke, in New York's Rensselaer County, had its King Tom, and the city of Albany its King Charles. Both Schaghticoke and Albany were once part of New Netherland and preserved a distinctively Dutch character until the early nineteenth century. This explains why their largest folk festival continued to be called Pinkster, the Dutch term for Pentecost.[34]

During the Pentecost holidays, enslaved people received considerable leeway to organize their own festivities. An anonymous source about the

1803 Pinkster celebrations in Albany reveals that the Black community took advantage of this to parade its "king" through town in a spectacle that attracted "a motley group of thousands." The parade honored "King Charles," who "after having passed through the principal streets in the city, is conducted in great style to *The Hill* already swarming with a multifarious crowd of gasping spectators." Before him was "borne a standard, on which significant colours are displayed, and a painting containing his *portrait*, and specifying what has been the duration of his reign." Two pedestrians "lead a superb steed, of a beautiful cream colour, on which their fictitious sovereign rides in all the pomp of an eastern *nabob*—whilst a large procession of the most distinguished and illustrious characters follow after."[35] The fact that the Albany processions during Charles's reign started in State Street, one of Albany's most noble districts, suggests that the city's elite was at least willing to tolerate the tradition and most likely offered support for it, similar to what occurred in New England. In his nineteenth-century childhood recollections from Albany, James Eights provided some more background by informing that "Charles originally came from . . . Angola" and that the festivities were coordinated by the Black community, whose "master of ceremonies . . . was Adam Blake, then body servant to the old *patroon*," a Dutch term for landowner.[36] In 1867 the Albany publisher Joel Munsell added that the dances performed by Black people on Pinkster Hill were "the original Congo dances as danced in their native Africa," a "double-shuffle" with "heel-and-toe breakdown."[37]

Munsell's reference to "Congo dances" may explain Eileen Southern's assumption that "the entire performance of the Place Congo dance was in the same African tradition as the Pinkster dances in New York."[38] While Southern didn't provide any evidence to sustain this claim, there are, indeed, several references to Black "kings" in New Orleans. In fact, the election and celebration of a "king" is a practice that exists to this day in New Orleans's Black community, where it is organized by the Zulu Social Aid and Pleasure Club, a mutual-aid society that is also known as the Krewe of Zulu.[39]

While the King of Zulu parade has traditionally been understood as a Black parody, starting around 1909, of the Mardi Gras King Rex, the fact is that king celebrations in New Orleans's Black community have historical roots that predate the 1856 foundation of the city's racist "Mystick Krewe." In the winter of 1823, for instance, during a stop in New Orleans along his journey through the Mississippi valley, Timothy Flint witnessed a "great Congo dance," with "hundreds of negroes, male and female," who paraded with "the king of the wake." The latter "wags his head and makes grimaces," the Presbyterian missionary wrote, and "all the characters that follow him, of leading estimation, have their own peculiar dress, and their own contortions."[40] Flint's observations correspond to the information provided in the story "The Singing Girl of New Orleans" (1849) about a tall Black man who was called "King of Congo."[41]

That such king celebrations and parades were not isolated cases is confirmed by Constance Rourke, who wrote in the 1930s that "many who heard the minstrels in the Gulf States or along the lower Mississippi must have remembered those great holidays in New Orleans early in the nineteenth century when hundreds of Negroes followed through the streets a king chosen for his youth, strength, and blackness."[42] In later decades this tradition shifted to Mardi Gras. During an 1864 Mardi Gras celebration, George Sala saw Black men on Canal Street dressed like "walking caricatures of the late Emperor Soulouque."[43] This reference to Faustin-Élie Soulouque, who ruled Haiti in the mid-nineteenth century and dressed like a European emperor, shows that the tradition of Black men carrying European-style royal attributes (crown, scepter, cape) on Mardi Gras predates the King of Zulu. In fact, the New Orleans Illinois Club, founded in 1895, used to have a Black "royal court."[44] Moreover, Marcus Christian's research revealed how, between 1913 and 1930, a Black society called the Bulls Aid and Pleasure Club used to organize "an annual midsummer carnival." Starting from "back-of-town," they would turn out from South Rampart Street onto Girod and proceed over to Saint Charles Street to the City Hall with "decorated floats upon which a king and his dukes and counts followed in majestic splendor."[45] This attachment to symbols of royalty could also explain Saxon's surprise over the fact that, of all beneficiary and burial societies in New Orleans, "the ones that require the carrying of a sword are particularly favored [by the Black community]. There isn't anything that lends dignity and importance . . . like a big shiny sword."[46]

Louis Armstrong's comment that "it was the dream of every kid in my neighborhood" to be chosen the King of Zulu and that his own election as "king" in 1949 was the realization of a "life-long dream" shows that this practice meant more to members of the Black community than just entertainment.[47] Saxon's description in *Fabulous New Orleans* of how, in a parade, the Zulu king was followed by "a motley collection of horse-drawn carriages [with] various leaders of Negro society; heads of lodges and fraternal organizations, wearing high silk hats; heads of Negro unions, wearing badges and colored ribbons" reflects the prestige this "king" enjoyed within the Black community.[48]

Not just in New Orleans, but also elsewhere in the United States, king parades from the era of slavery continued to influence Black performance culture after abolition. On July 5, 1827 (Emancipation Day), for instance, "Grand Marshal" Samuel Hardenburgh paraded through the streets of New York City in virtually the same outfit that "King" Charles had been using during Pinkster processions. Hardenburgh was wearing a "cocked hat and drawn sword," and, "mounted on a milk-white steed," he was followed by "his aids on horseback, dashing up and down the line." Then, in due order, "splendidly dressed in scarfs of silk with gold-edgings, and with colored bands of music, and their banners appropriately lettered and painted followed The New York African Society for Mutual Relief, The Wilberforce Benevolent Society, and The Clarkson Benevolent Society."[49] Unlike Charles, however, Hardenburgh was no longer enslaved. He was a free man, and the organization he led was a registered fraternity. In the streets of New York, the Wilberforce Society proudly displayed its mutual-aid fund that was "raised by weekly subscription, which is employed in assisting sick and unfortunate blacks."[50]

As Hodges explained, not only in New York, but also in New Jersey, "Masonic and other fraternal organizations" replaced "eighteenth-century gathering moments such as Pinkster" and provided "permanent forms for black camaraderie, self-help, and benevolence."[51] The name "Angola Society," of a similar society in Philadelphia, clearly suggests the continuation of a tradition that already existed prior to abolition.[52] Another example can be found in the *New England Galaxy & Masonic Magazine* from 1820, where a parade of "five to six hundred Negroes, with a band of music, pikes, swords, epaulettes, sashes, cocked hats, and standards" is described that bears striking similarities with Election Day.[53] Similar scenes were recorded in Virginia, where the leaders of Black fraternities paraded in "aristocratic garments" with bands and banners, and were called "Grand Emperor, Ruler, Potentate, or whatever may be the title of His Highness."[54]

Of particular interest is the case of Luke Belcher, who, while being enslaved, had been elected as "governor of the Africans" on Election Day in Massachusetts and, later, became a prominent freemason as a free man.

As Chernoh Sesay Jr. has argued, Belcher's trajectory suggests that the social roots of Black freemasonry "were planted firmly in inclusive communal traditions that also established social distinction through popular slave festivals."[55] We could also mention the case of Adam Blake, president of the prestigious (Black) Burdett-Coutts Benevolent Association in Albany, who happened to be the son or grandson of an enslaved man with the same name and whom James Eights recalled as "master of ceremonies" in King Charles's Pinkster parades.[56] The most impressive case of social promotion is that of Eben Bassett, son of the Black "governor" Eben Tobias and grandson of "king" Tobias Pero, who helped to enlist Black soldiers for the Union Army during the Civil War, in recognition of which President Grant appointed him as U.S. ambassador to Haiti.[57]

These African American traditions have many characteristics in common with the fraternal practices we observed in Latin America and the Caribbean. They reveal that, all over the Americas, from New England to Argentina, Black communities formed mutual-aid societies and elected leaders with royal titles. As Thornton confirms, "The election of kings and queens [was] widespread in the society of Afro-American slaves in all parts of the Americas. In Iberian America, the annual elections were public events, while in other areas they were acknowledged, if not recognized."[58]

One way to explain this phenomenon is by pointing to pan-African communalities, in the assumption that enslaved Africans with different ethnic backgrounds shared a common desire to honor their leaders with noble titles and parades and that, over time, an assimilation process took place, which resulted in the Pinkster kings, Election Day kings, and Congo Square kings. John Storm Roberts, for instance, identified a series of parallels between "the *rara* bands of Haiti, the highly danceable *marchas* of Brazil, the New Orleans marching bands, and the Trinidadian *calenda* groups" and claimed that all these phenomena are "to be traced to African origins in royal and religious ceremonial in such old kingdoms as the Ashanti, Yoruba, and Fon," whereas Katherine Harris argued that enslaved Africans from "Angola, Nigeria, Cameroon, Ghana, and other areas where intricate systems of checks and balances prevailed . . . reclaimed this political heritage and transformed it using the language of English-speaking America," adopting "the titles 'Governor' and 'King.'"[59]

The aristocratic titles, however, are not the only European element of these parade traditions. The recurrent use of European-style symbols of royalty such as crowns, scepters, and swords; the firing of salutes; and the carrying of banners should caution us not to reduce this phenomenon to indigenous African traditions only. Moreover, as Souza has argued, even when we see scenes of enslaved people in the Americas proudly displaying cultural elements rooted in European aristocratic traditions, we may discern a link to "an African past that was already infused with European elements . . . since the beginning of the sixteenth century."[60] The parallels to what we observed in Latin America and the frequent references to Kongo/Angola justify an alternative explanation that relates these king parades to Afro-Iberian brotherhood traditions.

In his study *Carnival, American Style* (1990), Samuel Kinser became intrigued with the fact that, in Louisiana and different parts of the Caribbean, Black people used virtually the same European royal symbols during such parades; he raised the question whether these "African kings" might not have descended from African prototypes but, rather, followed an old "Hispano-Portuguese custom."[61] Unfortunately, he discarded this possibility and opted for pan-African communalities instead. Contradicting Kinser, who believed that "the black people of New Orleans did not have the numbers or the political space to develop the regal order . . . which is apparent in the *cabildos* of Havana," Ned Sublette has argued that there existed "a cultural continuum" between Havana and New Orleans during the Spanish era. Speaking about Black brotherhoods or *cabildos* under Spanish rule, he added, "It is clear that the idea of such societies was already well established among free people of color in Cuba and Saint-Domingue, and existed in New Orleans as well." To strengthen his argument, Sublette referred to the abundance of Black benevolent societies in nineteenth-century New Orleans, many of which carried the names of Catholic saints.[62]

Long before Sublette, the Cuban folklorist Ortiz had already identified parallels between Black benevolent societies in New Orleans and Havana. Ortiz also showed that, in the case of Cuba, virtually all of these societies had developed out of ancient confraternities led by "kings."[63] A similar continuum of brotherhood culture existed between Spanish Florida and Cuba. Data from 1688 show that Saint Augustine counted no fewer than seven confraternities, one of which was made up of the town's Native American population.[64] "While there are no specific references to black *cabildos* in Florida," Landers argued, "other informal associations along tribal, geographic, and kingship lines are noted, and the long-lived religious associations so well documented in Cuba probably had at least an informal Florida counterpart."[65]

These assumptions sustain Jon Sensbach's argument that "in large Spanish sections of the American South the colonial period did not end in 1783, and continuities with a long Catholic past persisted."[66] It would be wrong, however, to limit the existence of Black mutual-aid and burial organizations modeled upon Afro-Iberian brotherhoods to North American territories with a Spanish colonial history. While the European aspects of the above-described king parades in New England or New York could in theory also be the result of English or Dutch influences, the parallels with Latin American variants make it more likely that this custom has Afro-Iberian roots.

One could, in this respect, draw a parallel between the development of mutual-aid societies and that of Black militias, another tradition with Iberian roots that flourished in Dutch, French, Danish, and British colonies. As we have seen, Black people in New Netherland formed a type of militia under the leadership of the *ladino* Bastiaen. Similar to what typically occurred in Iberian societies, this practice required the Dutch authorities to negotiate a deal with a group of enslaved men, who subsequently petitioned for liberty. This had happened earlier in Dutch Brazil, where the establishment of Black militias had forced the Dutch authorities to start negotiations with a group of enslaved men who seized the opportunity to petition their freedom.[67] In the Danish Virgin Islands, Oldendorp observed the same phenomenon. There, too, the Black community had formed "its own company" for which it chose "a captain from their own" with the Iberian name [Do]mingo. Whenever the Danish authorities faced a threat, he and his men "were ready to help."[68]

Considering the prestige of confraternities in Iberian societies and parts of Africa with a historically strong Portuguese influence, Afro-Atlantic Catholics who arrived in North America were undoubtedly familiar with mutual-aid and burial societies, and, as Jorge Cañizares-Esguerra, Matt Childs, and James Sidbury have pointed out, "Approved institutional structures authorized by the Catholic Church were not always necessary for Africans and their descendants to build fraternal structures."[69] Moreover, as Thornton and Heywood have argued, Afro-Atlantic Catholics, thanks to their familiarity with European traditions, possessed "the means to set down their own cultural pattern in the Americas, even where they were subsequently outnumbered by new arrivals."[70] This could explain not only why Afro-Atlantic Catholics established mutual-aid associ-

ations and leadership positions in accordance with the Afro-Iberian fraternal model they were familiar with, but also why these societies became a
prototype that Black communities continued to use in later decades.

With the arrival of abolition, however, a new generation of African
American community leaders felt the need to distance itself from the ancient fraternal practices.[71] *Freedom's Journal*, the nation's first Black newspaper, was particularly engaged in this endeavor, with the argument that
"nothing is more disgraceful to the eyes of a reflecting man of colour than
one of these grand processions."[72] In August 1840, Charles Bennett Ray's
The Colored American also complained that, during an August 1 celebration, "a number came in from the country, with a drum and fife, formed a
procession, which was fallen in with by a few of the more thoughtless of
the place, all of whom conducted themselves in a manner deeply morti-
fying to the mass of our people in Newark."[73] Frederick Douglass lashed
out at those participating in parades as the "vastly undue proportion of
the most unfortunate, unimproved, and unprogressive class of the colored
people."[74] In his newspaper, *The North Star*, Douglass accused Black societies of "swallowing up the best energies of many of our best men, con-
tenting them with the glittering follies of artificial display, and indisposing
them to seek for solid and important realities."[75] To Douglass, the election
and celebration of Black kings were nothing but circuses that ultimately
served the interests of slaveholders because "to enslave men successfully
and safely it is necessary to keep their minds occupied with thoughts and
aspirations short of the liberty of which they are deprived."[76]

As Joseph Reidy has argued about Election Day, "Generally unmindful
of its earlier positive contributions, [post-abolition Black community lead-
ers] saw it only as an anachronism devoid of any tactical or strategic relevance."[77] Since they were the first African Americans to have access to the
press, the new Black elite successfully wiped out memories of this legacy.

The following section will reveal a parallel evolution in the formation
of the first African American evangelical churches.

FROM MUTUAL-AID SOCIETIES TO CHURCHES

By the time the Dutch Reformed Church in New Netherland adopted a
restrictive baptismal policy for the children of enslaved Africans in the
1650s, a small Black Protestant community had already been formed in

Manhattan. The eagerness of enslaved parents in the Dutch colony to have their children baptized makes one suspect that this community could have been much larger had the Reformed Church not revised its policy. This calls for a reflection on the reason(s) why so many members of the Manhattan charter generation had an interest in joining the Dutch Reformed Church.

As we have seen, the decision by the Reformed Church to reach out to the Black population resulted from a desire not only to proselytize but also to combat Catholic, Iberian influences in the colony. Black Catholics in New Netherland, however, appeared to harbor no reservations about having their children baptized in a Protestant church. This is intriguing considering that the Catholic nobility in Kongo had always fiercely resisted Protestant attempts to proselytize. King Garcia II allegedly went as far as to publicly burn a stack of Calvinist books in 1642.[78] Not only in Africa, but also in Europe and the Americas, we find examples of such Black Catholic zeal. For instance, Mark Ponte's research on the Black community in seventeenth-century Amsterdam, which originated from parts of Africa with a historically strong Portuguese influence, revealed that many of its members had their children baptized in the Catholic house church Moyses.[79] This was a clandestine church, since the public display of Catholic services was not tolerated in Amsterdam. Something similar occurred in the South African Cape Colony, where the French priest Nicolas Étienne was, during his short stay in this Dutch colony in 1661, approached by "a Catholic enslaved Black man, who had been captured from the Portuguese by the Dutch" with the request to baptize two of his daughters.[80] In Barbados, Biet alleged that Black Catholics complained about having to live on an "island of heretics."[81] In Curaçao, we observed that Black people largely ignored Reformed ministers and flocked to Spanish Catholic priests. On that same island we also found examples of Black Catholic zeal turning into intolerance of Jews and unbaptized Africans. A similar scene, this time involving Protestants, can be found in Dutch Brazil, where, in 1641, the Reformed Church reported that members of the Black confraternity of Our Lady of the Rosary in Sirinhaém had not only violated Dutch rules by staging "a procession of the idol *Rosário*," but also that "good [i.e., Protestant] Christians . . . who witnessed it and refused to honor [the Virgin]" were "not only treated disrespectfully but at several occasions beaten up."[82] Even in New Netherland, where many members of the Black community joined the Reformed Church, "Abraham Jansen, called the Mulatto" provocatively refused to pay the obligatory "six guilders for the support of Dominee Polhemius" in 1658 with the argument that he "was Catholic."[83]

These scenes of Catholic zeal contrast, however, with the fact that at least fifty-six Black children were baptized by Reformed ministers in New Netherland and no fewer than six hundred in Dutch Brazil. Since the Dutch administration in Brazil tolerated the Catholic Church, parents had opted for a baptism in the Reformed Church despite the Catholic alternative.[84] Even in Curaçao, a handful of Black people opted for a baptism in the Reformed Church instead of procuring Catholic Spanish missionaries. The same occurred in the 1640s during the brief Dutch occupation of Luanda, where a handful of African parents reached out to the Dutch minister Nicolaus Ketel with a request to baptize their children.[85] These examples show that the desire among members of the Black population in New Netherland to have their children baptized in the Reformed Church was not exceptional, in spite of their Afro-Catholic roots.

A parallel could be drawn to the late nineteenth century, when a British Baptist missionary post was set up in Mbanza Kongo, the capital of the Kongo kingdom. The Baptists were well received by the population and successful in their missionary efforts.[86] Although Baptist missionaries themselves downplayed any continuities, Adrian Hastings argued that "it would be very hard not to explain this quite extensive popular enthusiasm for Christianity coming so soon after the missionary arrival other than in terms of the revival of an ancient religion."[87] In reference to this apparently smooth transition from a Kongolese variant of Catholicism to Baptist Protestantism, Jelmer Vos argued that "the difference between both religions was only slight from an African perspective." Ras Michael Brown argued similarly that "Even those who had extensive experience with Catholic Christian rituals and spirits would not have felt compelled to differentiate between [Catholicism and Protestantism] to a great extent."[88]

Heywood and Thornton used a similar argument when speaking about the Black community in seventeenth-century New Netherland. In their view, what mattered to these people "was the assertion of a Christian identity rather than a sectarian Catholic one."[89] Berlin argued in the same vein, "That the church was Catholic rather than Anglican or Dutch Reformed was less important than that membership knit black people together in bonds of kinship and certified incorporation into the larger community."[90]

Material support is an important factor to consider in this context, however. As Ponte pointed out, one had to be a member of the Reformed Church in order to receive financial benefits, which could explain why most children born in Amsterdam's seventeenth-century Black community were (clandestinely) baptized in a Catholic church, while most marriages within this community took place in a Dutch Reformed Church.[91] It is, in this respect, also interesting to note that early references to Black people taking the initiative to approach Protestant churches in North America reveal that they often did so with a request for aid. For instance, Cotton Mather's diary on life in colonial Massachusetts refers to "a company of poor Negroes" who, in December 1693, "of their own accord" approached him with "a design which they had, of erecting . . . a meeting for the welfare of their miserable nation that were servants among us."[92] We could also mention the case of the "mulatto named Antoni," who, in 1748, "came for a visit" to the Moravian Church in Bethlehem, Pennsylvania, and requested "several pounds in gold to pay his debts," with the promise to work off the debt.[93] An interesting case in the Dutch Reformed Church is that of Bassie de Neger. As the deacons' accounts from the year 1671 show, this Black man requested and obtained food and money from the Reformed Church in Rensselaerswyck when he was in financial need. Later, the church also paid for his coffin and funeral, including the brandy for the reception that followed.[94] In an Iberian context, such requests would typically have been dealt with by one's confraternity.

Equally important is that, ever since the Portuguese introduced Christianity in Africa, it had been associated with the perception that conversion could improve one's living conditions and possibly lead to freedom. This connection between conversion and freedom has been stressed by Sweet, who argued that "Central Africans quickly came to understand that Christian practices (however Catholicized or Africanized) were a potential passageway to an improved condition, perhaps even freedom."[95] If applied to New Netherland, it would imply that the desire of enslaved Africans to have their children baptized in the Reformed Church may have been primarily intended as a symbolic act to build trust and, later, to capitalize on that trust to demand privileges and, ultimately, manumission. If so, their eagerness to have their children baptized and get married in the Reformed Church had more to do with tactics than with faith. Such a mindset would also explain why so many enslaved people in New Neth-

erland made a point of identifying themselves as Christians in their petitions for freedom and why Black families frequently asked members of the
White community to serve as witnesses for their children's baptisms. One
of them, Anthony Ferdinandus, even chose Paulus Heymans, the Dutch
overseer of the enslaved, as witness at his son's baptism.[96] Here, again, we
see a parallel with Iberian colonies. As Gerald Cardoso has shown, once an
Iberian slaveholder accepted a request to be the godparent of an enslaved
child, this would "free the Negro baby at the baptismal font."[97]

The liberal baptismal policy of the Reformed Church in the early decades of New Netherland may, in this way, have contributed to the growth
of a free Black community that, by the time the English took over the
Dutch colony in 1664, consisted of at least seventy-five people.[98] This
view is in line with the argument used by New Netherland minister Henricus Selijns to justify the change in baptismal policy. When writing to the
classis in 1664, Selijns explained that he and his colleagues had decided to
henceforth reject requests by enslaved people to baptize their children
"partly because of their lack of knowledge of the faith, and partly because
of the material and wrong aim on the part of the aforementioned Negroes
who sought nothing else by it than the freeing of their children from material slavery, without pursuing piety and Christian virtues."[99] Similar
complaints could be heard in Anglican circles. In 1739, for instance, Reverend James Blair wrote from Virginia, "I doubt not some of the Negroes
are sincere converts, but the far greater part of them . . . only are in hopes
that they will meet with so much more respect, and that some time or
other Christianity will help them to their freedom."[100]

These words echo a common reproach in Iberian societies of *ladinos*,
who had the reputation of being opportunists, to the point that the adjec-
tive *ladino* over time acquired a new meaning in the Spanish and Portuguese language: guileful or cunning. One could hypothesize that enslaved
Africans familiar with Iberian practices may have brought a *ladino* mindset to New Netherland and understood conversion to the Reformed
Church as a logical step in their transition from Iberian *ladinos* into Dutch
ladinos. Research on early Protestant conversions in the West Indies points
in this direction. The earliest enslaved people to be welcomed to the Anglican Church all tended to stand close to the ruling class, either because
they had a White father or because they occupied leading positions, such
as that of overseer, which, according to Katharine Gerbner, "suggests that

the most important factor leading to baptism for adults was maintaining a close relationship with a master or mistress."[101] Similar to the *ladino* status in Iberian colonies, being Christian tended, as such, to be perceived by enslaved people as something distinctive that sealed an alliance with the ruling class. Consequently, when missionaries of the Moravian Church began to reach out to the entire enslaved community, they faced opposition not only from slaveholders, but also from the Black elite.[102] As Oldendorp confirms, the Moravian Church in the Danish Virgin Islands mainly attracted enslaved people who had been unsuccessful in improving their position in other ways, whereas "of those slaves who enjoyed the greatest freedom to convert, very few showed interest."[103]

If applied to New Netherland, such a *ladino* mindset would explain not only the decision of the "black Captain" Bastiaen, who featured as baptismal witness in at least four cases, to fight on the side of the Dutch and even assist them in the capturing of escapees, but also why those who joined the Reformed Church in Manhattan gradually switched from Iberian to Dutch names. Significantly, the abovementioned Bassie was known by the Dutch variant of his originally Iberian name Sebastián/Sebastião, whereas Bastiaen's son, who was to become a communicant member in the Dutch Reformed Church, used not the Portuguese name Francisco but the Dutch variant Franciscus. In good *ladino* tradition, he changed his name again after the English conquered the Dutch colony, this time to Francis.[104] Just how easily *ladinos* would switch sides can also be illustrated with reference to "the black *ladino* from Kongo," whom the Capuchin Juan de Santiago encountered on a Dutch ship that, in the mid-seventeenth century, was captured by the Portuguese near the island of Príncipe. This man, who had been baptized as Catholic in Kongo, was captured by the Dutch and taken to Amsterdam, where he had converted to Protestantism and started to work as a sailor on Dutch ships. Now that he had been captured again, this time by the Portuguese, he reconverted to Catholicism.[105] In this respect, the conversion of enslaved Black people in New Netherland may have paralleled that of the Native American Mohawk community. According to Mark Meuwese, Mohawks who converted to the Dutch Reformed Church in the 1690s rarely intended to abandon their traditional beliefs or the Catholic customs they had adopted from French Jesuits. Some Mohawks were even witnessed praying the rosary while attending Calvinist church services![106]

The latter case opens up yet another question, namely, whether Afro-Atlantic Catholics who converted to a Protestant church had the genuine intention of leaving their entire Afro-Catholic heritage behind. Ponte's research findings on the Black community in seventeenth-century Amsterdam question this, since they reveal that many of those who had married in the Dutch Reformed Church nevertheless decided to have their children baptized (clandestinely) at a Catholic church.[107] What occurred in seventeenth-century Amsterdam renders credibility to Willem Frijhoff's theory that one of the main reasons for the decision by the Reformed Church to adopt a more restrictive baptismal policy in New Netherland was disappointment over the continuous attachment among Black converts to certain Afro-Iberian, Catholic traditions.[108]

In the absence of further evidence, we can only speculate about the underlying reasons Black people in New Netherland had for conversion. Those reasons may, after all, have differed from individual to individual. This also applies to those who converted to the Anglican Church and its Society for the Propagation of the Gospel (SPG) after the English conquered the Dutch colony and renamed it New York and New Jersey. The first new wave of Black conversions in the area came with the French Huguenot turned Anglican Élie (Elias) Neau. Profoundly influenced by his humiliating condemnation, due to his Protestant faith, to row in a galley after being captured by a French privateer near Jamaica, Neau shared a contempt of Catholicism with his Dutch Reformed predecessors in Manhattan. This was accompanied, however, by an admiration of Catholic missionary success. Neau knew, of course, about concerns among English slaveholders regarding the consequences of baptism but let himself be inspired by "the Fr[ench] & the Span[ish]," who "baptize all their slaves w[i]thout giving them Temporall Liberty" and, therefore, also the "slaves of the English" should, in his view, after being baptized, "continue slaves."[109]

Nevertheless, by 1712, Neau had more than one hundred and fifty Black students and baptized thirty-one of them. After he passed away in 1722, his successor William Huddelston allegedly found "swarms of Negroes coming about my door & asking if I would be pleased to teach them."[110] Other SPG ministers in the region experienced similar reactions. In Hempstead, Long Island, Johan Thomas had "many Negroes who are constant hearers" at his church in 1709, while, in Albany, Thomas Barclay had forty Black catechumens and seventeen baptized by 1714. "If I wanted to," Barclay wrote, "I could quickly form a congregation alone of the slaves."[111] We could also mention the intriguing case of Aree [Arie] van Guinee, a free Dutch-speaking Black man who had come to New York via Suriname and hosted the first Lutheran service by Reverend Justus Falckner at his house near today's Franklin Township, New Jersey, in August 1714.[112] Black people also continued to approach the Reformed Church after the demise of New Netherland.[113] In 1788, for instance, Peter Lowe, the Reformed minister in Kings County (present-day Brooklyn), considered a group of Black men who requested full membership in the church "worthy . . . to the privileges of the Gospel," but his Dutch American congregants disagreed, claiming that "Negroes have no souls," that "their pretended zeal . . . is nothing else than vain parade and ostentation," and that "they clan together on Sunday evenings, and do what they ought not to do—pray and sing together, not the psalms of David—but hymns & spiritual songs." In their defense, Lowe wrote that "the hymns they sing are Dr. Watts and other pious authors of blessed memory."[114]

Eighteenth-century reports about Christianized Black people refer not only to different forms of worship but also to initiatives to conduct preaching and teaching activities on their own. When, for instance, the SPG missionary Pierre Stoupe reached out to the Black population in New Rochelle, New York, in 1728, he observed to his surprise that some already "have had some instruction" by other Black people, who were versed in "the fundamentals of Christian faith"; this reveals that Andreas, who, in December 1742, joined a group of Moravian preachers "to itinerate among the Negroes in the New York countryside" was likely not the first Black person to spread the gospel in the region.[115]

Black preachers also show up frequently in runaway advertisements. In 1740, for instance, the *Pennsylvania Gazette* referred to an escapee called Simon from New Jersey who "pretended to be a doctor and very religious, and says he is a churchman."[116] In 1775 an advertisement in *Rivington's New-York Gazetteer* mentioned the case of Mark, from Bergen County, who allegedly was a "preacher," and, in 1783, the *New York Gazette and the Weekly Mercury* posted an advertisement for Anthony who "pretends to be a preacher, and sometimes officiates in that capacity among the blacks."[117] It is important to stress that all of this occurred *before* the spiritual awakenings on the banks of the James River that Berlin identified as the beginning of African American enthusiasm for Christianity.

Some of these references even predate the arrival of John Wesley and George Whitefield in America, which gives credit to Bonomi's plea to erase "the artificial line between pre- and post-Great Awakening black Christianity."[118]

If we follow Bonomi's suggestion, the question becomes whether the presence of Afro-Atlantic Catholics in North America's charter generations may, in any form, have influenced the development of Black Protestantism. This question is all the more pertinent considering that those who converted to the Dutch Reformed Church in seventeenth-century Manhattan all came from Catholic backgrounds. That many of the earliest Black converts to Protestantism in North America were former Catholics should, thus, not be a matter of debate. More difficult to know, however, is how strong their impact was on the genesis and further development of African American Christianity.

This question brings us back to Hodges's assumption that the charter generation in New Netherland established a mutual-aid society modeled upon Afro-Iberian confraternities. It is, in fact, not inconceivable that the Black community in New Netherland cared only about the administration of sacraments, not unlike Catholics in isolated parts of Africa who would, at best, see a priest once a year and otherwise took the organization of all forms of spiritual and social aid into their own hands. If this was indeed the case, one could imagine a connection with the Pinkster king parades in parts of New York with a Dutch colonial history. It is, in this respect, important to recall that these parades used to take place on Pentecost/Whitsuntide. Hodges has speculated that Dutch settlers in America may have used their Pinkster festival to engage in a "religious interaction" with the enslaved, whereby "ecstatic moments of the Holy Wind" during Pentecost allowed for a "spiritual conversion" or "spiritual baptisms."[119] It is doubtful whether this is true. The religious celebration of Pentecost in the Reformed Church and the popular Pinkster festival, known in Dutch as *Pinkster kermis*, were two very different things. Devout Calvinists considered these *kermises* a "popish" vestige from the pre-Reformation era, and the Reformed Church did everything it could to keep its members away from them.[120] It is hard to imagine that those who ignored objections by church authorities would have considered the bacchanalian Pinkster *kermises* an opportunity to have a "religious interaction" with the Black community.

This does not necessarily mean that the Pinkster celebrations had no religious meaning whatsoever to the Black population. An intriguing characteristic of the way they celebrated Pinkster, for instance, is that it involved a parade or procession. Claire Sponsler and Donna Merwick have speculated that Black king parades during Pinkster may have been modeled upon ancient Dutch procession traditions that, over time, were mixed with indigenous African elements.[121] This is doubtful too. Under Calvinist pressure, processions had been prohibited in the Dutch Republic, and, although the Reformed Church begrudgingly tolerated the boisterous Pinkster *kermises*, it would never have allowed Dutch or other European settlers to introduce (Catholic) procession traditions in New Netherland.[122] There are no indications that the small European Catholic minority in New Netherland ever defied the mighty Reformed Church by manifesting itself publicly during religious holidays. As Jaap Jacobs confirms, "Incidents did not take place with the Roman Catholics. Only a few of them lived in New Netherland, and they seem to have obeyed the edicts against conventicles and probably limited their worship to the family circle."[123]

If the Black Pinkster king parades had any Christian meaning at all, its roots must be found outside of the Netherlands. This is also the opinion of Frijhoff, who suggested that "The religious practices of blacks in New Netherland were strongly influenced by Portuguese Catholicism" and "One can assume that this Catholic heritage survived for a long time, which explains the origin of the Pinkster processions."[124] This opinion can be supported with reference to one of the few African American eyewitness accounts of the festival: that of John Williams, a formerly enslaved man from Albany, who claimed that "Pinkster Day was in Africa a religious day, partly pagan and partly Christian, like our Christmas day."[125] Williams's statement is astonishing because it reveals that—similar to Cabrera's interviewees in Cuba—some members of the Black population in nineteenth-century New York may have been aware of the existence of syncretic Afro-Christian traditions in Africa. The fact that the Albany King Charles allegedly had Angolan roots and danced "Congo dances" strengthens this assumption.[126] Equally intriguing is the discovery, during excavations in Albany in the 1970s, of a perforated coin, probably minted in Portugal in the 1690s and found on a site where enslaved people used to live. Such coins—often depicting a cross symbol on one side and Saint Anthony on the other—were commonly used in the Kongo region as amulets.[127] What renders further credibility to this theory is that the Pinkster king parade, as it was recorded in Albany in 1803, followed a pattern that corresponds remarkably well to that of the Portuguese Feast of the Divine Holy Spirit. As we have seen, this festival was one of the most important celebrations in early modern Portugal and the most popular performance on Portuguese ships during the nation's overseas expansion.

Similar to what occurred in Albany's Black community, the Portuguese Feast of the Divine involved the election and parade of a "king" and his "court" during Pentecost. At the front of these parades typically marched a standard-bearer holding the brotherhood's banner. In Albany, such a standard-bearer also walked at the front of the parade, allegedly carrying a banner with "a painting" of King Charles, "containing his *Portrait*, and specifying what has been the duration of his reign." In the Feast of the Divine, the banner displayed an image not of the brotherhood's king, but rather of its patron saint and/or the crown of the Divine, and the year on display refers not to the duration of the emperor/king's reign but to the foundation of the association. While we can only speculate whether the anonymous Anglo-American observer in Albany mistook the image of a (Black) saint and a crown for that of the society's king, it is interesting to note that yet another characteristic of the Portuguese Feast of the Divine can be identified in the 1803 report from Albany, namely that of the *bodo*, the banquet that followed the parade. Such a Pentecost banquet is visible not only in the author's reference to "apartments . . . stored with fruit, cakes, cheese, beer and liquors of various kinds" at the Pinkster celebrations in Albany, but also in the investigations surrounding the 1741 New York plot.[128] In their confessions, several Black people involved in the plot linked their first knowledge of the conspiracy to a banquet on Pentecost in 1740. The constables Joseph North and Peter Lynch argued in court that "that there was a cabal of Negroes at Hughson's last Whitsuntide was twelve months" and that, when they entered the room, "the Negroes were round a table, eating and drinking, for there was meat on the table, and knives and forks; and the Negroes were calling for what they wanted."[129]

While scholars have traditionally been inclined to discard Judge Horsmanden's suspicion that the 1741 conspiracy was part of a "popish plot," it is important to note that many of those involved were Catholic. While all White culprits were Irish Catholics, at least thirteen of the Black culprits were "Spanish Negroes."[130] Although there is good reason to doubt the trustworthiness of Mary Burton's allegations, there may have been some truth in her testimony about a Catholic priest in disguise named John Ury, who allegedly baptized the conspirators while holding a crucifix over their heads. Ury's secret missionary work among the Black population was confirmed by other witnesses, and his journal contains evidence that—although not ordained—he pretended to be a Catholic priest. One witness, Elias DeBrosse, argued that Ury had approached him to buy sacramental wafers for a Mass, while another, William Kane, claimed to have witnessed Ury performing the baptism of a Black child by putting "salt into the child's mouth," which corresponds to a typically Kongolese Catholic custom.[131]

We could also draw parallels to Pentecost celebrations among Afro-Catholic confraternities in Latin America. As Carlos Hernández Soto and Edis Sánchez explained with reference to the Cofradía de los Congos del Espíritu Santo in the Dominican Republic, "On the eve before the feast [of Pentecost], Saturday night, the kings representing the different communities in Villa Mella gather at the church square, wearing their crowns." Initiated by fireworks, "the kings, the gathered public and members of the brotherhood carrying musical instruments enter the church, where the rituals of the last night of the nine days of prayer [in anticipation of the arrival of the Holy Spirit on Pentecost] take place." Following Mass, "a procession takes place through the village" and, after that, "all members of the brotherhood gather in the park of Villa Mella where they play their songs and drink rum. They play music, sing, and dance."[132] These Pentecost celebrations also have a spiritual component whereby members "call" the Holy Spirit by creating a form of trance that is obtained by the constant repetition of the same rhythm, chants, and dance movements.[133]

This deep, personal connection to the Holy Spirit in Afro-Catholic brotherhood traditions can also be found in evangelical communities. The calls on the Holy Spirit by members of the Cofradía de los Congos del Espíritu Santo remind one of the Holiness Movement and other forms of Black Protestant Christianity that emphasize the importance of personal contacts with the Holy Spirit. In particular, they echo Black evangelical congregations in Jamaica that provoke spiritual experiences by performing penance and fasting and became known as "Spirit Baptists."[134]

The entrancement brought on by constant repetition of chants and dance movements also recalls the North American "ring shouts," described by Thomas Higginson in 1862 as "men, singing at the top of their voices, in one of their quaint, monotonous, endless, Negro-Methodist chants, with obscure syllables recurring constantly, and slight variations interwoven, all accompanied with a regular drumming of the feet and clapping of the hands, like castanets."[135] When Higginson made these comments, ring shouts were typically associated with Black mutual-aid and burial societies, known as "bands." As Richard Wade explains, these bands were "religious in impulse," yet "usually existed outside of church supervision. White ministers knew they existed and worried about their influence."[136] Even Black ministers had concerns about the rituals practiced by bands. Daniel Payne, one of the leaders of the African Methodist Episcopal Church, wrote about an encounter with a "band" in 1878 whose members performed "a ring" after the sermon, and "with coats off sung, clapped their hands and stamped their feet in a most ridiculous and heathenish way." Upon his urging that they put an end to this, "they stopped their dancing and clapping of hands, but remained singing and rocking their bodies to and fro" and told Payne that "sinners won't get converted unless there is a ring."[137]

Ring shouts have traditionally been associated with indigenous African rituals.[138] As early as 1862, Laura Towne wrote to a friend that, shortly after her arrival on Saint Helena Island, in South Carolina, she had "been to a 'shout,'" which she believed to be "certainly the remains of some old idol worship."[139] In his influential work *Slave Culture* (1988), Stuckey considered ring shouts one of the most important unifying elements of pre-Christian, indigenous African spirituality in the American diaspora.[140]

David Daniels, however, presented an alternative theory by suggesting that "ring shouts" may have been "framed by Kongolese Christianity."[141] Considering their connection to mutual-aid and burial societies, it is worth further exploring Daniels's theory and investigating whether ring shouts may, indeed, have evolved out of African rituals that appealed to a Catholic saint and the Christian Holy Spirit rather than an indigenous African divinity or ancestor spirit.

Certain Afro-Catholic brotherhood rituals have, in fact, much in common with North American ring shouts. For instance, an eighteenth-century source from the island of Príncipe noted that the local population used to express their gratitude for surviving a shipwreck "or other danger" by meeting "in a large room of the house, with a strum, to which one of the company . . . sings" while the others "close to the petitions, take it in their turns . . . to step round, called dancing, the whole clapping their hands continually," and repeating the same words over and over again. These spiritual exercises could last for "three or four days" and "perhaps twelve or sixteen hours at a time."[142] As José de Almada Negreiros explained, prayer sessions in the form of a ring dance were also common on the nearby island of São Tomé and essentially functioned as ex-votos to Catholic saints. The gatherings were organized by brotherhoods and known as *assembleias*. They typically involved a band, with drummers and flute players, and others dancing in the form of a circle, with one man standing in the middle, holding the brotherhood's banner.[143]

Similar ring dances accompanied by songs in call-and-response form occur, to this day, in Black Catholic brotherhoods' prayer sessions in Latin America. In Venezuela, for instance, Juan Liscano explained that *velorios* in honor of Saint John typically involve scenes in which "the men and women make a circle and sing and dance . . . taking each other by the hand."[144] A similar practice was identified by Iyanaga with regard to Brazilian *rezas*, where Catholic prayer sessions involve circle dances accompanied by drum music, handclapping, and call-and-response singing, known as *samba de roda* (samba of the circle). "On certain occasions," Iyanaga explains, this "*samba* can prompt possession trance dancing."[145]

We could also point to parallels between Payne's description of a shout and the ceremony John Codman observed when visiting a plantation near Rio de Janeiro in the 1860s. According to the American sea captain and writer, members of the Black community had "organized a church of their own" with "a priest from their own number." Services were started "by a general shout" that was followed by "a long, silent prostration of all hands upon the floor" and then "a chattering song . . . in African, with the exception of the chorus of 'Sancta Maria, ora pro nobis.'" It was performed by the congregation "sitting upon their haunches . . . clapp[ing] their hands" and ended with the priest "cross[ing] himself in every direction, whirling about like a dervish, then threw[ing] himself down, and [rising] again." After that, there was "music again, and that always vocal, while the congregation, standing, beat time both with hands and feet."[146]

These parallels to ring dances and shouts call for a reflection on other characteristics Black evangelical communities have in common with Afro-Catholic brotherhoods. One such commonality relates to the settling of conflicts and the imposing of discipline. Similar to "judges" in Afro-Catholic brotherhoods, William Francis Allen observed that, within early

Black Baptist communities, "the church was their court and all matters should be settled within it."[147] Moreover, as Sylvia Frey indicated, "spiritual pastors" often combined the functions of "ritual leaders, moral advisors, and political leaders" and "served as intermediaries between the slave and free communities," which corresponds to the functions of kings in Afro-Catholic brotherhoods.[148]

The most striking parallel between confraternities and Black evangelical churches is undoubtedly the combination of spirituality with forms of social and material support. As Sobel has argued, the earliest Black Baptist churches in North America "were technically no more than mutual-aid societies."[149] Thus, it was not by accident that Martha Jackson, born on a Louisiana plantation in 1836, recalled that "Our boss let us have our church and our 'sociation."[150] One could not thrive without the other. This characteristic was also highlighted by W. E. B. Du Bois, who observed in 1899, "The Negro church has become a center of social intercourse to a degree unknown in white churches," that "All movements for social betterment are apt to center in the churches," and that "Beneficial societies in endless number are formed here."[151] E. Franklin Frazier, in his classic study *The Negro Church in America* (1964), also explained the popularity of Black evangelical churches with reference to the provision of social aid and social cohesion, two essential characteristics of brotherhoods. As an example, he mentioned the African Methodist Episcopal Church in Philadelphia, dating to the 1790s, that developed out of the Free African Society, a fraternity that had been established several years earlier.[152]

There exist myriads of other examples of Black evangelical churches that developed out of or in connection to benevolent societies.[153] Similar to Afro-Catholic brotherhoods, these churches gave great importance to burial procedures. One of the first actions of the African Society, founded in the 1790s as the first Black evangelical church community in New York City, was the purchase of land for a cemetery. It also supported the purchase of coffins for those in need.[154] In Charleston, the Brown Fellowship Society, established in 1790, not only procured a burial ground for its members but also organized deathbed visitations, just like Afro-Catholic brotherhoods.[155] According to the authors of the Virginia Federal Writers' Program, African Americans dedicated so much of their attention to funerals that "the accusation that Negroes spend more on their loved ones' burials than they spend on them while alive is hardly an exaggeration."

The Writers' Program description of a Black funeral scene in Virginia reveals that Black evangelical funeral practices followed a basic structure that
parallels ancient Afro-Catholic brotherhood practices remarkably well.
When a member died, everyone "came quickly to pay his respects [and] all
night long friends would 'set' with the family and sing and chant over the
body," for proper respect to the departed required that "the body not be
left unattended until burial." During the wake, "The others would build
or purchase a coffin, clothe their departed brother decently, and accompany him to the Negro burying ground, chanting hymns along the way."[156]

This practice of chanting hymns, including the hand clapping, foot
tapping, and antiphonal singing that are so typical of African American
gospel music, also thrived in the context of Afro-Catholic brotherhoods.
The rhythmic singing in call-and-response form has characterized the way
in which African Catholics pray the rosary for centuries. For example, in his
report on a late seventeenth-century journey up the Congo River, Merolla
da Sorrento observed how in a marketplace in Lemba, a "large crowd, divided into two choirs" was singing "the rosary in the Kongolese tongue." He
also noted that people reacted to his sermon with "a great clapping of hands
and humming, which are tokens of great joy among these people," and that
"the rosary was being sung by women while they were working in the
fields."[157] We could also refer to the Cape Verde islands, where local folklorists demonstrated that certain drum rhythms accompanied by call-and-response songs, which to outsiders may seem like indigenous African surviv-
als, are derived from ancient "ritual enactments of the rosary prayer."[158]

Other practices of evangelical churches are virtual copies of Afro-
Catholic brotherhood customs. In nineteenth-century Missouri, for instance, the members of an African Methodist church used to elect their
"king," and in 1911 a report in the *Owego Gazette* revealed how members
of the Bethel African Methodist Church in New York's Tioga County used
to organize colorful parades accompanied by the beating of a drum. Not
unlike those who had in previous decades marched in one of the region's
Pinkster processions, participants "were grotesquely costumed, representing historical personages, who were gorgeously arrayed in discarded regalia
of fraternal societies."[159]

These many parallels shed new light on Giggie's observation that African American evangelical churches "appropriate[ed] many of the institutional resources and rituals of Black fraternal culture."[160] They also suggest

that scholars in past decades may have wrongly reduced the genesis of African American evangelical churches to a mixture of White Protestant and indigenous African elements and thereby overlooked a third source of influence, that of fraternal practices rooted in ancient Afro-Atlantic Catholic traditions. If seen from this perspective, the birth of Black evangelicalism should be understood not as a radical break with the past but, rather, as a process of transition from fraternal structures to new forms of community building that increasing numbers of Black people deemed necessary in view of rapidly changing social conditions. We should not forget that the old fraternal societies mainly served to attenuate the hardships, humiliation, oppression, and pain of slavery. The approaching abolition required the development of new societies adjusted to life in a postslavery society.

Interpreting the genesis of Black evangelical church communities/societies as a process that evolved out of mutual-aid and burial societies rooted in ancient Afro-Catholic brotherhood traditions also provides an answer to one of the greatest enigmas in the history of these churches: the sudden rejection of dancing. The "repudiation of dancing was neither eccentric nor an isolated phenomenon," Dena Epstein confirms, "but widespread and quite general among both white and black converts to various evangelical sects."[161] When Charles Lyell visited the Hopeton plantation in Georgia in the 1840s, he enthusiastically reported that "above twenty violins have been silenced by the Methodist missionaries."[162] Such efforts would not have succeeded, however, had Black community leaders not encouraged this. The rejection of dancing by Black evangelicals was, in fact, largely a voluntary decision. Significantly, Willis Winn of Texas recalled, "When I joined the Church, I burned my fiddle up."[163]

A revealing example of this radical change in attitude toward dancing can be found in Zephaniah Kingsley's report on the arrival of a new group of enslaved people from Georgia and South Carolina on his plantation on the banks of Saint Johns River, Florida, in 1812. They were accompanied by a man "calling himself a minister," who encouraged the enslaved individuals to form "private societies under church regulations, where all were brothers and sisters, and, under an oath of the most horrid penalty, never to tell or divulge any crime that would bring any brother or sister into trouble," but rather "to lay all the blame on those who had not united with them, and who, of necessity, were obliged to join the fraternity, as soon as possible, in their own defense." Ultimately, all those who had initially been reluctant to give up the old traditions joined the new fraternity. As a result, Kingsley explained, "Myself and the overseer became completely divested of all authority over the Negroes. The latter even went as far as to consult the head men of the church whether or not, according to their religion, my orders ought to be obeyed." Remarkably, Kingsley reacted to this development by encouraging "as much as possible dancing, merriment, and dress," which was countered by the Black minister, who preached that it was "sinful to dance" and "if they did, they were to go to a place where they would be tormented with fire and brimstone for all eternity."[164]

Scholars have long been puzzled about the apparent ease with which Black converts abandoned dancing. After all, this decision stands in contrast to claims that African Americans adapted Protestant rituals to fit indigenous African traditions.[165] John Catron confirmed that the rejection of dancing in Black evangelical churches contradicts "claims by many authors that blacks chose evangelicalism because it allowed them to freely express their African cultures," but failed to provide an explanation for why dancing suddenly lost its appeal other than that it was opposed by missionaries.[166]

If viewed from an Afro-Catholic perspective, however, this rejection was a logical decision. We should not forget that, in a brotherhood tradition, dancing was never intended as a form of entertainment. Not unlike fasting or praying, it was closely associated with the making of vows and with the belief in purgatory. With the arrival of evangelical Christianity, however, people ceased to believe in purgatory and the power of saints. As a result, vows became meaningless and hence also the tradition of specific performances to honor them. What had once contributed to one's ascension to heaven now came to be seen as a potential obstacle to reaching that very goal.

Nowhere in North America has this transition from mutual-aid societies with Afro-Atlantic Catholic roots to evangelical churches been more clearly documented than in the Georgia and South Carolina Lowcountry.

MUTUAL-AID SOCIETIES AND CHURCHES
IN THE LOWCOUNTRY

One of the most eccentric African American evangelical churches is the United House of Prayer for All People of the Church on the Rock of the

Apostolic Faith, established in the early twentieth century by Charles Manuel "Sweet Daddy" Grace. It is known for its colorful brass-band and flag-bearer parades, described by a member of Georgia's Writer's Program in Savannah as featuring "the Holy Prophet" Grace, seated "upon a lofty throne" in the company of his "queen" and protected by a "double line of uniformed guards."[167] Grace, whose real name was Marcelino Manuel da Graça, had immigrated from the Cape Verde islands to the United States in 1902, when he was in his twenties. It is, therefore, probably not by accident that his use of banners, music, and a king and queen guarded by soldiers echoes Cape Verdean *tabanca* parading traditions. Yet, as Gary McDonogh observed, none of this was perceived as strange or exotic by African Americans because similar parading traditions were "deeply engrained in black Savannah folklore."[168]

McDonogh was right. As an example, we could refer to Henry Benjamin Whipple's description of the Black society parade in Saint Marys, near the Georgia Sea Islands, in December 1843. According to the Episcopalian bishop, it consisted of "a corps of staff officers with red sashes, mock epaulettes & goose quill feathers, and a band of music composed of 3 fiddles, 1 tenor & 1 bass drum, 2 triangles & 2 tambourines and they are marching up & down the streets in great style." They were followed by "others, some dancing, some walking & some hopping, other singing, all as lively as lively can be. . . . Here they come again with flags flying and music enough to deafen one & they have now two fifes to increase their noise." While Whipple didn't mention the presence of a king, he noticed that they "levy contributions on all the whites they see," which recalls brotherhood practices.[169] Other sources from the Lowcountry Sea Islands mention that Black community leaders in the region once used royal titles. Rosanna Williams, for instance, told an interviewer of the George Writers' Program that her "granpapa wuz 'Golla' Dennerson, King uh his tribe"—with *Golla* being an abbreviation of *Angola*[170]—and Sam Gadsden, a Black man born on Edisto Island in 1882, recalled, "We had some black kings around here in the old days . . . and they really ruled the colored people."[171]

These references to Black kings can be associated with Thomas Howard's observation in 1888 that, among Black Baptists on the Sea Islands, "Those united in church fellowship are usually banded for mutual assistance. The congregation is a community; if one member suffers, the other members relieve," and with William Francis Allen's argument, in 1861, that "The Sea Islands had myriad societies" and "To a great extent, every black church was a society."[172] In order to explain these parallels to brotherhoods, it is worth making a connection to Catron's 2016 study on Black evangelicalism, where we read that "Lowcountry South Carolina and Georgia in the eighteenth century were the most culturally African regions in British North America," and yet "more black Christians lived in the Lowcountry than anywhere else in the Anglophone world." The reason, Catron argued, is the exceptionally high number of enslaved Africans in the region who had roots in Kongo/Angola and who identified as Catholic.[173] Jason Young, too, is convinced that their "prior experience and exposure . . . to Christianity in Kongo undoubtedly colored their interactions with Protestant missionaries."[174]

It is, in this respect, important to realize that the presence of Catholic elements in the South Carolina and Georgia Black communities represented more than just a religious concern to the colonial authorities. After all, the struggle against Iberian, Catholic dominance in the Americas had been an important rallying cry in support of England's colonial ambitions from the outset. As Rebecca Anne Goetz pointed out, "Almost all pro-colonization literature emphasized plans for stemming the Catholic tide."[175] In a border region such as the Carolinas, which had been conquered from the Spanish and had experienced decades of Anglo-Iberian warfare, these concerns were particularly relevant. We should not forget that many, if not most, of the Native Americans in the region—who made up as much as to 30 percent of the initial enslaved population—had been influenced by Spanish Catholicism. As Brown has indicated, "In a world in which Roman Catholic Spanish . . . settlers presented a threat to British colonial interests in North America, the religious rivalry would have resulted in a close scrutiny of any group that openly presented itself as Roman Catholic."[176]

Moreover, this was also a region where slaveholders lived with a constant concern about enslaved people fleeing to Spanish-controlled Florida and, as the 1739 Stono Rebellion revealed, organizing armed uprisings to reach that goal. It is not by accident that, in the immediate aftermath of this rebellion, the South Carolina Assembly decided to place a prohibitive duty on the import of enslaved people and to use this money to stimulate, instead, the settlement of "poor [European] Protestants."[177] By 1752 it had become clear that replacing enslaved Africans with "poor Protestants" to do the backbreaking work in the colony was an illusion, and the duty was repealed. Yet, plantation owners now deliberately avoided Africans from the region of Kongo/Angola and preferred to purchase West Africans, who, as Henry Laurens explained in a letter of 1756, were "better esteemed by our people than Angolas."[178]

These concerns applied even more in Georgia, due to its geographical proximity to the Florida border. While the 1732 vision of Georgia as a colony of yeoman farmers, without slavery, has traditionally been explained in terms of the desired salvation of the English poor through labor and of European Protestants from Catholic persecution, there can be no doubt that James Oglethorpe and the Georgia Trustees must have been aware of the difficulties in preventing enslaved people from escaping to Florida. In a letter of 1739 to the Crown, for instance, Scottish Presbyterians from Darian pointed out that "the nearness of the Spaniard, who have proclaimed freedom to all slaves who run away from their masters, makes it impossible for us to keep them without more labour to guard them."[179] Johann Martin Boltzius, a German-born minister who associated with a group of (Protestant) Salzburger settlers in Georgia, even spoke of enslaved Africans and Spanish Florida as "cruel enemies within & without."[180]

It is well known that Whitefield sided with colonists who (successfully) advocated for the introduction of slavery in Georgia in 1748, which justifies the critique by recent scholars against the tradition of reading abolition into early Protestant missions. As Gerbner has argued, early Protestant missionaries were responsible for "a series of laws and opinions that strengthened slavery in order to encourage slave conversion."[181] These Protestant missions could also be understood from a political perspective, however, since they ultimately aligned with a broader British policy to fight Iberian influence in the Americas and, especially in the case of South Carolina and Georgia, to find strategies to discourage enslaved people from fleeing to Catholic territory.

The first to report on Catholic elements among the enslaved population in South Carolina was the former French Huguenot turned SPG missionary Francis Le Jau. During his 1710 campaign in the Saint James parish of Goose Creek, Le Jau learned that some among the enslaved population "were born and baptized among the Portuguese" and "express a great desire to receive the H. communion amongst us." This prompted him to establish that these men, whom he believed to originate from the Portuguese island of Madeira, would only be admitted to communion upon "abjuring the errors of the Romish Church." Le Jau clarified that he "framed a short model of submission grounded upon some Popish tenets which they told me of their own accord, without troubling them with things they know not: I require of them their renouncing of those particular points, the chief of which is praying to the saints." In a later report he also referred to a Black woman from Guadeloupe, whom he forced to abjure Catholicism in order to be admitted to communion. Le Jau shared Neau's mixture of contempt for Catholicism with admiration for its missionary strategy, which he copied when employing converted Black people as catechists and taking "all the care I can that they instruct one another when they have time; there are a few men in several plantations to whom I have recommended to do that good service to the others, those men are religious, zealous, honest, they can read well."[182]

The gradual expansion of Protestantism among the enslaved did not imply that the latter spontaneously gave up all their religious and social traditions. That the earliest Black Protestant communities in the region held on to certain Afro-Atlantic Catholic elements is visible in the reports of the Methodist missionary Thomas Turpin. When Turpin reached out to the Black population on the South Carolina Sea Islands in 1833, he reported that "almost all of them [were] under Baptist influence." However, he added that they "scarcely ever saw the pastor of the Church to which they belonged" and, for this reason, "had societies organized among themselves." The latter "appeared to be very much under the influence of Roman Catholic principles." Members of these societies "do penance" for their "sins," and "there were three degrees of punishment for three degrees of offenses." Turpin reassured his Methodist readers, however, that he had managed to "establish a better principle of religion among them" and that "those societies are nearly broken up."[183]

It is surprising that Margaret Washington Creel, in her classic study *"A Peculiar People"* (1988), rejected Turpin's observation that Black Baptist societies on the Sea Islands were influenced by Catholic traditions with the blunt comment "Obviously they were not."[184] Her assumption that, on the Sea Islands, "early black exposure to Christianity" had nothing to do with Catholicism but "was largely the work of those previously influenced by George Whitefield, and of post-war Methodists" is questionable considering that the vast majority of enslaved Black people arriving on the Sea Islands up to the 1740s originated from the Kongo/Angola region, where Catholicism was part of the religious culture that many had grown up with.[185] In fact, when Creel observed that Black people on the Sea Islands embraced Christianity selectively, "fusing Christianity with African traditions," she was referring not to a new phenomenon but to a syncretic process initiated in Kongo in the fifteenth century.[186] We could also refer to the earlier quoted report mentioning Portuguese-speaking, Catholic Black people from Angola in the context of the Stono Rebellion; to escapees who arrived in Florida saying their Catholic prayers in Kikongo; and to Le Jau's explicit confirmation of the existence of Black Catholics in the region. That Kongolese influences were passed on for several generations can also be illustrated with reference to language. When, in the context of the Federal Writers' Project in the 1930s, members of the Sea Islands' Black community were asked to identify some "Golla words," Tonie Houston mentioned "*musungo* tobacco, *mulafo* whiskey, and *sisure* chicken. A cow was called *gombay* and a hog *gulluh*."[187] Every single one of these words derives from Kikongo: *musungo* from *(n)sung(a)* (tobacco/perfume), *mulafo* from *(ma)lafu* or *malavu* (alcohol), *sisure* from *(n)sus(s)u* (chicken), *gombay* from *ngombe* (cow), and *gulluh* from *ngulu* (hog). The continuous use of these words, albeit in a creolized form, proves that Kongolese elements continued to be passed on among Black people living on the Sea Islands until at least the early twentieth century.

In order to explain why Turpin later excused himself for his report, Creel commented that the readers of Methodist literature "wanted favorable, optimistic reports" and were much more interested in stories about "the conversion of an old African-born slave than to outline what appeared to be latent types of 'Roman Catholic' ceremonies," which suggests that other missionary encounters with Afro-Atlantic Catholics may have remained unmentioned.[188] We could also rephrase Creel's words by stating that, more than just a matter of favorable reports, this information touched the core identity of Baptist and Methodist Churches. After all, the evangelical credo of both churches reflected itself in a missionary ethos, one that, in adverse circumstances, had opened the eyes of the blind to let them behold the Christian light. This self-image required brave missionary stories about heroic work among the heathen rather than reports on how people were being lured away from their Afro-Catholic traditions.

While Turpin's case is exceptional in its recognition of Catholic elements in the region, the earliest ethnographic studies of Black societies on the Sea Islands confirm strong parallels with Afro-Catholic brotherhood traditions. For instance, when Mason Crum was doing fieldwork on the islands of Edisto and Saint Helena, he pointed out that people were attached to funerals in great style, to which "the secret societies turn out in force with all members in full regalia."[189] In his study about Saint Helena, Thomas Jackson Woofter spoke of "lodges and societies" that "hold their principal annual 'turn out' in connection with the church," to which they come "with banners, sashes, and embroidered aprons," and "the minister gives them a special sermon" because "they remember their dead and honor their living."[190]

These "lodges and societies" undoubtedly relate to the "bury leagues" described by the South Carolina author Julia Mood Peterkin in her attempted ethnography *Roll, Jordan, Roll* (1933). As Melissa Cooper has shown, Peterkin's work needs to be considered with caution due to the author's tendency to embellish historical facts.[191] Her detailed descriptions of mutual-aid and burial societies, however, are credible and largely correspond to Creel's research findings that such organizations were "organized by the slaves themselves" and allowed them to practice "their own version of Christianity."[192] According to Peterkin, "every neighborhood has a local chapter," and members "pay a small sum each week to a common fund which provides for the next funeral." They are also "required to attend every burial unless hindered by providence. They all wear white gloves, and women carry white paper flowers, and officers who carry the banners of the organization wear large gaudy badges." The dues "must be paid promptly and every member must visit the sick and take presents of money or food. To fail in the least of these obligations means to be dropped from the League, but nobody fails." She also explained that their burial services "were long with much mourning and praying and singing," and "lightwood torches gave light for the burial and for marching round and round the grave." This way, "The dead are helped by thoughtfulness just as the living are, and the very poorest people must struggle to pay insurance dues to the Bury League, not only for themselves but for every member of their families." In what is perhaps one of the most touching scenes written about Black life on the Sea Islands, Peterkin showed the grief of a father who had postponed paying the dues for his baby son, and, upon the son's sudden death, couldn't count on the Bury League. He was, therefore, forced to give his child a shameful burial "in a simple box of pine boards."

The carpenter consoled the weeping father by reassuring him that "the child was too young to have sin and was bound to reach heaven," which recalls the Catholic folk belief that one should not cry over the death of innocent children because one's tears would wet these little angels' wings and thereby make their flight to heaven harder.[193]

Here, again, scholars have traditionally pointed to a variety of indigenous African societies to explain the origins of the Sea Islands' mutual-aid and burial societies.[194] It reflects a tendency to take for granted that the development of Black Christianity was characterized by a welcoming attitude vis-à-vis indigenous African influences, a phenomenon that Brown labeled as the "*kalunga*," the "all-encompassing physical and conceptual world inhabited by African-descended people."[195] One wonders, however, why Afro-Atlantic Catholic communities in the Sea Islands would have displayed such an all-embracing *kalunga* attitude, whereas similar communities in Curaçao and Haiti disdained unbaptized newcomers as "asses" or "horses," and in the Virgin Islands even forced them to submit to a humiliating whipping ritual. While it is certainly true that the variants of Catholicism that developed in Kongo and other parts of Africa with a historically strong Portuguese influence built on pre-Christian traditions, it is questionable to deduce thereby that such variants were characterized, as Young suggested, "by a notable fluidity and adaptability of belief," to the point that Kongolese Catholics in the Lowcountry would have eagerly embraced rituals from indigenous African societies.[196] If we compare the situation in the Lowcountry to that of other parts of the Americas with a high concentration of Afro-Atlantic Catholics, it is much more likely that the mutual-aid and burial societies in the region have their roots in Afro-Atlantic Catholic brotherhoods. Significantly, one such society was called The Brother and Sister of the Weeping Mary.[197]

The assumption that Black communities in the region were organized in fraternities prior to being approached by Protestant missionaries also provides an explanation for the reason why, after their conversion, they continued to self-organize material and spiritual assistance. Reports on this desire can be found as early as in 1784, when the German Johann Schoepf noted in Saint Augustine that a group of Black people who had entered Florida with Loyalist settlers from Georgia and South Carolina had formed "an association . . . of the Anabaptist sect . . . in which one of their own countrymen, who has set himself up to be their teacher, holds services."[198] That Black people would form their own "associations," build "pray's/praise houses," and have their own "teachers" holding "services" was not what Protestant missionaries had hoped for. Le Jau was convinced that "those men have not judgment enough to make a good use of their learning" and Turpin made no secret of his ambition to replace Black societies by "a better principle of religion."[199] Not surprisingly, thus, we find endless complaints by White missionaries about Black societies being "in the hands of the colored people who are actively engaged against us" and exercising an "influence against us which is remarkably strong"; about Black evangelicalism being riddled with "fatal doctrines," "idolatrous extravagances and superstitions," which made it into a "pseudo religion"; and about surreptitious attempts by Black people to "incorporate their superstitious rites with a purer system of instruction, producing thereby a hybrid, crude, and undefinable medley of truth and falsehood."[200]

As Henry Louis Gates Jr. has rightly argued, "It should not surprise us that enslaved Africans in North America did not accept Christianity . . . exactly as white Americans practiced it or pictured it" and decided to reshape it "in their own images, to satisfy their own spiritual and practical needs."[201] Indeed, for communities that had been accustomed to organizing themselves into fraternities, the only acceptable Christian congregation was one under their own control.

In spite of their initial skepticism, White Baptist and Methodist church leaders ultimately understood the importance of granting African Americans the necessary leeway to build their own congregations. As Catron confirms, "One of the key reasons for the evangelicals' success among people of African descent arose from their willingness to allow blacks to preach to their fellows and to have real power within their churches."[202] Even in the South, Raboteau adds, White control over Black congregations was only nominal, "since black exhorts and deacons functioned in reality as the pastors of their people. . . . American blacks made evangelical Christianity their own by assuming, whenever possible, leadership of their own religious life."[203]

This desire for autonomy should not be restricted to evangelical communities, however. As early nineteenth-century reports indicate, it existed just as much among African American Catholics. When visiting Jekyll Island, in Georgia, in the 1840s, Bishop Ignatius Reynolds learned that Black Catholics there had their own chapel, known as the "Negro chapel."

His predecessor, John England, had noted that Black Catholics "have great charity in assisting each other in time of sickness or distress, not only with temporal aid, if it be required, but by spiritual reading, prayer, and consolation," and are "exceedingly attentive to have the funeral of an associate respectably attended, and not only to have the offices of the church performed, but to continue the charity of prayer for a considerable time after death, for the repose of the souls of their friends."[204] These words reveal how deeply their understanding of Catholicism was influenced by brotherhood practices. It should, as such, be no surprise that in mid-nineteenth-century Charleston, Black people established numerous charitable organizations, such as Saint John's Burial Society and Saint Joseph's Benevolent Society, modeled upon confraternities.[205] In Baltimore, Black Catholics formed an independent Society of the Holy Family in 1843 that sponsored Masses for the dead, engaged in charity activities, and gathered to sing hymns and recite the rosary. "The self-governing feature of this group is noteworthy," Morris MacGregor pointed out, "because it occurred during an era when church authorities . . . kept close control over all lay organizations."[206] In fact, Davis's well-known criticism that Black Catholics in America "had to fight for their faith, but their fight was often with members of their own household" also applies to autonomously operating confraternities.[207] As Gillard explained, church authorities monitored Black confraternities closely because they tended to perceive Black societies as "a hindrance to conversions" and believed that Black "benevolent societies and social organizations" had a "negative effect" on people's behavior.[208]

Considering their own fraternal roots, it is not without irony that Black evangelical church leaders reacted with similar suspicion when, in the aftermath of the Civil War, American society experienced a new fraternity boom. As Giggie explained, the popularity of new fraternities—such as the Odd Fellows, the Knights of Pythias, the Mosaic Templars, the United Brotherhood of Friendship, the Grand Compact Masons, and the Prince Hall Masons—caused fears among evangelical leaders that "lodges might displace churches as the dominant voluntary institution in black life." The Baptist preacher T. O. Fuller even decided that "Members were not received into the Tabernacle Baptist Church . . . if they held membership in a secret society." Encouraged by the fact that these fraternities "banned some of their more objectionable public practices, such as parading on Sundays," church leaders ultimately opted for cooperation instead of conflict upon the "realization that most blacks viewed fraternal orders and churches as partners in the new emerging structural ecology of their religion." As a concession to the fraternities, they also agreed to pay "far more attention to the role of insignia in church life."[209]

As will be shown in the next section, the historical evolution from mutual-aid societies, rooted in ancient Afro-Atlantic Catholic brotherhood traditions, to evangelical church communities can also be illustrated with reference to individual converts.

WILLFULLY FORGETTING

In 1872, the *Albany Daily Evening Times* reported on Diana Mingo, a formerly enslaved woman from Schodack, in New York's Rensselaer County, whose name [Do]mingo reveals Afro-Iberian heritage. The newspaper informed its readers that, in her youth, Mingo used to "take part in the unique celebrations of her race on 'Pinxter' . . . hill . . . in the company of 'King Charley' (a sort of leviathan Ethiopian dressed in scarlet coat with gold lace trimmings and other showy uniform)." After joining "the organization of the colored Methodist Church," however, Mingo became "an exemplary member," and "this half-heathen observance was strongly contrasted by the religious character of her long life in church."[210]

A similar trajectory can be observed in the life of Sojourner Truth, formerly called Isabel, who was born in 1797 in a predominantly Dutch-speaking village in New York's Ulster County. Research by Margaret Washington revealed that she may have had Kongolese roots.[211] In spite of the fact that her mother had acculturated to Dutch customs and only spoke Dutch to her child, she did, in fact, give her daughter the typically Iberian name Isabel rather than a Dutch one. Her heritage may also explain Truth's active participation at the annual king elections during Pinkster and her connection to a type of "society" that allowed enslaved people to "use their influence" to obtain concessions from slaveholders, as we read in her *Narrative* from 1850.[212] Moreover, the many references to Mary in Truth's songs and speeches, including the famous "Are'n't I a Woman?," as well as her decision to literally bargain with God over His assistance — "I could help you, as you can me" — and to fast in order to obtain grace, point more toward an Afro-Catholic than a Dutch Calvinist approach to the Divine.[213]

Similar to Mingo, Truth radically distanced herself from this heritage after she joined an evangelical church. It is interesting to note that, in her *Narrative*, she made an explicit link between her rebirth as evangelical Christian and the annual Pinkster celebration on Pentecost. After escaping from slavery, she voiced a surprising desire to return to John Dumont, the slaveholder who had beaten her, broken his promise to grant her freedom, and sold her son Peter. Her justification for looking "back into Egypt" was the approaching Pinkster festival, where everything looked "so pleasant." At that very moment, we read, "God revealed himself to her, with all the suddenness of a flash of lightning," which made her decide to embrace a new life as an evangelical Christian.[214] She subsequently dropped her Afro-Catholic name and henceforth called herself Sojourner Truth, decided to no longer participate at the annual Pinkster king festivities, and, later, even claimed that "she never had any learning" and did not even know "that Jesus Christ was the Son of God" until the day she joined an evangelical community.[215] These words are surprising, considering that she herself acknowledged in her *Narrative* that her mother had taught her the Lord's Prayer.[216] It seems that, rather than conveying a factual truth, these words reflect a desire to willfully forget her previous beliefs after her rebirth as an evangelical Christian.

Truth's decision to turn her back on the Pinkster king celebrations and drop a name rooted in her community's Afro-Iberian history could also be understood in a broader context as a symbolic moment of change in the history of African American Christianity. It reflects a conviction that, with the arrival of abolition, a new era was beginning, one in which the ancient Afro-Catholic heritage would no longer be of use. With this mindset, it should not be a surprise that African Americans began to distance themselves from king elections and Iberian Catholic names such as Isabel and (Do)mingo. To these newborn Christians, this heritage had become an embarrassment that only brought back memories of a time when they and their fellow brothers and sisters still lived a life in slavery.

CONCLUSION

The core idea of this final chapter is that the genesis of African American evangelical churches should not be reduced to a mixture of White Protestant and indigenous African elements, and that a third source of influence

deserves to be highlighted: elements rooted in mutual-aid and burial societies modeled upon ancient Afro-Atlantic Catholic traditions.

As an example of how this new perspective encourages us to look at the
history of African American Christianity with different eyes, we could
mention Clarence Deming's observations about some of the earliest Black
churches in the nineteenth-century Mississippi Delta. During his visit to
the region in 1883, Deming noticed that the common structure of these
houses of worship was a "rough, barn-like exterior, whitewashed, and with
seating capacity for perhaps a hundred auditors." Inside, there were "coarse
benches, cobwebbed board walls, a long desk and platform made of unfin-
ished lumber, [and] a dingy kerosene chandelier with one or two lights,"
and "behind the so-called pulpit" one could see "a line of tawdry colored
prints pasted on the boards depicting scriptural themes like Moses and the
burning bush, the ark on Ararat, and Daniel with the lions." Deming concluded by highlighting that one object, in particular, was greatly desired
though often beyond the financial means of congregations: a church bell.
Undeterred by this constraint, they worked out creative solutions, one of
which consisted of "a rusty buzz-saw hung by a rope" that, "when stuck by
a stone," gave a "cracked note to summon worshippers together."[217]

If analyzed from a traditional perspective, the fact that these Black
congregations went to great lengths to produce the sound of a bell would
typically be explained as reflecting the desire to have a church with the
same characteristics as those attended by the White elite. Scholars who
have stressed that Black communities were eager to incorporate indigenous
African elements into their church rituals would question that assumption
and, rather, explore the importance of bell sounds in African traditions. As
an example, they might hold up the importance in Kongolese culture of
the double bell or *lunga*, which, in remembrance of the legendary first king
who introduced iron technology to his people, was rung at royal ceremonies and the departure of the army for war.[218]

The new perspective introduced in this book underscores the importance of including the long African history of Catholicism into our analysis. In doing so, we come to realize that church bells have played a crucial
role in the dissemination of Christianity in Africa and that African Catholics developed a strong emotional attachment to this musical instrument.
One of the earliest references to it can be found in Rui de Pina's fifteenth-century account of the Kingdom of Kongo, where we read that the

Portuguese King João II sent not only crucifixes, chalices, banners, and candlesticks to Kongo, but also church bells.[219] The importance bells acquired among African Christians can be illustrated with a Portuguese report about the *praça* of Bissau from the 1790s, in which Bernardino António de Andrade claimed that "the number of Christians dispersed through the distant hinterlands is infinite" and that whenever a priest went there, his arrival was announced by the ringing of a bell. Thereupon, "all these dispersed Christians gather . . . next to a cross . . . some to confess or to receive the sacrament of the Eucharist, others to be baptized [or to request] prayers for the souls of their parents and family members who are buried in the fields."[220] In Kongo, the importance of church bells was such that the kingdom's capital, and, by extension, the kingdom itself, became popularly known as *Kongo dia Ngunga* (Kongo of the Bell).[221]

This historical connection cautions us not to automatically assume that church bells were a phenomenon new to enslaved Africans upon their arrival in the Americas, or to spontaneously relate the emotional connection Black church communities in America developed with this instrument to the imitation of White customs or to indigenous African traditions. Naturally, such assumptions remain speculative because we will never know what drove congregations in nineteenth-century Mississippi to go to such lengths in producing something that sounded like a church bell. What can be said with certainty, however, is that the ancient name of Kongo's capital city was passed on for generations, to the point that the Alliance of Bakongo resistance movement in (the then still Belgian colony of) Congo called its periodical *Kongo dia Ngunga*.[222] Data from Cuba reveal that the recollection of this history was also passed on among descendants of enslaved Kongolese in the Americas. In fact, when interviewed in the early twentieth century, a formerly enslaved man recalled that "the *Congo Reales* are Kongos who in Africa are called *Angunga* because, in their city, they used to have a church bell (*angunga*)."[223] This recollection of Kongo's religious culture also has relevance to the United States. As we have seen, interviews conducted by the Federal Writers' Project reveal that members of the Sea Islands' Black community still used Kikongo terms in the 1930s. This evidence of the long-lasting influence of cultural elements from the Kongo region in North America renders legitimacy to the plea not to ignore Africa's long Catholic history when studying the development of African American Christianity.

We may conclude with a reference to Richard Burton's report from the 1860s on a visit to Soyo, the western part of the ancient Kongo kingdom. When entering an old church in Pinda, the region's capital, the British geographer saw "a lot of old church gear, the Virgin (our Lady of Pinda), saints, and crucifixes, a tank-like affair of iron that acted as font, and tattered bundles of old music-scores in black and red ink." Nevertheless, he concluded that "all traces of Catholicism had disappeared." Burton did notice one more object of particular importance, "a bell" that "hung to a dwarf gallows" and was "dated 1700." It bore the inscription "Si Deus com nobis qis (sic) contra nos?"[224]

Conclusion

In October 1991, workers in Lower Manhattan accidentally discovered a burial ground dating back to the seventeenth century that contained the intact remains of 419 Black people. They were taken to Howard University for anthropological examination and, in 2003, returned to Manhattan to be solemnly reburied in what is now known as the African Burial Ground National Monument. Along the way they were honored in a series of tribute ceremonies, staring at Howard University's Rankin Memorial Chapel and continuing to Maryland's Prince Hall Masonic Lodge, the Mother African Union Church in Wilmington, the Mother Bethel A. M. E. Church in Philadelphia, the Bethany Baptist Church in Newark, and Liberty State Park in Jersey City. After an Arrival Ceremony at South and Wall Streets, where New York's slave market used to be, they proceeded to the African Burial Ground Memorial Site, where a commemorative vigil took place before the final Public Tribute and Reinterment Ceremony on October 4, 2003.[1] No memorial service at a Catholic church was included. This is unfortunate considering the likelihood that at least some of the people whose remains had been uncovered identified as Catholic.

The fact that no Catholic memorial service took place is regrettable, though not surprising. The history of African American Christianity in this nation has been studied almost exclusively from a Protestant perspective. "Black Catholics have been left on the margins of inquiry," Matthew Cressler wrote, because they fail to fit "into our comfortable narratives."[2] Scholars are naturally aware of the presence of Black Catholics in colonial America, but these have typically been perceived as a passive community. "Catholicism among black slaves in America," Randall Miller argued, "left no legacy of resistance" and "built no solid foundation for future black social and political activity."[3]

Black expressions of Protestant Christian devotion, however, have traditionally enjoyed a much more favorable interpretation. Black evangelicalism tends to be associated with the African American striving for cultural and spiritual autonomy. Theirs is not a history of passivity, but of Black people as heroic agents who bravely organized secret gatherings and held inflammatory sermons, risking their livelihood in defense of faith and paving a path to liberation that would ultimately lead to Martin Luther King Jr. and the civil rights movement. In this heroic narrative, Black Catholics have remained conspicuously absent. "In the midst of celebrations of black pride and rediscoveries of black culture," Raboteau wrote, "some wondered where black Catholics fit. . . . Were they not, after all, blacks in a white church [and] had not African American culture been overwhelmingly Protestant?"[4]

This book sought to challenge this narrative by pointing to the importance of an Afro-Atlantic Catholic substratum in the history of African American Christianity. It argued that the traditional focus on Protestantism has led to a distorted understanding of the meaning of the Christian faith to African Americans and failed to answer questions of crucial importance: Why did Black people embrace the religion of the very same people who were responsible for the enslavement of their ancestors? If, as some have argued, Christianity was thrust upon these people by those who bore responsibility for an African cultural and religious genocide, how then are we to understand that so many of their descendants have come to embrace this faith in such a passionate way?

This book did not react to these challenging questions by insisting on the indigenous African features of early Black evangelical churches; rather, it stressed the importance of acknowledging that Christianity is also an African religion and that it was perceived as such by many enslaved people. It provided historical evidence that unequivocally demonstrated that charter generations all over the Americas included substantial numbers of Afro-Atlantic Catholics, who were as proud of their Christian identity as of their African origins. Their legacy, it claimed, is of crucial importance to understanding the further evolution of Black Christianity in the Americas because these charter generations built the foundations for future Black religious, social, and political activity.

The book started with a reference to Andrew Saxon, an escapee in eighteenth-century New York, who was labeled as Roman Catholic by his owner. The latter also seemed convinced that, even as a fugitive, Saxon would continue to take pride in his Catholic faith, displaying it openly via the crosses embroidered on his clothing. This man's decision to publicly identify himself as Catholic in a profoundly hostile environment teaches us that we misconceive Black pride if we associate it exclusively with indigenous African or Islamic heritage. In fact, as the Brazilian scholar Marina de Mello e Souza has argued, to many enslaved Africans, especially those originating from the Kongo region, "Catholicism represented a link to their native Africa."[5]

It is, therefore, a mistake to relate Black Catholicism to passivity or to assume that theirs is a history devoid of resistance. Considering the virulent anti-Catholic mood in eighteenth-century New York, Saxon's defense of his faith can unquestionably be classified as an expression of Black pride and resistance. As the circumstances leading up to the 1739 Stono Rebellion show, Catholicism even inspired enslaved Africans to one of the largest uprisings in North American history.

In order to understand the underlying reasons for this, it is important to move away from the simplistic view of Africa during the era of the transatlantic slave trade as a virgin, untouched continent, where only indigenous traditions were considered truly African. After all, the African history of Catholicism started in the fifteenth century, and the religion was embraced by locals long before the first enslaved Africans arrived on North American shores. Not unlike Islam, Catholicism was, in multiple African variants, the faith they had grown up with. It was *their* religion.

While the total number of Afro-Atlantic Catholics was small in comparison to the millions of others who arrived in the Americas without any knowledge of Christianity, they still had a profound influence on the development of Black diaspora communities. In many, if not most, places in the Americas, Afro-Atlantic Catholics played a dominant role in the charter generations that laid the social foundations on which enslaved communities were to be built. Using their shared familiarity with Iberian social practices, Afro-Atlantic Catholics were the first Black community to transcend ethnic boundaries in America. Even as far north as Manhattan, Africans from Cape Verde, São Tomé, Kongo, and other parts of Africa with a historically strong Portuguese influence bonded over the Afro-Iberian identity markers they shared.

Historical documents reveal the importance of one identity marker in particular: brotherhoods. Hence, this book concludes that the history of African American Christianity goes hand in hand with that of Black mutual-aid and burial societies and that, in spite of major transformations triggered by changing local conditions, the charter generations' fraternal structures proved of key importance to the development of Black Christianity in the Americas. The crucial factor in understanding the remarkable longevity of these structures is the importance of solidarity, care, leadership, assistance, consolation, respectability, and pride, to which successive generations of enslaved communities continued to respond with the organization of mutual-aid societies modeled upon the charter generation's brotherhoods. They did so because the only people they could really trust were each other.

The theory that Black Baptist and Methodist churches in North America built on older layers rooted in Afro-Iberian fraternal traditions represents a revolutionary new perspective on the history of African American Christianity. It rejects the problematic assumption of the Great Awakening that Black people had lived in darkness until the day White preachers opened their eyes to behold the Christian light. Rather, it argues that the foundations of African American Christianity date back to the charter generations and that the later wave of evangelical conversion should be understood as the continuation of a process that was initiated in the fifteenth century on the Iberian Peninsula and the African Atlantic islands.

When the focus shifts to Afro-Atlantic Catholics, the image of Black Catholics in the broader history of African American Christianity changes dramatically. From passive bystanders they transform into active pioneers who adjusted and subsequently disseminated in America a form of Christianity with African roots: pre-Tridentine in nature, skeptical of outside control, and with a firm commitment to mutual aid and solidarity. A form of Christianity, in other words, composed of brothers and sisters who proudly call their churches "African" in the awareness that there is no contradiction in being Christian and being proud of one's African heritage.

NOTES

1. *The New-York Gazette,* August 27, 1733.

2. Hodges, *Root and Branch*, 93–98; Linebaugh and Rediker, *The Many-Headed Hydra*, 186–90; Lepore, *New York Burning*, 181.

3. Horsmanden, *The New York Conspiracy*, 139, 149, 182, 378.

4. *The New-York Weekly Journal,* August 17, 1741.

5. Biet, *Voyage*, 277, 292.

6. "Classis of Amsterdam. Act of the Deputies" (October 25, 1660), in Hastings and Corwin, *Ecclesiastical Records,* 1:493.

7. Judd, "Frederick Philipse," 354–74; Maika, "Encounters," 35–72.

8. "Apontamentos do embaixador do Rei do Congo" (March 31, 1607); "Embaixada do Rei do Congo" (June 12, 1607); "Carta do Rei do Congo a D. Feilipe II" (October 23, 1615); "Relação do Bispo do Congo a El-Rei" (September 7, 1619), in Brásio, *Monumenta missionária Africana: Primeira série,* 5:191–292; 5:314; 6:231; 6:380–82 [hereafter *MMA-PS*].

9. Dicomano, "Informazione sul regno del Congo," http://arlindo-correia.com/121208.html.

10. Sarmento, *Os sertões*, 49.

11. Sarmento, *Os sertões*, 49. A variant of this oath can be found in Farinha, *A expansão da fé*, 183.

12. Heywood and Thornton, "Intercultural Relations," 192–203; Dewulf, *The Pinkster King*, 35–41.

13. P. Wood, *Black Majority*, 340–41; Littlefield, *Rice and Slaves*, 113.

14. Quoted in Sublette, *The World That Made New Orleans*, 107.

15. Vila Vilar, *Hispano-América y el comercio de esclavos*, 144–53.

16. Heywood and Thornton, *Central Africans, Atlantic Creoles*, ix.

17. J. Miller, "Central Africans during the Era of the Slave Trade," 61.

18. Berlin, "From Creole to African," 251–88.

19. Ibid., 258–59.

20. Ibid., 288.

21. Mintz and Price, *The Birth of African-American Culture*, 42.

22. Thornton, "The Development of an African Catholic Church," 147–67; Thornton, "On the Trail," 261–78; Thornton, *Africa and Africans*, 254.

23. Brooks, "The Observance of All Souls' Day," 10.

24. Fromont, *The Art of Conversion*, 15–19.

25. Brásio, *História e missiologia*, 126.

26. Fromont, *The Art of Conversion*, 271.

27. Gillard, *The Catholic Church*, 223–25, 227, 250–51.

28. C. Davis, *The History of Black Catholics*, 25.

29. C. Davis, "God of Our Weary Years," 29.

30. Giggie, "For God and Lodge," 199.

CHAPTER ONE. PORTUGAL

1. Pinto da França, *A influência portuguesa*, 43–44, 64–67.

2. "Carta do ouvidor geral, João Vieira de Andrade, ao rei D. José" (July 26, 1762), in D. Pereira, *Estudos da história*, 337–40.

3. Barcellos, *Subsídios para a história*, 1:28–30; Green, *The Rise of the Trans-Atlantic Slave Trade*, 105.

4. Bethencourt, "A Igreja," 385–86.

5. Winston-Allen, *Stories of the Rose*, 130; Rawlings, *Church, Religion and Society*, 92–97; W. Christian, *Local Religion*, 161–68; Beirante, *Confrarias medievais*, 1; Beirante, *Territórios do sagrado*, 185; Paiva, "A recepção e aplicação do concilio de Trento," 13–40.

6. Bruneau, *The Church in Brazil*, 23.

7. Hoornaert, *História da igreja*, 2:155–56, 234–35, 246, 274–75, 287, 383, 385, 386.

8. Marques, *Daily Life in Portugal*, 227.

9. Ibid., 207, 227.

10. Ibid., 227.

11. Ibid., 224.

12. W. Christian, *Local Religion*, 141, 148.

13. Santa Maria, *Santuario Mariano*, 3:67.

14. E. Oliveira, *Festividades cíclicas*, 224.

15. Quoted in Chaves, *Folclore religioso*, 147.

16. Quoted in García y García and Cantelar Rodriguez, *Synodicon Hispanum II*, 108.

17. Gallop, *Portugal*, 131–35; Sanchis, *Arraial*, 49–50, 86–93; Penteado, *Peregrinos da memória*, 171; W. Christian, *Local Religion*, 23–69; Rawlings, *Church, Religion and Society*, 90–91; Rowe, *Black Saints*, 92.

18. Gallop, *Portugal*, 49–83; Boxer, *The Church Militant*, 104–5; T. Walker, *Doctors*, 45; Rawlings, *Church, Religion and Society*, 80; Marques, *Daily Life in Portugal*, 207–8; Rowe, *Black Saints*, 90–91.

19. A. Marques, *Daily Life in Portugal*, 227.

20. Griffiths, "Popular Religious Scepticism," 83.

21. Brandão, *Sacerdotes de viola*, 241.

22. Beirante, *Confrarias medievais*, 29; Rawlings, *Church, Religion and Society*, 17, 95.

23. Quoted in Beirante, *Territórios do sagrado*, 182.

24. Vilar, *A vivência da morte*, 180–81; Sá, *Quando o rico se faz pobre*, 23–52.

25. Braga, *O povo portuguez*, 2:283–84.

26. Gallop, *Portugal*, 98–100, 181–82; A. Marques, *Daily Life in Portugal*, 225–26; Beirante, *Territórios do sagrado*, 32–76; Vilar, *A vivência da morte*, 180–91; Beirante, *Confrarias medievais*, 2–17; Pina-Cabral, *Sons of Adam*, 229.

27. A. Marques, *Daily Life in Portugal*, 276; Rawlings, *Church, Religion and Society*, 87; Beirante, *Territórios do sagrado*, 27.

28. Quoted in Pina, "Ritos e imaginários," 125.

29. Letts, *The Travels of Leo of Rozmital*, 112–13.

30. Vilar, *A vivência da morte*, 211, 305.

31. Azevedo, "O compromisso da Confraria do Espírito Santo," 14; Mattoso, "O pranto fúnebre," 206–7; Braga, *O povo portuguez*, 1:200–14.

32. Braga, *O povo portuguez*, 1:219–28; Becoña Iglesias, *La Santa Compaña*, 45–67; Vilar, *A vivência da morte*, 215; Pina, "Ritos e imaginários," 129; Beirante, *Territórios do sagrado*, 31, 182; A. Marques, *Daily Life in Portugal*, 274–79; Boxer, *The Church Militant*, 104–5; Pina-Cabral, *Sons of Adam*, 227–29; Chaves, *Portugal além*, 155, 161; Gallop, *Portugal*, 183; Lima and Carneiro, "A encomendação das almas," 3–21; Dias and Dias, *A encomendação das almas*, 5–36, 48, 56–71.

33. Fonseca, *Escravos e senhores*, 353–59.

34. Beirante, *Territórios do sagrado*, 181; Mattos, *Santo António*, 16, 29–35, 54, 72–80; Braga, *O povo portuguez*, 2:47, 297.

35. Guattini and Carli, *La Mission au Kongo*, 154.

36. Lahon, "Esclavage et confréries noires," 567; E. Oliveira, *Festividades cíclicas*, 119–77; Gallop, *Portugal*, 139–46, 177.

37. Serrão, *Em nome do Espírito Santo*, 9; Beirante, *Territórios do sagrado*, 178; Abreu, "Confrarias do Espírito Santo," 51–60; Chaves, *Portugal além*, 70, 90–91; Chaves, *Folclore religioso*, 98–110, 144, 185–96; Leal, *As festas do Espírito Santo*, 21–162.

38. Moura, *Teatro a bordo de naus*, 97–109.

39. Cortesão, *Obras completas*, 5:91–114.

40. Quoted in Viterbo, *Artes e artistas*, 247.

41. Viterbo, *Artes e artistas*, 242–45; J. Marques, "A confraria do Corpo de Deus," 223–47; I. Gonçalves, "As festas do Corpus Christi," 3–23; A. Marques, *Daily Life in Portugal*, 217–18; Beirante, *Territórios do sagrado*, 179; Lacerda, *Folclore da Madeira*, 88; Chaves, *Folclore religioso*, 136–38; Sanchis, *Arraial*, 121–22; Sardinham, *Danças populares*, 44; E. Oliveira, *Festividades cíclicas*, 273–86; Braga, *O povo portuguez*, 2:162–63, 291–94; Gallop, *Portugal*, 163–66; B. Santos, *O corpo de Deus*, 23–56.

42. Beirante, *Territórios do sagrado*, 174; A. Marques, *Daily Life in Portugal*, 224; Chaves, *Folclore religioso*, 41–42, 136–38; Chaves, *Danças*, 8; Beirante, *Confrarias medievais*, 15–16, 43; Alford, "Midsummer and Morris," 218–35; Viterbo, *Artes e artistas*, 244–45; Gallop, *Portugal*, 166–67; E. Oliveira, *Festividades cíclicas*, 149–50; M. Harris, *Carnival*, 52–53.

43. A. Marques, *Daily Life in Portugal*, 216; Penteado, *Peregrinos da memória*, 163, 170–73, 182–83, 195–96, 213–14; Chaves, *Portugal além*, 107, 120; E. Oliveira, *Festividades cíclicas*, 222; Sanchis, *Arraial*, 86, 158; Gallop, *Portugal*, 126, 131, 138, 157, 161, 166–67.

44. Godinho, *A estrutura na antiga sociedade*, 204–6.

45. C. Oliveira, *Lisboa em 1551*, 101.

46. W. Phillips, *Slavery in Medieval and Early Modern Iberia*, 24; Fonseca, *Escravos e senhores*, 82–104; Fonseca, *Escravos em Évora*, 15; Henriques, *A herança africana*, 10–11, 44–45, 54; Lahon, *O Negro*, 13; Lahon "Os escravos negros," 69–78; Caldeira and Feros, "Black Africans," 261–80.

47. Quoted in Braga, *O povo portuguez*, 1:186–87.

48. "Baptismo dos escravos da Guiné" (March 24, 1514); "Carta de El-Rei D. Manuel I ao vigário da Conceição de Lisboa" (June 26, 1516); both in Brásio, *Monumenta missionária Africana: Segunda série*, 2:69, 2:122 [hereafter *MMA-SS*]; "Consulta da Junta sobre o baptismo dos Negros adultos" (June 27, 1623), in Brásio, *MMA-PS*, 7:124–25; Brásio, *Os pretos*, 15–16; Saunders, *A Social History*, 40–41; Fonseca, *Escravos e senhores*, 361–76.

49. Brockey, "Jesuit Pastoral Theater," 35.

50. Telles, *Crônica da Companhia de Jesus*, 2:223–24.

51. Simão Cardoso, "Carta dos Mezes Setembro e Outubro de 88 desta Casa de São Roque da Companhia de Jesus" (November 1, 1588), quoted in Brockey, "Jesuit Pastoral Theater," 32.

52. Fonseca, *Escravos e senhores*, 367.

53. Arquivo Histórico da Câmara Municipal, Lisbon, Câmara Municipal de Lisboa, livro 3, doc. 27, fol. 203. In its 1565 constitution, however, Lisbon's Brotherhood of Our Lady of the Rosary of the Black Men claimed that its origins dated back to the year 1460. I. Pereira, "Dois compromissos," 13.

54. Moreno, *La Antigua Hermandad*, 25–56; Gual Camarena, "Una cofradía," 457–66; Phillips, *Slavery in Medieval and Early Modern Iberia*, 94–95; Fonseca, *Religião e liberdade*, 17; Díaz Rodriguez, "La cofradía," 359–484; Ireton, "They Are Blacks," 603–6; Blumenthal, "'La Casa dels Negres,'" 225–46; Blumenthal, *Enemies and Familiars*, 101–2; Rowe, *Black Saints*, 58–65; Vincent, "Les confréries de noirs," 17–28; Mira Caballos, "Confradías étnicas," 57–88.

55. I. Pereira, "Dois compromissos," 11, 28; Fonseca, *Religião e liberdade*, 23.

56. Quoted in Winston, "Tracing the Origins," 634.

57. Winston-Allen, *Stories of the Rose*, 4, 24, 66, 78–79, 117; Winston, "Tracing the Origins," 619–36; Rubin, *Mother of God*, 332–38.

58. Saunders, *A Social History*, 152; Tinhorão, *Os Negros*, 126–27; Sweet, *Recreating Africa*, 207.

59. Reginaldo, "África em Portugal," 305–6; Lahon, *O Negro*, 59–60; Fonseca, *Religião e liberdade*, 21.

60. Quoted in Henriques, *A herança africana*, 147.

61. "Carta de El-Rei D. João III" (July 9, 1526), in Brásio, *MMA-PS*, 1:472–73; I. Pereira, "Dois compromissos," 10, 15; Fonseca, *Escravos e senhores*, 410–11; Fonseca, *Religião e liberdade*, 99; Lahon, "Vivencia Religiosa," 129; Tinhorão, *Os Negros*, 142; Saunders, *A Social History*, 151–55; Reginaldo, "África em Portugal," 302–6.

62. I. Pereira, "Dois compromissos," 9–47; Brásio, *Os pretos*, 76; Lahon, *O Negro*, 296; Pimentel, *Viagem*, 53; Lahon, "Exclusion," 286–87.

63. "Embaixador do Rei de Angola" (April 6, 1600), in Brásio, *MMA-PS*, 5:7; Fonseca, *Religião e liberdade*, 103–4; Fonseca, *Escravos e senhores*, 434–35; Henriques, *A herança africana*, 111; Lahon, "Esclavage," 364.

64. Lahon, "Esclavage," 336–63; Lahon, *O Negro*, 61–62; Lahon, "Vivencia Religiosa," 129; Fonseca, *Escravos e senhores*, 403–6, 438–40; Fonseca, *Religião e liberdade*, 23–31, 438–39.

65. Fonseca, *Religião e liberdade*, 31–37, 109–11; Lahon, *O Negro*, 66–67; Lahon "Vivencia Religiosa," 130–31; Reginaldo, "África em Portugal," 307.

66. Cadornega, *História geral das guerras angolanas*, 3:26–28; Reginaldo, "África em Portugal," 309–10; Fonseca, *Religião e liberdade*, 35; Lahon, "Vivencia Religiosa" 126–27; Rowe, *Black Saints*, 26–45, 82–83. A statue of Saint Benedict and Saint Antonio da Noto, in the company of the (also Black) Saints Elesban and Efigenia can still be found at the altar dedicated to Our Lady of Rosary in Lisbon's Our Lady of the Grace Church as well as in the Cathedral of Braga.

67. Lahon, "Vivencia Religiosa," 147–48; Fonseca, *Religião e liberdade*, 107.

68. Quoted in I. Pereira, "Dois compromissos," 23.

69. Lahon, "Esclavage," 382–85, 475, 505; Fiume, "St. Benedict," 25; Fonseca, *Religião e liberdade*, 110–11.

70. Cadornega, *Descrição de Vila Viçosa*, 28–29.

71. Fonseca, *Religião e liberdade*, 110–11.

72. Graubart, "'So color,'" 47–48.

73. M. Andrade, *Obras completas*, 2:19–20; Bastide, *African Civilisations*, 182; Boschi, *Os leigos*, 138–39.

74. Lahon, *O Negro*, 71; Saunders, *A Social History*, 105–7, 150–65; Phillips, *Slavery in Medieval and Early Modern Iberia*, 96–97; Rowe, *Black Saints*, 56–72, 93–100; Graubart, "'So color,'" 48–49; Bristol, *Christians*, 95–107.

75. Gray, *Black Christians*, 11–27; A. Hastings, *The Church in Africa*, 125; Blackburn, *The Making of New World Slavery*, 330; Rowe, *Black Saints*, 99–105.

76. "Lettere della S. Congregazione" (March 6, 1684), quoted in Aubert, "'To Establish One Law and Definite Rules,'" 31.

77. Fonseca, *Religião e liberdade*, 104–5.

78. Brásio, *História e missiologia*, 216–43; Newitt, *The Portuguese*, 13.

79. Lahon, "Esclavage," 390, 507, 531; Fonseca, *Religião e liberdade*, 78.

80. Simão Cardoso, "Carta e Relação do Recebimento que se fez às Santas Relliquias que deu Dom João de Borja em Janeiro de 88" (February 1588?), quoted in Brockey, "Jesuit Pastoral Theater," 23.

81. *Folheto de ambas Lisboas,* October 6, 1730.

82. Dezoteux, "Voyage du ci-devant duc du Châtelet," 116.

83. Saunders, *A Social History*, 150.

84. António and Araújo, *Breve extracto*, 5–7.

85. Henriques, *A herança africana*, 156; Fonseca, *Escravos e senhores*, 449; Tinhorão, *Os Negros*, 190; Sweet, "The Hidden Histories," in Cañizares-Esguerra, Childs, and Sidbury, *The Black Urban Atlantic in the Age of the Slave Trade*, 243–44; Lahon, "Vivencia Religiosa," 144.

86. Quoted in Fonseca, *Religião e liberdade*, 111–18.

87. Merveilleux, *Mémoires instructifs*, 1:174, 2:133.

88. A. P. D. G., *Sketches of Portuguese Life*, 286–93.

89. Bonaparte-Wyse, "Le Portugal," 403.

CHAPTER TWO. AFRICA

1. Curran, *Papist Devils*, 121.
2. Purple, *Marriages,* 10–30; Evans, *Records*, 10–38.
3. Thornton, "Central African Names," 729.
4. Schoeman, *Early Slavery,* 60–61.
5. Tachard, "Tachard's First Voyage," 106–7.
6. Guattini and Carli, *La Mission au Kongo*, 56.
7. Merolla da Sorrento and Piccardo, *Breve e succinta relatione*, 7.
8. Guerreiro, *Relação anual*, 1:400.
9. "Lembranças de D. Francisco de Moura para sua Majestade ver" (c. 1622), in Brásio, *MMA-SS*, 702–3.
10. Sandoval, *Un tratado*, 384.
11. Torrão, "Rotas comerciais," 2:17–124, in Albuquerque and Madeira Santos, *História Geral*; Carreira, *Cabo Verde*, 271–72; Pereira, *Estudos da história*, 228.
12. Faro, *André de Faro's Missionary Journey*, 45.
13. Sarró and Barros, "History," 105–24; Havik, *Silences*, 190–91; Brooks, *Eurafricans*, 242, 280.
14. Sandoval, *Un tratado*, 382.
15. Thornton, *Africa and Africans*, 254.
16. F. Almeida, *História da igreja*, 1:332–40, 2:222–32; Brásio, *História e missiologia*, 3–20; Rema, *História das missões católicas*, 42–50; Bethencourt, "A igreja," 1:369–73; Boxer, *The Church Militant*, 78–80; Neill, *Christian Missions*, 141; S. Costa, "Trento e o clero secular," 197–214; Santos and Soares, "Igreja," 2:475–77, in Albuquerque and Madeira Santos, *História Geral*; Blackburn, *The Making of New World Slavery*, 100–106; Maxwell, *Slavery and the Catholic Church*, 53–55.
17. Peres, *Viagens de Luís de Cadamosto*, 149; Boxer, *The Church Militant*, 3; Brásio, *História e missiologia*, 886–925; J. Costa, "D. João II," 405–16.
18. Vasconcelos, *Itinerário do Dr. Jerónimo Münzer*, 61–62.
19. Raboteau, *Slave Religion*, 6.
20. Wheat, *Atlantic Africa*, 222.
21. Sandoval, *Un tratado*, 139.
22. Barcellos, *Subsídios para a história*, 1:33–57; Scelle, *Histoire politique de la traite nègrière*, 1:121–22, 300–301; E. Andrade, *Les Isles du Cap-Vert*, 29–48, 68–71; Blake, *Europeans in West Africa*, 1:64–67, 95–96; Carreira, *Cabo Verde*, 79–284; Russell-Wood, *The Portuguese Empire,* 40–41; Riley, "Ilhas atlânticas," 1:137–62; Green, *The Rise of the Trans-Atlantic Slave Trade*, 95–119, 135–42.
23. Carreira, *Cabo Verde*, 259–80; Wheat, *Atlantic Africa*, 216–52; Havik, "Kriol without Creoles," 41–74.

24. Pereira, *Estudos da história*, 205; Blake, *Europeans in West Africa*, 1:39; Cabral, *A primeira elite*, 42, 95–97; Rego, *The Dialogic Nation*, 26–27.

25. Cabral, *A primeira elite*, 107, 131; Barreto, *História da Guiné*, 88.

26. Barrow, *A Voyage to Cochinchina*, 66.

27. Pereira, *Estudos da história*, 61.

28. Cabral, *A primeira elite*, 97, 126; Carreira, *Cabo Verde*, 313; Newitt, *Emigration and the Sea*, 48–53.

29. Blake, *European Beginnings*, 88; Torrão, "Actividade comercial," 1:237–346, in Albuquerque and Madeira Santos, *História Geral*; Green, *The Rise of the Trans-Atlantic Slave Trade*, 12, 115–74, 187–88; Carreira, *Cabo Verde*, 56–78, 85, 268, 314; Rema, *História das missões*, 66–74; M. Santos, "Lançados," 64–78; Havik, *Silences and Soundbites*, 150–51; G. Brooks, *Eurafricans*, 49–69, 89–90; Nafafe, "Lançados," 49–71; Rego, *The Dialogic Nation*, 24–27.

30. Carreira, *Cabo Verde*, 56; A. Matos, "Santiago," vol. 3, bk. 2, 221–29, in Joel Serrão and Oliveira Marques, *Nova história*; Torrão, "Actividade comercial," 1:237–346, in Albuquerque and Madeira Santos, *História Geral*; Torrão, "Rotas comerciais," 2:17–124, in Albuquerque and Madeira Santos, *História Geral*; Green, *The Rise of the Trans-Atlantic Slave Trade*, 260–77.

31. Sandoval, *Un tratado*, 139.

32. Bowser, *The African Slave*, 79. See also Bennett, *Africans in Colonial Mexico*, 43–44.

33. Konetzke, *Colección de documentos*, 1:80–81.

34. "Deposition of William Fowler of Ratcliffe, Merchant" (April 30, 1569), in Donnan, *Documents*, 1:72. See also Antonil, *Cultura e opulência*, 92; E. Andrade, *Les Isles du Cap-Vert*, 109; Rego, *The Dialogic Nation*, 20. According to Bowser, however, the price of a *ladino* in early colonial Peru was sometimes lower than that of a *bozal*. See Bowser, *The African Slave*, 235.

35. Carreira, *Cabo Verde*, 267–68.

36. Green, *A Fistful of Shells*, 99.

37. Brásio, *História e missiologia*, 160; Chelmicki and Varnhagen, *Corografia cabo-verdiana*, 177; Barcellos, *Subsídios para a história*, 1:9, 104–5; Barreto, *História da Guiné*, 76; Bethencourt, "A igreja," 1:374–75; Costa, "Trento e o clero secular," 197–214.

38. Quoted in Monteiro Junior, *Os rebelados*, 39.

39. Rema, *História das missões*, 89–90; Vicente, "Quatro séculos de vida cristã," 109–11.

40. N. Gonçalves, "A igreja e a cultura," vol. 3, bk. 2, 204–20, in Joel Serrão and Oliveira Marques, *Nova história*; Pereira, *Estudos da história*, 143; Costa, "Trento e o clero secular," 197–214.

41. "Carta do Padre António Vieira ao Padre André Fernandes" (December 25, 1652), in Brásio, *História e missiologia*, 731.

42. Costa, "Trento e o clero secular," 204–6.

43. "Relação de Francisco de Andrade sobre as Ilhas de Cabo Verde" (January 26, 1582), in Brásio, *MMA-SS,* 3:97–107; Santos and Soares, "Igreja," 2:455–66, in Albuquerque and Madeira Santos, *História Geral*; Bethencourt, "A igreja," 1:385; Costa, "Trento e o clero secular," 202.

44. Carreira, *Cabo Verde*, 273–76; N. Gonçalves, "A Igreja e a cultura," vol. 3, bk. 2, 216–17, in Joel Serrão and Oliveira Marques, *Nova história*; Santos and Soares, "Igreja," 2:378, 485, in Albuquerque and Madeira Santos, *História Geral*; Meintel, *Race*, 76–78.

45. Costa, "Trento e o clero secular," 199.

46. Quoted in Baleno, "Povoamento e formação," 1:128, in Albuquerque and Madeira Santos, *História Geral*; Barcellos, *Subsídios para a história*, 1:119, 173.

47. Monteiro Junior, *Os rebelados*, 90.

48. L'Honoré Naber, "Het dagboek van Hendrik Haecxs," 167.

49. Costa, "Trento e o clero secular," 204–6; Rego, *The Dialogic Nation*, 140–45.

50. G. Brooks, "The Observance of All Souls' Day," 2.

51. Senna, *Dissertação sobre as ilhas de Cabo Verde*, 92.

52. Chelmicki and Varnhagen, *Corografia cabo-verdiana*, 2:150.

53. N. Cabral, *Le moulin*, 98, 101–2; Meintel, *Race*, 105; Monteiro Junior, *Os rebelados*, 83.

54. "Carta do ouvidor geral, João Vieira de Andrade, ao rei D. José" (July 26, 1762), in Pereira, *Estudos da história*, 337–40.

55. Senna, *Dissertação sobre as ilhas de Cabo Verde*, 92–95.

56. Braga, *O povo portuguez*, 1:212–13.

57. F. Monteiro, "Tabanca," 6:14–18, 7:19–26.

58. C. Monteiro, "Literatura e folklore," 50; Monteiro Junior, *Os rebelados*, 187–94; F. Monteiro, "Tabanca," 6:18; Saraiva, "Rituais funerários," 121–56; Correia, "Txoru falado," 221; Tavares, *Aspectos evolutivos*, 45; Mendes, *Ritual de 'apanha de espírito' em Santiago*, 118–60; Rego, *The Dialogic Nation*, 123–34.

59. J. Lima, *Ensaios sobre a statística*, 1:108.

60. Farinha, *A expansão da fé*, 91; Pereira, *Estudos da história*, 353; Green, *The Rise of the Trans-Atlantic Slave Trade,* 105; Rowe, *Black Saints*, 70.

61. Santos and Soares, "Igreja," 2:472–73 in Albuquerque and Madeira Santos, *História Geral*.

62. Torrão, "Rotas comerciais," 2:360–61, in Albuquerque and Madeira Santos, *História Geral*; Pereira, *Estudos da história*, 55–56.

63. "Carta do ouvidor geral, João Vieira de Andrade, ao rei D. José" (July 26, 1762); "Carta do desembargador João Gomes Ferreira" (1764), both in Pereira, *Estudos da história*, 337–41.

64. Barcellos, *Subsídios para a história*, 2:244–45.

65. "Registo de um Bando proibindo Zambunas, Choros e Reinados" (September 16, 1772), in Pereira, *Estudos da história*, 342–43.

66. Braga, *O povo portuguez*, 1:298–300.

67. F. Monteiro, "Tabanca," 6:14–18, 7:19–26; N. Cabral, *Le moulin*, 124–30; Trajano Filho, "Os cortejos das tabancas," 37–73; Trajano Filho, "As cores nas tabancas," 339–66; P. Cardoso, *Folclore Caboverdeano*, 39, 43; Pereira, *Estudos da história*, 352; Kohl, *A Creole Nation*, 138–39; Meintel, *Race*, 144–45; Tavares, *Aspectos evolutivos*, 46–48; C. Gonçalves, *Kab Verd Band*, 28–34.

68. F. Monteiro, "Bandeiras," 9–22; C. S. Monteiro, "Literatura e folklore," 52–53; Semedo and Turano, *Cabo Verde*, 59–90; Meintel, *Race*, 110–21; E. Andrade, *Les Isles du Cap-Vert*, 57; M. Ferreira, *A aventura crioula*, 102–8; C. Gonçalves, *Kab Verd Band*, 35–43.

69. Semedo and Turano, *Cabo Verde*, 13–14, 40, 62, 111.

70. Monteiro Junior, *Os rebelados*, 93–95, 124; Meintel, *Race*, 144–46; Rego, *The Dialogic Nation*, 135–56.

71. "Viagens de Cadamosto e Pedro de Sintro," in Brásio, *MMA-SS*, 1:350–73.

72. Hair, "Early Sources on Sierra Leone," 5, IV:90, 95, 98 and 6, II:60; Northrup, *Africa's Discovery*, 26.

73. Isichei, *A History of Christianity*, 58–59; Strathern, "Catholic Missions," 173–75.

74. Horta, "Ensino e cristianização informais," 418.

75. Almada, *Tratado breve*, 46–48, 60. See also "Relação de Lopo Soares de Albergaria sobre a Guiné de Cabo Verde" (c. 1600), in Brásio, *MMA-SS*, 4:3–5.

76. Blake, *Europeans in West Africa*, 1:80–86; Brásio, *História e missiologia*, 893; Hair, "Christian Influences," 3–14; Thornton, "On the Trail," 264–67; Brooks, "Historical Perspectives," 25–54; Brooks, *Eurafricans*, 51–54, 91, 128; Havik, "Traders," 197–226; Havik, *Silences and Soundbites*, 45–53, 129–45; Kohl, *A Creole Nation*, 19–30, 50–54; Green, *The Rise of the Trans-Atlantic Slave Trade*, 12, 85–88; Horta, "Evidence for a Luso-African Identity," 99–130; Horta, "Ensino e cristianização informais," 407–18; Mark, "The Evolution of 'Portuguese' Identity," 173–91.

77. Faro, *André de Faro's Missionary Journey*, 2–7; Kenny, *The Catholic Church*, 61–67; N. Gonçalves, *Os Jesuítas e a missão de Cabo Verde*, 123–91; Mota, *Guiné Portuguesa*, 2:21–22; Anguiano, *Misiones capuchinas*, 2:62–215; Bane, *Catholic Pioneers*, 74–82.

78. Jobson, *The Discovery of River Gambra*, 97–98.

79. Villault, *Relation des costes d'Afrique*, 82.

80. Courbe, *Premier voyage du sieur de la Courbe*, 192–93, 211.

81. Donelha, *An Account of Sierra Leone*, 149.

82. Brooks, *Eurafricans*, 233.

83. Saint-Lô, *Relations du voyage*, 125–26.

84. Loyer, *Relation du voyage*, 56–57.

85. W. Smith, *A New Voyage to Guinea*, 25.

86. Moore, *Travels into the Inland Parts*, 29.

87. Kohl, "Luso-Creole Culture," 47.

88. Coelho, *Duas descrições,* 49, 149, 158; Barcellos, *Subsídios para a historia*, 1:106; Rema, *História das missões católicas*, 166–68; Vicente, "Quatro séculos de vida cristã," 99–117.

89. Farinha, *A expansão da fé*, 46–55, 64, 70–71; Havik, *Silences and Soundbites*, 133; Coelho, *Duas descrições,* 60, 168, 234–35.

90. Quoted in Hair, "Hamlet," 32.

91. Mota, *As viagens do Bispo D. Frei Vitoriano Portuense*, 146; Rema, *História das missões*, 254.

92. Moore, *Travels into the Inland Parts*, 29; Matthews, *A Voyage*, 13–14.

93. Havik, *Silences and Soundbites*, 57, 140.

94. Demanet, *Nouvelle histoire*, 122–23.

95. Barreto, *História da Guiné*, 186; Havik, *Silences and Soundbites*, 133–34; Seibert, "Creolization," 49; Kohl, *A Creole Nation*, 50, 131–62; Barry, *Senegambia*, 76–78.

96. Barreto, *História da Guiné*, 155.

97. Brooks, *Eurafricans*, 216; Havik, *Silences and Soundbites*, 134.

98. Hair, "Hamlet," 34.

99. "Carta ânua do P. B. Barreira ao P. Jerónimo Dias, provincial, Santiago" (January 1, 1610), in Brásio, *MMA-SS,* 4:444–45.

100. J. Almeida, *Um mez na Guiné*, 50.

101. Carvalho, *Guiné*, 74–75.

102. Brooks, "The Observance of All Souls' Day," 3.

103. Trigoso, *Viagem de Lisboa*, 51–52.

104. Garfield, *A History of São Tomé*, 15–16, 102–20; Pinheiro, "O Povoamento," 3, II:239–59; Caldeira, "A sociedade," vol. 3, bk., 2, 389–424, in Joel Serrão and Oliveira Marques, *Nova história*; Riley, "Ilhas atlânticas," 1:137–62; Newitt, *Emigration and the Sea*, 48–58; Henriques, *São Tomé e Príncipe*, 63–92.

105. Alencastro, *O trato dos viventes*, 63–70; Klein, "The Atlantic Slave Trade," 204–8; Schwartz, *Sugar Plantations*, 13–9, 65–72.

106. Sandoval, *Un tratado*, 139–40.

107. Blake, *European Beginnings*, 100–102; Riley, "Ilhas atlânticas," 1:159–60.

108. Crone, *The Voyages of Cadamosto*, 115.

109. "Diogo D'Alvarenga to King Manuel, São Jorge da Mina" (August 18, 1503); "Affonso Caldeira to King Manuel, São Jorge da Mina" (January 2, 1513); "Duarte Pires to King Manuel, Benin" (October 20, 1516), in Blake, *Europeans in West Africa*, 1:95, 113, 124.

110. Castilho, "A província de S. Tomé," 813–14.

111. Ward-Price, *Dark Subjects*, 238.

112. Bane, *Catholic Pioneers*, 83–95; Anguiano, *Misiones capuchinas*, 2:23–58, 219–66; Kenny, *The Catholic Church*, 25–60; Isichei, *A History of Christianity*, 59–63; Strathern, "Catholic Missions," 170–72; Hastings, *The Church in Africa*, 77–79, 118–20; Law, "Religion," 42–77; Sanneh, *West African Christianity*, 42–51

113. Dapper, *Naukeurige beschrijvinge*, 507–8.

114. Adams, *Sketches*, 36–37.

115. King, *Extraits de relation inédite*, 318.

116. Marees, *Beschryvinghe*, 76–77.

117. Barbot, *Barbot on Guinea*, 2:381.

118. "De kerkraad van St. George D'Elmina" (February 15, 1743), in Eekhof, *De negerpredikant*, 78.

119. Cruickshank, *Achttien jaren*, 1:9–10, 2:113.

120. Wiltgen, *Gold Coast Mission*, 139.

121. Wiltgen, *Gold Coast Mission*, 143–44; Wartemberg, *Sao Jorge d'El Mina*, 98–99, 152–53; Todd, *African Mission*, 104; Obeng, *Asante Catholicism*, 104–7.

122. Villault, *Relation des costes d'Afrique*, 403.

123. "Carta dos habitantes de S. Tomé a El-Rei" (July 27, 1499); "Palavras de D. João II, Rei de Portugal, sobre a ilha de S. Tomé" (1494), in Brásio, *MMAPS*, 1:163–65, 4:16–20; Vasconcelos, *Itinerário do Dr. Jerónimo Münzer*, 61–62; Caldeira and Neves, "A igreja e a cultura," vol. 3, bk. 2, 425–43, in Joel Serrão and Oliveira Marques, *Nova história*; Bethencourt, "A igreja," 1:374; Costa, "Trento e o clero secular," 201; Boxer, *Race Relations*, 16.

124. "Carta do ouvidor geral ao Príncipe Regente" (March 6, 1683), in Brásio, *MMA-PS*, 9:540.

125. Quoted in Caldeira and Neves, "A igreja e a cultura," vol.3, bk. 2, 425–43, in Joel Serrão and Oliveira Marques, *Nova história*.

126. Barbot, *Barbot on Guinea*, 2:724–25.

127. Bosman, *Nauwkeurige beschryving*, 205, 207.

128. "Carta de El-Rei D. João III" (July 9, 1526), in Brásio, *MMA-PS*, 1:472–74; Pinheiro, "O Povoamento," 3, II:256.

129. "Lettere da S. Tomé" (April 4, 1693), in Salvadorini, *Le missioni*, 211.

130. Birmingham, *Trade and Conflict*, 42–161; Thornton, "The Portuguese in Africa," 150–53.

131. Valdez, *Six Years of a Traveller's Life*, 2:63.

132. Seibert, *Camaradas*, 41–61.

133. Santa Maria, *Santuario Mariano*, 10:440–41.

134. Quoted in Farinha, *A expansão da fé*, 151.

135. Matos, *Compêndio histórico*, 148.

136. Moraes, *Um breve esboço*, 15; Negreiros, *História ethnográphica*, 205–6; Pereira, *Das Tchiloli*, 285.

137. Negreiros, *História ethnográphica*, 167, 173.

138. Ambrósio, "O Danço Congo," 341–44.

139. Seibert, "Performing Arts," 685.

140. "Primeira missão enviada ao Congo" (1490); "Os primeiros missionários do Congo" (1490–1508), both in Brásio, *MMA-PS*, 1:78–85; 1:86–103; Brásio, *História do Reino do Congo*, 49–76; Brásio, *História e missiologia*, 446; Pigafetta, *A Report*, 70–78; Radulet, *O cronista Rui de Pina*, 97–133; Thornton, "The Development of an African Catholic Church," 147–67.

141. "Reinado de D. Afonso I do Congo" (1493?–1543); "Carta do Rei do Congo aos senhores do reino" (1512); "Carta do Rei do Congo a seus povos" (1512), in Brásio, *MMA-PS*, 1:141–47; 1:256–59; 1:266–69; Brásio, *História do Reino do Congo*, 77–80; Pigafetta, *A Report*, 70–89.

142. Góis, *Crónica do Felicíssimo Rei*, 3:149–53.

143. "Regimento de D. Manuel a Simão da Silva" (1512), in Brásio, *MMAPS*, 1:228–46; Brásio, *História e missiologia*, 209–15; Cuvelier, *L'ancien royaume*, 97–103; Amaral, *O reino do Congo*, 27–31; Thornton, "The Kingdom of Kongo," 87–118; Fromont, *The Art of Conversion*, 21–33.

144. "Alvará régio a Rui Leite" (August 14, 1514); "Carta do Rei do Congo a D. Manuel" (May 27, 1517); "Carta do Rei do Congo a D. João III" (August 25, 1526), in Brásio, *MMA-PS*, 1:287–88, 1:406–7, 1:483–84; Brásio, *História do Reino do Congo*, 82–87; Brásio, *História e missiologia*, 888–92.

145. "Carta do Vigário Rui de Aguiar a El-Rei D. Manuel" (May 25, 1516), in Brásio, *MMA-PS*, 1:361–63.

146. "Carta do Rei do Congo, a D. Manuel I" (October 5, 1514), in Brásio, *MMA-PS*, 1:294–323.

147. "Carta do Rei do Congo, a D. Manuel I" (October 5, 1514); "Carta do Rei do Congo a D. Manuel I" (May 31, 1515); "Carta do Vigário Rui de Aguiar a El-Rei D. Manuel" (May 25, 1516); "De algumas coisas que tocam ao Rei do Congo" (1516), in Brásio, *MMA-PS*, 1:294–323, 1:335–38; 1:361–63; 1:373–75; Brásio, *História do Reino do Congo*, 82–83; Góis, *Crónica do Felicíssimo*

Rei, 1:180–81; Amaral, *O reino do Congo*, 90–92; Thornton, "The Development of an African Catholic Church," 154–56; Thornton, "Afro-Christian Syncretism," 61–62; M. Souza, *Além do visível*, 228–30.

148. Brásio, *História e missiologia*, 209–10.

149. "Carta do Rei do Congo a D. João III" (August 25, 1526), in Brásio, *MMA-PS,* 1:476–82.

150. "Carta do Rei do Congo a D. Manuel I" (October 5, 1514), in Brásio, *MMA-PS,* 1:294–323.

151. "Rol de objetos a enviar para o Congo" (1512); "Carta do Rei do Congo aos Senhores do Reino" (1512), in Brásio, *MMA-PS,* 1:247–53, 1:256–59; Brásio, *História do Reino do Congo*, 81; Pigafetta, *A Report*, 109; A. Gonçalves, "As influências do Cristianismo," 5:523–39; Heywood and Thornton, *Central Africans, Atlantic Creoles,* 135–43; Heywood and Thornton "Central African Leadership," 222–23; Thornton, "Portuguese-African Relations," 57–63; Thornton, "Religious and Ceremonial Life," 86, in Heywood, *Central Africans and Cultural Transformations*; M. Souza, *Além do visível*, 79–80. Hastings, *The Church in Africa*, 73–77; Sá, "Ecclesiastical Structures," 270–71; Fromont, *The Art of Conversion*, 47–59, 71, 130.

152. Van den Broecke, *Journal of Voyages*, 59.

153. Brun, *Schiffarten*, 28.

154. "Corte beschrijvinge van de principaelste plaetsen gelegen in Angola te weten Commo, Goby, Maiomba, Loango, Cacongo, Molemboe, Zarry, Sonho, Congo, en aderen omleggende plaetsen" (March 1642), Archives of the Old/First West India Company, no. 46:5, National Archives, The Hague.

155. "Regimento de D. Manuel a Simão da Silva" (1512); "Carta do Rei do Congo, a D. Manuel I" (October 5, 1514); "Carta do Padre Cristóvão Ribeiro" (July 31, 1548), in Brásio, *MMA-PS,* 1:228–46, 1:294–323, 15:161–63; Brásio, *História do Reino do Congo*, 67–90; Cuvelier, *L'ancien royaume de Congo*, 104–12, 143–53; Balandier, *Daily Life in the Kingdom of the Kongo*, 42–58; Hilton, *The Kingdom of the Kongo*, 62–64; Amaral, *O reino do Congo*, 21–32; J. Miller, "Worlds Apart," 227–80; Heywood and Thornton, "Central African Leadership," 202, 212; Thornton, *The Kingdom of Kongo*, 65; Thornton, "Religious and Ceremonial Life," 83–88, in Heywood, *Central Africans and Cultural Transformations*; Fromont, *The Art of Conversion*, 26–33, 47–59, 71, 130, 177.

156. "Carta de D. João III ao Rei do Congo" (Fins de 1529); "Apontamentos do embaixador do Rei do Congo" (March 31, 1607); "Embaixada do Rei do Congo" (June 12, 1607); "Carta do Rei do Congo a D. Filipe II" (October 23, 1615); "Relação do Bispo do Congo a El-Rei" (September 7, 1619), in Brásio, *MMA-PS,* 1:521–539, 5:280–93, 5:310–15, 6:230–33, 6:375–84; Heywood

and Thornton, "Central African Leadership," 203–7; Heywood and Thornton, "The Kongo Kingdom and European Diplomacy," 52–57, in Cooksey, Poynor, and Vanhee, *Kongo Across the Waters*; Fromont, *The Art of Conversion*, 173–77.

157. Birmingham, *Trade and Conflict*, 42–161; Hilton, *The Kingdom of the Kongo*, 104–12; Thornton, "The Portuguese in Africa," 150–53; J. Miller, "Worlds Apart," 261–64.

158. "Supplique des ambassadeurs du roi du Congo" (May 9, 1648), in Jadin, *L'Ancien Congo et l'Angola*, 2:987; Kenny, *The Catholic Church*, 20–32; Hastings, *The Church in Africa*, 79–94; Thornton, "The Development of an African Catholic Church," 147–67; Fromont, *The Art of Conversion*, 26–33; Bethencourt, "A igreja," 1:375.

159. Anguiano, *Misiones capuchinas*, 1:157–64; Jadin, "Le clergé séculier," 185–483; Hastings, *The Church in Africa*, 94–102; Gray, "Como vero prencipe Catolico," 39–54; Thornton, *The Kingdom of Kongo*, 56–68.

160. "Annexe-Relation de Pieter Moortamer à la Chambre de Zélande" (June 29, 1643); "Les directeurs C. Nieulant et Hans Mols aux XIX" (June 10, 1643), in Jadin, *L'Ancien Congo et l'Angola*, 1:355, 429–31; Jadin, "Le clergé séculier," 206; Ratelband, *Nederlanders in West-Afrika*, 91–283; Fromont, *The Art of Conversion*, 155–64; Noorlander, *Heaven's Wrath*, 179–80.

161. "Brief (kopie) van Dom Garcia, Koning van Kongo, Angola et cetera . . . aan Gouverneur-Generaal Johan Maurits van Nassau" (May 12, 1642), Archives of the Old/First West India Company, no. 58:211, National Archives, The Hague.

162. Rome, *Brève relation*, 112.

163. "Provisão de D. Garcia Afonso II sobre o Padre Jorge de Geel" (March 2, 1653), in Brásio, *MMA-PS*, 11:264–67.

164. "Relação da batalha de Ambuíla" (October 29, 1665), in Brásio, *MMA-PS*, 12:582–91.

165. Caltanissetta, *Diaire Congolais*, 36.

166. Jadin, "Les survivances chrétiennes," 137–85; Farinha, *A expansão da fé*, 272–74; Kenny, *The Catholic Church*, 31–33.

167. Savona, "Aperçu de la situation," 380.

168. Proyart, *Histoire de Loango*, 317.

169. Quoted in Farinha, *A expansão da fé*, 205.

170. Sapede, *Muana Congo*, 89–120.

171. Vide, Couto Godinho, and Miranda, "Relação da Viagem," 64–65; Vide, "Viagem e Missão."

172. Jadin, "Recherches dans les archives," 946–66; Hastings, *The Church in Africa*, 194–96; Kenny, *The Catholic Church*, 33.

173. Necessidades, "Factos memoráveis," 1–2.

174. Quoted in J. Santos, *Apenas um punhado*, 200.

175. Barroso, "O Congo," 234; Cerqueira, *Vida social indígena*, 85; Vos, *Kongo in the Age of Empire*, 60; Hastings, *The Church in Africa*, 109–18, 385–88.

176. Thornton, *The Kingdom of Kongo*, 69–113; Birmingham, *Central Africa*, 146–48; Fromont, *The Art of Conversion*, 2–8; Vos, "Kongo Cosmopolitans," 235–53.

177. "Relação dos Carlemitas descalços" (1584), in Brásio, *MMA-PS*, 4:413.

178. "Apontamentos do Padre Sebastião de Souto" (1561); "Fábrica da Sé do Congo" (January 19, 1600), in Brásio, *MMA-PS*, 2:477–81, 5:3–5; Heywood and Thornton, "Central African Leadership," 212–13.

179. "Relatório de D. Frei Francisco do Soveral na visit ad 'Sacra Limini'" (April 1, 1631), in Brásio, *MMA-PS*, 8:11–25.

180. Fromont, *The Art of Conversion*, 103.

181. Thornton, *The Kongolese Saint Anthony*, 17.

182. Hastings, *The Church in Africa*, 90–93; Jadin, "Le clergé séculier," 203.

183. Cavazzi, *Istorica descrizione*, 420; Jadin, "Le clergé séculier," 247; Brinkman, "Kongo Interpreters," 255–76; Strathern, "Catholic Missions," 151.

184. "Carta do Rei do Congo a D. Manuel I" (October 5, 1514), in Brásio, *MMA-PS*, 294–323; Jadin, "Le clergé séculier," 186; Hastings, *The Church in Africa*, 92; Thornton, "The Development of an African Catholic Church," 165–66; Thornton, "Religious and Ceremonial Life," 71–90, in Heywood, *Central Africans and Cultural Transformations*; Thornton, "Rural People," 33–44; Thornton, "Afro-Christian Syncretism," 53–77; Fromont, *The Art of Conversion*, 5–12, 143–52; M. Souza, *Além do visível*, 228–32, 235–49.

185. "Apontamentos do Padre Sebastião de Souto" (1561), in Brásio, *MMA-PS*, 2:477–81.

186. Parco, "Informations sur le royaume du Congo," 371.

187. Savona, "Aperçu de la situation," 371.

188. "Interrogatória de statu regni congensis fact ulissipone" (1595), in Brásio, *MMA-PS*, 3:500–504.

189. Franco, *Synopsis*, 249, 253–56.

190. "Terceira missão dos Dominicanos ao Reino do Congo" (1610), in Brásio, *MMA-PS*, 5:605–14; "Érection du diocese de San Salvador" (1595), in Cuvelier and Jadin, *L'Ancien Congo*, 187; Lucques, *Relations sur le Congo*, 202; Atri, *L'anarchia Congolese*, 205; Gray, "A Kongo Princess," 140–54; Fromont, *The Art of Conversion*, 202–6; Thornton, "The Development of an African Catholic Church," 147–67; Heywood, "Mbanza Kongo/São Salvador," 385.

191. "Processo canónico do Bispo do Congo" (December 19, 1603–January 31, 1604); "Relatório da Diocesa do Congo e Angola" (December 19, 1609); "Terceira missão dos Dominicanos ao Reino do Congo" (1610), in Brásio, *MMA-PS*, 5:64–80, 524–32, 605–14; Thornton, *The Kingdom of Kongo*, 66–67; Heywood and Thornton, "Central African Leadership," 213.

192. Anguiano, *Misiones capuchinas*, 1:109–11, 115, 349; Franco, *Synopsis*, 250, 253; MacGaffey, *Religion and Society*, 203–8; Thornton, "The Development of an African Catholic Church," 163–64; Hilton, *The Kingdom of the Kongo*, 97; Gray, *Black Christians*, 34–56; Fromont, *The Art of Conversion*, 202–6.

193. Hildebrand, *Le martyr Georges de Geel*, 251–54.

194. "Giuseppe Maria da Busseto au procureur général" (April 18, 1674), in Jadin, "Rivalités luso-néerlandaises," 290.

195. Franco, *Synopsis*, 249, 253–56.

196. Caltanissetta, *Diaire Congolais*, 199.

197. Anguiano, *Misiones capuchinas*, 1:205.

198. Caltanissetta, *Diaire Congolais*, 24.

199. Jadin, "Le Congo et la secte des Antoniens," 454–59.

200. Guattini and Carli, *La Mission au Kongo*, 125.

201. "Giuseppe Maria da Busseto au procureur général" (April 18, 1674), in Jadin, "Rivalités luso-néerlandaises, " 291.

202. Pavia, "Voyages apostoliques," 446–48.

203. Ibid., 444–45.

204. "Relatório de D. Frei Francisco do Several na visita 'ad sacra limina'" (September 22, 1640), in Brásio, *MMA-PS*, 8:441–50.

205. Guattini and Carli, *La Mission au Kongo*, 237; Caltanissetta, *Diaire Congolais*, 62; Jadin, "Rivalités luso-néerlandaises," 291.

206. "Carta de Frei Boaventura de Alessano ao Secretário da Propaganda Fide" (August 4, 1649), in Brásio, *MMA-PS*, 10:385; Anguiano, *Misiones capuchinas*, 1:112.

207. Quoted in Guattini and Carli, *La Mission au Kongo*, 233, 258.

208. "Capítulos do regimento do Rei do Congo" (1553); "Carta do Padre Mateus Cardoso ao Rei do Congo" (1624); "Carta de Frei Boaventura de Alessano ao Secretário da Propaganda Fide" (August 4, 1649); "Carta do Padre António de Teruel aos Cardeais da Propaganda" (February 18, 1662), in Brásio, *MMA-PS*, 2:325–26, 7:287–90, 10:379–86, 12:369–71; Brásio, *História e missiologia*, 457–58; Bontinck, "Le Vocabularium Latinum," 529–35; Kind, Schryver, and Bostoen, "Pushing Back the Origin," 159–94; Brinkman and Bostoen, "'To Make Book,'" 216–34; Brewer-García, *Beyond Babel*, 107–15.

209. Hilton, *The Kingdom of the Kongo*, 94–98; MacGaffey, "The West in Congolese Experience," 57; Heusch, *Le roi de Kongo*, 83; Thornton, "The Development of an African Catholic Church," 147–67, 156–57; Thornton, "Afro-Christian Syncretism," 67–77; Isichei, *A History of Christianity*, 65–66.

210. Cavazzi, *Istorica descrizione*, 117.

211. Dicomano, "Informazione sul regno del Congo."

212. Heywood and Thornton, "Central African Leadership," 215–16.

213. Thornton, "Religious and Ceremonial Life, in Heywood, *Central Africans and Cultural Transformations*," 71–90.

214. MacGaffey, *Religion and Society*, 63–135.

215. MacGaffey, "Constructing a Kongo Identity," 180.

216. Horta, "Africanos e portugueses," 301–21.

217. Caltanissetta, *Diaire Congolais*, 68–69.

218. Merolla da Sorrento and Piccardo, *Breve e succinta relatione*, 212.

219. Fromont, *The Art of Conversion*, 79.

220. Bouveignes and Cuvelier, *Jérôme de Montesarchio*, 156–57.

221. Jadin, "Le Congo et la secte des Antoniens," 411–614; MacGaffey, *Religion and Society*, 203–11; Hilton, *The Kingdom of the Kongo*, 206–7; Rodrigues, "Aculturação artística," 5:541–53; Thornton, *The Kongolese Saint Anthony*; Janzen, "Renewal," 132–42, in Cooksey, Poynor, and Vanhee, *Kongo Across the Waters*; Fromont, *The Art of Conversion*, 206–12; Strathern, "Catholic Missions," 161; A. Gonçalves, "Kimpa Vita," 323–38.

222. Jadin, "Le Congo et la secte des Antoniens," 494, 515.

223. "Carta do Padre Francisco de Gouveia ao Geral da Companhia" (March 20, 1592), in Brásio, *MMA-PS*, 15:317.

224. Lucques, *Relations sur le Congo*, 109.

225. Dapper, *Naukeurige beschrijvinge*, 588.

226. "Schriftelijck Rapport van Pieter Mortamer" (June 29, 1643), Archives of the Old/First West India Company, no. 46, National Archives, The Hague.

227. C. Thomas, *Adventures and Observations*, 268.

228. Dennett, *Seven Years among the Fjort*, 44–45.

229. Nassau, *Fetichism in West Africa*, 212.

230. Thornton, "The Development of an African Catholic Church," 154; Heywood and Thornton, "Central African Leadership," 217.

231. MacGaffey, "A Central African Kingdom," 57; MacGaffey, "Dialogues of the Deaf," 260–61.

232. Hilton, *Kingdom of Kongo*, 62–64, 90–103; MacGaffey, *Religion and Society*, 189–216; Bastide, *The African Religions*, 89; Sweet, *Recreating Africa*, 103–17, 194, 205; Young, *Rituals of Resistance*, 57–59; J. Miller, "Worlds Apart," 227–80; Berlin, *Many Thousands Gone*, 21.

233. Hastings, *The Church in Africa*, 74.

234. "Relatório de D. Frei Francisco do Soveral na visita ad 'Sacra Limini'" (April 1, 1631), in Brásio, *MMA-PS*, 8:11–25; Heywood and Thornton, "Central African Leadership," 214; Thornton, "Rural People," 36.

235. Jadin, "Le Congo et la secte des Antoniens," 481–83.

236. Jadin, "Les survivances chrétiennes," 137–85; Thornton, "The Development of an African Catholic Church," 166–67; Vanhee and Vos, "Kongo in the Age of Empire," 78–89, in Cooksey, Poynor, and Vanhee, *Kongo Across the Waters*; Fromont, *The Art of Conversion*, 215–65.

237. Sarmento, *Os sertões*, 80.

238. Tuckey, *Narrative*, 139.

239. Carrie, "Une visite à Saint Antoine," 473, 496–97.

240. Heintze, *Max Buchners Reise*, 520–22.

241. Bentley, *Pioneering on the Congo*, 1:35.

242. Bastian, *Ein Besuch in San Salvador*, 162; Fromont, *The Art of Conversion*, 243–45; "Charles Callewaert: Fetish hut in Lutele" (1883), Archives de particuliers — Histoire colonial, no. HO.0.1.3114, Royal Museum for Central Africa, Tervuren, Belgium.

243. "Carta do Padre Baltasar Afonso para o Padre Miguel de Sousa" (July 4, 1581); "Relatório de Frei Serafim de Cortona sobre a Cristandade de Angola" (December 9, 1658), in Brásio, *MMA-PS*, 3:198–207, 12:195–203; Kenny, *The Catholic Church*, 18–20; Heintze, "Luso-African Feudalism," 111–31; M. Souza, *Além do visível*, 85–142; J. Miller, "Worlds Apart," 263–66.

244. Heywood and Thornton, "Central African Leadership," 219.

245. "Carta de Fernão de Sousa a El-Rei" (August 15, 1624), in Brásio, *MMA-PS*, 7:248–50; Cavazzi, *Istorica descrizione*, 721–22; Jadin, "Le clergé séculier," 227; Skidmore-Hess, "Njinga," 123–42; Heywood, *Njinga*, 223–28; M. Souza, *Além do visível*, 143–224; Strathern, "Catholic Missions," 156–68.

246. "Apontamentos das cousas de Angola" (1563); "Carta do Padre Francisco de Gouveia ao Geral da Companhia" (November 1, 1564), in Brásio, *MMA-PS*, 2:518–21, 15:228–35.

247. "Estado religioso e político de Angola" (1588), in Brásio, *MMA-PS*, 3:375–82; Felner, *Angola*, 145.

248. "Carta do Padre Pedro Tavares ao Reitor do Colégio de Luanda" (October 14, 1631), in Brásio, *MMA-PS*, 8:169.

249. Thornton, "Religious and Ceremonial Life, in Heywood, *Central Africans and Cultural Transformations*," 87–88.

250. "Carta do Padre Manuel Ribeiro sobre a missão de 1672–1673" (January 15, 1674), in Brásio, *MMA-PS*, 13:248–74.

251. Merolla da Sorrento and Piccardo, *Breve e succinta relatione*, 259; Heywood, "Portuguese into African," in Heywood, *Central Africans and Cultural Transformations*, 91–113; Klein, "The Atlantic Slave Trade," 211–12.

252. Corrêa, *História de Angola*, 2:197.

253. Heintze, *Afrikanische Pioniere*, 159.

254. Heintze, *Max Buchners Reise*, 386–87.

255. Ibid., 523–24.

256. "Cofradía da Nossa Senhora do Rosário aos Cardinais da Propaganda" (June 29, 1658), in Brásio, *MMA-PS*, 12:164–65; "Resposta do governador de Angola à carta régia de 10 de Março de 1692 sobre missões" (April 24, 1693), in Jordão, *História do Congo*, 318–39; Jadin, "Le clergé séculier," 148; Jadin, "Relations sur le Congo," 438; Merolla da Sorrento and Piccardo, *Breve e succinta relatione*, 251; Zucchelli, *Relazioni del viaggio*, 113; Gabriel, *Padrões da fé*, 123; Caldeira, "Luanda," 93–94; Heywood and Thornton, *Central Africans, Atlantic Creoles*, 188; R. Ferreira, *Cross-Cultural Exchange*, 91–92.

257. Cadornega, *História geral*, 3:26–28.

258. R. Ferreira, *Cross-Cultural Exchange*, 181.

259. Zucchelli, *Relazioni del viaggio*, 108.

260. Parco, "Informations sur le royaume du Congo," 362; Caldeira, "Luanda," 97; R. Ferreira, *Cross-Cultural Exchange*, 182; Dananoja, "Healers," 459–62; Reginaldo, *Os rosários dos Angolas*, 58; Heywood, "Portuguese into African," 99–100.

261. Corrêa, *História de Angola*, 1:87–89.

262. Corrêa, *História de Angola*, 1:74.

263. Farinha, *A expansão da fé*, 221.

264. "Relação das festas que a residência de Angolla fez na Beatificação do Beato Padre Francisco de Xavier" (1620), in Felner, *Angola*, 531–43.

265. Birmingham, "Carnival," 93–103; Ribas, *Izomba*, 44, 46, 74, 92, 100; Comissão Nacional Prepatória do Carnaval da Vitória, *Carnaval*, 26, 51.

266. Gray, *Black Christians*, 43; Fromont, *The Art of Conversion*, 183–84.

267. S. Johnson, *African American Religions*, 17.

268. "Carta Régia aos Governadores de Portugal" (December 9, 1622); "Carta Régia ao Governador do Brasil" (March 18, 1624), in Brásio, *MMA-PS*, 7:64–65, 7:220.

269. Randles, *L'ancien royaume*, 149.

270. Hastings, *The Church in Africa*, 113.

271. J. Miller, "Central Africans during the Era of the Slave Trade," 61, in Heywood, *Central Africans and Cultural Transformations*.

272. Thornton, "Portuguese-African Relations," 63.

273. Bennett, *African Kings*, 4.

CHAPTER THREE. THE AMERICAS

1. Rueda, *Obras de Lope de Rueda*, 1:180.
2. Cabrera, *Reglas de Congo,* 108–9.
3. Merolla da Sorrento and Piccardo, *Breve e succinta relatione*, 160.
4. Selka, "Black Catholicism," 288.
5. Quoted in Pereira, *Compêndio Narrativo*, 140.
6. M. Souza, "Reis do Congo," 83.
7. Sandoval, *Un tratado*, 413; Splendiani and Aristizábal, *Proceso de beatificación*, 88, 108–9, 113, 222–25; Brewer-García, *Beyond Babel*, 123–32.
8. Konetzke, *Colección de documentos*, 1:237–40.
9. "Visitas dos Padres," quoted in Metcalf, "Millenarian Slaves?," 1547.
10. Benci, *Economia cristã*, 93–94.
11. Antonil, *Cultura e opulência*, 93.
12. "Visitas dos Padres," quoted in Metcalf, "Millenarian Slaves?," 1547.
13. Wheat, *Atlantic Africa*, 252; Chaudenson and Mufwene, *Creolization of Language*, 74, 92.
14. Stevenson, *Historical and Descriptive Narrative*, 1:303.
15. Thornton, *Africa and Africans*, 254, 262.
16. "Denúnia contra Pedro" (December 25, 1764), in Arquivo Nacional da Torre do Tombo, Lisbon, Inquisição de Lisboa, manuscript no. 16001.
17. Aguado, *Historia de Venezuela*, 1:218–20, 253–58; 2:107–10.
18. Troconis de Veracoechea, *Documentos*, 79–80.
19. Larrazabal Blanco, *Los negros*, 151–52; Ricourt, *Cimarrones*, 91.
20. Quoted in Landers, "The African Landscape," in Cañizares-Esguerra, Childs, and Sidbury, *The Black Urban Atlantic in the Age of the Slave Trade*, 155–56.
21. Alegre, *Historia de la provincia*, 2:175–80; Palmer, *Slaves of the White God*, 128–30; G. Cardoso, *Negro Slavery*, 54–58; Thornton, *Africa and Africans*, 269; Tardieu, *Resistencia de los Negros*, 15–68; Carroll, *Blacks in Colonial Veracruz*, 90–92.
22. Baerle, *The History of Brazil*, 236; Kent, "Palmares," 166–68.
23. Nieuhof, *Gedenkweerdige Brasiliaense Zee- en Lantreize*, 14.
24. "Relação das guerras feitas aos Palmares de Pernambuco no tempo do governador Dom Pedro de Almeida" (1675–78), in Gomes, *Mocambos*, 222.
25. Hoornaert, *História da igreja*, 2:263.
26. "Visitas dos Padres," quoted in Metcalf, "Millenarian Slaves?," 1547.
27. Quoted in Bowser, *The African Slave*, 248.
28. Quoted in Leite, *Cartas dos primeiros jesuítas*, 1:325–26.
29. Klein, "The Atlantic Slave Trade," 206; Bowser, *The African Slave*, 247–48; Tardieu, *Los negros*, 1:517; Reis, *A morte é uma festa*, 49–72; Karasch, *Slave*

Life, 86; Soares, *Devotos da cor*, 13; Rowe, *Black Saints*, 105–16; Graubart, "'So color,'" 47–48; Mulvey, "Black Brothers," 253–79.

30. Sandoval, *Un tratado*, 238, 422.

31. Benzoni, *History of the New World*, 94.

32. Quoted in Rojas, "Algunos datos," 1285.

33. Querol y Roso, *Negros y mulatos*, 30; Chimalpahin, *Diario*, 286.

34. Bristol, *Christians*, 102.

35. Konetzke, *Colección de documentos*, 2:88.

36. Heywood, "The Angolan-Afro-Brazilian Cultural Connections," 21. For Mexico, see Germeten, "Black Brotherhoods," in Cañizares-Esguerra, Childs, and Sidbury, *The Black Urban Atlantic in the Age of the Slave Trade*, 252; for Peru, see Graubart, "'So color,'" 47.

37. Reginaldo, *Os rosários dos Angolas*, 75, 102–3, 121–22.

38. F. Costa, *Anais pernambucanos*, 2:468–69.

39. Quoted in Reginaldo, *Os rosários dos Angolas*, 167.

40. Quoted by Russell-Wood, "Atlantic Bridge," 162–63.

41. Hesperióphylo, "Idea de las congregationes públicas," 48:112–17, 49:120–25.

42. Ortiz Fernández, *Los bailes*, 288, 439–41; Bettelheim, Bridges, and Yonker, "Festivals," 143; Thornton, "The Kingdom of Kongo and Palo Mayombe," 11.

43. Bremer, *The Homes*, 2:382–83.

44. W. Goodman, *The Pearl*, 137.

45. Koster, *Travels*, 243–44.

46. Quoted in C. Andrade, *Poesia completa*, 810–15.

47. R. Lima, *Folguedos*, 37–38.

48. Kiddy, "Who Is the King of Congo?," 159, 171, in Heywood, *Central Africans and Cultural Transformations*.

49. Ortiz Fernández, *Ensayos etnográficos*, 12.

50. Cabrera, *Reglas de Congo*, 15, 78.

51. Ramos, *O folklore negro*, 38.

52. M. Andrade, *Obras completas*, 1:357; 2:17, 38.

53. Fromont, "Dancing for the King of Congo," 199; Fromont, *The Art of Conversion*, 60–62.

54. Burton, *Explorations*, 1:237–38.

55. Moraes Filho, *Festas e tradições*, 95; Cascudo, *Dicionário do folclore*, 242–45; R. Lima, *Folguedos populares*, 29–30, 198–215; Zuluar, *Os homens de Deus*, 78; Meyer, *De Carlos Magno*, 17–60; Borges, *Escravos e libertos*, 189–90; Poel, *Dicionário da religiosidade popular*, 241–45, 272–73; Lara, "Significados cruzados," 81; Fromont, "Dancing for the King of Congo," 184–208; Fromont,

"Envisioning Brazil's Afro-Christian Congados," 117–39, in Fromont, *Afro-Catholic Festivals.*

56. Macedo, "Mouros e Cristãos," 7.

57. Bettelheim, "Carnaval of Los Congos," 287–309.

58. R. Smith, "Arroz Colorao," 239–66.

59. Lipski, *The Speech of the Negros*, 67–114; Craft, *When the Devil Knocks*, 56–107.

60. Rome, *Brève relation*, 130–31.

61. Merolla da Sorrento and Piccardo, *Breve e succinta relatione*, 157.

62. Fromont, *The Art of Conversion*, 24–26.

63. M. Souza, "Kongo King Festivals," 43.

64. Andrews, *Afro-Latin America*, 19.

65. Ramos, *A aculturação negra*, 273.

66. Hoornaert, *História da igreja*, 2:348.

67. Vainfas, *Dicionário do Brasil*, 67–68.

68. Antonil, *Cultura e opulência*, 97–98.

69. Brandão, *Os deuses do povo*, 169–98; Brandão, *Sacerdotes de viola*, 236–41; Pollak-Eltz, *La religiosidad popular*, 127–29; M. Davis, *Voces del purgatório*, 31–41, 49–53, 169; Whitten, *Black Frontiersmen*, 137–38; Brandt, *Estudio etnomusicológico*, 55–56; Prien, *Christianity in Latin America*, 223–42.

70. Stein, *Vassouras*, 203.

71. Lay Bravo, *Kinfuiti*, 23, 27–28.

72. Ricourt, *Cimarrones*, 124–30.

73. Pavia, "Voyages apostoliques," 448.

74. R. Lima, *Folclore das festas cíclicas*, 71–90; Poel, *Dicionário da religiosidade popular*, 106–7.

75. Sojo, *Estudios del Folklore*, 172; Pollak-Eltz, *Black Culture*, 42–61; Pollak-Eltz, *La religiosidad popular*, 57–61; Liscano, *La fiesta de San Juan*, 47–61; Guss, "The Selling of San Juan," 451–73. For similar practices in the Dominican Republic, see Lizardo and Muñoz Victoria, *Fiestas patronales*, 76–77.

76. Pollak-Eltz, *Black Culture*, 44; Pollak-Eltz, *La religiosidad popular*, 118–19, 130–31; Reis, *A morte é uma festa*, 104, 122–23, 139–40; Hevia Lanier, *Prácticas religiosas*, 46, 56–57; Lipner and Lipner, *Dances of Venezuela*, 4; M. Davis, *Voces del purgatório*, 44; Poel, *Dicionário da religiosidade popular*, 161, 648.

77. M. Davis, "Music and Black Ethnicity," 124–29; M. Davis, "Dominican Folk Dance," 138–39; Hernández Soto and Sánchez, "Los Congos," 297–316; Lizardo, *Danzas y bailes*, 104–14; Santana and Sánchez, *La música folclórica*, 209–54; Roberts, *Black Music*, 33; Reis, *A morte é uma festa*, 61–66.

78. Reily, *Voices of the Magi*, 36.

79. Iyanaga, "Por que se canta?," 163–90; Iyanaga, "Why Saints Love Samba," 119–47; Iyanaga, "On Hearing Africas," 165–89, in Fromont, *Afro-Catholic Festivals*.

80. Hoornaert, *História da igreja*, 2:386.

81. Bruneau, *The Church in Brazil*, 25; T. Walker, "The Queen of los Congos," 311–12; Rivas Aliaga, "Danzantes negros," 35–63.

82. Quoted in Chacón, *Curiepe*, 33.

83. Ibid., 58.

84. Pérez Rodríguez, *El carnaval*, 1:124.

85. F. Ferreira, *Inventando Carnavais*, 32, 76, 132–45; F. Ferreira, *O livro de ouro*, 269–96; Chasteen, *National Rhythms*, 181–82.

86. B. Jacobs, *Origins of a Creole*, 316.

87. Laet, *Iaerlyck verhael*, 4:101–4.

88. Ibid., 4:266, 305.

89. Gehring and Schiltkamp, *Curaçao Papers*, 23; Hamelberg, *Documenten*, 48.

90. M. Goodman, "The Portuguese Element," 361–405.

91. Emmanuel and Emmanuel, *History of the Jews*, 1:41–47.

92. Gehring and Schiltkamp, *Curaçao Papers*, 81.

93. Klooster, *The Dutch Moment*, 175–82.

94. Emmanuel and Emmanuel, *History of the Jews*, 1:75; Rupert, *Creolization*, 82–83, 143; Klooster, "Curaçao as a Transit Center," 28.

95. Gehring and Schiltkamp, *Curaçao Papers*, 157, 163.

96. Ibid., 123.

97. Ibid., 162.

98. Hastings and Corwin, *Ecclesiastical Records*, 1:493.

99. Cardot, *Curazao Hispánico*, 392–93, 404–6, 412.

100. Konetzke, *Colección de documentos*, 3:248–49.

101. Lampe, "Christianity and Slavery," 142; Rupert, "'Seeking the Water of Baptism,'" 106–14.

102. Rupert, *Creolization*, 87. A reproduction of the 1677 baptismal book was published as an attachment to Schunck, "Intolerante tolerantie," 239–84.

103. Rupert, *Creolization*, 179.

104. Brenneker, *Zjozjoli*, 41; Panhuys, "Folklore van Bonaire," 319. The *West-Indisch Plakaatboek* includes more references to festive parades of Black people playing instruments, singing songs, and carrying flags in the streets of Curaçao that parallel brotherhood practices. See Schiltkamp and De Smidt, *West-Indisch Plakaatboek*, 1:271, 2:518, 831.

105. "Faesch aan kamer Amsterdam" (August 6, 1740), Archives of the New/ Second West India Company, no. 588:57r–59r, National Archives, The Hague.

106. Barcia, *Los ilustres apellidos*, 89–90; Rossi, *Cosas de negros*, 68.

107. Brenneker, *Sambumbu*, 3:516; 5:1087, 1100–1104, 1151, 1158, 1240; 6:1372–73; 7:1853; 9:2325–27; 10:2508; Streefkerk, "Godsdienstige gebruiken," 48; Lampe, "Christianity and Slavery," 139; R. Allen, *Di ki manera?*, 241–50.

108. Stein, *Vassouras*, 203; Randles, *L'ancien royaume*, 150–51; Wannyn, *L'Art ancien*, 36.

109. Brenneker, *Sambumbu*, 1:53–55, 188–90, 206; 5:1151, 1240; 7:1693–94, 1851; 10:1151, 2546; Streefkerk, "Godsdienstige gebruiken," 50; Rosalia, *Tambú*, 97, 208; R. Allen, *Di ki manera?*, 241.

110. Brenneker, *Sambumbu*, 1:186; 6:1507 ; 9:2276–77; Brenneker, *Zjozjoli*, 50, 247; Pereira, *Das Tchiloli*, 285; Karasch, *Slave Life*, 275–77; R. Lima, *Folclore das festas cíclicas*, 37; Brandão, *Sacerdotes de viola*, 195; Lizardo and Muñoz Victoria, *Fiestas Patronales*, 95–96; Pollak-Eltz, *La religiosidad popular*, 105–6.

111. Klooster, *Illicit Riches*, 65–66.

112. Green, *The Rise of the Trans-Atlantic Slave Trade*, 229; Santos and Soares, "Igreja," 2:497, in Albuquerque and Madeira Santos, *História Geral*; Fra Molinero, *La imagen de los Negros*, 45.

113. Brenneker, *Curaçaoensia*, 17; Brenneker, *Sambumbu*, 1:105; 5:1091, 1106–7; 10:2487–89; Hoefnagels and Hoogenbergen, *Antilliaans spreekwoordenboek*, 76; Abraham, *Van je familie*, 233.

114. Jordaan, *Slavernij en Vrijheid*, 150.

115. Schabel, "Notitia," 139; Brenneker, *Sambubu*, 3:555; 5:1092–93.

116. Brenneker, *Curaçaoensia*, 63.

117. Lampe, "Christianity and Slavery," 131.

118. Hoetink, *Het patroon*, 71; Nooijen, *De slavenparochie*, 28–29.

119. Baxter, *A Grammar of Kristang*, 8.

120. Kihm, *Kriyol Syntax*, 2.

121. Klooster, "Subordinate but Proud," 291.

122. Ibid.

123. Schiltkamp and De Smidt, *West-Indisch Plakaatboek*, 1:246; Rupert, *Creolization*, 152.

124. R. Allen, *Di ki manera?*, 165; Rosalia, *Tambú*, 105, 208.

125. Voorhoeve, "Historical and Linguistic Evidence," 142; Megenny, "África en América," 207–60; Perl, "Zur Präsenz des kreolisierten Portugiesisch," 131–48.

126. Abbenhuis, *De katholieke kerk in Suriname*, 118; Vernooij, *De regenboog*, 13–14.

127. Wolbers, *Geschiedenis van Suriname*, 146; Junker, "Eenige mededelingen," 449–80; Linde, *Surinaamse suikerheren*, 97.

128. Berkel, *The Voyages*, 153.

129. Quoted in Klinkers, *Op hoop van vrijheid*, 33.

130. Renselaar and Voorhoeve, "Messianism and Nationalism," 195–97; Abbenhuis, *De katholieke kerk in Suriname*, 119; Klinkers, *Op hoop van vrijheid*, 33.

131. Quoted in Gaspar, *Bondmen*, 23–24; Westergaard, *The Danish West Indies*, 161; Rupert, "'Seeking the Water of Baptism,'" 199–231.

132. Oldendorp, *Historie der caribischen Inseln*, vol. 2, part 1, 16–29.

133. Oldendorp, *Historie der caribischen Inseln*, vol. 2, bk. 2, 176–77; Sensbach, *Rebecca's Revival*, 92–96; Catron, *Embracing Protestantism*, 73–74; Frey and Wood, *Come Shouting*, 104–5; Gerbner, *Christian Slavery*, 138–63.

134. Oldendorp, *Historie der caribischen Inseln*, vol. 2, bk. 2, 188.

135. Ibid., vol. 2, bk. 1, 172–73, 186.

136. Sensbach, *Rebecca's Revival*, 53–60, 87.

137. Ibid., 92–93.

138. Quoted in Ibid., 87.

139. Oldendorp, *Historie der caribischen Inseln*, 1:445–48.

140. Ibid., 1:446–47; vol. 2, bk. 2, 758.

141. Ibid., 1:448, 647, 741–43.

142. Sensbach, *Rebecca's Revival*, 92–93.

143. Warner-Lewis, *Central Africa in the Caribbean*, 186.

144. P. Murphy, *The Moravian Mission*, 16; N. Hall, *Slave Society*, 200.

145. Campbell, "St. Thomas Negroes," 65.

146. Weed, *Letters from Europe*, 345.

147. *St. Croix Avis,* January 4, 1856.

148. Nicholls, *The Jumbies' Playing Ground*, 79, 95.

149. Biet, *Voyage*, 276–77, 292.

150. "Carta do secretário da Propaganda Fide aos povos do Reino do Congo" (October 6, 1660), in Brásio, *MMA-PS*, 12:312–13.

151. Merolla da Sorrento and Piccardo, *Breve e succinta relatione*, 135.

152. Savona, "Aperçu de la situation," 372; Thornton, *The Kongolese Saint Anthony*, 102–3; Heywood, "Slavery and Its Transformation," 20.

153. Lucques, *Relations sur le Congo*, 63, 181–82.

154. "James Barbot's Voyage to the Congo River" (August 28, 1700), in Donnan, *Documents*, 1:452.

155. Quoted in Palacios Preciado, *La trata de negros*, 348.

156. Winthrop, *Winthrop's Journal*, 2:227.

157. Ligon, *A True & Exact History*, 1–2.

158. Ratelband, *Nederlanders in West-Afrika*, 224–25; Wätjen, *Das holländisches Kolonialreich*, 314; Stokes, *The Iconography*, 4:106.

159. Maika, "Encounters," 35–72.

160. Ligon, *A True & Exact History*, 52.

161. Gaspar, "'Subjects of the King of Portugal,'" 99, 111.

162. Quoted in Shaw, *Everyday Life*, 123, 147.

163. Quoted in Gaspar, *Bondmen*, 227, 236–37.

164. Catron, *Embracing Protestantism*, 65–66.

165. Phillippo, *Jamaica*, 93, 102–4.

166. Schuler, "Myalism," 65–79; V. Brown, *The Reaper's Garden*, 226; Curtin, *Two Jamaicas*, 33–34; Turner, *Slaves and Missionaries*, 57–59.

167. Morales Padrón, *Spanish Jamaica*, 157, 212, 257; Mullin, *Africa in America*, 26; Amussen, *Caribbean Exchanges*, 164–67.

168. Beckwith, *Black Roadways*, 104; Abrahams and Szwed, *After Africa*, 39–47.

169. Rodway, *History of British Guiana*, 2:295–97.

170. Crookall, *British Guiana*, 132.

171. Northcroft, *Sketches*, 67–68.

172. Powles, *The Land of the Pink Pearl*, 147.

173. H. Johnson, "Friendly Societies," 184–87.

174. Quoted in Adderley, *"New Negroes,"* 203–6.

175. Quoted in Warner-Lewis, *Central Africa in the Caribbean*, 65.

176. *The Port of Spain Gazette,* November 12, 1853.

177. *The New Era,* November 8, 1889.

178. Cothonay, *Trinidad*, 64, 303–4.

179. Stewart, "The Orisha House," 153, in Fromont, *Afro-Catholic Festivals*.

180. Atwood, *The History of the Island of Dominica*, 268.

181. Quoted in Peabody, "A Dangerous Zeal," 53–54.

182. Mongin, "L'évangélisation des esclaves," 110, 120.

183. Peabody, "A Dangerous Zeal," 63–66.

184. Mongin, "L'évangélisation des esclaves," 86.

185. Quoted in Peabody, "A Dangerous Zeal," 67.

186. Wells and Wells, *Friendly Societies*, 11–12, 46.

187. H. Breen, *St. Lucia*, 192; Crowley, "La Rose and La Marguerite," 549–50.

188. Aubert, "To Establish One Law," 21–43.

189. Quoted in Wiesinger, "Acteurs et échanges."

190. Rochefort, *The History of the Caribby Islands*, 201.

191. Bouton, *Relation de l'établissement des françois*, 98, 100, 134.

192. Tertre, *Histoire générale des Isles*, 474–75; Tertre, *Histoire générale des Antilles*, 1:63–64, 2:518.

193. Chevillard, *Les desseins*, 193.

194. Labat, *Nouveau voyage*, 4:440.

195. Binder, "Die Zeeländische Kaperfahrt," 42–43.

196. Tertre, *Histoire générale des Antilles*, 1:460–65; 2:492, 494–95.

197. Biet, *Voyage*, 147.

198. Quoted in Wiesinger, "Acteurs et échanges."

199. Jennings and Pfänder, *Inheritance and Innovation*, 55–69.

200. Long, *The History of Jamaica*, 2:430.

201. Peabody, "A Dangerous Zeal," 79.

202. Debbasch, "Les associations serviles," 122, 127.

203. Peabody, "A Dangerous Zeal," 88–90.

204. Debbasch, "Les associations serviles," 124.

205. Ibid., 139.

206. Quoted in Peytraud, *L'Esclavage*, 182–83.

207. Charlevoix, *Histoire de l'Isle Espagnole*, 2:501.

208. Moreau de Saint-Méry, *Description topographique*, 1:53–55.

209. V. Brown, *The Reaper's Garden*, 223.

210. "Arrêt de Réglement du Conseil du Cap" (February 18, 1761), in Moreau de Saint-Méry, *Loix et constitutions*, 4:352–55.

211. Carteau, *Soirées bermudiennes*, 81.

212. Cabon, *Notes sur l'Histoire Religieuse*, 91.

213. Candler, *Brief Notices*, 150.

214. Vanhee, "Central African Popular Christianity," 261, in Heywood, *Central Africans and Cultural Transformations*.

215. Herskovits, *Life in a Haitian Valley*, 113, 141, 144, 157, 177, 207–13, 272, 277, 288.

216. Labouret and Rivet, *Le Royaume d'Ardra*, 31–35; Anguiano, *Misiones capuchinas*, 251–66.

217. Thornton, "On the Trail of Voodoo," 267; Thornton, "I Am the Subject," 206–14; Vanhee, "Central African Popular Christianity," 243–64, in Heywood, *Central Africans and Cultural Transformations*; Rey, "Kongo Catholic Influences," 265–85; Rey: "The Virgin Mary," 341–69.

218. Guerra, *Teatralización del folklore*, 41.

219. Deren, *Divine Horsemen*, 177; Polk, *Haitian Vodou Flag*, 15–16; Polk, "Sacred Banners," 325–47.

220. Cosentino, "It's All for You," 250.

221. Murell, *Afro-Caribbean Religions*, 75; Rigaud, *La tradition Voudoo*, 257; Heusch, *Le roi de Kongo*, 343–49; Thomas, *Roots of Haiti's Vodou-Christian Faith*, 88, 90, 111.

222. Métraux, *Le Vaudou Haïtien*, 287.

223. Hebblethwaite, *Vodou Songs*, 59. Compare to Randles, *L'ancien royaume*, 150–51.

224. Quoted in Thornton, "'I Am the Subject of the King of Kongo,'" 208.

225. Madiou, *Histoire d'Haïti*, 1:181; Thornton, "'I Am the Subject of the King of Kongo,'" 181–85, 204; J. Miller, "Central Africans during the Era of the Slave Trade," 56–57, in Heywood, *Central Africans and Cultural Transformations*. It should also be noted that "Dos Reis Magos" (lit. From the Magi) was the surname of a prestigious Kongolese family; see Thornton, "Central African Names," 734.

226. Quoted in Geggus, "The Slaves and Free People," in Cañizares-Esguerra, Childs, and Sidbury, *The Black Urban Atlantic in the Age of the Slave Trade*, 118.

227. Schoelcher, *Colonies étrangères*, 2:299–30.

228. Seabrook, *The Magic Island*, 191–93.

229. R. Hall, "The Société Congo," 685 700; Métraux, *Le Vaudou Haïtien*, 143; Dunham, *Dances of Haiti*, 32; Laguerre, "Bizango," 147–60; W. Davis, *Passage of Darkness*, 241–84.

230. Fick, *The Making of Haiti*, 127; Rey, "The Virgin Mary," 341–69.

231. Dubois, *Haiti*, 62.

232. Bastian, *Ein Besuch in San Salvador*, 134.

233. Sobel, *Trabelin' On*, xxiii.

234. J. Jacobs, *New Netherland*, 380–88.

235. "Letter of Reverend Jonas Michaëlius to Adrian Smoutius" (August 11, 1628), in Hastings and Corwin, *Ecclesiastical Records,* 1:62.

236. O'Callaghan, *Voyages of the Slavers*, 178–80, 194–200, 205–6, 214–25; O'Callaghan, Fernow, and Brodhead, *Documents*, 14:477; Gehring and Schiltkamp, *Curaçao Papers*, 125, 141, 168, 174, 177–79, 186–87; Dewulf, *The Pinkster King*, 37–39; Maika, "To 'Experiment with a Parcel of Negros,'" 33–69.

237. "Report on the Surrender of New Netherland" (1666), in O'Callaghan, Fernow, and Brodhead, *Documents*, 2:430.

238. Purple, *Marriages*, 10–30; T. Evans, *Records*, 10–38; Laer, *New York Historical Manuscripts*, 1:23 and 4:35, 53, 60, 62, 96–100, 208–9, 212–13; Gehring, *New York Historical Manuscripts: Dutch, Volumes GG, HH & II*, 55; Sypher, *Liber A*, 3–37.

239. Fernow, *The Records of New Amsterdam*, 4:56–57.

240. Ibid., 4:41–42, 56–57.

241. O'Callaghan, Fernow, and Brodhead, *Documents*, 2:23–47.

242. Dankers and Sluyter, *Journal of a Voyage*, 137.

243. "Order Increasing the Salary of Resolved Waldron" (June 10, 1657), New Netherland Council: Dutch Colonial Council Minutes, 1638–1665, series A1809, vol. 8, New York State Archives, Albany, NY.

244. Laet, *Iaerlyck verhael*, 2:146, 3:209, 4:13; O'Callaghan, Fernow, and Brodhead, *Documents*, 13:142–43, 152, 273, 328, 330, 338, and 14:52; Evans,

Records, 21–23; Laer, *New York Historical Manuscripts*, 4:333; Gehring, *Council Minutes, 1652–1654*, 129–30; Christoph, "The Freedmen," 159; G. Hodges, *Root and Branch*, 11–12; C. Moore, "A World of Possibilities," 47–48; Romney, *New Netherland Connections*, 215–17.

245. Gehring, *Council Minutes 1655–1656*, 77; Donnan, *Documents*, 3:414–15, 4:49–50; Breen and Innes, *"Myne Owne Ground,"* 71.

246. "Fernando Appeals His Suit to the General Court" (1667), in Billings, *The Old Dominion*, 200.

247. Fernow, *The Records of New Amsterdam*, 1:362–63; Eekhof, *De Hervormde kerk*, 2:155.

248. Brüser and Santos, *Dicionário do Crioulo*, 652; Rougé, *Petit dictionnaire*, 128.

249. In his research on the Black community in seventeenth-century Amsterdam, which was similar in origin to the one in New Amsterdam, Mark Ponte observed that whenever members of this community needed an interpreter, they opted for someone speaking Spanish or Portuguese. Moreover, the Black community integrated people with roots in Portuguese colonies in Asia (Goa, Malacca), which indicates that familiarity with Iberian culture and language were important community-building factors. Ponte, "'Al de swarten,'" 56–57.

250. Sobel, *Trabelin' On*, 40.

251. J. Jacobs, *New Netherland*, 312–18; Mosterman, *Spaces of Enslavement*, 39–43.

252. Deursen, *Bavianen*, 137.

253. Ibid., 139.

254. Schalkwijk, *The Reformed Church*, 151; Joosse, *Geloof in de Nieuwe Wereld*, 507–8.

255. "Acta Deputatorum ad res Exteras" (November 19, 1641), in Hastings and Corwin, *Ecclesiastical Records*, 1:142.

256. Joosse, *Geloof in the Nieuwe Wereld*, 242.

257. Boxer, *The Dutch in Brazil*, 32–66; Joosse, *Geloof in the Nieuwe Wereld*, 425–26; Dewulf, "Emulating," 3–36.

258. Teensma and Nielsen, *Seventeen Letters*, 11–12; J. Jacobs, *New Netherland*, 313.

259. Quoted in Schoeman, *Early Slavery*, 83, 167.

260. Hovy and Streefkerk, *"Zoo is 't,"* 95.

261. Dewulf, *The Pinkster King*, 45–46.

262. Quoted in Lampe, "The Dutch Reformed Church," 111.

263. "Classis of Amsterdam. Act of the Deputies" (September 12, 1650), in Hastings and Corwin, *Ecclesiastical Records*, 1:280–81.

264. "Act of the Deputies. Letter to Rev. Van Beaumont" (July 9, 1661), in Hastings and Corwin, *Ecclesiastical Records*, 1:508; "Beaumont to the Amsterdam Classis" (December 5, 1662), in Archief van de Nederlandse Hervormde Kerk, Classis Amsterdam, nos. 157:425, 224:17–21.

265. "Vice Director Beck to Petrus Stuyvesant, Curaçao" (November 15, 1664), in Gehring and Schiltkamp, *Curaçao Papers*, 451; "Rev. Henry Selyns, Minister at Brooklyn, L.I., to the Classis of Amsterdam" (October 4, 1660), in Hastings and Corwin, *Ecclesiastical Records*, 1:479; Bonomi, "'Swarms of Negroes,'" 43.

266. Canin, *Acta Synodi Nationalis*, 47–50; Shell, "Civic Status," 28–63.

267. Udemans, *'T geestelyk roer*, 183.

268. Brumund, "Bijdragen tot de geschiedenis der kerk in Batavia," 52.

269. Quoted in G. Hodges, *Slavery*, 37.

270. "John Rolfe to Sir Edwin Sandys" (January 1919/20), in Kingsbury, *The Records*, 3:243; Thornton, "The African Experience," 421–34.

271. Thornton, "The African Experience," 434.

272. Donnan, *Documents*, 4:49.

273. Heywood and Thornton, "'Canniball Negroes,'" 81–82; Breen and Innes, *"Myne Owne Ground,"* 130; Berlin, *Many Thousands Gone*, 36–39.

274. Hotten, *Original Lists*, 172–73, 241, 244; Breen and Innes, *"Myne Owne Ground,"* 69–70; Writers' Program Virginia, *The Negro in Virginia*, 12–17; Goetz, *The Baptism of Early Virginia*, 95–96.

275. Writers' Program Virginia, *The Negro in Virginia*, 12; Deal, *Race and Class*, 166, 229; Breen and Innes, *"Myne Owne Ground,"* 18, 77; Berlin, *Many Thousands Gone*, 36–46; Billings, *The Old Dominion*, 177.

276. Writers' Program Virginia, *The Negro in Virginia*, 11, 87.

277. Ibid., 15.

278. Ibid., 17; Donnan, *Documents*, 4:68.

279. Raboteau, *Slave Religion*, 97–99; Bonomi, *Under the Cope of Heaven*, 119–20; Bonomi, "'Swarms of Negroes,'" 34–58; Goetz, *The Baptism of Early Virginia*, 86–111; Beasley, *Christian Ritual*, 67–68; Glasson, "'Baptism Doth Not Bestow Freedom,'" 279–318; Porter, *Religion versus Empire*, 25. For opposition to slave baptism in the Caribbean, see Dunn, *Sugar and Slaves*, 249–50; Amussen, *Caribbean Exchanges*, 114–16; Gerbner, *Christian Slavery*, 91–111.

280. Donnan, *Documents*, 4:68.

281. Quoted in Johnston, *Slavery in Rhode Island*, 11–12.

282. T. Murphy, *Jesuit Slaveholding*, 17, 35–37, 45, 91–122.

283. Hughes, *History of the Society of Jesus*, 1:213; Heywood and Thornton, *Central Africans, Atlantic Creoles*, 283–84.

284. Menard, "The Maryland Slave Population," 29–54; W. Johnson, "The Origin and Nature of African Slavery," 236–45.

285. Donnan, *Documents*, 3:434.

286. Bonomi, "'Swarms of Negroes,'" 47.

287. Hodes, *White Women*, 19–23.

288. Sweet, "African Identity," 247.

289. Winthrop, *Winthrop's Journal*, 1:260.

290. Donnan, *Documents*, 3:19; Heywood and Thornton, "'Canniball Negroes,'" 76–94; Warren, *New England Bound*, 120–22, 137, 164–65, 177–78, 198–99, 243; Sanborn, "Angola," 119–29.

291. P. Wood, *Black Majority*, 332–41.

292. Thornton, "African Dimensions," 1103–5.

293. Salley, *Warrants*, 1:112; 2:44, 59, 63, 79, 80, 83; 3:176, 187–88, 212; P. Wood, *Black Majority*, 44.

294. "Account of the Negroe Insurrection in South Carolina" (1739), in Mark Smith, *Stono*, 14.

295. Ibid., 108–23.

296. Wright, "Dispatches of Spanish Officials," 144–95.

297. Landers, *Black Society*, 32, 48, 110, 113; Landers, "The Central African Presence," 227–41, in Heywood, *Central Africans and Cultural Transformations*; Landers, "Free and Slave," 172; Kapitzke, *Religion*, 9.

298. Gannon, *The Cross*, 84–85; Berlin, *Many Thousands Gone*, 154; Woods, *A History of the Catholic Church*, 30–31.

299. McDonogh, *The Florida Negro*, 10.

300. Higginson, "Slave Songs," 115; W. Allen, *Slave Songs*, 45.

301. Iberville, *Iberville's Gulf Journals*, 154.

302. Ru, *Journal*, 71.

303. Pratz, *Histoire de la Louisiane*, 1:342.

304. G. Hall, *Africans in Colonial Louisiana*, 57–60; G. Hall, "The Formation of Afro-Creole Culture," 66–71; Lachance, "The Growth of the Free and Slave Populations," 204–43.

305. G. Hall, *Slavery and African Ethnicities*, 176; G. Hall, "Epilogue," 291–309; Sublette, *The World That Made New Orleans*, 107.

306. Lachance, "The 1809 Immigration," 245–84; G. Hall, "The Formation of Afro-Creole Culture," 58–90; Dessens, *From Saint-Domingue*, 1–5, 154–62.

307. Lachance, "The Foreign French," 117.

308. Baudry des Lozières, *Second voyage*, 108–46; Glaunec, "'Un Nègre,'" 107; G. Hall, *Africans in Colonial Louisiana*, 283; G. Hall, *Slavery and African Ethnicities*, 70–74; Dessens, *From Saint-Domingue*, 244–64; F. Evans, *Congo Square*, 48; Dewulf, *From the Kingdom of Kongo*, 1–21, 123–44.

309. Baudier, *The Catholic Church*, 74; Gillard, *The Catholic Church*, 17; Vidal, *Caribbean New Orleans*, 148–61; Woods, *A History of the Catholic Church*, 102–3; Aubert, "'To Establish One Law,'" 21–43; Sensbach, "'The Singing,'" 24–25; Raboteau, *Slave Religion*, 134; Pasquier, *Fathers on the Frontier*, 181–83.

310. "Raphaël de Luxembourg to Jean Baptiste Raguet" (May 15, 1725), in Rowland, Sanders, and Galloway, *Mississippi Provincial Archives*, 2:480–82.

311. Gould and Nolan, *No Cross*, xxvi; Woods, *A History of the Catholic Church*, 193; Blassingame, *Black New Orleans*, 16; Ochs, *Black Patriot*, 13; Gould, "The Parish Identities," 1–10; Wheat, "My Friend," 117–31.

312. Watson, "Notitia," vol. 2, no. 1: 234; Robin, *Voyage*, 58, 248.

313. Latrobe, *Impressions*, 35, 62, 94, 122–23, 164–65.

314. Coleman, *Creole Voices*, 58–59; Nolan, *A History of the Archdiocese of New Orleans*, 9–20.

315. Quoted in Pasquier, *Fathers on the Frontier*, 177.

316. Clark and Gould, "The Feminine Face," 420, 427.

317. Martineau, *Retrospect*, 1:259–60.

318. Gillard, *Colored Catholics*, 58–59.

319. Ingersoll, *Mammon*, 111–13.

320. Sobel, *Trabelin' On*, xvii, 55.

321. Berlin, *Many Thousands Gone*, 349.

322. Pasquier, "Creole Catholicism," 274.

323. Latrobe, *Impressions*, 137–38.

324. Quoted in Tardieu, *Los negros*, 1:558–59.

325. Letts, *The Travels of Leo of Rozmital*, 112–13.

326. F. Monteiro, "Tabanca," 18; Saraiva, "Rituais funerários," 141.

327. Latrobe, *Impressions*, 164–65.

328. Saxon, *Fabulous New Orleans*, 17.

329. M. Christian, "The Negro in Louisiana," chapter 11, "Voodooism and Mumbo-Jumbo" https://louisianadigitallibrary.org/islandora/object/uno-p15140coll42%3A21; Jacobs and Kaslow, *The Spiritual Churches*, 64; Dawdy, *Building the Devil's Empire*, 139–40; Cooksey, Poynor, and Vanhee, *Kongo Across the Waters*, 248–49; Pasquier, "Creole Catholicism," 276.

330. "Dédé/McKinney interview," in Louisiana Writers' Project, folder 25, Federal Writers' Collection, Watson Memorial Library, Northwestern State University, Natchitoches, LA.

331. Brandão, *Sacerdotes de viola*, 85–87; Slenes, "Saint Anthony," 238; Stein, *Vassouras*, 203; "Raphael/Breaux-Villere interview," in Louisiana Writers' Project, folder 587, Federal Writers' Collection, Watson Memorial Library, Northwestern State University, Natchitoches, LA; Long, *A New Orleans Vodou Priestess*, 134.

332. "Oscar Felix/Edmund Burke interview," in Louisiana Writers' Project, folder 25, Federal Writers' Collection, Watson Memorial Library, Northwestern State University, Natchitoches, LA.

333. Reprint, *Democratic Pharos,* August 16, 1871.

334. Reis, *A morte é uma festa,* 104; Hevia Lanier, *Prácticas religiosas,* 46, 56–57.

335. Saxon, *Fabulous New Orleans,* 33–34.

336. L. Brooks, *The Dances,* 3–4, 54; Ruiz, *A King Travels,* 266–92; Chaves, *Danças,* 9–23; Very, *The Spanish Corpus Christi Procession,* 15, 37, 44–45, 91–99; E. Oliveira, *Festividades cíclicas,* 273–86.

337. O'Neill, *New Orleans Carnival,* 192–93.

338. Braga, *O povo portuguez,* 2:268–69; F. Ferreira, *O livro de ouro,* 149–50.

339. Barbinais, *Nouveau voyage,* 3:173–74.

340. Braga, *O povo portuguez,* 2:268–69; Chasteen, *National Rhythms,* 35.

341. Saxon, *Fabulous New Orleans,* 15–16.

342. Ortiz, *Los bailes,* 441–46, 483–84; S. Walker, "Congo Kings," 130.

343. Creecy, *Scenes in South,* 43–45.

344. Very, *The Spanish Corpus Christi Procession,* 26, 44, 73, 82–83, 91.

345. Saxon, *Fabulous New Orleans,* 15–16.

346. Epstein, *Sinful Tunes,* 84; Logsdon and Bell, "The Americanizaton," 236; Crété, *Daily Life,* 71, 207; Tallant, *Mardi Gras,* 107; Sensbach, "'The Singing,'" 28–30.

347. Russell, *Pictures,* 93–96.

348. Paxton, *The New-Orleans Directory,* 40–41.

349. Quoted in Long, *A New Orleans Voudou Priestess,* 107.

350. Niehaus, *The Irish,* 28–36; Nau, *The German People,* 4–5; R. Miller, "The Failed Mission," 156–57; Woods, *A History of the Catholic Church,* 277–78, 359.

351. Baudier, *The Catholic Church,* 354–55; R. Miller, "Slaves," 142.

352. Newman, *Desegregating Dixie,* 65–82; Logsdon and Bell, "The Americanizaton," 201–61; Baudier, *The Catholic Church,* 489; Ochs, *Desegregating,* 34–37; Woods, *A History of the Catholic Church,* 194, 300; R. Miller, "The Failed Mission," 166–69.

353. Saxon, Dreyer, and Tallant, *Gumbo Ya-Ya,* 242.

354. Quoted in Jacobs and Kaslow, *The Spiritual Churches,* 16.

355. Michael Smith, *Spirit World,* 35.

356. *The Daily Picayune,* June 25, 1874.

357. Michael Smith, *Mardi Gras Indians,* 25–29, 51; Dewulf, *From the Kingdom of Kongo,* 123–94.

358. Tallant, *Mardi Gras,* 241.

359. Draper, "The Mardi Gras Indians," 23.

360. Kinser, *Carnival*, 174; Berry, Foose, and Jones, "In Search," 210.

361. A. Kennedy, *Big Chief Harrison*, 30, 71–72, 223, 307, 338.

CHAPTER FOUR. THE CATHOLIC ROOTS OF AFRICAN AMERICAN CHRISTIANITY

1. Osgood, Keep, and Nelson, *Minutes of the Common Council*, 4:86–88.

2. Seeman, *Death in the New World*, 197, 230. For similar prohibitions in the Caribbean, see Beasley, *Christian Ritual*, 121.

3. "Morte de D. Álvaro III, Rei do Congo, e eleição de D. Pedro II Afonso" (1622), in Brásio, *MMA-PS*, 15:485–86.

4. Debien, "La Christianisation des esclaves," 534; Mintz and Price, *The Birth of African-American Culture*, 42; G. Hall, *Slavery*, 169; Heywood and Thornton, *Central Africans, Atlantic Creoles*, 262; Wheat, *Atlantic Africa*, 252; Epstein, *Sinful Tunes*, 79; Mufwene, "The Founder Principle," 83–134; Chaudenson and Mufwene, *Creolization*, 74, 92; Sensbach, *Rebecca's Revival*, 92.

5. Robin, *Voyages*, 3:169–70.

6. Berlin, *Many Thousands Gone*, 92, 102–3, 189, 272.

7. Laing, "'Heathens and Infidels,'" 200, 218.

8. *The New-York Gazette*, August 27, 1733; Hodges, *Root and Branch*, 124; *The Pennsylvania Gazette*, March 27, 1740; Donnan, *Documents*, 3:27, 4:29–34; Hodes, *White Women*, 41; Morgan, *Slave Counterpoint*, 592; *The Virginia Gazette or The American Advertiser*, Nov. 13, 1784.

9. C. Davis, "God," 26; C. Davis, *The History of Black Catholics*, 86–88, 102–3.

10. "Governor Hunter to the Lords of Trade" (June 23, 1712), in O'Callaghan, Fernow, and Brodhead, *Documents*, 5:342.

11. Hodges and Brown, *Pretends to Be Free*, 134.

12. Horsmanden, *The New York Conspiracy*, 149, 378; Meehan, "Mission Work," 125.

13. McManus, *Black Bondage*, 101.

14. Bonomi, "'Swarms of Negroes,'" 47.

15. Phillippo, *Jamaica*, 93, 102–4.

16. Sharpe, "Proposals," 341.

17. Medford, *Historical Perspectives*, 13–23, 65–76.

18. Hodges, *Root and Branch*, 28.

19. Felt, *Annals of Salem*, 2:419–20.

20. M. Wade, "'Shining in Borrowed Plumage,'" 228.

21. Earle, *Customs and Fashions*, 225–26; Reidy, "'Negro Election Day,'" 102–17; White, "'It Was a Proud Day,'" 13–50; Fowler, *History of Durham*, 162.

22. Caulkins, *History of Norwich*, 330–31.

23. Stuart, *Hartford*, 38–39; K. Harris, "In Remembrance," 41.

24. Updike, *History of the Episcopal Church*, 178.

25. Greene, *The Negro*, 249–50; McManus, *Black Bondage*, 96–97.

26. Platt, "Negro Governors," 318–25; Piersen, *Black Yankees*, 134–35.

27. Greene, *The Negro*, 255.

28. *The Massachusetts Centinel*, August 19, 1786.

29. Quoted in J. Phillips, *Salem*, 272.

30. "An Act for Preventing Insurrection among Slaves" (June 1680), in Billings, *The Old Dominion*, 205.

31. Harris, "In Remembrance," 40–43.

32. Horsmanden, *The New York Conspiracy*, 327.

33. Stuckey, *Going through the Storm*, 73.

34. Niles, *The Hoosac Valley*, 415, 488; White, "Pinkster in Albany," 191–99; Dewulf, "Pinkster," 245–71; Dewulf, *The Pinkster King*, 35–74.

35. *The Albany Centinel*, June 13, 1803.

36. Eights, "Pinkster Festivities," 2:323–27.

37. J. Munsell, "Theatrical Reminiscences," 2:56.

38. Southern, *The Music of Black Americans*, 138.

39. Kinser, *Carnival*, 46–47, 233–36; Mitchell, *All on a Mardi Gras Day*, 151–84; O'Neill, *New Orleans Carnival*, 184–88.

40. Flint, *Recollections*, 103.

41. Dewulf, "The Missing Link," 83–95.

42. Rourke, *American Humor*, 88.

43. Sala, *America Revisited*, 350.

44. Gill, *Lords of Misrule*, 157–58.

45. M. Christian, "The Negro in Louisiana," chapter 41, "Carnival Groups and Social, Aid, and Pleasure Clubs," https://louisianadigitallibrary.org/islandora/object/uno-p15140coll42%3A29.

46. Saxon, Dreyer, and Tallant, *Gumbo Ya-Ya*, 308–9.

47. Armstrong, *Satchmo*, 127.

48. Saxon, *Fabulous New Orleans*, 24–29, 49–50.

49. J. Smith, *Introduction*, 24–25.

50. Bernhard, *Travels*, 127.

51. Hodges, *Black New Jersey*, 69.

52. Kachun, *Festivals of Freedom*, 36.

53. *The New England Galaxy & Masonic Magazine*, July 14, 1820.

54. Writers' Program Virginia, *The Negro in Virginia*, 324, 331–32.

55. Sesay, "Emancipation," 21–22.

56. Reynolds, *Albany Chronicles*, 629; W. Kennedy, *O Albany!*, 254–55; Williams-Myers, *Long Hammering*, 136.

57. Greene, *The Negro*, 252; K. Harris, "In Remembrance," 35; K. Harris, "The Black Governors," 75–76.

58. Thornton, "'I Am the Subject of the King of Kongo,'" 200.

59. Roberts, *Black Music*, 67; K. Harris, "In Remembrance," 36.

60. M. Souza, "Kongo King Festivals," 43.

61. Kinser, *Carnival*, 43.

62. Sublette, *The World That Made New Orleans*, 110–15, 295.

63. Ortiz Fernández, *Los cabildos*, 11–13, 18.

64. Kapitzke, *Religion*, 24.

65. Landers, *Black Society*, 110.

66. Sensbach, "Religion," 636.

67. Mello, *Nederlanders in Brazilië*, 184, 197–98; Baerle, *The History of Brazil*, 51; Joosse, *Geloof in de Nieuwe Wereld*, 505; L'Honoré Naber, *Reisebeschreibungen*, 1:32, 59; Dewulf, "Emulating," 3–36.

68. Oldendorp, *Historie der caribischen Inseln*, 1:608.

69. Cañizares-Esguerra, Childs, and Sidbury, *The Black Urban Atlantic*, 9.

70. Heywood and Thornton, "Central African Leadership," 238.

71. Kachun, *Festivals of Freedom*, 5, 20.

72. *Freedom's Journal*, July 18, 1828.

73. *The Colored American*, August 15, 1840.

74. Quoted in White and White, *Stylin'*, 137.

75. *The North Star*, July 14, 1848.

76. Douglass, *My Bondage*, 253.

77. Reidy, "'Negro Election Day,'" 113.

78. Rome, *Brève relation*, 112.

79. Ponte, "Al de swarten," 58.

80. Vincent de Paul, *Correspondence*, 8:501.

81. Biet, *Voyage*, 276–77, 292.

82. Grothe, "Classicale Acta van Brazilië," 402.

83. Gehring and Venema, *Council Minutes, 1656–1658*, 431–32.

84. Schalkwijk, *The Reformed Church*, 151; Joosse, *Geloof in de Nieuwe Wereld*, 507–8.

85. "Nicolaus Ketel te Luanda" (February 18–March 4, 1642), Archives of the States-General, part 2, nos. 5756:145–47, National Archives, The Hague; Noorlander, *Heaven's Wrath*, 179–80.

86. Vos, *Kongo in the Age of Empire*, 60;

87. Hastings, *The Church in Africa*, 385–87.

88. Vos, *Kongo in the Age of Empire*, 78; R. Brown, "The Immersion," 251.

89. Heywood and Thornton, *Central Africans, Atlantic Creoles*, 272.

90. Berlin, *Many Thousands Gone*, 75–76.

91. Ponte, "Al de swarten," 58.

92. Mather, *Diary*, 1:176.

93. Quoted in Catron, *Embracing Protestantism*, 122–23.

94. Venema, *Deacons' Accounts*, 223–24.

95. Sweet, "African Identity," 246.

96. Mosterman, *Spaces of Enslavement*, 108; T. Evans, *Records*, 26. For parallels to English colonies, see Goetz, *The Baptism of Early Virginia*, 101.

97. G. Cardoso, *Negro Slavery*, 140–41.

98. Christoph, "The Freedmen," 163–65.

99. "Henricus Selijns. Second Letter" (June 9, 1664), in Linde, *Old First Dutch Reformed Church*, 230–31.

100. Quoted in Raboteau, *Slave Religion*, 123.

101. Gerbner, *Christian Slavery*, 79.

102. Gerbner, *Christian Slavery*, 138–63; Beasley, *Christian Ritual*, 74–77.

103. Oldendorp, *Historie der caribischen Inseln*, 2, I:337.

104. Purple, *Marriages*, 14, 71.

105. Faria, "Fr. João de Santiago," 323.

106. Meuwese, "Dutch Calvinism," 118–41.

107. Ponte, "Al de swarten," 58

108. Frijhoff, *Wegen van Evert Willemsz*, 779.

109. Quoted in Gerbner, *Christian Slavery*, 118.

110. Quoted in Bonomi, "'Swarms of Negroes,'" 53.

111. Ibid.

112. Wittwer, *The Faithful*, 7; Hodges, *Black New Jersey*, 19.

113. Evans, *Records*, 99–111, 116–17, 120, 122, 127, 130, 137, 140, 142, 149–51, 154, 158, 162, 169; Purple, *Marriages*, 32, 35–38, 46–48, 51, 53, 64, 68, 71, 85–86, 138, 220, 227, 231, 241; Goodfriend, *Who Should Rule*, 178–97; Mosterman, *Spaces of Enslavement*, 112–13.

114. Mosterman, "'I Thought They Were Worthy,'" 610–16.

115. Quoted in Bonomi, "'Swarms of Negroes,'" 53; K. Hamilton, *The Bethlehem Diary*, 121, 134–35.

116. *The Pennsylvania Gazette*, September 11, 1740.

117. *Rivington's New-York Gazetteer*, June 8, 1775; *The New York Gazette and the Weekly Mercury*, November 10, 1783.

118. Bonomi, "'Swarms of Negroes,'" 58.

119. Hodges, *Slavery and Freedom*, 31, 58, 153; Hodges, *Root and Branch*, 63, 87–88; Hodges, *Black New Jersey*, 23. Others have built on this idea: see Armstead, *Mighty Change*, 6; L. Harris, *In the Shadow of Slavery*, 41.

120. Deursen, *Plain Lives*, 108–9; Frijhoff and Spies, *Nederlandse cultuur*, 351–432.

121. Merwick, *Possessing Albany*, 75; Sponsler, *Ritual Imports*, 48.

122. Frijhoff, *Wegen van Evert Willemsz*, 775; Deursen, *Plain Lives*, 108–9; Frijhoff and Spies, *Nederlandse cultuur*, 351–432; Kosterman, *Het aanzien*, 61–63.

123. J. Jacobs, *New Netherland*, 312.

124. Frijhoff, *Wegen van Evert Willemsz*, 774.

125. Quoted in Howell and Tenny, *History of the County of Albany*, 725.

126. Eights, "Pinkster Festivities," 2:323–27; Munsell, "Theatrical Reminiscences," 2:56.

127. Huey, "A New Look at an Old Object," 22–23; Fromont, *Art of Conversion*, 150–51; Mosterman, *Spaces of Enslavement*, 130–31.

128. *The Albany Centinel*, June 13, 1803.

129. Horsmanden, *The New York Conspiracy*, 130.

130. Horsmanden, *The New York Conspiracy*, 139, 182; Hodges, *Root and Branch*, 93–98; Linebaugh and Rediker, *The Many-Headed Hydra*, 186–90; Lepore, *New York Burning*, 181.

131. Horsmanden, *The New York Conspiracy*, 349, 418; Hoffer, *The Great New York Conspiracy*, 138–51, 346.

132. Hernández Soto and Sánchez, "Los Congos," 298.

133. M. Davis, *Voces del purgatório*, 71.

134. Waddell, *Twenty-Nine Years*, 26, 36; V. Brown, *The Reaper's Garden*, 226; Curtin, *Two Jamaicas*, 33–34; Turner, *Slaves and Missionaries*, 57–59.

135. Higginson, *Army Life*, 17–18.

136. R. Wade, *Slavery in the Cities*, 171.

137. Payne, *Recollections*, 255.

138. Pollitzer, "The Relationship," 60; Lomax and Lomax, *Folk Song*, 335; Courlander, *Negro Folk Music*, 196; Frey and Wood, *Come Shouting*, 123; Washington, "Community Regulation," 71.

139. Towne, *Letters and Diary*, 20.

140. Stuckey, *Slave Culture*, 12, 16, 24.

141. Daniels, "Kongolese Christianity," 226.

142. "Of Captain Howell Davis and His Crew" (1724), in Defoe and Davis, *A General History*, 190.

143. Negreiros, *História ethnográphica*, 167, 173.

144. Liscano, *La fiesta*, 54.

145. Iyanaga, "On Hearing Africas," 172, in Fromont, *Afro-Catholic Festivals*.

146. Codman, *Ten Months in Brazil*, 90–91.

147. W. Allen, *Slave Songs*, 158.

148. Frey, "'The Year of Jubilee,'" 111.

149. Sobel, *Trabelin' On*, 129.

150. Quoted in Saxon, Dreyer, and Tallant, *Gumbo Ya-Ya*, 229.

151. Du Bois, *The Philadelphia Negro*, 204–7.

152. Frazier, *The Negro Church*, 3–19.

153. C. Jacobs, "Benevolent Societies," 21–33; Gravely, "The Rise of African Churches," 139–40; L. Harris, *In the Shadow of Slavery*, 82–84; Hodges, *Root and Branch*, 183; Harvey, *Through the Storm*, 37; Hackett, "The Prince Hall Masons," 770–802; Giggie, "For God and Lodge," 198–218; Giggie, "The Mississippi River," 113–29.

154. Swan, *New Amsterdam Gehenna*, 425–26; Hodges, *Root and Branch*, 183; L. Harris, *In the Shadow of Slavery*, 83–84; Alexander, *African or American?*, 9; Berlin, *Many Thousands Gone*, 252; Hodges, *Slavery and Freedom*, 188.

155. Seeman, *Death in the New World*, 118–19.

156. Writers' Program Virginia, *The Negro in Virginia*, 84, 324, 331–32.

157. Merolla da Sorrento and Piccardo, *Breve e succinta relatione*, 216, 218, 229.

158. Semedo and Turano, *Cabo Verde*, 13–14, 40, 62.

159. Owen, "Among the Voodoos," 240–42; *The Owego Gazette,* July 27, 1911.

160. Giggie, "For God and Lodge," 200.

161. Epstein, *Sinful Tunes*, 209.

162. Lyell, *A Second Visit*, 1:269–70.

163. Levine, *Black Culture*, 18.

164. Kingsley, *A Treatise*, 21–22.

165. See, for instance, Sobel, *Trabelin' On*, xvii, 79–98; Raboteau, *Slave Religion*, 15, 65.

166. Catron, *Embracing Protestantism*, 9.

167. Writers' Program Georgia, *Drums and Shadows*, 47–48.

168. McDonogh, *Black and Catholic*, 51.

169. Whipple, *Bishop's Whipple's Southern Diary*, 51.

170. While several theories have been presented on the origin of the terms *Golla* and *Gulla(h)* in the Sea Islands, the study of historical sources in combination with data from other parts of the Americas leaves little doubt that the terms originally referred to Angola. See J. Hamilton, *Negro Plot*, 22; Gonzales,

The Black Border, 9; Teenstra, *De landbouw*, 2:180–84; Pollitzer, *The Gullah People*, 108.

171. Writers' Program Georgia, *Drums and Shadows*, 70; Lindsay, *An Oral History*, 72.

172. Howard, "Before and After Emancipation," 142–43, W. Allen, *Slave Songs*, 412.

173. Catron, *Embracing Protestantism*, 150.

174. Young, *Rituals of Resistance*, 45.

175. Goetz, *The Baptism of Early Virginia*, 20.

176. R. Brown, *African-Atlantic Cultures*, 187–88, 190–96, 210.

177. Littlefield, *Rice and Slaves*, 116; Olwell, *Masters, Slaves, and Subjects*, 28.

178. Donnan, *Documents*, 4:363.

179. "Anti-slavery petition" (January 3, 1739), in Scott, *Cornerstones*, 34

180. Quoted in B. Wood, *Slavery in Colonial Georgia*, 68.

181. Gerbner, *Christian Slavery*, 4.

182. Le Jau, *The Carolina Chronicle*, 69, 77, 102, 120, 133.

183. Turpin, "May and New River Mission," 34.

184. Creel, *"A Peculiar People,"* 182.

185. Thornton, "African Dimensions," 1103–5.

186. Creel, *"A Peculiar People,"* 4, 131.

187. Writers' Program Georgia, *Drums and Shadows*, 66.

188. Creel, *"A Peculiar People,"* 186.

189. Crum, *Gullah*, 97.

190. Woofter, *Black Yeomanry*, 230.

191. Cooper, *Making Gullah*, 19–23.

192. Creel, *"A Peculiar People,"* 185, 231.

193. Peterkin, *Roll, Jordan, Roll*, 205–10.

194. Kuyk, "The African Derivation," 559–92; Kuyk, *African Voices*, 95–143; Creel, *"A Peculiar People,"* 45–54, 181–82; Washington, "Community Regulation," 47–79; Gomez, *Exchanging*, 99–102; Glass, *African American Dance*, 77; R. Brown, *African-Atlantic Cultures*, 198–250; Young, *Rituals of Resistance*, 78–80, 95.

195. R. Brown, "The Immersion," 246–55.

196. Young, *Rituals of Resistance*, 80, 101.

197. Chlotilde R. Martin, "Negro Burial Societies," Folder D-4–27B, and Mildred Hare, "Burial Societies and Lodges," Folder S-260–264-N, Works Progress Administration Federal Writers' Project Manuscript Collection, South Carolina Library, University of South Carolina.

198. Schoepf, *Travels*, 2:230.

199. Quoted in Gerbner, *Christian Slavery*, 230; Turpin, "May and New River Mission," 34.

200. *Christian Advocate and Journal,* January 22, 1836, and July 22, 1836; *The Southern Christian Advocate,* February 16, 1844, and October 30, 1846.

201. Gates, *The Black Church*, 16.

202. Catron, *Embracing Protestantism*, 82, 151.

203. Raboteau, "The Black Experience," 93.

204. Quoted in Krebsbach, "Black Catholics," 147–48.

205. Krebsbach, "Black Catholics," 157–59; Madden, *Catholics*, 68–69; Tate, *Catholics' Lost Cause*, 174–75.

206. MacGregor, *The Emergence*, 29.

207. C. Davis, *The History of Black Catholics*, 259.

208. Gillard, *The Catholic Church*, 223–25, 227, 250–51.

209. Giggie, "The Mississippi River," 117–18; Giggie, "For God and Lodge," 210.

210. *The Albany Daily Evening Times,* July 30, 1872.

211. Washington, *Sojourner Truth's America*, 10.

212. Truth, *Narrative*, 16, 48.

213. Truth, *Narrative*, 7, 53; Fitch and Mandziuk, *Sojourner Truth*, 77, 107, 125, 141, 218.

214. Truth, *Narrative*, 48–50.

215. Fitch and Mandziuk, *Sojourner Truth*, 146, 153; Mabee, *Sojourner Truth*, 128.

216. Truth, *Narrative*, 7.

217. Deming, *By-Ways of Nature*, 359–60; Giggie, "The Mississippi River," 123.

218. Brásio, *História e missiologia*, 236–37; Fromont, *Art of Conversion*, 41–44.

219. Pina, *Relação do Reino do Congo*, 105.

220. B. Andrade, *Planta da praça de Bissau*, 53–54.

221. "Apontamentos do Padre Sebastião de Souto" (1561); "Fábrica da Sé do Congo" (January 19, 1600), in Brásio, *MMA-PS*, 2:477–81, 5:3–5; Heywood and Thornton, "Central African Leadership," 212–13; Thornton, "Mbanza Kongo/São Salvador," 67.

222. Martins, *Contacto de culturas no Congo Português*, 119; Lemarchant, "The Bases of Nationalism," 344–54; MacGaffey, "Kongo and the King of the Americans," 171–81.

223. Guanche, *Africanía y etnicidad*, 237.

224. "If God is with us, who can be against us." Burton, *Two Trips*, 2:76, 317.

CONCLUSION

1. "Reinterment"; "An African-American Homecoming"; "Teaching with Historic Places," from The African Burial Ground, National Park Service, U.S. General Services Administration.

2. Cressler, *Authentically Black*, 11.

3. R. Miller, "The Failed Mission," 149.

4. Raboteau, *A Fire in the Bones*, 134.

5. Souza, "Reis do Congo," 83.

BIBLIOGRAPHY

ARCHIVES

Academia de Ciências, Lisbon, Portugal.

Archief van de Nederlandse Hervormde Kerk; Classis Amsterdam. Amsterdam City Archives, The Netherlands.

Archives de particuliers—Histoire colonial. Royal Museum for Central Africa, Tervuren, Belgium.

Archives of the Congregation of the Most Holy Redeemer, Jean Cuvelier Papers. KADOC Documentation and Research Centre on Religion, Culture, and Society, KU Leuven, Belgium.

Arquivo Histórico da Câmara Municipal, Lisbon, Portugal.

Arquivo Histórico Ultramarino, Lisbon, Portugal.

Arquivo Nacional da Torre do Tombo, Lisbon, Portugal.

Engel Sluiter Historical Documents Collections. Bancroft Library, University of California, Berkeley.

Federal Writers' Collection. Watson Memorial Library, Cammie G. Henry Research Center, Northwestern State University, Natchitoches, LA.

Marcus Christian Collection. Earl K. Long Library, Louisiana and Special Collections Department, University of New Orleans.

National Archives, The Hague, The Netherlands.

New York State Archives, Albany, NY.

Works Progress Administration Federal Writers' Project Manuscript Collection. South Carolina Library, University of South Carolina.

NEWSPAPERS AND PERIODICALS

The Albany Centinel (Albany, NY, 1797–1806).
The Albany Daily Evening Times (Albany, NY, 1869–1881).
Christian Advocate and Journal (New York, 1833–1865).
The Colored American (New York, 1836–1842).
The Daily Picayune (New Orleans, 1837–1914).
Democratic Pharos (Logansport, IN, 1844–1874).
Folheto de ambas Lisboas (Lisbon, Portugal, 1730–1831).
Freedom's Journal (New York, 1827–1829).
Louisiana Courier (New Orleans, 181?–1824).
The Massachusetts Centinel (Boston, 1787–1789).
The New England Galaxy & Masonic Magazine (Boston, 1817–1820).
The New Era (Trinidad, 1870–1891).
The New-York Gazette (New York, 1725–1744).
The New-York Gazette and the Weekly Mercury (New York, 1768–1783).
The New-York Weekly Journal (New York, 1733–1751).
The North Star (New York, 1847–1851).
The Owego Gazette (Owego Village, NY, 1814–1967).
The Pennsylvania Gazette (Philadelphia, 1728–1800).
The Port of Spain Gazette (Trinidad, 1825–1956).
Rivington's New-York Gazetteer (New York, 1773–1775).
The Southern Christian Advocate (Charleston, SC/Augusta, GE/Macon, GE/ Columbia, SC/ Greenville, SC, 1837–1948).
St. Croix Avis (St. Croix, Virgin Islands, 1844–present).
The Virginia Gazette, or, The American Advertiser (Richmond, 1781–1786).

WORKS CITED

A. P. D. G. *Sketches of Portuguese Life, Manners, Costume, and Character.* London: Geo. B. Whittaker, 1826.

Abbenhuis, M. F. *De katholieke kerk in Suriname. Vox Guyanae* 2, no. 3 (September 1956): 117–44.

Abraham, Eva. *Van je familie moet je het hebben: Curaçaose verwantschappen.* Zutphen: Walburg Pers, 2013.

Abrahams, Roger D., and John F. Szwed. *After Africa: Extracts from British Travel Accounts and Journals of the Seventeenth, Eighteenth, and Nineteenth Centuries Concerning the Slaves, Their Manners, and Customs in the British West Indies.* New Haven, CT: Yale University Press, 1983.

Abreu, Laurinda. "Confrarias do Espírito Santo e Misericórdias: Um percurso histórico moldado pela intervenção régia." In *Em nome do Espírito Santo: História de um culto*, edited by José Vicente Serrão, 51–60. Lisbon: Torre do Tombo, 2004.

Adams, John. *Sketches Taken During Ten Voyages to Africa, between the Years 1786 and 1800*. New York: Johnson Reprint, 1970.

Adderley, Rosanne Marion. *"New Negroes from Africa": Slave Trade, Abolition and Free African Settlement in the Nineteenth-Century Caribbean*. Bloomington: Indiana University Press, 2006.

African Burial Ground, National Park Service, U.S. General Services Administration. "Reinterment." https://www.nps.gov/afbg/learn/historyculture/reinterment.htm.

———. "An African-American Homecoming." http://www.africanburial ground.gov/ABG_AnAfricanAmericanHomecoming.htm, available at archive.org.

———. "Teaching with Historic Places." https://www.nps.gov/afbg/learn /education/upload/Twhp-Lesson_AfricanBurialGroundNM2017.pdf.

Aguado, Pedro de. *Historia de Venezuela, escrita en 1581 por Fray Pedro de Aguado*. Edited by Rafael Andrés y Alonso and Pedro César Domínici. 2 vols. Caracas: Imprensa nacional, 1913–15.

Albuquerque, Luís de, and Maria Emília Madeira Santos, eds. *História Geral de Cabo Verde*. 3 vols. Lisbon: Centro de Estudos de História e Cartografia Antiga, 2001.

Alegre, Francisco Javier. *Historia de la provincia de la Compañía de Jesús de Nueva España*. Edited by Ernest J. Burrus y Félix Zubillaga. 4 vols. Rome: Institutum Historicum, 1956–60.

Alencastro, Luiz Felipe de. *O trato dos viventes: Formação do Brasil no Atlântico Sul, séculos XVI e XVII*. São Paulo: Companhia das Letras, 2000.

Alexander, Leslie M. *African or American? Black Identity and Political Activism in New York City, 1784–1861*. Urbana: University of Illinois Press, 2008.

Alford, Violet. "Midsummer and Morris in Portugal." *Folklore* 44, no. 2 (June 1933): 218–35.

Allen, Rose Mary. *Di ki manera? A Social History of Afro-Curaçaoans, 1863–1917*. Amsterdam: SWP, 2007.

Allen, William Francis. *Slave Songs of the United States*. New York: A. Simpson, 1867.

Almada, André Alvares d'. *Tratado breve dos Rios de Guiné de Cabo Verde (1594)*. Edited by Diogo Köpke. Porto: Tipografia Commercial Portuense, 1841.

Almeida, Fortunato de. *História da igreja em Portugal*. 2 vols. Coimbra: Impressa Académica, 1912.

Almeida, Januário Correia de. *Um mez na Guiné.* Lisbon: Typographia Universal, 1859.

Amaral, Ilídio do. *O reino do Congo, os Mbundu (ou Ambundos), o reino dos 'Ngola' (ou de Angola) e a presença portuguesa, de finais do século XV a meados do século XVI.* Lisbon: Ministério de Ciência e da Tecnologia, 1996.

Ambrósio, António. "O Danço Congo de São Tomé e as suas origens." *Leba: Estudos de Quaternário, Pré-História e Arqueologia* (1992): 341–44.

Amussen, Susan Dwyer. *Caribbean Exchanges: Slavery and the Transformation of English Society, 1640–1700.* Chapel Hill: University of North Carolina Press, 2007.

Andrade, Bernardino António Alvares de. *Planta da praça de Bissau e suas adjacentes.* Edited by Damião Peres. Lisbon: Academia portuguesa da história, 1952.

Andrade, Carlos Drummond de. *Poesia completa e prosa.* Rio de Janeiro: Companhia José Aguilar Editora, 1973.

Andrade, Elisa Silva. *Les Isles du Cap-Vert de la 'découverte' à l'indépendance nationale (1460–1975).* Paris: L'Harmattan, 1996.

Andrade, Mário de. *Obras completas de Mário de Andrade: Danças dramáticas do Brasil.* Edited by Oneyda Alvarenga. Vols. 1–3. São Paulo: Martins, 1959.

Andrews, George Reid. *Afro-Latin America, 1800–2000.* New York: Oxford University Press, 2004.

Anguiano, Mateo de. *Misiones capuchinas en África.* 2 vols. Madrid: Instituto Santo Toribio de Mogrevejo, 1950–57.

Antonil, André João. *Cultura e opulência do Brasil por suas drogas e minas.* Edited by Andrée Mansuy Diniz Silva. Lisbon: Comissão Nacional para as Comemorações dos Descobrimentos Portugueses, 2001.

António, Gonçalo, and Estácio de Novaes e Araújo. *Breve extracto do Augustíssimo Triunfo, que a Augusta Braga prepara em obsequio do Santíssimo Sacramento.* Coimbra: Real Colégio das Artes da Companhia de Jesu, 1731.

Armstead, Myra B. Young. *Mighty Change, Tall Within: Black Identity in the Hudson Valley.* Albany: State University of New York Press, 2003.

Armstrong, Louis. *Satchmo: My Life in New Orleans.* New York: Prentice-Hall, 1954.

Atri, Marcellino d'. *L'anarchia Congolese nel sec. XVII: La relazione inedita di Marcellino d'Atri (1702).* Edited by Carlo Toso. Genova: Bozzi Editore, 1984.

Atwood, Thomas. *The History of the Island of Dominica.* London: J. Johnson, 1791.

Aubert, Guillaume. "'To Establish One Law and Definite Rules': Race, Religion, and the Transatlantic Origins of the Louisiana Code Noir." In *Louisiana: Crossroads of the Atlantic World,* edited by Cecile Vidal, 21–43. Philadelphia: University of Pennsylvania Press, 2014.

Azevedo, Rui. "O compromisso da Confraria do Espírito Santo de Benavente." *Lusitania Sacra* 6 (1963): 7–23.

Baerle, Caspar van. *The History of Brazil under the Governorship of Count Johan Maurits of Nassau, 1636–1644.* Edited and translated by Blanche T. van Berckel-Ebeling Koning. Gainesville: University Press of Florida, 2011.

Balandier, Georges. *Daily Life in the Kingdom of the Kongo from the Sixteenth to the Eighteenth Century.* New York: Pantheon Books, 1968.

Bane, Martin J. *Catholic Pioneers in West Africa.* Dublin: Clonmore and Reynolds, 1956.

Barbinais, Le Gentil de la. *Nouveau voyage autour du monde.* 3 vols. Paris: Briasson, 1728.

Barbot, Jean. *Barbot on Guinea: The Writings of Jean Barbot on West Africa 1678–1712.* Edited by P. E. H. Hair, Adam Jones, and Robin Law. 2 vols. London: Hakluyt Society, 1992.

Barcellos, Christiano José de Senna. *Subsídios para a história da Guiné e Cabo Verde.* 7 vols. Lisbon: Typographia da Academia Real das Ciências de Lisboa, 1899–1913.

Barcia, María del Carmen. *Los ilustres apellidos: Negros en La Habana colonial.* Havana: Editorial de Ciencias Sociales, 2009.

Barreto, João. *História da Guiné, 1418–1918.* Lisbon: Edição do autor, 1938.

Barroso, António. "O Congo, seu passado, seu presente e seu futuro." *Boletim da Sociedade de Geografia de Lisboa* 8, 3–4 (1888–1889): 162–235.

Barrow, John. *A Voyage to Cochinchina, in the Years 1792 and 1793.* London: T. Cadell and W. Davies, 1806.

Barry, Boubacar. *Senegambia and the Atlantic Slave Trade.* Translated by Ayi Kwei Armach. Cambridge: Cambridge University Press, 1998.

Bastian, Adolf. *Ein Besuch in San Salvador, der Hauptstadt des Königreichs Congo: Ein Beitrag zur Mythologie und Psychologie.* Bremen: Heinrich Strack, 1859.

Bastide, Roger. *African Civilisations in the New World.* Translated by Peter Green. New York: Harper, 1971.

———. *The African Religions of Brazil: Toward a Sociology of the Interpretation of Civilizations.* Translated by Helen Sebba. Baltimore, MD: Johns Hopkins University Press, 1978.

Baudier, Roger. *The Catholic Church in Louisiana.* New Orleans: Privately printed, 1939.

Baudry des Lozières, Louis Narcisse. *Second voyage à la Louisiane, faisant suite au premier de l'auteur de 1794 à 98.* Paris: Chez Charles, 1803.

Baxter, Alan N. *A Grammar of Kristang, Malacca Creole Portuguese.* Canberra: Australian National University, 1998.

Beasley, Nicholas M. *Christian Ritual and the Creation of British Slave Societies, 1650–1780.* Athens: University of Georgia Press, 2009.

Becoña Iglesias, Elisardo. *La Santa Compaña, el urco y los muertos.* La Coruña: Magoygo, 1982.

Beckwith, Martha Warren. *Black Roadways: A Study of Jamaican Folk Life.* Chapel Hill: University of North Carolina Press, 1929.

Beirante, Maria Ângela Godinho Vieira da Rocha. *Confrarias medievais portuguesas.* Lisbon: Maria Ângela Beirante, 1990.

———. *Territórios do sagrado: Crenças e comportamentos na Idade Média em Portugal.* Lisbon: Colibri, 2011.

Benci, Jorge. *Economia cristã dos senhores no governo dos escravos: Livro brasileiro de 1700.* Edited by Pedro de Alcântara Figueira and Claudinei M. M. Mendes. São Paulo: Editorial Grijalbo, 1977.

Bennett, Herman L. *Africans in Colonial Mexico: Absolutism, Christianity, and Afro-Creole Consciousness, 1570–1640.* Bloomington: Indiana University Press, 2003.

———. *African Kings and Black Slaves: Sovereignty and Dispossession in the Early Modern Atlantic.* Philadelphia: University of Pennsylvania Press, 2019.

Bentley, William Holman. *Pioneering on the Congo.* 2 vols. London: Religious Tract Society, 1900.

Benzoni, Girolamo. *History of the New World, by Girolamo Benzoni, of Milan. Shewing His Travels in America from A.D. 1541 to 1556.* Edited by W. H. Smyth. London: Hakluyt Society, 1857.

Berkel, Adriaan van. *The Voyages of Adriaan van Berkel to Guiana.* Edited by Martijn van den bel, Lodewijk Hulsman, and Lodewijk Wagenaar. Leiden: Sidestone Press, 2014.

Berlin, Ira. "From Creole to African: Atlantic Creoles and the Origins of African-American Society in Mainland North America." *William and Mary Quarterly* 53, no. 2 (1996): 251–88.

———. *Many Thousands Gone: The First Two Centuries of Slavery in North America.* Harvard, MA: Belknap Press, 1998.

Bernhard, Duke of Saxe-Weimar Eisenach, *Travels in North America.* Philadelphia: Carey, Lea & Carey, 1828.

Berry, Jason, Jonathan Foose, and Tad Jones. "In Search of the Mardi Gras Indians." In *When Brer Rabbit Meets Coyote: African-Native American Literature,* edited by Jonathan Brennan, 197–217. Urbana: University of Illinois Press, 2003.

Bethencourt, Francisco. "A Igreja." In *História da Expansão Portuguesa.* 5 vols. Edited by Francisco Bethencourt and Kirti Chaudhuri, 1:369–86. Lisbon: Círculo de Leitores, 1998.

Bettelheim, Judith. "Carnaval of Los Congos of Portobelo, Panama: Feathered Men and Queens." In *African Diasporas in the New and Old Worlds: Consciousness and Imagination*, edited by Geneviève Fabre and Klaus Benesch, 287–309. Amsterdam: Rodopi, 2004.

Bettelheim, Judith, Barbara Bridges, and Dolores Yonker. "Festivals in Cuba, Haiti, and New Orleans." In *Caribbean Festival Arts: Each and Every Bit of Difference*, edited by John W. Nunely and Judith Bettelheim, 137–64. Seattle: University of Washington Press, 1988.

Biet, Antoine. *Voyage de la France équinoxiale en l'Isle de Cayenne.* Paris: Chez François Clouzier, 1664.

Billings, Warren M., ed. *The Old Dominion in the Seventeenth Century: A Documentary History of Virginia, 1606–1700.* Rev. ed. Chapel Hill: University of North Carolina Press, 2007.

Binder, Franz. "Die Zeeländische Kaperfahrt." *Mededelingen van het Koninklijk Zeeuwsch Genootschap der Wetenschappen* (1976): 40–92.

Birmingham, David. "Carnival at Luanda." *Journal of African History* 29 (1988): 93–103.

———. *Central Africa to 1870: Zambezia, Zaïre and the South Atlantic.* Cambridge: Cambridge University Press, 1981.

———. *Trade and Conflict in Angola: The Mbundu and Their Neighbours under the Influence of the Portuguese 1483–1790.* Oxford: Clarendon Press, 1966.

Blackburn, Robin. *The Making of New World Slavery: From the Baroque to the Modern, 1492–1800.* London: Verso, 2010.

Blake, John W. *European Beginnings in West Africa, 1454–1578.* Westport, CT: Greenwood Press, 1937.

———., ed. *Europeans in West Africa, 1450–1560.* 2 vols. London: Hakluyt Society, 1942.

Blassingame, John W. *Black New Orleans 1860–1880.* Chicago: University of Chicago Press, 1973.

Blumenthal, Debra. *Enemies and Familiars: Slavery and Mastery in Fifteenth-Century Valencia.* Ithaca, NY: Cornell University Press, 2009.

———. "'La Casa dels Negres': Black African Solidarity in Late Medieval Valencia." In *Black Africans in Renaissance Europe*, edited by T. F. Earle and K. J. P. Lowe, 225–46. Cambridge: Cambridge University Press, 2005.

Bonaparte-Wyse, Marie, Princesse Rattazzi. "Le Portugal à vol d'oiseau (1879)." In *Voyages au Portugal aux XVIIIe et XIXe siècles*, edited by Claude Mafre, 399–437. Urrugne: Pimientos, 2005.

Bonomi, Patricia U. "'Swarms of Negroes Comeing about My Door': Black Christianity in Early Dutch and English North America." *Journal of American History* 103, no. 1 (June 2016): 34–58.

————. *Under the Cope of Heaven: Religion, Society and Politics in Colonial America*. Oxford: Oxford University Press, 2003.

Bontinck, François. "Le Vocabularium Latinum, Hispanicum et Congonse: Nouvelles notes marginales." *Annales Aequatoria* 1 (1980): 529–35.

Borges, Célia Maia. *Escravos e libertos nas irmandades do Rosário: Devoção e solidariedade em Minas Gerais, séculos XVIII e XIX*. Juiz de Fora: Editora UFJF, 2005.

Boschi, Caio César. *Os leigos e o poder: Irmandades leigos e política colonizadora em Minas Gerais*. São Paulo: Editora Ática, 1986.

Bosman, Willem. *Nauwkeurige beschryving van de Guinese Goud- Tand- en Slavekust*. Utrecht: Anthony Schouten, 1704.

Bouton, Jacques. *Relation de l'établissement des françois depuis l'an 1635 en l'Isle de Martinique, l'une des Antilles de l'Amérique*. Paris: Cramoisy, 1640.

Bouveignes, O. de, and J. Cuvelier, eds. *Jérôme de Montesarchio: Apôtre du Vieux Congo*. Namur: Collectio Lavigreie, 1951.

Bowser, Frederick P. *The African Slave in Colonial Peru, 1524–1650*. Stanford, CA: Stanford University Press, 1974.

Boxer, C. R. *The Church Militant and Iberian Expansion 1440–1770*. Baltimore: Johns Hopkins University Press, 1978.

————. *The Dutch in Brazil, 1624–1654*. Oxford: Clarendon Press, 1957.

————. *Race Relations in the Portuguese Colonial Empire, 1415–1825*. Oxford: Clarendon Press, 1963.

Braga, Theophilo. *O povo portuguez nos seus costumes, crenças e tradições*. 2 vols. Lisbon: Ferreira, 1885.

Brandão, Carlos Rodrigues. *Os deuses do povo: Um estudo sobre a religião popular*. São Paulo: Livraria Brasiliense, 1980.

————. *Sacerdotes de viola: Rituais religiosos do catolicismo popular em São Paulo e Minas Gerais*. Petrópolis: Vozes, 1981.

Brandt, Max Hans. *Estudio etnomusicológico de três conjuntos de tambores afrovenezolanos de Barlovento*. Caracas: Centro para las Culturas Populares y Tradicionales, 1987.

Brásio, António, ed. *História do Reino do Congo (Ms. 8080 da Biblioteca Nacional de Lisboa)*. Lisbon: Centro de Estudos Históricos Ultramarinos, 1969.

————, ed. *História e missiologia: Inéditos e esparsos*. Luanda: Instituto de Investigação Científica de Angola, 1973.

————, ed. *Monumenta missionária Africana: Primeira série [MMA-PS]*. 15 vols. Lisbon: Agência Geral do Ultramar/Academia Portuguesa da História, 1952–88.

————, ed. *Monumenta missionária Africana: Segunda série [MMA-SS]*. 5 vols. Lisbon: Agência Geral do Ultramar/Academia Portuguesa da História, 1958–79.

———. *Os pretos em Portugal*. Lisboa: Agência Geral das Colónias, 1944.

Breen, Henry H. *St. Lucia: Historical, Statistical, and Descriptive*. London: Longman, Brown, Green, and Longmans, 1844.

Breen, T. H., and Stephen Innes. *"Myne Owne Ground": Race and Freedom on Virginia's Eastern Shore, 1640–1676*. New York: Oxford University Press, 1980.

Bremer, Frederika. *The Homes of the New World: Impressions of America*. Translated by Mary Howitt. 2 vols. New York: Harper, 1858.

Brenneker, Paul. *Curaçaoensia: Folkloristische aantekeningen over Curaçao*. Curaçao: Boekhandel St. Augustinus, 1961.

———. *Sambumbu: Volkskunde van Curaçao, Aruba en Bonaire*. 10 vols. Curaçao: Drukkerij Scherpenheuvel, 1969–75.

———. *Zjozjoli: Gegevens over de volkskunde van Curaçao, Aruba en Bonaire*. Curaçao: Publisidat Antiano, 1986.

Brewer-García, Larissa. *Beyond Babel: Translations of Blackness in Colonial Peru and New Granada*. Cambridge: Cambridge University Press, 2020.

Brinkman, Inge. "Kongo Interpreters, Traveling Priests, and Political Leaders in the Kongo Kingdom (15th–19th Century)." *International Journal of African Historical Studies* 49, no. 2 (2016): 255–76.

Brinkman, Inge, and Koen Bostoen. "'To Make Book': A Conceptual Historical Approach to Kongo Book Cultures (Sixteenth–Nineteenth Centuries)." In *The Kongo Kingdom: The Origins, Dynamics and Cosmopolitan Culture of an African Polity*, edited by Koen Bostoen and Inge Brinkman, 216–34. Cambridge: Cambridge University Press, 2018.

Bristol, Joan Cameron. *Christians, Blasphemers, and Witches: Afro-Mexican Ritual Practice in the Seventeenth Century*. Albuquerque: University of New Mexico Press, 2007.

Brockey, Liam M. "Jesuit Pastoral Theater on an Urban Stage: Lisbon, 1588–1593." *Journal of Early Modern History* 9, no. 1 (2005): 1–50.

Brooks, George E. *Eurafricans in Western Africa: Commerce, Social Status, Gender, and Religious Observance from the Sixteenth to the Eighteenth Century*. Athens: Ohio University Press, 2003.

———. "Historical Perspectives on the Guinea-Bissau Region, Fifteenth to Nineteenth Centuries." In *Mansas, escravos, grumetes e gentio: Cacheu na encruzilhada de civilizações*, edited by Carlos Lopes, 25–54. Lisbon: Imprensa Nacional-Casa da Moeda, 1993.

———. "The Observance of All Souls' Day in the Guinea-Bissau Region: A Christian Holy Day, an African Harvest Festival, an African New Year's Celebration, or All of the Above(?)." *History in Africa* 11 (1984): 1–34.

Brooks, Lynn Matluck. *The Dances of the Processions of Seville in Spain's Golden Age*. Kassel: Reichenberger, 1988.

Brown, Ras Michael. *African-Atlantic Cultures and the South Carolina Lowcountry*. Cambridge: Cambridge University Press, 2012.

———. "The Immersion of Catholic Christianity in Kalunga." *Journal of Africana Religions* 2, no. 2 (2014): 246–55.

Brown, Vincent. *The Reaper's Garden: Death and Power in the World of Atlantic Slavery*. Cambridge, MA: Harvard University Press, 2008.

Brumund, J. F. G. "Bijdragen tot de geschiedenis der kerk in Batavia." *Tijdschrift voor Indische Taal-, Land- en Volkenkunde* 13, no. 4 (1864): 1–189.

Brun, Samuel. *Schiffarten in etliche newe Länder und Insulen*. Edited by Walter Hirschberg. Graz: Akademische Druck- u. Verlagsanstalt, 1969.

Bruneau, Thomas C. *The Church in Brazil: The Politics of Religion*. Austin: University of Texas Press, 1982.

Brüser, Martina, and André dos Reis Santos. *Dicionário do Crioulo da Ilha de Santiago (Cabo Verde)*. Tübingen: G. Narr, 2002.

Burton, Richard F. *Explorations of the Highlands of the Brazil*. 2 vols. London: Tinsley Brothers, 1869.

———. *Two Trips to Gorilla Land and the Cataracts of the Congo*. 2 vols. London: Sampson Low, Marston, Low and Searle, 1876.

Cabon, Adolphe. *Notes sur l'Histoire Religieuse d'Haïti: De la Révolution au Concordat (1789–1860)*. Port-au-Prince: Petit Séminaire Collège St. Martial, 1933.

Cabral, Iva Maria de Ataíde Vilhena. *A primeira elite colonial atlântica: Dos 'homens honrados brancos' de Santiago à 'nobreza da terra'. Finais do séc. XV-início do séc. XVII*. Praia: Livraria Pedro Cardoso, 2015.

Cabral, Nelson E. *Le moulin et le pilon: Les Îles de Cap-Vert*. Paris: L'Harmattan, 1980.

Cabrera, Lydia. *Reglas de Congo, palo monte, mayombe*. Miami: Peninsular Printing, 1979.

Cadornega, António de Oliveira de. *Descrição de Vila Viçosa*. Edited by Heitor Gomes Teixeira. Lisbon: IN-CM, 1982.

———. *História geral das Guerras Angolanas*. Edited by José Matias Delgado. 3 vols. Lisbon: Agência-Geral do Ultramar, 1972.

Caldeira, Arlindo Manuel. "Luanda in the Seventeenth Century: Diversity and Cultural Interaction in the Process of Forming an Afro-Atlantic City." *Nordic Journal of African Studies* 22, nos. 1–2 (2013): 72–104.

Caldeira, Arlindo, and Antonio Feros. "Black Africans in the Iberian Peninsula (1400–1820)." In *The Iberian World, 1450–1820*, edited by Fernando Bouza, Pedro Cardim, and Antonio Feros, 261–90. London: Routledge, 2020.

Caltanissetta, Luca da. *Diaire Congolais (1690–1701)*. Edited and translated by François Bontick. Louvain: Editions Nauwelaerts, 1970.

Campbell, Albert. "St. Thomas Negroes: A Study in Personality and Culture." *Psychological Monographs* 55, no. 5 (1943): 1–90.

Candler, John. *Brief Notices of Hayti: With its Condition, Resources, and Prospects.* London: T. Ward, 1842.

Canin, Isaac Jansz. *Acta Synodi Nationalis.* Dordt: Typis Isaaci Ioannidis Caninii, 1620.

Cañizares-Esguerra, Jorge, Matt D. Childs, and James Sidbury, eds. *The Black Urban Atlantic in the Age of the Slave Trade.* Philadelphia: University of Pennsylvania Press, 2013.

Cardoso, Gerald. *Negro Slavery in the Sugar Plantations of Veracruz and Pernambuco, 1550–1680.* Washington, DC: University Press of America, 1983.

Cardoso, Pedro Monteiro. *Folclore Caboverdeano.* Porto: Maranus, 1933.

Cardot, Carlos Felice. *Curazao Hispánico (Antagonismo flamenco-español).* Caracas: Ediciones de la Presidencia de la República, 1982.

Carreira, António. *Cabo Verde: Formação e extinção de uma sociedade escravocrata (1460–1878).* Praia: Estudos e Ensaios, 2000.

Carrie, R. P. "Une visite à Saint Antoine de Sogno (Congo)." *Les missions Catholiques* 487 (October 4, 1878), 488 (October 11 and 18, 1878): 472–74, 485–89, 496–98.

Carroll, Patrick J. *Blacks in Colonial Veracruz: Race, Ethnicity and Regional Development.* Austin: University of Texas Press, 2001.

Carteau, Félix. *Soirées bermudiennes, ou entretiens sur les événemens qui ont opéré la ruine de la partie française de l'isle Saint-Domingue.* Bordeaux: Pellier-Lawalle, 1802.

Carvalho, Henrique Augusto Dias de. *Guiné: Apontamentos inéditos.* Lisbon: Agência Geral das Colónias, 1944.

Cascudo, Luís da Câmara. *Dicionário do folclore brasileiro.* São Paulo: Melhoramentos, 1979.

Castilho, Augusto de. "A província de S. Tomé e o Golfo de Benim." *Boletim da Sociedade de Geografia de Lisboa* 9, no. 14 (1895): 777–819.

Catron, John W. *Embracing Protestantism: Black Identities in the Atlantic World.* Gainesville: University Press of Florida, 2016.

Caulkins, Frances Manwaring. *History of Norwich, Connecticut: From its Possession by the Indians to the Year 1866.* Hartford, CT: Caulkins, 1866.

Cavazzi, Giovanni Antonio. *Istorica descrizione de' tre' regni Congo, Matamba et Angola.* Bologna: Per Giacomo Monti, 1687.

Cerqueira, Ivo de. *Vida social indígena na colónia de Angola (usos e costumes).* Lisbon: Agência Geral das Colónias, 1947.

Chacón, Alfredo. *Curiepe: Ensayo sobre la realización del sentido en la actividad mágicorelgiosa de un pueblo venezolano.* Caracas: Universidad Central de Venezuela, 1979.

Charlevoix, Pierre-François-Xavier de. *Histoire de l'Isle Espagnole ou de St. Domingue: Écrite particulièrement sur des mémoires manuscrits du P. Jean-Baptiste Le Pers*. 2 vols. Paris: Chez François Barois, 1731.

Chasteen, John Charles. *National Rhythms, African Roots: The Deep History of Latin American Popular Dance*. Albuquerque: University of New Mexico Press, 2004.

Chaudenson, Robert, and Salikoko S. Mufwene. *Creolization of Language and Culture*. London: Routledge, 2001.

Chaves, Luís. *Danças, bailados & mímicas guerreiras*. Lisbon: Ethnos, 1942.

———. *Folclore religioso*. Porto: Portucalense, 1945.

———. *Portugal além*. Gaia: Edições Pátria, 1932.

Chelmicki, José Conrado Carlos de, and Francisco Adolfo de Varnhagen. *Corografia cabo-verdiana ou descripção geográfico-histórica da provincínia das Ilhas de Cabo Verde e Guiné*. Lisbon: L. C. da Cunha, 1841.

Chevillard, André. *Les desseins de son Eminence le cardinal de Richelieu pour l'Amérique ce qui s'est passé de plus remarquable depuis l'établissement des colonies*. Rouen: n.p., 1659.

Chimalpahin, Domingo. *Diario*. Translated by Rafael Tena. Mexico City: Conaculta, 2001.

Christian, Marcus. "The Negro in Louisiana." Marcus Christian Collection, Earl K. Long Library, Louisiana and Special Collections Department, University of New Orleans. Louisiana Digital Library, https://louisianadigitallibrary.org/islandora/object/uno-p15140coll42:collection.

Christian, William A., Jr. *Local Religion in Sixteenth-Century Spain*. Princeton, NJ: Princeton University Press, 1981.

Christoph, Peter R. "The Freedmen of New Amsterdam." In *A Beautiful and Fruitful Place: Selected Rensselaerswijck Seminar Papers*, edited by Nancy A. M. Zeller, 157–70. New York: New Netherland, 1991.

Clark, Emily, and Virginia Meacham Gould. "The Feminine Face of Afro-Catholicism in New Orleans, 1727–1852." *William and Mary Quarterly* 59, no. 2 (April 2002): 409–48.

Codman, John. *Ten Months in Brazil: Notes on the Paraguayan War*. New York: James Miller, 1872.

Coelho, Francisco de Lemos. *Duas descrições seiscentistas da Guiné*. Edited by Damião Peres. Lisbon: Academia Portuguesa da História, 1953.

Coleman, Edward Maceo, ed. *Creole Voices: Poems in French by Free Men of Color*. Washington, DC: Associated Publishers, 1945.

Comissão Nacional Preparatória do Carnaval da Vitória. *Carnaval da Vitória: Entre a tradição e a modernidade*. Luanda: Comissão Nacional Preparatória do Carnaval da Vitória, 1985.

Cooksey, Susan, Robin Poynor, and Hein Vanhee, ed. *Kongo Across the Waters.* Gainesville: University Press of Florida, 2013.

Cooper, Melissa L. *Making Gullah: A History of Sapelo Islanders, Race, and the American Imagination.* Chapel Hill: University of North Carolina Press, 2017.

Corrêa, Elias Alexandre da Silva. *História de Angola,* 2 vols. Lisbon: Atica, 1937.

Correia, Maria Madalena da Veiga. "Txoru falado e txoru cantado: Representações sociais da morte no espaço rural da Achada Falcão." In *Ensaios Etnográficos na ilha de Santiago de Cabo Verde: Processos identitários na Contemporaneidade,* edited by Maria Elizabeth Lucas and Sérgio Baptista da Silva, 183–228. Praia: Edições Uni-CV, 2009.

Cortesão, Jaime. *Obras completas.* 33 vols. Lisbon: Portugália/Livros Horizonte, 1964–85.

Cosentino, Donald J. "It's All for You, Sen Jak!" In *Sacred Arts of Haitian Vodou,* edited by Donald J. Cosentino, 243–63. Los Angeles: UCLA Fowler Museum of Cultural History, 1995.

Costa, Francisco Augusto Pereira da, ed. *Anais pernambucanos.* 10 vols. Recife: Arquivo Público Estadual, 1951–66.

Costa, João Paulo A. O. "D. João II e a cristianização de África." In *Congresso Internacional Bartolomeu Dias e a sua Época: Actas.* 5 vols., 1:405–16. Porto: Universidade do Porto, 1989.

Costa, Susana Goulart. "Trento e o clero secular nas ilhas atlânticas." In *O concílio de Trento em Portugal e nas suas conquistas: Olhares novos,* edited by António Camões Gouveia, David Sampaio Barbosa, and José Pedro Paiva, 197–214. Lisbon: CEHR, 2014.

Cothonay, Marie Bertrand de. *Trinidad: Journal d'un missionnaire dominicain des Antilles anglaises.* Paris: V. Retaux et fils, 1893.

Courbe, Michel Jajolet de La. *Premier voyage du sieur de la Courbe fait à la coste d'Afrique en 1685.* Edited by P. Cultru. Paris: E. Champion, 1913.

Courlander, Harold. *Negro Folk Music U.S.A.* New York: Columbia University Press, 1963.

Craft, Renee Alexander. *When the Devil Knocks: The Congo Tradition and the Politics of Blackness in Twentieth-Century Panama.* Columbus: Ohio State University Press, 2015.

Creecy, James. *Scenes in South, and Other Miscellaneous Pieces.* Washington, DC: T. McGill, 1860.

Creel, Margaret Washington. *'A Peculiar People': Slave Religion and Community Culture among the Gullahs.* New York: New York University Press, 1988.

Cressler, Matthew J. *Authentically Black and Truly Catholic: The Rise of Black Catholicism in the Great Migration.* New York: New York University Press, 2017.

Crété, Liliane. *Daily Life in Louisiana 1815–1830.* Translated by Patrick Gregory. Baton Rouge: Louisiana State University Press, 1981.

Crone, G. R., ed. *The Voyages of Cadamosto and Other Documents on Western Africa in the Second Half of the Fifteenth Century.* Nendeln: n.p., 1967.

Crookall, L. *British Guiana; or, Work and Wanderings among the Creoles and Coolies, the Africans and Indians of the Wild Country.* London: T. F. Unwin, 1898.

Crowley, Daniel J. "La Rose and La Marguerite Societies in St. Lucia." *Journal of American Folklore* 71, no. 282 (1958): 541–52.

Cruickshank, Brodie. *Achttien jaren aan de Goudkust. Uit het Engelsch vertaald en met eene inleiding vermeerderd door D.P.H.J. Weijtingh.* 2 vols. Amsterdam: Weijtingh & Van der Haart, 1855.

Crum, Mason. *Gullah: Negro Life in the Carolina Sea Islands.* Durham, NC: Duke University Press, 1940.

Curran, Robert Emmett. *Papist Devils: Catholics in British America, 1574–1783.* Washington, DC: Catholic University of American Press, 2014.

Curtin, Philip D. *Two Jamaicas: The Role of Ideas in a Tropical Colony, 1830–1865.* Cambridge, MA: Harvard University Press, 1955.

Cuvelier, Jean. *L'ancien royaume de Congo.* Brussels: De Brouwer, 1946.

Cuvelier, Jean, and Louis Jadin, eds. *L'Ancien Congo d'après les archives romaines, 1518–1640.* Brussels: Académie Royale des Sciences Coloniales, 1954.

Dananoja, Kalle. "Healers, Idolaters, and Good Christians: A Case Study of Creolization and Popular Religion in Mid-Eighteenth-Century Angola." *International Journal of African Historical Studies* 43, no. 3 (2010): 443–65.

Daniels, David D. "Kongolese Christianity in the Americas of the 17th and 18th Centuries." In *Polycentric Structures in the History of World Christianity*, edited by Klaus Koschorke and Adrian Hermann, 215–26. Wiesbaden: Harrassowitz, 2014.

Dankers, Jasper, and Peter Sluyter. *Journal of a Voyage to New York and a Tour in Several of the American Colonies in 1679–80.* Edited by Henry Murphy. Brooklyn, NY: Long Island Historical Society, 1867.

Dapper, Olfert. *Naukeurige beschrijvinge der Afrikaensche gewesten.* Amsterdam: Jacob van Meurs, 1668.

Davis, Cyprian. "God of Our Weary Years: Black Catholics in American Catholic History." In *Taking Down Our Harps: Black Catholics in the United States,* edited by Diana L. Hayes and Cyprian Davis, 17–46. New York: Maryknoll, 1998.

———. *The History of Black Catholics in the United States.* New York: Crossroad, 1990.

Davis, Martha Ellen. "Dominican Folk Dance and the Shaping of National Identity." In *Caribbean Dance from Abakuá to Zouk: How Movement Shapes Identity*, edited by Susanne Sloat, 127–51. Gainesville: University of Florida Press, 2002.

———. "Music and Black Ethnicity in the Dominican Republic." In *Music and Black Ethnicity: The Caribbean and South America*, edited by Gerard H. Béhague, 119–55. New Brunswick, NJ: Transaction, 1992.

———. *Voces del purgatório: Estudio de la salve dominicana*. Santo Domingo: Museu del Hombre Dominicano, 1981.

Davis, Wade. *Passage of Darkness: The Ethnobiology of the Haitian Zombie*. Chapel Hill: University of North Carolina Press, 1988.

Dawdy, Shannon Lee. *Building the Devil's Empire: French Colonial New Orleans*. Chicago: University of Chicago Press, 2008.

Deal, J. Douglas. *Race and Class in Colonial Virginia: Indians, Englishmen, and Africans on the Eastern Shore during the Seventeenth Century*. New York: Garland, 1993.

Debbasch, Yvan. "Les associations serviles à la Martinique au XIXe siècle." In *Études d'Histoire du Droit Privé offertes à Pierre Petot*, 121–30. Paris: Éditions Montchrestien, 1959.

Debien, Gabriel. "La Christianisation des esclaves des Antilles Françaises aux XVIIe et XVIIIe siècles." *Revue d'histoire de l'Amérique française* 20, no. 4 (March 1967): 524–55.

Defoe, Daniel, and Manuel Schonhorn Davis, eds. *A General History of the Pyrates*. Mineola, NY: Dover Publications, 1999.

Demanet, M. *Nouvelle histoire de l'Afrique Françoise*. Paris: Veuve Duchesne, 1767.

Deming, Clarence. *By-Ways of Nature and Life*. New York: G. P. Putnam's Sons, 1884.

Dennett, R. E. *Seven Years among the Fjort: Being an English Trader's Experiences in the Congo District*. London: S. Low, Marston, Searle, & Rivington, 1887.

Deren, Maya. *Divine Horsemen: The Living Gods of Haiti*. New York: Chelsea House, 1953.

Dessens, Nathalie. *From Saint-Domingue to New Orleans: Migration and Influences*. Gainesville: University of Florida Press, 2007.

Deursen, Arie T. van. *Bavianen en slijkgeuzen: Kerk en kerkvolk ten tijde van Maurits en Oldenbarnevelt*. Assen: Van Gorcum, 1974.

———. *Plain Lives in a Golden Age: Popular Culture, Religion and Society in Seventeenth-Century Holland*. Translated by Maarten Ultee. Cambridge: Cambridge University Press, 1991.

Dewulf, Jeroen. "Black Brotherhoods in North America: Afro-Iberian and West-Central African Influences." *African Studies Quarterly* 15, no. 3 (June 2015): 19–38.

———. "Emulating a Portuguese Model: The Slave Policy of the West India Company and the Dutch Reformed Church in Dutch Brazil (1630–1654) and New Netherland (1614–1664) in Comparative Perspective." *Journal of Early American History* 4 (2014): 3–36.

———. "Flying Back to Africa or Flying to Heaven? Competing Visions of Afterlife in the Lowcountry and Caribbean Slave Societies." *Religion and American Culture: A Journal of Interpretation* 31, no. 2 (2021): 222–61.

———. "From Papiamentu to Afro-Catholic Brotherhoods: An Interdisciplinary Analysis of Iberian Elements in Curaçaoan Popular Culture." *Studies in Latin American Popular Culture* 36 (2018): 69–94.

———. "From the *Calendas* to the *Calenda*: On the Afro-Iberian Substratum in Black Performance Culture in the Americas." *Journal of American Folklore* 131, no. 519 (Winter 2018): 3–29.

———. *From the Kingdom of Kongo to Congo Square: Kongo Dances and the Origins of the Mardi Gras Indians.* Lafayette: University of Louisiana at Lafayette Press, 2017.

———. "Iberian Linguistic Elements among the Black Population in New Netherland (1614–1664)." *Journal of Pidgin and Creole Languages* 34, no. 1 (2019): 49–82.

———., ed. "The Missing Link between Congo Square and the Mardi Gras Indians? The Anonymous Story of 'The Singing Girl of New Orleans' (1849)." *Louisiana History* 60, no. 1 (Winter 2019): 83–95.

———. "Pinkster: An Atlantic Creole Festival in a Dutch-American Context." *Journal of American Folklore* 126, no. 501 (2013): 245–71.

———. *The Pinkster King and the King of Kongo: The Forgotten History of America's Dutch-Owned Slaves.* Jackson: University Press of Mississippi, 2017.

———. "Rethinking the Historical Development of Caribbean Performance Culture from an Afro-Iberian Perspective: The Case of Jankunu." *New West Indian Guide* (2021): 1–31.

Dezoteux, Pierre, Baron de Cormantin. "Voyage du ci-devant duc du Châtelet, en Portugal (1798)." In *Voyages au Portugal aux XVIIIe et XIXe siècles*, edited by Claude Mafre, 113–18. Urrugne: Pimientos, 2005.

Dias, Margot, and Jorge Dias. *A encomendação das almas.* Porto: Imprensa Portuguesa, 1953.

Díaz Rodriguez, Vicente. "La cofradía de los morenos de los primeros años de los dominicos en Cádiz." *Communio* 39, no. 2 (2006): 359–484.

Dicomano, Raimondo da. "Informazione sul regno del Congo di Fra Raimondo da Dicomano (1798)." Arquivo Histórico Ultramarino, Lisbon, Diversos, caixa 823, sala 12. Edited by Arlindo Correia. http://arlindo-correia.com /121208.html.

Dillard, J. L. *Lexicon of Black English.* New York: Seabury Press, 1977.

Donelha, André. *An Account of Sierra Leone and the Rivers of Guinea of Cape Verde (1625).* Edited by Avelino Teixeira da Mota, translated by P. E. H. Hair. Lisbon: Junta de Investigações Científicas do Ultramar, 1977.

Donnan, Elizabeth, ed. *Documents Illustrative of the History of the Slave Trade to America.* 4 vols. Washington, DC: Carnegie Institute, 1930–35.

Douglass, Frederick. *My Bondage and My Freedom.* New York: Arno Press, 1969.

Draper, David Elliott. "The Mardi Gras Indians: The Ethnomusicology of Black Associations in New Orleans." Ph.D. dissertation, Tulane University, 1973.

Dubois, Laurent. *Haiti: The Aftershocks of History.* New York: Metropolitan Books, 2012.

Du Bois, W. E. B. *The Philadelphia Negro: A Social Study.* Philadelphia: Publications of the University of Pennsylvania, 1899.

Dunham, Katherine. *Dances of Haiti.* Los Angeles: UCLA Center for Afro-American Studies, 1983.

Dunn, Richard S. *Sugar and Slaves: The Rise of the Planter Class in the English West Indies, 1624–1713.* Chapel Hill: University of North Carolina Press, 2000.

Earle, Alice Morse. *Customs and Fashions in Old New England.* Detroit: Omnigraphics, 1990.

Eekhof, Albert. *De Hervormde kerk in Noord-Amerika (1624–1664).* 2 vols. The Hague: M. Nijhoff, 1913.

———. *De negerpredikant Jacobus Elisa Joannes Capitein, 1717–1747.* The Hague: M. Nijhoff, 1917.

Eights, James. "Pinkster Festivities in Albany Sixty Years Ago." In *Collections on the History of Albany,* 4 vols., edited by Joel Munsell, 2:323–27. Albany, NY: Munsell, 1865–71.

Emmanuel, Isaac S., and Suzanne A. Emmanuel. *History of the Jews of the Netherlands Antilles.* 2 vols. Cincinnati, OH: American Jewish Archives, 1970.

Epstein, Dena J. *Sinful Tunes and Spirituals: Black Folk Music to the Civil War.* Urbana: University of Illinois Press, 1977.

Evans, Freddi Williams. *Congo Square: African Roots in New Orleans.* Lafayette: University of Louisiana at Lafayette Press, 2011.

Evans, Thomas Grier, ed. *Records of the Reformed Dutch Church in New Amsterdam and New York: Baptisms from 25 December 1639, to 27 December 1730.* New York: Clearfield, 1901.

Faria, F. Leite de. "Fr. João de Santiago e a sua relação sobre os Capuchinhos no Congo." *Portugal em África* 59 (1953): 316–33.

Farinha, António Lourenço. *A expansão da fé na África e no Brasil: Subsídios para a história colonial.* Lisbon: Agência Geral das Colónias, 1942.

Faro, André de. *André de Faro's Missionary Journey to Sierra Leone in 1663–64.* Edited by P. E. H. Hair. Freetown: Institute of African Studies, University of Sierra Leone, 1982.

Felner, Alfredo de Albuquerque, ed. *Angola: Apontamentos sobre a ocupação e início do estabelecimento dos Portugueses no Congo, Angola e Benguela extraídos de documentos históricos.* Coimbra: Imprensa da Universidade, 1933.

Felt, Joseph Barlow. *Annals of Salem.* 2 vols. Salem, MA: W. & S. B. Ives, 1845–49.

Fernow, Berthold, ed. *The Records of New Amsterdam from 1653 to 1674.* 7 vols. New York: Knickerbocker Press, 1897.

Ferreira, Felipe. *Inventando Carnavais. O surgimento do carnaval carioca no século XIX e outras questões carnavalescas.* Rio de Janeiro: Editora UFRJ, 2005.

———. *O livro de ouro do carnaval brasileiro.* Rio de Janeiro: Ediouro, 2004.

Ferreira, Manuel. *A aventura crioula.* Lisbon: Plátano Editora, 1985.

Ferreira, Roquinaldo. *Cross-Cultural Exchange in the Atlantic World: Angola and Brazil during the Era of the Slave Trade.* Cambridge: Cambridge University Press, 2012.

Fick, Carolyn E. *The Making of Haiti: The Saint-Domingue Revolution from Below.* Knoxville: University of Tennessee Press, 1990.

Fitch, Suzanne P., and Roseann M. Mandziuk. *Sojourner Truth as Orator: Wit, Story and Song.* Westport, CT: Greenwood Press, 1997.

Fiume, Giovanna. "St. Benedict the Moor: From Sicily to the New World." In *Saints and Their Cults in the Atlantic World*, edited by Margaret Cormack, 16–51. Columbia: University of South Carolina Press, 2007.

Flint, Timothy. *Recollections of the Last Ten Years in the Valley of the Mississippi.* Edited by George R. Brooks. Carbondale: Southern Illinois University Press, 1968.

Fonseca, Jorge. *Escravos em Évora no século XVI.* Évora: Câmara Municipal de Évora, 1997.

———. *Escravos e senhores na Lisboa quinhentista.* Lisbon: Colibri, 2010.

———. *Religião e liberdade: Os Negros nas irmandades e confrarias portuguesas (séculos XV a XIX).* V. N. Famalicão: Humus, 2016.

Fowler, William Chauncey. *History of Durham, Connecticut, from the First Grant of Land in 1662 to 1866.* Hartford, CT: Press of Wiley, 1866.

Fra Molinero, Baltasar. *La imagen de los Negros en el teatro del Siglo de Oro.* Madrid: Siglo Veintiuno, 1995.

França, António Pinto da. *A influência portuguesa na Indonésia*. Lisbon: Prefácio, 2003.

Franco, António. *Synopsis Annalium Societatis Jesu in Lusitania ab 1540 usque ad annum 1725*. Augsburg: Sumptibus Philippi, Martini, & Joannis Veith, Haeredum, 1726.

Frazier, E. Franklin. *The Negro Church in America*. New York: Schocken Books, 1966.

Frey, Sylvia R. "'The Year of Jubilee Is Come': Black Christianity in the Plantation South in Post-Revolutionary America." In *Religion in a Revolutionary Age*, edited by Ronald Hoffman and Peter J. Albert, 87–124. Charlottesville: University Press of Virginia, 1994.

Frey, Sylvia R., and Betty Wood. *Come Shouting to Zion: African American Protestantism in the American South and British Caribbean to 1830*. Chapel Hill: University of North Carolina Press, 1998.

Frijhoff, Willem. *Wegen van Evert Willemsz: Een Hollands weeskind op zoek naar zichzelf 1607–1647*. Nijmegen: SUN, 1995.

Frijhoff, Willem, and Marijke Spies. *Nederlandse cultuur in Europese context: 1650. Bevochten eendracht*. The Hague: Sdu Uitgevers, 1999.

Fromont, Cécile, ed. *Afro-Catholic Festivals in the Americas: Performance, Representation, and the Making of Black Atlantic Tradition*. University Park: Pennsylvania State University Press, 2019.

———. *The Art of Conversion: Christian Visual Culture in the Kingdom of Kongo*. Chapel Hill: University of North Carolina Press, 2014.

———. "Dancing for the King of Congo from Early Modern Central Africa to Slavery-Era Brazil." *Colonial Latin American Review* 22, no. 2 (2013): 184–208.

Gabriel, Manuel Nunes. *Padrões da fé: Igrejas antigas de Angola*. Luanda: Arquidiocese de Luanda, 1981.

Gallop, Rodney. *Portugal: A Book of Folk-Ways*. Cambridge: Cambridge University Press, 1936.

Gannon, Michael V. *The Cross in the Sand: The Early Catholic Church in Florida, 1513–1870*. Gainesville: University of Florida Press, 1965.

García y García, António, and Francisco Cantelar Rodriguez, eds. *Synodicon Hispanum II, Portugal*. Madrid: Biblioteca de Autores Cristianos, 1982.

Garfield, Robert. *A History of São Tomé Island 1470–1655: The Key to Guinea*. San Francisco: Mellen Research University Press, 1992.

Gaspar, David Barry. *Bondmen and Rebels: A Study of Master-Slave Relations in Antigua*. Baltimore, MD: John Hopkins University Press, 1985.

———. "'Subjects of the King of Portugal': Captivity and Repatriation in the Atlantic Slave Trade (Antigua, 1724)." In *The Creation of the British Atlantic*

L

World, edited by Elizabeth Mancke and Carole Shammas, 93–114. Baltimore, MD: Johns Hopkins University Press, 2005.

Gates, Henry Louis, Jr. *The Black Church: This Is Our Story, This Is Our Song.* New York: Penguin Press, 2021.

Gehring, Charles T., ed. *Council Minutes, 1652–1654: New York Historical Manuscripts.* Baltimore, MD: Genealogical Publishing, 1983.

———., ed. *Council Minutes 1655–1656.* Syracuse, NY: Syracuse University Press, 1995.

———., ed. *New York Historical Manuscripts: Dutch, Volumes GG, HH & II, Land Papers.* Baltimore, MD: Genealogical Publishing, 1980.

Gehring, Charles T., and J. A. Schiltkamp, eds. *Curaçao Papers 1640–1665.* Interlaken, NY: Heart of the Lakes, 1987.

Gehring, Charles T., and Janny Venema, eds. *Council Minutes, 1656–1658.* Syracuse, NY: Syracuse University Press, 2018.

Gerbner, Katharine. *Christian Slavery: Conversion and Race in the Protestant Atlantic World.* Philadelphia: University of Pennsylvania Press, 2018.

Giggie, John M. "For God and Lodge: Black Fraternal Orders and the Evolution of African American Religion in the Postbellum South." In *The Struggle for Equality: Essays on Sectional Conflict, the Civil War, and the Long Reconstruction*, edited by Orville Vernon Burton, Jerald Podair, and Jennifer L. Weber, 198–218. Charlottesville: University of Virginia Press, 2011.

———. "The Mississippi River and the Transformation of Black Religion in the Delta 1877–1915." In *Gods of the Mississippi*, edited by Michael Pasquier, 113–29. Bloomington: Indiana University Press, 2013.

Gill, James. *Lords of Misrule: Mardi Gras and the Politics of Race in New Orleans.* Jackson: University Press of Mississippi, 1997.

Gillard, John T. *The Catholic Church and the American Negro.* Baltimore, MD: St. Joseph's Society Press, 1928.

———. *Colored Catholics in the United States.* Baltimore, MD: Josephite Press, 1941.

Glass, Barbara S. *African American Dance: An Illustrated History.* Jefferson, NC: McFarland, 2007.

Glasson, Travis. "'Baptism Doth Not Bestow Freedom': Missionary Anglicanism, Slavery, and the Yorke-Talbot Opinion, 1701–30." *William and Mary Quarterly* 67 (April 2010): 279–318.

Glaunec, Jean-Pierre Le. "'Un Nègre nommè [sic] Lubin ne connaissas pas Sa Nation': The Small World of Louisiana Slavery." In *Louisiana: Crossroads of the Atlantic World*, edited by Cécile Vidal, 103–22. Philadelphia: University of Pennsylvania Press, 2013.

Godinho, Vitorino Magalhães. *A estrutura na antiga sociedade portuguesa*. Lisbon: Arcádia, 1977.

Goetz, Rebecca Anne. *The Baptism of Early Virginia: How Christianity Created Race*. Baltimore, MD: Johns Hopkins University Press, 2012.

Góis, Damião de. *Crónica do Felicíssimo Rei Dom Manuel*. 4 vols. Coimbra: Imprensa da Universidade, 1954.

Gomes, Flávio, ed. *Mocambos de Palmares: História e fontes (séc. XVI-XIX)*. Rio de Janeiro: 7Letras, 2010.

Gomez, Michael A. *Exchanging our Country Marks: The Transformation of African Identities in the Colonial and Antebellum South*. Chapel Hill: University of North Carolina Press, 1998.

Gonçalves, António Custódio. "As influências do Cristianismo na organização política do Reino do Congo." In *Congresso Internacional Bartolomeu Dias e a sua época: Actas*, 5 vols., 5:523–39. Porto: Universidade do Porto, 1989.

———. "Kimpa Vita: Simbiose de tradição e de modernidade." In *Actas do seminário 'Encontro de Povos e Culturas' em Angola*, 323–38. Lisbon: Comissão Nacional para as Comemorações dos Descobrimentos Portugueses, 1997.

Gonçalves, Carlos Filipe. *Kab Verd Band*. Praia: Instituto do Arquivo Histórico Nacional, 2006.

Gonçalves, Iria. "As festas do Corpus Christi do Porto na segunda metade do século XV: A participação do concelho." *Estudos medievais* 4–5 (1985): 3–23.

———. *Os Jesuítas e a missão de Cabo Verde (1604–1642)*. Lisbon: Brotéria, 1996.

Gonzales, Ambrose E. *The Black Border: Gullah Stories of the Carolina Coast*. Columbia, SC: State Company, 1922.

Goodfriend, Joyce D. *Who Should Rule at Home? Confronting the Elite in British New York City*. Ithaca, NY: Cornell University Press, 2017.

Goodman, Morris. "The Portuguese Element in the American Creoles." In *Pidgin and Creole Languages*, edited by Glenn G. Gilbert, 361–405. Honolulu: University of Hawaii Press, 1987.

Goodman, Walter. *The Pearl of the Antilles, or An Artist in Cuba*. London: Henry S. King, 1873.

Gould, Virginia Meacham. "The Parish Identities of Free Creoles of Color in Pensacola and Mobile, 1698–1860." *U.S. Catholic Historian* 14, no. 3 (Summer 1996): 1–10.

Gould, Virginia Meacham, and Charles E. Nolan, eds. *No Cross, No Crown: Black Nuns in Nineteenth-Century New Orleans. Sister Mary Bernard Deggs*. Bloomington: Indiana University Press, 2001.

Graubart, Karen B. "'So color de una cofradía': Catholic Confraternities and the Development of Afro-Peruvian Ethnicities in Early Colonial Peru." *Slavery & Abolition* 33, no. 1 (2012): 43–64.

Gravely, Will B. "The Rise of African Churches in America (1786–1822): Re-Examining the Contexts." In *African-American Religion: Interpretative Essays in History and Culture*, edited by Timothy E. Fulop and Albert J. Raboteau, 133–52. New York: Routledge, 1997.

Gray, Richard. *Black Christians and White Missionaries*. New Haven, CT: Yale University Press, 1990.

———. "*Como vero prencipe Catolico*: The Capuchins and the Rulers of Soyo in the Late Seventeenth Century." *Africa* 53, no. 3 (1983): 39–54.

———. "A Kongo Princess, the Kongo Ambassadors and the Papacy." *Journal of Religion in Africa* 29, no. 2 (May 1999): 140–54.

Green, Toby. *A Fistful of Shells: West Africa from the Rise of the Slave Trade to the Age of Revolution*. Chicago: University of Chicago Press, 2019.

———. *The Rise of the Trans-Atlantic Slave Trade in Western Africa, 1300–1589*. Cambridge: Cambridge University Press, 2012.

Greene, Lorenzo Johnston. *The Negro in Colonial New England, 1620–1776*. Port Washington, NY: Kennikat Press, 1966.

Griffiths, Nicholas. "Popular Religious Skepticism and Idiosyncrasy in Post-Tridentine Cuenca." In *Faith and Fanaticism in Early Modern Spain*, edited by Lesley K. Twomey, 95–126. Aldershot: Ashgate, 1997.

Grothe, J. A., ed. "Classicale Acta van Brazilië." *Kroniek van het Historisch Genootschap* 29.6, no. 4 (1874): 298–419.

Gual Camarena, Miguel. "Una cofradía de negros libertos en el siglo XV." *Estudios de la Edad Media en la Corona de Aragón* 5 (1952): 457–66.

Guanche, Jesús. *Africanía y etnicidad en Cuba: Los componentes étnicos africanos y sus múltiples denominaciones*. Havana: Editorial de Ciencias Sociales, 2009.

Guattini, Michelangelo, and Dionigi Carli. *La Mission au Kongo des pères Michelangelo Guattini et Dionigi Carli*. Translated by Cheyron d'Abzac. Paris: Chandeigne, 2006.

Guerra, Ramiro. *Teatralización del folklore y otros ensayos*. Havana: Editorial Letras Cubanas, 1989.

Guerreiro, Fernão. *Relação anual das coisas que fizeram os padres da Companhia de Jesus*. 3 vols. Coimbra: Imprensa Universidade/Imprensa Nacional, 1930–42.

Guss, David. "The Selling of San Juan: The Performance of History in an Afro-Venezuelan Community." *American Ethnologist* 20, no. 2 (1993): 451–73.

Hackett, David G. "The Prince Hall Masons and the African American Church: The Labors of Grand Master and Bishop James Hood, 1831–1918." *Church History* 69, no. 4 (December 2000): 770–802.

Hair, P. E. H. "Christian Influences in Sierra Leone before 1787." *Journal of Religion in Africa* 27, no. 1 (February 1997): 3–14.

———. "Early Sources on Sierra Leone." *African Research Bulletin* 5, no. 4 (1975): 81–118, and 6, no. 2 (1976): 45–70.

———. "Hamlet in an Afro-Portuguese Setting: New Perspectives on Sierra Leone in 1607." *History in Africa* 5 (1978): 21–42.

Hall, Gwendolyn Midlo. *Africans in Colonial Louisiana: The Development of Afro-Creole Culture in the Eighteenth Century*. Baton Rouge: Louisiana State University Press, 1992.

———. "Epilogue: Historical Memory, Consciousness, and Conscience in the New Millennium." In *French Colonial Louisiana and the Atlantic World*, edited by Bradley G. Bond, 291–309. Baton Rouge: Louisiana State University Press, 2005.

———. "The Formation of Afro-Creole Culture." In *Creole New Orleans: Race and Americanization*, edited by Arnold R. Hirsch and Joseph Logsdon, 66–71. Baton Rouge: Louisiana State University Press, 1992.

———. *Slavery and African Ethnicities in the Americas: Restoring the Links.* Chapel Hill: University of North Carolina Press, 2005.

Hall, Neville A. T. *Slave Society in the Danish West Indies: St. Thomas, St. John and St. Croix*. Edited by B. W. Higman. Baltimore, MA: Johns Hopkins University Press, 1992.

Hall, R. B. "The Société Congo of the Ile à Gonave." *American Anthropologist* 31, no. 4 (1929): 685–700.

Hamelberg, J. H. J., ed. *Documenten behoorende bij de Nederlanders op de West-Indische Eilanden. I. Curaçao, Bonaire, Aruba*. Amsterdam: J. H. de Bussy, 1901.

Hamilton, James, Jr. *Negro Plot: An Account of the Late Intended Insurrection among a Portion of the Blacks of the City of Charleston*. South Carolina. Boston: J. W. Ingraham, 1822.

Hamilton, Kenneth G., ed. *The Bethlehem Diary*. Bethlehem, PA: Archives of the Moravian Church, 1971.

Harris, Katherine J. "The Black Governors, 1780 to 1856." In *African American Connecticut Explored*, edited by Elizabeth J. Normen, 69–79. Middletown, CT: Wesleyan University Press, 2013.

———. "In Remembrance of Their Kings of Guinea: The Black Governors and the Negro Election, 1749 to 1800." In *African American Connecticut Explored*, edited by Elizabeth J. Normen, 35–44. Middletown, CT: Wesleyan University Press, 2013.

Harris, Leslie M. *In the Shadow of Slavery: African Americans in New York City, 1626–1863*. Chicago: University of Chicago Press, 2003.

Harris, Max. *Carnival and Other Christian Festivals: Folk Theology and Folk Performance.* Austin: University of Texas Press, 2003.

Harvey, Paul. *Through the Storm, Through the Night: A History of African American Christianity.* Lanham, MD: Rowman & Littlefield, 2011.

Hastings, Adrian. *The Church in Africa 1450–1950.* Oxford: Clarendon Press, 1994.

Hastings, Hugh, and Edward Tanjore Corwin, eds. *Ecclesiastical Records, State of New York.* 7 vols. Albany, NY: State Historian, 1901–16.

Havik, Philip J. "Kriol without Creoles: Rethinking Guinea's Afro-Atlantic Connections (Sixteenth to Twentieth Centuries)." In *Cultures of the Lusophone Black Atlantic,* edited by Nancy Priscilla Naro, Roger Sansi-Roca, and David H. Treece, 41–74. London: Palgrave Macmillan, 2007.

———. *Silences and Soundbites: The Gendered Dynamics of Trade and Brokerage in the Pre-Colonial Guinea Bissau Region.* Münster: Lit Verlag, 2004.

———. "Traders, Planters and Go-betweens: The Kristons in Portuguese Guinea." *Portuguese Studies Review* 19, no. 1/2 (2011): 197–226.

Hebblethwaite, Benjamin. *Vodou Songs in Haitian Creole and English.* Philadelphia: Temple University Press, 2012.

Heintze, Beatrix. *Afrikanische Pioniere: Trägerkarawanen im westlichen Zentralafrika.* Frankfurt am Main: Lembeck, 2002.

———. "Luso-African Feudalism in Angola? The Vassal Treaties of the 16th to the 18th Centuries." *Revista Portuguesa de História* 37 (1980): 111–31.

———., ed. *Max Buchners Reise nach Zentralafrika, 1878–1882, Briefe, Berichte, Studien.* Cologne: Köppe Verlag, 1999.

Henriques, Isabel Castro. *A herança africana em Portugal.* Lisbon: CTT, 2009.

———. *São Tome e Príncipe: A invenção de uma sociedade.* Lisbon: Vega, 2000.

Hernández Soto, Carlos, and Edis Sánchez, "Los Congos de Villa Mella, República Dominicana." *Revista de música latinoamericana* 18, no. 2 (1997): 297–316.

Herskovits, Melville J. *Life in a Haitian Valley.* New York: Knopf, 1937.

Hesperióphylo [Joseph Rossi y Rubí]. "Idea de las congregationes públicas de los negros bozales." *Mercurio Peruano* 48 (June 16, 1791): 112–17, 49 ; (June 19, 1791): 120–25.

Heusch, Luc de. *Le roi de Kongo et les monstres sacrés: Mythes et rites bantous III.* Paris: Gallimard, 2000.

Hevia Lanier, Oilda. *Prácticas religiosas de los negros en la colonia.* Havana: Editora Historia, 2010.

Heywood, Linda M. "The Angolan-Afro-Brazilian Cultural Connections." *Slavery & Abolition: A Journal of Slave and Post-Slave Studies* 20, no. 1 (1999): 9–23.

————, ed. *Central Africans and Cultural Transformations in the American Diaspora.* Cambridge: Cambridge University Press, 2002.

————. "Mbanza Kongo/São Salvador: Culture and the Transformation of an African City, 1491 to 1670s." In *Africa's Development in Historical Perspective*, edited by Emmanuel Akyeampong, Robert H. Bates, Nathan Nunn, and James A. Robinson, 366–92. Cambridge: Cambridge University Press, 2014.

————. *Njinga of Angola: Africa's Warrior Queen.* Cambridge, MA: Harvard University Press, 2017.

————. "Slavery and Its Transformation in the Kingdom of Kongo, 1491–1800." *Journal of African History* 50, no. 1 (2009): 1–22.

Heywood, Linda M., and John K. Thornton. "'Canniball Negroes': Atlantic Creoles, and the Identity of New England's Charter Generation." *African Diaspora* 4 (2011): 76–94.

————. "Central African Leadership and the Appropriation of European Culture." In *The Atlantic World and Virginia, 1550–1624*, edited by Peter C. Mancall, 194–224. Chapel Hill: University of North Carolina Press, 2007.

————. *Central Africans, Atlantic Creoles, and the Foundation of the Americas, 1585–1660.* Cambridge: Cambridge University Press, 2007.

————. "Intercultural Relations between Europeans and Blacks in New Netherland." In *Four Centuries of Dutch-American Relations 1609–2009*, edited by Hans Krabbendam, Cornelis A. van Minnen, and Giles Scott-Smith, 192–203. Albany: State University of New York Press, 2009.

Higginson, Thomas Wentworth. "Slave Songs and Spirituals." In *African American Religious History: A Documentary Witness*, edited by Milton C. Sernett, 112–36. Durham, NC: Duke University Press, 1999.

————. *Army Life in a Black Regiment.* Boston: Fields, Osgood, 1870.

Hildebrand, P. *Le martyr Georges de Geel et les débuts de la mission au Congo, 1645–1652.* Antwerp: Archives des Capucins, 1940.

Hilton, Anne. *The Kingdom of the Kongo.* Oxford: Clarendon Press, 1985.

Hodes, Martha. *White Women, Black Men: Illicit Sex in the Nineteenth-Century South.* New Haven, CT: Yale University Press, 1997.

Hodges, Graham Russell Gao. *Black New Jersey: 1664 to the Present Day.* New Brunswick, NJ: Rutgers University Press, 2018.

————. *Root and Branch: African Americans in New York & East Jersey 1613–1863.* Chapel Hill: University of North Carolina Press, 1999.

————. *Slavery, Freedom & Culture among Early American Workers.* Armond, NY: M. E. Sharpe, 1998.

Hodges, Graham Russell, and Alan Edward Brown, eds. *Pretends to Be Free: Runaway Slave Advertisements from Colonial and Revolutionary New York and New Jersey.* New York: Garland, 1994.

Hoefnagels, Peter, and Shon W. Hoogenbergen. *Antilliaans spreekwoordenboek.* Curaçao: De Curaçaosche Courant, 1980.

Hoetink, Harry. *Het patroon van de oude Curaçaose samenleving: Een sociologische studie.* Aruba: De Wit, 1959.

Hoffer, Peter Charles. *The Great New York Conspiracy of 1741: Slavery, Crime, and Colonial Law.* Lawrence: University Press of Kansas, 2003.

Hoornaert, Eduardo. *História da igreja no Brasil: Ensaio de interpretação a partir do povo.* 2 vols. Petrópolis: Vozes, 1977.

Horsmanden, Daniel. *The New York Conspiracy.* Edited by Thomas J. Davis. Boston: Beacon Press, 1971.

Horta, José da Silva. "Africanos e portugueses na documentação inquisitorial de Luanda a Mbanza Kongo (1596–1598)." In *Actas do seminário 'Encontro de Povos e Culturas' em Angola*, 301–21. Lisbon: Comissão Nacional para as Comemorações dos Descobrimentos Portugueses, 1997.

———. "Ensino e cristianização informais: Do contexto luso-africano à primeira 'escola' jesuíta na Senegâmbia (Biguba, Buba—Guiné-Bissau, 1605–1606)." In *Rumos e Escrita da História: Estudos em Homenagem a A. A. Marques de Almeida*, 407–18. Lisbon: Edições Colibri, 2006.

———. "Evidence for a Luso-African Identity in 'Portuguese' Accounts on 'Guinea of Cape Verde' (Sixteenth–Seventeenth Centuries)." *History in Africa* 27 (2000): 99–130.

Hotten, John C. *Original Lists of Persons of Quality, 1600–1700.* Baltimore, MD: Genealogical Publishing, 1980.

Hovy, L., and C. Streefkerk. *"Zoo is 't dat wij daarin ander willende voorzien": Prolegomena voor een Ceylonees plakkaatboek.* Amsterdam: VU, 1985.

Howard, Thomas D. "Before and After Emancipation." *Unitarian Review* (August 1888):136–44.

Howell, George R., and Jonathan Tenny. *History of the County of Albany, from 1609 to 1886.* Albany, NY: W. W. Munsell, 1886.

Huey, Paul. "A New Look at an Old Object." *New York State Preservationist* 8, no. 2 (2004): 22–23.

Hughes, Thomas, ed. *History of the Society of Jesus in North America; Colonial and Federal.* 4 vols. Cleveland, OH: Burrows Brothers, 1907–17.

Iberville, Pierre Le Moyne d'. *Iberville's Gulf Journals (1698–1702).* Edited by Richebourg Gaillard McWilliams. Tuscaloosa: University of Alabama Press, 1981.

Ingersoll, Thomas N. *Mammon and Manon in Early New Orleans: The First Slave Society in the Deep South, 1718–1819.* Knoxville, TN: University of Tennessee Press, 1999.

Ireton, Chloe. "'They Are Blacks of the Caste of Black Christians': Old Christian Black Blood in the Sixteenth- and Early Seventeenth-Century Iberian Atlantic." *Hispanic American Historical Review* 97, no. 4 (2017): 579–612.

Isichei, Elizabeth. *A History of Christianity in Africa from Antiquity to the Present.* Grand Rapids, MI: William B. Eerdmans, 1995.

Iyanaga, Michael. "Por que se canta? Rezando os santos católicos no Recôncavo baiano." In *Vozes, performances e arquivos de saberes*, edited by Edil Silva Costa, Nerivaldo Alves Araújo, and Frederico Augusto Garcia Fernandes, 163–90. Salvador: EDUNEB, 2018.

———. "Why Saints Love Samba: A Historical Perspective on Black Agency and the Rearticulation of Catholicism in Bahia, Brazil." *Black Music Research Journal* 35, no. 1 (Spring 2015): 119–47.

Jacobs, Bart. *Origins of a Creole: The History of Papiamentu and its African Ties.* Berlin: De Gruyter Mouton, 2002.

Jacobs, Claude F. "Benevolent Societies of New Orleans during the Late Nineteenth and Early Twentieth Centuries." *Louisiana History* 29 (Winter 1988): 21–33.

Jacobs, Claude F., and Andrew J. Kaslow. *The Spiritual Churches of New Orleans: Origins, Beliefs, and Rituals of an African-American Religion.* Knoxville: University of Tennessee Press, 1991.

Jacobs, Jaap. *New Netherland: A Dutch Colony in Seventeenth-Century America.* Leiden: Brill, 2005.

Jadin, Louis, ed. *L'Ancien Congo et l'Angola 1639–1655 d'après les archives romaines, portugaises, néerlandaises et espagnoles.* 3 vols. Brussels: Institut Historique Belge de Rome, 1975.

———. "Le clergé séculier et les capucins du Congo et d'Angola aux XVIe et XVIIe siècles: Conflits de juridiction, 1700–1726." *Bulletin de l'Institut Historique Belge de Rome* 36 (1964): 185–483.

———. "Le Congo et la secte des Antoniens: Restauration du Royaume sous Pedro IV et la 'Saint Antoine' congolaise (1694–1718)." *Bulletin de l'Institut Historique Belge de Rome* 32 (1961): 411–614.

———. "Recherches dans les archives et bibliothèques d'Italie et du Portugal sur l'ancien Congo." *Bulletin de L'Académie Royale des Sciences Coloniales* 2 (1956): 951–90.

———. "Relations sur le Congo et l'Angola tirées des archives de la Compagnie de Jésus, 1621–1631." *Bulletin de l'Institut Historique Belge de Rome* 39 (1968): 332–453.

———. "Rivalités luso-néerlandaises du Sohio, Congo, 1600–1675." *Bulletin de l'Institut Historique Belge de Rome* 37 (1966): 137–360.

————. "Les survivances chrétiennes au Congo au XIXe siècle." Études d'Histoire Africaine 1 (1970): 137–85.

Jennings, William, and Stefan Pfänder. *Inheritance and Innovation in a Colonial Language: Towards a Usage-Based Account of French Guianese Creole.* Cham: Palgrave Macmillan, 2018.

Jobson, Richard. *The Discovery of River Gambra (1623).* Edited by David P. Gamble and P. E. H. Hair. London: Hakluyt Society, 1999.

Johnson, Howard. "Friendly Societies in the Bahamas, 1834–1910." *Slavery and Abolition* 12, no. 3 (December 1991): 183–99.

Johnson, Sylvester A. *African American Religions, 1500–2000: Colonialism, Democracy, and Freedom.* Cambridge: Cambridge University Press, 2015.

Johnson, Washington B. "The Origin and Nature of African Slavery in Seventeenth Century Maryland." *Maryland Historical Magazine* 73, no. 3 (Fall 1978): 236–45.

Johnston, W. *Slavery in Rhode Island, 1755–1776.* Providence, RI: n.p., 1894.

Joosse, Leendert Jan. *Geloof in de Nieuwe Wereld: Ontmoeting met Afrikanen en Indianen 1600–1700.* Kampen: Kok, 2008.

Jordaan, Hans. *Slavernij en Vrijheid op Curaçao.* Zutphen: Walburg Pers, 2013.

Jordão, Levy Maria, ed. *História do Congo: Obra posthuma do Visconde de Paiva Manso.* Lisbon: Typographia da Academia, 1877.

Judd, Jacob. "Frederick Philipse and the Madagascar Trade." *New-York Historical Society Quarterly* 55 (1971): 354–74.

Junker, L. "Eenige mededelingen over de Saramakkaner Boschnegers." *De West-Indische gids* 4 (1922): 449–80.

Kachun, Mitch. *Festivals of Freedom: Memory and Meaning in African American Emancipation Celebrations, 1808–1915.* Amherst: University of Massachusetts Press, 2003.

Kapitzke, Robert L. *Religion, Power, and Politics in Colonial St. Augustine.* Gainesville: University Press of Florida, 2001.

Karasch, Mary C. *Slave Life in Rio de Janeiro 1808–1850.* Princeton, NJ: Princeton University Press, 1987.

Kennedy, Al. *Big Chief Harrison and the Mardi Gras Indians.* Gretna, LA: Pelican, 2010.

Kennedy, William. *O Albany! Improbable City of Political Wizards, Fearless Ethnics, Spectacular Aristocrats, Splendid Nobodies, and Underrated Scoundrels.* New York: Viking Press, 1983.

Kenny, Joseph. *The Catholic Church in Tropical Africa, 1445–1850.* Ibadan: Ibadan University Press, 1983.

Kent, R. K. "Palmares: An African State in Brazil." *Journal of African History* 6, no. 2 (1965): 161–75.

Kihm, Alain. *Kriyol Syntax: The Portuguese-Based Creole Language of Guinea-Bissau*. Amsterdam: John Benjamin, 1994.

Kind, Jasper De, Gilles-Maurice de Schryver, and Koen Bostoen. "Pushing Back the Origin of Bantu Lexicography: The Vocabularium Congense of 1652, 1928, 2012." *Lexikos* (December 2012): 159–94.

King, John. "Extraits de relation inédite d'un voyage fait, en 1820, aux royaumes de Benin et de Warree." In *Journal des Voyages*, vol. 13, edited by J.-T. Verneur, 313–18. Paris: Colnet, Roret et Roussel, Arthus Bertrand, 1822.

Kingsbury, Susan Myra, ed. *The Records of the Virginia Company of London*. 4 vols. Washington DC: Government Printing Office, 1906–35.

Kingsley, Zephaniah. *A Treatise on the Patriarchal System of Society, as it Exists in Some Governments and Colonies in America, and in the United States, under the Name of Slavery, with Its Necessity and Advantages by an Inhabitant of Florida*. n.l.: n.p., 1834.

Kinser, Samuel. *Carnival, American Style: Mardi Gras at New Orleans and Mobile*. Chicago: University of Chicago Press, 1990.

Klein, Herbert. "The Atlantic Slave Trade to 1650." In *Tropical Babylons: Sugar and the Making of the Atlantic World, 1450–1680*, edited by Stuart B. Schwartz, 201–36. Chapel Hill: University of North Carolina Press, 2004.

Klinkers, Elisabeth Maria Leonie. *Op hoop van vrijheid: Van slavensamenleving naar creoolse gemeenschap in Suriname, 1830–1880*. Utrecht: Vakgroep Culture Antropologie, 1997.

Klooster, Wim. "Curaçao as a Transit Center to the Spanish Main and the French West Indies." In *Dutch Atlantic Connections, 1680–1800: Linking Empires, Bridging Borders*. Leiden: Brill, 2014.

———. *The Dutch Moment: War, Trade, and Settlement in the Seventeenth-Century Atlantic World*. Ithaca, NY: Cornell University Press, 2016.

———. *Illicit Riches: Dutch Trade in the Caribbean, 1648–1795*. Leiden: KITLV, 1998.

———. "Subordinate but Proud: Curaçao's Free Blacks and Mulattoes in the Eighteenth Century." *NWIG* 68, nos. 3 and 4 (1994): 283–300.

Kohl, Christoph. *A Creole Nation: National Integration in Guinea-Bissau*. New York: Bergbahn, 2018.

———. "Luso-Creole Culture and Identity Compared: The Cases of Guinea-Bissau and Sri Lanka." In *The Upper Guinea Coast in Global Perspective*, edited by Jacqueline Knörr and Christoph Kohl, 40–57. New York: Bergbahn, 2016.

Konetzke, Richard, ed. *Colección de documentos para la historia de la formación social de Hispanoamérica, 1493–1810*. 3 vols. Madrid: Consejo Superior de Investigaciones Científicas, 1953–62.

Koster, Henry. *Travels in Brazil.* London: Longman, Hurst Rees, Orme and Brown, 1816.

Kosterman, Hans. *Het aanzien van een millennium: De Unie van Utrecht.* Utrecht: Spectrum, 1999.

Krebsbach, Suzanne. "Black Catholics in Antebellum Charleston." *South Carolina Historical Magazine* 108, no. 2 (April 2007): 143–59.

Kuyk, Betty M. "The African Derivation of Black Fraternal Orders in the United States." *Comparative Studies in Society and History* 25, no. 4 (1983): 559–92.

———. *African Voices in the African American Heritage.* Bloomington: Indiana University Press, 2003.

Labat, Jean-Baptiste. *Nouveau voyage aux isles de l'Amérique.* 8 vols. Paris: Ch. J. B. Delespine, 1742.

Labouret, Henri, and Paul Rivet. *Le Royaume d'Ardra et son évangélisation au XVII siècle.* Paris: Institut d'ethnologie, 1929.

Lacerda, Francisco de. *Folclore da Madeira e Porto Santo.* Lisbon: Colibri, 1994.

Lachance, Paul. "The 1809 Immigration of Saint-Dominque Refugees." In *The Road to Louisiana: The Saint-Domingue Refugees, 1792–1809,* edited by Carl A. Brasseaux and Glenn R. Conrad, 245–84. Lafayette: Center for Louisiana Studies, 1992.

———. "The Foreign French." In *Creole New Orleans: Race and Americanization,* edited by Arnold R. Hirsch and Joseph Logsdon, 101–30. Baton Rouge: Louisiana State University Press, 1992.

———. "The Growth of the Free and Slave Populations of French Colonial Louisiana." In *French Colonial Louisiana and the Atlantic World,* edited by Bradley G. Bond, 204–43. Baton Rouge: Louisiana State University Press, 2005.

Laer, Arnold J. F. van, ed. *New York Historical Manuscripts: Dutch.* 4 vols. Baltimore, MD: Genealogical Publishing, 1974.

Laet, Johannes de. *Iaerlyck verhael van de verrichtingen der Geocroyeerde West-Indische Compagnie.* Edited by S. P. L'Honoré Naber and J. C. M. Warnsinck. 4 vols. The Hague: M. Nijhoff, 1931–1937.

Laguerre, Michel. "Bizango: A Voodoo Secret Society in Haiti." In *Secrecy: A Cross-Cultural Perspective,* edited by Stanton K. Tefft, 147–60. New York: Human Science Press, 1980.

Lahon, Didier. "Esclavage et confréries noires au Portugal durant l'Ancien Régime (1441–1830)." Ph.D. dissertation, EHESS, 2001.

———. "Exclusion, intégration et métissage dans les confréries noires de Portugal (XVIe-XIVe siècles)." In *Negros, Mulatos, Zambaigos: Derroteros africanos en los mundos ibéricos,* edited by Berta Ares Queija and Alessandro Stella, 275–311. Seville: EEHA, 2000.

————. "Os escravos negros em Portugal." In *Os Negros em Portugal—sécs. XV a XIX*, edited by Ana Maria Rodrigues, 69–78. Lisbon: Comissão Nacional para as Comemorações dos Descobrimentos Portugueses, 1999.

————. *O Negro no coração do Império: Uma memória a resgatar—Séculos XV–XIX*. Lisbon: Secretariada Coordenador dos Programas Multiculturais—Ministério da Educação, 1999.

————. "Vivencia Religiosa." In *Os Negros em Portugal—sécs. XV a XIX*, edited by Ana Maria Rodrigues, 127–64. Lisbon: Comissão Nacional para as Comemorações dos Descobrimentos Portugueses, 1999.

Laing, Annette. "'Heathens and Infidels'? African Christianization and Anglicanism in the South Carolina Low Country, 1700–1750." *Religion and American Culture: A Journal of Interpretation* 12, no. 2 (Summer 2002): 197–228.

Lampe, Armando. "Christianity and Slavery in the Dutch Caribbean." In *Christianity in the Caribbean: Essays on Church History*, edited by Armando Lampe, 126–53. Barbados: University of the West Indies Press, 2001.

————. "The Dutch Reformed Church and Catholicism in Curaçao (17th–18th Century)." In *Christen und Gewürze: Konfrontation und Interaktion kolonialer und indigener Christentumsvarianten*, edited by Klaus Koschorke, 106–16. Göttingen: Vandenhoeck & Ruprecht, 1998.

Landers, Jane. *Black Society in Spanish Florida*. Urbana: University of Illinois Press, 1999.

————. "Free and Slave." In *The New History of Florida*, edited by Michael Gannon, 167–82. Gainesville: University Press of Florida, 1996.

Lara, Silvia Hunold. "Significados cruzados: Um reinado de Congos na Bahia setecentista." In *Carnavais e outras f(r)estas: Ensaios de história social da cultura*, edited by Maria Clementina Pereira Cunha, 71–100. Campinas: Editora Unicamp, 2002.

Larrazabal Blanco, Carlos. *Los negros y la esclavitud en Santo Domingo*. Santo Domingo: Julia D. Postigo, 1975.

Latrobe, Benjamin Henry Boneval. *Impressions Respecting New Orleans: Diary and Sketches 1818–1820*. Edited by Samuel Wilson Jr. New York: Columbia University Press, 1951.

Law, Robin. "Religion, Trade, and Politics on the 'Slave Coast': Roman Catholic Missions in Allada and Whydah in the Seventeenth Century." *Journal of Religion in Africa* 21 (1991): 42–77.

Lay Bravo, Mercedes. *Kinfuiti: Cantos y toques en la fiesta de San Antonio de Padua*. Havana: Cidmuc, 2013.

Leal, João. *As festas do Espírito Santo nos Açores: Um estudo de antropologia social*. Lisbon: Dom Quixote, 1994.

Leite, Serafim, ed. *Cartas dos primeiros jesuítas do Brasil*. 3 vols. São Paulo: Comissão do IV Centenário da Cidade de São Paulo, 1954.

Le Jau, Francis. *The Carolina Chronicle of Dr. Francis Le Jau 1706–1717*. Edited by Frank J. Klingberg. Berkeley: University of California Press, 1956.

Lemarchant, René. "The Bases of Nationalism among the Bakongo." *Africa: Journal of the International African Institute* 31, no. 4 (October 1961): 344–54.

Lepore, Jill. *New York Burning: Liberty, Slavery, and Conspiracy in Eighteenth-Century Manhattan*. New York: Alfred A. Knopf, 2005.

Letts, Malcom, ed. *The Travels of Leo of Rozmital through Germany, Flanders, England, France, Spain, Portugal and Italy, 1465–1467*. Cambridge: Hakluyt Society, 1957.

Levine, Lawrence W. *Black Culture and Black Consciousness: Afro-American Folk Thought from Slavery to Freedom*. New York: Oxford University Press, 1977.

L'Honoré Naber, S. P. "Het dagboek van Hendrik Haecxs, Lid van den Hoogen Raad van Brazilië (1645–1654)." *Bijdragen en Mededelingen van het Historisch Genootschap* 46 (1925): 126–311.

———., ed. *Reisebeschreibungen von deutschen Beamten und Kriegsleuten im Dienst der niederländishen West- und Ost-Indischen Kompagnien 1602–1797*. 10 vols. The Hague: Martinus Nijhoff, 1930.

Ligon, Richard. *A True & Exact History of the Island of Barbados*. London: Printed for Humphrey Moseley, 1657.

Lima, Augusto César Pires de, and Alexandre Lima Carneiro. "A encomendação das almas." *Douro Litoral* 4, nos. 3–4 (1951): 3–21.

Lima, José Joaquim Lopes de. *Ensaios sobre a statística das possessões portuguezas na África occidental e oriental*. 5 vols. Lisbon: Imprensa nacional, 1844–62.

Lima, Rossini Tavares de. *Folclore das festas cíclicas*. São Paulo, Irmãos Vitale, 1971.

———. *Folguedos populares do Brasil*. São Paulo: Ricordi, 1962.

Linde, A. P. G. J. van der, ed. *Old First Dutch Reformed Church of Brooklyn, New York: First Book of Records, 1660–1752*. New York Historical Manuscripts: Dutch. Baltimore, MD: Genealogical Publishing, 1983.

Linde, J. M. van der. *Surinaamse suikerheren en hun kerk: Plantagekolonie en handelskerk ten tijde van Johannes Basseliers, predikant en planter in Suriname, 1667–1689*. Wageningen: H. Veenman en zonen, 1966.

Lindsay, Nick, ed. *An Oral History of Edisto Island: Sam Gadsden Tells the Story*. Goshen College, IN: Pinchpenny Press, 1975.

Linebaugh, Peter, and Marcus Rediker. *The Many-Headed Hydra: Sailors, Salves, Commoners, and the Hidden History of the Revolutionary Atlantic*. Boston: Beacon Press, 2000.

Lipner, Ronnie, and Stu Lipner. *Dances of Venezuela*. New York: Folkways Records, 1958.

Lipski, John M. *The Speech of the Negros Congos of Panama*. Amsterdam: John Benjamins, 1989.

Liscano, Juan. *La fiesta de San Juan el Bautista*. Caracas: Monte Avila Editores, 1973.

Littlefield, Daniel C. *Rice and Slaves: Ethnicity and the Slave Trade in Colonial South Carolina*. Baton Rouge: Louisiana State University Press, 1981.

Lizardo, Fradique. *Danzas y bailes folklóricos dominicanos*. Santo Domingo: Taller, 1974.

Lizardo, Fradique, and J. P. Muñoz Victoria. *Fiestas patronales y juegos populares dominicanos*. Santo Domingo: Fundación García-Arévalo, 1979.

Logsdon, Joseph, and Caryn Cossé Bell. "The Americanization of Black New Orleans." In *Creole New Orleans: Race and Americanization*, edited by Arnold R. Hirsch and Joseph Logsdon. Baton Rouge: Louisiana State University Press, 1992.

Lomax, John A., and Alan Lomax. *Folk Song U.S.A.* New York: Ducil, Sloan and Pearce, 1947.

Long, Carolyn Morrow. *A New Orleans Voudou Priestess: The Legend and Reality of Marie Laveau*. Gainesville: University of Florida Press, 2006.

Long, Edward. *The History of Jamaica or, General Survey of the Antient and Modern State of the Island*. 3 vols. London: T. Lownudes, 1774.

Loyer, Godefroy. *Relation du voyage du royaume d'Issyny, Côte d'Or, païs de Guinée, en Afrique*. Paris: A. Seneuze, 1714.

Lucques, Laurent de [Lorenzo da Lucca]. *Relations sur le Congo du Père Laurent de Lucques (1700–1718)*. Edited by J. Cuvelier. Brussels: Institut Royal Colonial Belge, 1953.

Lyell, Charles. *A Second Visit to the United States of North America*. 2 vols. New York: Harper & Bros, 1849.

Mabee, Carleton. *Sojourner Truth: Slave, Prophet, Legend*. New York: New York University Press, 1993.

Macedo, José Rivair. "Mouros e Cristãos. A ritualização da conquista no velho e no Novo Mundo." *BUCEMA* 2 (2008): 2–10.

MacGaffey, Wyatt. "A Central African Kingdom: Kongo in 1480." In *The Kongo Kingdom: The Origins, Dynamics and Cosmopolitan Culture of an African Polity*, edited by Koen Bostoen and Inge Brinkman, 42–59. Cambridge: Cambridge University Press, 2018.

———. "Constructing a Kongo Identity: Scholarship and Mythopoesis." *Comparative Studies in Society and History* 58, no. 1 (2016):159–80.

———. "Dialogues of the Deaf: Europeans on the Atlantic Coast of Africa." In *Implicit Understandings: Observing, Reporting, and Reflecting on the Encounters between Europeans and Other People in the Early Modern Era*, edited by Stuart B. Schwartz, 249–67. Cambridge: Cambridge University Press, 1994.

———. "Kongo and the King of the Americans." *Journal of Modern African Studies* 6, no. 2 (August 1968): 171–81.

———. *Religion and Society in Central Africa: The BaKongo of Lower Zaire.* Chicago: University of Chicago Press, 1986.

———. "The West in Congolese Experience." In *Africa and the West: Intellectual Responses to European Culture*, edited by Philip D. Curtin, 49–74. Madison: University of Wisconsin Press, 1972.

MacGregor, Morris J. *The Emergence of a Black Catholic Community. St. Augustine's in Washington.* Washington, DC: Catholic University of America Press, 1999.

Madden, Richard C. *Catholics in South Carolina: A Record.* Lanham, MD: University Press of America, 1985.

Madiou, Thomas. *Histoire d'Haïti.* 3 vols. Port-au-Prince: J. Courtois, 1904.

Maika, Dennis J. "Encounters: Slavery and the Philipse Family, 1680–1751." In *Dutch New York: The Roots of Hudson Valley Culture*, edited by Roger Panetta, 35–72. Bronx, NY: Fordham University Press, 2009.

———. "To 'Experiment with a Parcel of Negros': Incentive, Collaboration, and Competition in New Amsterdam's Slave Trade." *Journal of Early American History* 10 (2020): 33–69.

Marees, Pieter de. *Beschryvinghe ende historische verhael van het Gout koninckrijck van Gunea anders de Gout-Custe de Mina genaemt liggende in het deel van Africa.* Edited by S. P. L'Honoré Naber. The Hague: M. Nijhoff, 1912.

Mark, Peter. "The Evolution of 'Portuguese' Identity: Luso-Africans on the Upper Guinea Coast form the Sixteenth to the Early Nineteenth Century." *Journal of African History* 40, no. 2 (July 1999): 173–91.

Marques, A. H. de Oliveira. *Daily Life in Portugal in the Late Middle Ages.* Translated by S. S. Wyatt. Madison: University of Wisconsin Press, 1971.

Marques, José. "A confraria do Corpo de Deus da cidade de Braga, no século XV." In *Homenagem a Lúcio Craveiro da Silva*, 223–47. Braga: Universidade do Minho, 1994.

Martineau, Harriet. *Retrospect of Western Travel.* 2 vols. London: Saunders and Otley, 1838.

Martins, Manuel Alfredo de Morais. *Contacto de culturas no Congo Português: Achegas para o seu estudo.* Lisbon: Estudos de Ciências Políticas e Sociais, 1958.

Mather, Cotton. *Diary of Cotton Mather, 1663–1728.* Edited by Worthington Chauncey Ford. 2 vols. Boston: Massachusetts Historical Society, 1911–12.

Matos, Raimundo J. da Cunha. *Compêndio histórico das possessões de Portugal na África.* Rio de Janeiro: Ministério de Justiça e Negócios Interiores, 1963.

Matthews, William. *A Voyage to the River Sierra-Leone: 1785, 1786, and 1787.* London: Frank Cass, 1966.

Mattos, Armando de. *Santo António de Lisboa na tradição popular.* Porto: Civilização, 1937.

Mattoso, José. "O pranto fúnebre na poesia trovadoresca Galego-Portuguesa." In *O Reino dos Mortos na Idade Média Peninsular,* edited by José Mattos, 201–16. Lisbon: Edições João Sá da Costa, 1995.

Maxwell, Francis. *Slavery and the Catholic Church: The History of Catholic Teaching Concerning the Moral Legitimacy of the Institution of Slavery.* Chichester: Barry Rose, 1975.

McDonogh, Gary W. *Black and Catholic in Savannah, Georgia.* Knoxville: University of Tennessee Press, 1993.

———., ed., *The Florida Negro: A Federal Writers' Project Legacy.* Jackson: University Press of Mississippi, 1993.

McManus, Edgar J. *Black Bondage in the North.* Syracuse, NY: Syracuse University Press, 1973.

Medford, Edna Greene, ed. *Historical Perspectives of the African Burial Ground: New York Blacks and the Diaspora.* Washington, DC: Howard University Press, 2009.

Meehan, Thomas F. "Mission Work among Colored Catholics." *Historical Records and Studies: United States Catholic Historical Society* 8 (June 1915): 116–28.

Megenny, William. "África en América, su herencia lingüística y su cultura literaria." *Montalban* 15 (1984): 207–60.

Meintel, Deirdre. *Race, Culture, and Portuguese Colonialism in Cabo Verde.* Syracuse, NY: Syracuse University Press, 1984.

Mello, José António Gonsalves de. *Nederlanders in Brazilië (1624–1654).* Edited by B. N. Teensma. Zutphen: Walburg, 2001.

Menard, Russell R. "The Maryland Slave Population, 1658 to 1730: A Demographic Profile of Blacks in Four Counties." *William and Mary Quarterly* 32, no. 1 (January 1975): 29–54.

Mendes, Arlindo. *Ritual de 'apanha de espírito' em Santiago de Cabo Verde.* Praia: Pedro Cardoso, 2018.

Merolla da Sorrento, Girolamo, and Angelo Piccardo. *Breve e succinta relatione del viaggio nel regno di Congo nell' Africa meridionale.* Naples: Francisco Mollo, 1692.

Merveilleux, David-François de. *Mémoires instructifs pour un voyageur dans les divers états de l'Europe: Contenant des anecdotes curieuses très propres à éclaircir l'histoire du tems; avec des remarques sur le commerce & l'histoire naturelle.* 2 vols. Amsterdam: H. Du Sauzet, 1738.

Merwick, Donna. *Possessing Albany, 1630–1710: The Dutch and English Experiences.* Cambridge: Cambridge University Press, 1990.

Metcalf, Alida C. "Millenarian Slaves? The Santidade de Jaguaripe and Slave Resistance in the Americas." *American Historical Review* 104, no. 5 (December 1999): 1531–59.

Métraux, Alfred. *Le Vaudou Haïtien.* Paris: Gallimar, 1958.

Meuwese, Mark. "Dutch Calvinism and Native Americans: A Comparative Study of the Motivations for Protestant Conversion among the Tupis in Northeastern Brazil (1630–1654) and the Mohawks in Central New York (1690–1710)." In *The Spiritual Conversion of the Americas*, edited by James Muldoon, 118–41. Gainesville: University of Florida Press, 2004.

Meyer, Marlyse. *De Carlos Magno e outras histórias: Cristãos e Mouros no Brasil.* Natal: Editora da UFRN, 1995.

Miller, Joseph C. "Worlds Apart: African's Encounters and Africa's Encounters with the Atlantic in Angola, before 1800." In *Actas do seminário 'Encontro de povos e culturas' em Angola*, 227–80. Lisbon: Comissão Nacional para as Comemorações dos Descobrimentos Portugueses, 1997.

Miller, Randall M. "The Failed Mission: The Catholic Church and Black Catholics in the Old South." In *Catholics in the Old South: Essays on Church and Culture*, edited by Randall M. Miller and Jon L. Wakelyn, 149–70. Macon, GA: Mercer University Press, 1983.

———"Slaves and Southern Catholicism." In *Masters & Slaves in the House of the Lord: Race and Religion in the American South 1740–1870*, edited by John B. Boles, 127–52. Lexington: University Press of Kentucky, 1988.

Mintz, Sidney, and Richard Price. *The Birth of African-American Culture: An Anthropological Perspective.* Boston: Beacon Press, 1992.

Mira Caballos, E. "Cofradías étnicas en la España moderna: Una aproximación al estado de la cuestión." *Hispania Sacra* 1, no. 16 (2014): 57–88.

Mitchell, Reid. *All on a Mardi Gras Day: Episodes in the History of New Orleans Carnival.* Cambridge, MA: Harvard University Press, 1995.

Mongin, Jean R. P. "L'évangélisation des esclaves au XVIIe siècle: Lettres du R. P. Jean Mongin." Edited by Marcel Chatillon. *Bulletin de la société d'histoire de la Guadeloupe* 61–62 (1984): 3–136.

Monteiro, Clarice Silva. "Literatura e folclore da Ilha do Fogo." *Boletim Geral das Colónias* 25, no. 292 (October 1949): 11–68.

Monteiro, Félix. "Bandeiras da Ilha do Fogo." *Claridade: Revista de Arte e Letras* 8 (May 1958): 9–22.

———. "Tabanca." *Claridade: Revista de Arte e Letras* 6 (July 1948): 14–18; 7 (December 1949): 19–26.

Monteiro Junior, Júlio. *Os rebelados da Ilha de Santiago, de Cabo Verde.* Lisbon: Sociedade Industrial Gráfica, 1974.

Moore, Christopher. "A World of Possibilities: Slavery and Freedom in Dutch New Amsterdam." In *Slavery in New York*, edited by Ira Berlin and Leslie M. Harris, 29–56. New York: New Press, 2005.

Moore, Francis. *Travels into the Inland Parts of Africa: Containing a Description of the Several Nations for the Space of Six Hundred Miles up the River Gambia.* London: Edward Cave, 1738.

Moraes, António Maria de Jesus Castro e. *Um breve esboço dos costumes de S. Thomé e Príncipe.* Lisbon: Typ. Adolpho de Mendonça, 1901.

Moraes Filho, Alexandre José de Mello. *Festas e tradições populares do Brazil.* Rio de Janeiro: Fauchon, 1895.

Morales Padrón, Francisco. *Spanish Jamaica.* Translated by Patrick E. Bryan. Kingston: Ian Randle, 2003.

Moreau de Saint-Méry, Médéric L. E. *Description topographique physique, civile, politique et historique de la partie Française de l'Isle Saint-Domingue.* 3 vols. Edited by Marcel Dorigny. Saint-Denis: Société française d'histoire d'outre-mer, 2004.

———. *Loix et constitutions des colonies françoises de l'Amérique sous le vent.* 6 vols. Paris: Chez l'auteur, 1784–1790.

Moreno, Isidoro. *La Antigua Hermandad de Los Negros de Sevilla: Etnicidad, poder y sociedad en 600 años de historia.* Sevilla: Universidad de Sevilla, 1997.

Morgan, Phillip D. *Slave Counterpoint: Black Culture in the Eighteenth-Century Chesapeake and Lowcountry.* Williamsburg: University of North Carolina Press, 1998.

Mosterman, Andrea. "'I Thought They Were Worthy': A Dutch Reformed Church Minister and His Congregation Debate African American Membership in the Church." *Early American Studies* (Summer 2016): 610–16.

———. *Spaces of Enslavement: A History of Slavery and Resistance in Dutch New York.* Ithaca, NY: Cornell University Press, 2021.

Mota, Avelino Teixeira da. *As viagens do Bispo D. Frei Vitoriano Portuense a Guiné e a Cristianização dos Reis de Bissau (1694–1696).* Lisbon: CECA/JICU, 1978.

———. *Guiné Portuguesa.* 2 vols. Lisbon: Agência Geral do Ultramar, 1954.

Moura, Carlos Francisco. *Teatro a bordo de naus portuguesas nos séculos XV, XVI, XVII e XVIII.* Rio de Janeiro: Instituto Luso-Brasileiro de História, 2000.

Mufwene, Salikoko S. "The Founder Principle in Creole Genesis." *Diacronica* 13, no. 1 (1996): 83–134.

Mullin, Michael. *Africa in America: Slave Acculturation and Resistance in the American South and the British Caribbean, 1736–1831.* Urbana: University of Illinois Press, 1992.

Mulvey, Patricia. "Black Brothers and Sisters: Membership in the Black Lay Brotherhoods of Colonial Brazil." *Luso-Brazilian Review* 17, no. 2 (1980): 253–79.

Munsell, Joel. "Theatrical Reminiscences." In *Collections on the History of Albany,* 4 vols., edited by Joel Munsell, 2:56. Albany, NY: J. Munsell, 1865–71.

Murell, Nathaniel Samuel. *Afro-Caribbean Religions: An Introduction to Their Historical, Cultural, and Sacred Traditions.* Philadelphia: Temple University Press, 2010.

Murphy, Patricia Shaubah. *The Moravian Mission to the African Slaves of the Danish West Indies 1732–1828,* St. Thomas: Caribbean Research Institute, 1969.

Murphy, Thomas. *Jesuit Slaveholding in Maryland, 1717–1838.* New York: Routledge, 2001.

Nafafe, José Lingna. "Lançados, Culture and Identity: Prelude to Creole Societies on the Rivers of Guinea and Cape Verde." In *Creole Societies in the Portuguese Colonial Empire,* edited by Philip J. Havik and Malyn Newitt, 49–71. Newcastle upon Tyne, UK: Cambridge Scholars, 2015.

Nassau, Robert Hamill. *Fetichism in West Africa.* London: Duckworth, 1904.

Nau, John Frederick. *The German People of New Orleans, 1850–1900.* Leiden: E. J. Brill 1958.

Necessidades, Francisco das. "Factos memoráveis da História de Angola." *Boletim Oficial do Governo Geral da Província de Angola,* 642 (January 16, 1858), 1–3.

Negreiros, José de Almada. *História ethnográphica da ilha de S. Thomé.* Lisbon: Bastos, 1895.

Neill, Stephen. *Christian Missions.* Baltimore, MA: Penguin, 1964.

Newitt, Malyn. *Emigration and the Sea: An Alternative History of Portugal and the Portuguese.* London: Hurst, 2015.

———., ed. *The Portuguese in West Africa, 1415–1670: A Documentary History.* Cambridge: Cambridge University Press, 2010.

Newman, Mark. *Desegregating Dixie: The Catholic Church in the South and Desegregation, 1945–1992.* Jackson: University Press of Mississippi, 2018.

Nicholls, Robert Wyndham. *The Jumbies' Playing Ground: Old World Influences on Afro-Creole Masquerades in the Eastern Caribbean.* Jackson: University Press of Mississippi, 2012.

Niehaus, Earl F. *The Irish in New Orleans, 1800–1860.* Baton Rouge: Louisiana State University Press, 1965.

Nieuhof, Johan. *Gedenkweerdige Brasiliaense Zee- en Lantreize.* Amsterdam: Weduwe van Jacob van Meurs, 1682.

Niles, Grace Greylock. *The Hoosac Valley, Its Legends and Its History.* New York: G. P. Putnam's Sons, 1912.

Nolan, Charles E. *A History of the Archdiocese of New Orleans.* New Orleans: Archdiocese of New Orleans, 2000.

Nooijen, R. H. *De slavenparochie van Curaçao rond het jaar 1750: Een demografie van het katholieke volksdeel.* Curaçao: Institute of Archaeology and Anthropology of the Netherlands Antilles, 1995.

Noorlander, D. L. *Heaven's Wrath: The Protestant Reformation and the Dutch West India Company in the Atlantic World.* Ithaca, NY: Cornell University Press, 2019.

Northcroft, George H. J. *Sketches of Summerland.* Nassau: Office of the Nassau Guardian, 1900.

Northrup, David. *Africa's Discovery of Europe, 1450–1850.* New York: Oxford University Library Press, 2002.

Obeng, Pashington. *Asante Catholicism: Religious and Cultural Reproduction among the Akan of Ghana.* Leiden: Brill, 1996.

O'Callaghan, Edmund B., ed. *Voyages of the Slavers St. John and Arms of Amsterdam.* Albany, NY: Munsell, 1867.

O'Callaghan, Edmund B., Berthold Fernow, and John R. Brodhead, eds. *Documents Relative to the Colonial History of the State of New York.* 15 vols. Albany, NY: Weed, Parsons & Company, 1853–87.

Ochs, Stephen J. *A Black Patriot and a White Priest: André Cailloux and Claude Paschal Maistre in Civil War New Orleans.* Baton Rouge: Louisiana State University Press, 2000.

———. *Desegregating the Altar: The Josephites and the Struggle for Black Priests, 1871–1960.* Baton Rouge: Louisiana State University Press, 1990.

Oldendorp, Christian Georg Andreas. *Historie der caribischen Inseln Sanct Thomas, Sanct Crux und Sanct Jan, insbesondere der dasigen Neger und der Mission der evangelischen Brüder unter denslehen.* Edited by Gudrun Meier, Stephan Palmié, Peter Stein, and Horst Ulbricht. 2 vols. Berlin: VWB, 2000.

Oliveira, Cristóvão Rodrigues de. *Lisboa em 1551. Sumário em que brevemente se contem algumas coisas assim eclesiásticas como seculares que há na cidade de Lisboa.* Edited by José da Felicidade Alves. Lisbon: Horizonte, 1987.

Oliveira, Ernesto Veiga de. *Festividades cíclicas em Portugal.* Lisbon: Dom Quixote, 1984.

Olwell, Robert. *Masters, Slaves, and Subjects: The Culture of Power in the South Carolina Low Country, 1740–1790*. Ithaca, NY: Cornell University Press, 1998.

O'Neill, Rosary. *New Orleans Carnival Krewes: The History, Spirit & Secrets of Mardi Gras*. Charleston, SC: History Press, 2014.

Ortiz Fernández, Fernando. *Los bailes y el teatro de los negros en el folklore de Cuba*. Havana: Editorial Letras Cubanans, 1985.

———. *Los cabildos y la fiesta afrocubanos del Día de Reyes*. Havana: Editorial de Ciencias Sociales, 1992.

———. *Ensayos etnográficos*. Edited by Miguel Barnet and Ángel L. Fernández. Havana: Editorial de Ciencias Sociales, 1984.

Osgood, Herbert L., Austin Baxter Keep, and Charles Alexander Nelson, eds. *Minutes of the Common Council of the City of New York, 1675–1776*. 8 vols. New York: Dodd, Mead, 1905.

Owen, Maria Alicia. "Among the Voodoos." In *The International Folklore Congress 1891: Papers and Transactions*, edited by J. Jacobs and Alfred Nutt, 230–48. London: Daid Nutt, 1892.

Paiva, José Pedro. "A recepção e aplicação do concilio de Trento em Portugal: Novos problemas, novas perspectivas." In *O concílio de Trento em Portugal e nas suas conquistas: Olhares novos*, edited by António Camões Gouveia, David Sampaio Barbosa, and José Pedro Paiva, 13–40. Lisbon: CEHR, 2014.

Palacios Preciado, Jorge. *La trata de negros por Cartagena de Indias (1650–1750)*. Tunja: Univ. Pedagógica y tecnológica, 1973.

Palmer, Colin A. *Slaves of the White God: Blacks in Mexico, 1570–1650*. Cambridge, MA: Harvard University Press, 1976.

Panhuys, L. C. van. "Folklore van Bonaire." *De West-Indische Gids* 16 (1933/1934): 318–20.

Parco, Rosario dal. "Informations sur le royaume du Congo et d'Angola du P. Rosario dal Parco, préfet des Capucins en Angola et Congo, 1760." Edited and translated by Louis Jadin. *Bulletin de L'Institut Historique Belge de Rome* 35 (1963): 358–76.

Pasquier, Michael. "Creole Catholicism before Black Catholicism: Religion and Slavery in French Colonial Louisiana." *Journal of Africana Religions* 2, no. 2 (2014): 271–79.

———. *Fathers on the Frontier: French Missionaries and the Roman Catholic Priesthood in the United States, 1789–1870*. Oxford: Oxford University Press, 2010.

Pavia, Andrea da. "Voyages apostoliques aux missions d'Afrique du P. Andrea da Pavia, Prédicateur Capucin 1685–1702." Edited and translated by Louis Jadin. *Bulletin de L'Institut Historique Belge de Rome* 41 (1970): 375–592.

Paxton, William. *The New-Orleans Directory and Register*. New Orleans: Private print, 1822.

Payne, Daniel Alexander. *Recollections of Seventy Years*. Edited by C. S. Smith. Nashville, TN: A. M. E. Sunday School Union, 1888.

Peabody, Sue. "A Dangerous Zeal: Catholic Missions to Slaves in the French Antilles, 1635–1800." *French Historical Studies* 25, no. 1 (Winter 2002): 53–90.

Penteado, Pedro. *Peregrinos da memória: O santuário de Nossa Senhora de Nazaré, 1600–1785*. Lisbon: Centro de Estudos da História Religiosa, 1998.

Pereira, Daniel A. *Estudos da história de Cabo Verde*. Praia: Alfa-Comunicaçoes, 2005.

Pereira, Isaias da Rosa. "Dois compromissos de irmandades de homens pretos." *Arqueologia e Historia* 9, no. 4 (1968): 9–47.

Pereira, Nuno Marques. *Compêndio Narrativo do Peregrino da América*. Lisbon: Oficina de Manoel Fernandes Costa, 1731.

Pereira, Pedro Paulo Alves. *Das Tchiloli von São Tomé: Die Wege des karolingischen Universums*. Frankfurt am Main: IKO, 2002.

Peres, Damião, ed. *Viagens de Luís de Cadamosto e Pedro de Sintra*. Lisbon: Academia Portuguesa de História, 1988.

Pérez Rodríguez, Nancy. *El carnaval santiaguero*. 2 vols. Santiago de Cuba: Editorial Oriente, 1988.

Perl, Matthias. "Zur Präsenz des kreolisierten Portugiesisch in der Karibik: Ein Beitrag zur Dialektologie des karibischen Spanisch." *Beiträge zur Romanischen Philologie* 28, no. 1 (1989): 131–48.

Peterkin, Julia. *Roll, Jordan, Roll*. New York: Robert O. Ballou, 1933.

Peytraud, Lucien. *L'Esclavage aux Antilles Françaises avant 1789 d'après des documents inédits des archives coloniales*. Paris: Hachette, 1897.

Phillippo, James M. *Jamaica: Its Past and Present State*. Philadelphia: J. M. Campbell, 1843.

Phillips, James Duncan. *Salem in the Eighteenth Century*. Boston: Houghton Mifflin, 1937.

Phillips, William D., Jr. *Slavery in Medieval and Early Modern Iberia*. Philadelphia: University of Pennsylvania Press, 2013.

Piersen, William D. *Black Yankees: The Development of an Afro-American Subculture in Eighteenth-Century New England*. Amherst: University of Massachusetts Press, 1988.

Pigafetta, Filippo. *A Report of the Kingdom of Congo and the Surrounding Countries; Drawn out of the Writings and Discourses of the Portuguese Duarte Lopez*. Edited by Margarite Hutchinson. New York: Negro Universities Press, 1969.

Pimentel, Maria do Rosário. *Viagem ao fundo das consciências. A escravatura na época moderna.* Lisbon: Colibri, 1995.

Pina, Isabel Castro. "Ritos e imaginários da morte em testamentos dos séculos XIV e XV." In *O Reino dos Mortos na Idade Média Peninsular*, edited by José Mattoso, 125–65. Lisbon: Edições João Sá da Costa, 1995.

Pina, Rui de. *Relação do Reino do Congo. Manuscrito inédito do Códice Riccardiano 1910.* Edited by Carmen M. Radulet. Lisbon: Imprensa Nacional—Casa da Moeda, 1992.

Pina-Cabral, João de. *Sons of Adam, Daughters of Eve: The Peasant Worldview of the Alto Minho.* Oxford: Clarendon Press, 1986.

Pinheiro, Luís da Cunha. "O Povoamento." In *Nova história da expansão portuguesa*, 11 vols., edited by Joel Serrão and A. H. de Oliveira Marques, 3, II:239–59. Lisbon: Editorial Stampa, 2005.

Platt, Orville. "Negro Governors." *New Haven Colony Historical Society Papers* 6 (1900): 315–35.

Poel, Francisco van der. *Dicionário da religiosidade popular: Cultura e Religião no Brasil.* Curitiba: Nossa Cultura, 2013.

Polk, Patrick Arthur. *Haitian Vodou Flag.* Jackson: University Press of Mississippi, 1997.

———. "Sacred Banners and the Divine Cavalry Charge." In *Sacred Arts of Haitian Vodou*, edited by Donald J. Cosentino, 325–47. Los Angeles: UCLA Fowler Museum of Cultural History, 1995.

Pollak-Eltz, Angelina. *Black Culture and Society in Venezuela.* Caracas: Public Affairs Dept. of Lagoven, 1994.

———. *La religiosidad popular en Venezuela.* Caracas: San Pablo, 1994.

Pollitzer, William S. *The Gullah People and Their African Heritage.* Athens: University of Georgia Press, 1999.

———. "The Relationship of the Gullah-Speaking People of Coastal South Carolina and Georgia to Their African Ancestors." *Historical Methods: A Journal of Quantitative and Interdisciplinary History* 26, no. 2 (1993): 53–67.

Ponte, Mark. "'Al de swarten die hier ter stede comen': Een Afro-Atlantische gemeenschap in zeventiende-eeuws Amsterdam." *Tijdschrift voor Economische en Sociale Geschiedenis* 15, no. 4 (2019): 33–62.

Porter, Andrew. *Religion versus Empire? British Protestant Missionaries and Overseas Expansion, 1700–1914.* Manchester, UK: Manchester University Press, 2004.

Powles, Louis Diston. *The Land of the Pink Pearl; or, Recollections of Life in the Bahamas.* London: S. Low, Marston, Searle, & Rivington, 1888.

Pratz, Antoine-Simon Le Page du. *Histoire de la Louisiane.* 3 vols. Paris: De Bure, 1758.

Prien, Hans-Jürgen. *Christianity in Latin America.* Translated by Stephen Buckwalter and Brian McNeil. Leiden: Brill, 2013.

Proyart, Liévin-Bonaventure. *Histoire de Loango, Kakongo, et autres royaumes d'Afrique: Rédigée d'après les mémoires des préfets apostoliques de la mission françoise.* Paris: C. P. Berton, N. Crapart, 1776.

Purple, Samuel S., ed. *Marriages from 1639 to 1801 in the Reformed Dutch Church, New Amsterdam, New York City.* New York: Genealogical and Biographical Society, 1940.

Querol y Roso, Luís. *Negros y mulatos de Nueva España (Historia de su alzamiento en Méjico en 1612).* Valencia: Hijo E. Vives Mora, 1935.

Raboteau, Albert J. "The Black Experience in American Evangelicalism: The Meaning of Slavery." In *African-American Religion: Interpretative Essays in History and Culture*, edited by Timothy E. Fulop and Albert J. Raboteau, 89–106. New York: Routledge, 1997.

———. *A Fire in the Bones: Reflections on African-American Religious History.* Boston: Beacon Press, 1995.

———. *Slave Religion: The 'Invisible Institution' in the Antebellum South.* Updated ed. New York: Oxford University Press, 2004.

Radulet, Carmen M., ed. *O cronista Rui de Pina e a 'Relação do Reino do Congo': Manuscrito inédito do 'Códice Riccardiano 1910.'* Lisbon: Imprensa Nacional—Casa da Moeda, 1992.

Ramos, Arthur. *A aculturação negra no Brasil.* São Paulo: Companhia Editora Nacional, 1942.

———. *O folklore negro no Brasil.* Rio de Janeiro: Livraria Editora, 1954.

Randles, W. G. L. *L'ancien royaume du Congo des origines à la fin du XIXe siècle.* Paris: Mouton, 1968.

Ratelband, Klaas. *Nederlanders in West-Afrika, 1600–1650. Angola, Kongo en São Tomé.* Edited by René Baesjou. Zutphen: Walburg Pers, 2000.

Rawlings, Helen. *Church, Religion and Society in Early Modern Spain.* New York: Palgrave, 2002.

Reginaldo, Lucilene. "África em Portugal: Devoções, irmandades e escravidão no Reino de Portugal, Século XVIII." *Historia* 28, no. 1 (2009): 289–319.

———. *Os rosários dos Angolas: Irmandades de africanos e crioulos na Bahia Setecentista.* São Paulo: Alameda, 2011.

Rego, Márcia. *The Dialogic Nation of Cape Verde: Slavery, Language, and Ideology.* Lanham, MD: Lexington Books, 2015.

Reidy, Joseph P. "'Negro Election Day' and Black Community Life in New England, 1750–1860." *Marxist Perspectives* 1, no. 3 (Fall 1978): 102–17.

Reily, Suzel Ana. *Voices of the Magi: Enchanted Journeys in Southeast Brazil.* Chicago: University of Chicago Press, 2002.

Reis, João José. *A morte é uma festa: Ritos fúnebres e revolta popular no Brasil do século XIX.* São Paulo: Companhia de Letras, 1991.

Rema, Henrique Pinto. *História das missões católicas da Guiné*. Braga: Editorial Franciscana, 1982.

Renselaar, H. van, and J. Voorhoeve. "Messianism and Nationalism in Surinam." *Bijdrage tot de Taal-, Land- en Volkenkunde* 118, no. 2 (1962): 193–216.

Rey, Terry. "The Virgin Mary and Revolution in Saint-Domingue: The Charisma of Romaine-la-Prophétesse." *Journal of Historical Sociology* 11, no. 3 (September 1998): 341–69.

Reynolds, Cuyler, ed., *Albany Chronicles of the City. Arranged Chronologically from the Earliest Settlement to the Present Time*. Albany, NY: J. B. Lyon Company, 1906.

Ribas, Óscar. *Izomba: Associativismo e recreio*. Luanda: Tip. Angolana, 1965.

Richshoffer, Ambrosius. *Reise nach Brasilien 1629–1632*. Edited by S. P. L'Honoré Naber. The Hague: M. Nijhoff, 1930.

Ricourt, Milagros. *Cimarrones: The Seeds of Subversion*. Ithaca, NY: Rutgers University Press, 2020.

Rigaud, Milo. *La tradition Voudoo et le Voudoo Haïtien: Son temple, ses mystères, sa magie*. Paris: Éditions Niclaus, 1953.

Riley, Carlos. "Ilhas atlânticas e costa africana." In *Historia da Expansão Portuguesa*, 5 vols., edited by Francisco Bethencourt and Kirti Chaudhuri, 1:137–62. Lisbon: Círculo de Leitores, 1998.

Rivas Aliaga, Roberto. "Danzantes negros en el Corpus Christi de Lima, 1756: 'Vos estis Corpus Christi.'" In *Etnicidad y discriminación racial en la historia del Perú*, edited by Elisa Dasso, 35–63. Lima: Pontíficia Universidad Católica del Perú, 2002.

Roberts, John Storm. *Black Music of Two Worlds*. New York: Schirmer Books, 1998.

Robin, C. C. *Voyage to Louisiana, 1803–1805*. Translated by Stuart O. Landry. New Orleans: Pelican, 1966.

Rochefort, Charles de. *The History of the Caribby Islands*. Translated by John Davies. London: T. Dring and J. Starkey, 1666.

Rodrigues, Adriano Vasco. "Aculturação artística e social no Reino do Congo resultante da evangelização após a chegada dos Portugueses." In *Congresso Internacional Bartolomeu Dias e a sua época: Actas*. 5 vols., 5:541–53. Porto: Universidade do Porto, 1989.

Rodway, James. *History of British Guiana*. 2 vols. Georgetown: J. Thomson, 1893.

Rojas, María Teresa. "Algunos datos sobre los negros esclavos y horros en La Habana del siglo XVI." *Miscelanea de estudios dedicados a Fernando Ortiz*. 2 vols., 2:1276–87. Havana: Impressores Úcar García, 1956.

Rome, Jean-François de [Giovanni Francesco Romano]. *Brève relation de la fondation de la mission des Frères Mineurs Capucins du Séraphique Père Saint François au Royaume de Congo (1648)*. Edited and translated by François Bontinck. Louvain: Nauwelaerts, 1964.

Romney, Susanah Shaw. *New Netherland Connections: Intimate Networks and Atlantic Ties in Seventeenth-Century America*. Chapel Hill: University of North Carolina Press, 2014.

Rosalia, René V. *Tambú: De legale en kerkelijke repressie van Afro-Curaçaose volkssuiting*. Zutphen: Walburg Pers, 1997.

Rossi, Vicente. *Cosas de negros*. Buenos Aires: Librería Hachette, 1958.

Rougé, Jean-Louis. *Petit dictionnaire étymologique du Kriol de Guinée-Bissau et Casamance*. Bissau: INEP, 1988.

Rourke, Constance. *American Humor: A Study of the National Character*. Tallahassee: Florida State University Press, 1986.

Rowe, Erin Kathleen. *Black Saints in Early Modern Global Catholicism*. Cambridge: Cambridge University Press, 2019.

Rowland, Dunbar, Albert Godfrey Sanders, and Patricia Kay Galloway. *Mississippi Provincial Archives*. 5 vols. Jackson: Press of the Mississippi Department of Archives and History, 1927–84.

Ru, Paul du. *Journal of Paul du Ru, Missionary Priest of Louisiana (February 1 to May 8, 1700)*. Edited by Ruth Lapham Butler. Chicago: Caxton Club, 1934.

Rubin, Miri. *Mother of God: A History of the Virgin Mary*. New Haven, CT: Yale University Press, 2009.

Rueda, Lope de. *Obras de Lope de Rueda: Edición de la Real Academia Española*. 2 vols. Edited by Emílio Cotarelo y Mori. Madrid: Suc. de Hernando, 1908.

Ruiz, Teofilo R. *A King Travels: Festive Traditions in Late Medieval and Early Modern Spain*. Princeton, NJ: Princeton University Press, 2012.

Rupert, Linda M. *Creolization and Contraband: Curaçao in the Early Modern Atlantic World*. Athens: University of Georgia Press, 2012.

———. "'Seeking the Water of Baptism': Fugitive Slaves and Imperial Jurisdiction in the Early Modern Caribbean." In *Legal Pluralism and Empires, 1500–1850,* edited by Richard J. Ross and Lauren Benton, 199–231. New York: New York University Press, 2013.

Russell, William Howard. *Pictures of Southern Life, Social, Political and Military, Written for the London Times*. New York: J. G. Gregory, 1861.

Russell-Wood, A. J. R. "Atlantic Bridge and Atlantic Divide: Africans and Creoles in Late Colonial Brazil." In *Creole Societies in the Portuguese Colonial Empire*, edited by Philip J. Havik and Malyn Newitt, 142–83. Newcastle upon Tyne: Cambridge Scholars, 2015.

———. *The Portuguese Empire, 1415–1808: A World on the Move.* Baltimore, MA: Johns Hopkins University Press, 1998.

Sá, Isabel dos Guimarães. "Ecclesiastical Structures and Religious Action." In *Portuguese Oceanic Expansion, 1400–1800,* edited by Francisco Bethencourt and Diogo Ramada Curto, 255–82. Cambridge: Cambridge University Press, 2007.

———. *Quando o rico se faz pobre: Misericórdias, caridade e poder no Império Português, 1500–1800.* Lisbon: Comissão Nacional para as Comemorações dos Descobrimentos Portugueses, 1997.

Saint-Lô, Alexis de. *Relations du voyage du Cap-Vert.* Paris: François Targa, 1637.

Sala, George Augustus. *America Revisited: From the Bay of New York to the Gulf of Mexico, and from Lake Michigan to the Pacific.* London: Vizetelly, 1886.

Salley, A. S., ed. *Warrants for Lands in South Carolina, 1672–1711.* 3 vols. Columbia: Historical Commission of South Carolina, 1910–15.

Salvadorini, Vittorio A., ed. *Le missioni a Benin e Warri nel XVII secolo: La relazione inedita di Bonaventura da Firenze.* Milan: Giuffrè, 1972.

Sanborn, Melinda Lutz. "Angola and Elizabeth: An African Family in the Massachusetts Bay Colony." *New England Quarterly* 72 (1999): 119–29.

Sanchis, Pierre. *Arraial, festa de um povo: As romarias portuguesas.* Translated by Madalena Mendes de Matos. Lisbon: Dom Quixote, 1983.

Sandoval, Alonso de. *Un tratado sobre la esclavitud.* Edited and translated by Vila Vilar. Enriqueta, Madrid: Alianza Editorial, 1987.

Sanneh, Lamin O. *West African Christianity: The Religious Impact.* London: C. Hurst, 1983.

Santa Maria, Agostinho de. *Santuario Mariano e história das imagẽs milagrosas de Nossa Senhora.* 10 vols. Lisboa: Officina de Antonio Pedrozo Galraõ, 1707–23.

Santana, Josué, and Edis Sánchez. *La música folclórica dominicana.* Santo Domingo: Instituto Panamericano de Geografía e Historia, 2010.

Santos, Beatriz Catão Cruz. *O corpo de Deus na América: A festa de Corpus Christi nas cidades da América portuguesa, século XVIII.* São Paulo: Annablume, 2005.

Santos, José Almeida. *Apenas um punhado de bravos!* Luanda: Câmara Municipal de Luanda, 1971.

Santos, Maria Emília. "Lançados na costa da Guiné: aventureiros e comerciantes." In *Mansas, escravos, grumetes e gentio: Cacheu na encruzilhada de civilizações,* edited by Carlos Lopes. Lisbon: Imprensa Nacional-Casa da Moeda, 1993.

Sapede, Thiago C. *Muana Congo, Muana Nzambi a Mpungu: Poder e Catolicismo no reino do Congo pós-restauração (1769–1795).* São Paulo: Alameda, 2014.

Saraiva, Maria Clara. "Rituais funerários em Cabo Verde: Permanência e inovação." *Revista da Faculdade de Ciências Sociais e Humanas* 12 (1998): 121–56.

Sardinham, José Alberto. *Danças populares do Corpus Christi de Penafiel.* Vila Verde: Tradisom, 2012.

Sarmento, Alfredo de. *Os sertões d'África: Apontamentos de viagem.* Lisbon: Francisco Arthur da Silva, 1880.

Sarró, Ramon, and Miguel de Barros. "History, Mixture, Modernity: Religious Pluralism in Guinea-Bissau Today." In *Guinea-Bissau: Micro-State to 'Narco-State,'* edited by Patrick Chabal and Toby Gree, 105–24. London: Hurst, 2016.

Saunders, A. C. de C. M. *A Social History of Black Slaves and Freedmen in Portugal, 1441–1555.* Cambridge: Cambridge University Press, 1982.

Savona, Cherubino da. "Aperçu de la situation du Congo et rite d'élection des rois en 1775, d'après Le P. Cherubino da Savona, missionnaire au Congo de 1759 à 1774." Edited and translated by Louis Jadin. *Bulletin de l'Institut Historique Belge de Rome* 35 (1963): 343–419.

Saxon, Lyle. *Fabulous New Orleans.* New Orleans: Robert L. Crager, 1952.

Saxon, Lyle, Edward Dreyer, and Robert Tallant, eds. *Gumbo Ya-Ya: A Collection of Louisiana Folk Tales.* Cambridge, MA: Riverside Press, 1945.

Scelle, Georges. *Histoire politique de la traite négrière aux Indes de Castille.* 2 vols. Paris: L. Larose & L. Tenin, 1906.

Schabel, Michael Joannes Alexius. "'Notitia de Coraçao, Bonayre, Oruba' (1705) and 'Diurnum' (1707–1708)." Edited by Christine W. M. Schunck. *Archivum Historicum Societatis Iesu* 66, no. 131 (Jan–Jun. 1997): 89–162.

Schalkwijk, Frans Leonard. *The Reformed Church in Dutch Brazil, 1630–1654.* Zoetermeer: Boekencentrum, 1998.

Schiltkamp, J. A., and J. Th. de Smidt, eds. *West-Indisch Plakaatboek: Publikaties en andere wetten alsmede de oudste resoluties betrekking hebbende op Curaçao, Aruba, Bonaire, 1638–1816.* 2 vols. Amsterdam: S. Emmering, 1978.

Schoelcher, Victor. *Colonies étrangères et Haiti.* 2 vols. Paris: Pagnerre, 1843.

Schoeman, Karel. *Early Slavery at the Cape of Good Hope, 1652–1717.* Pretoria: Protea, 2007.

Schoepf, Johann. *Travels in the Confederation, 1783–1784.* Edited by Alfred J. Morrison. 2 vols. Philadelphia: William, J. Campell, 1911.

Schuler, Monica. "Myalism and the African Religious Tradition in Jamaica." In *Africa and the Caribbean: The Legacies of a Link,* edited by Margaret E. Crahan and Franklin W. Knight, 65–79. Baltimore, MD: Johns Hopkins University Press, 1979.

Schunck, Christine Wilhelmina Maria. "Intolerante tolerantie: De geschiedenis van de katholieke missionering op Curaçao 1499–1776." Ph.D. dissertation, Radboud University, Nijmegen, 2019.

Schwartz, Stuart B. *Sugar Plantations in the Formation of Brazilian Society: Bahia, 1550–1835.* Cambridge: Cambridge University Press, 1985.

Scott, Thomas A., ed. *Cornerstones of Georgia History: Documents, which Formed a State.* Athens: University of Georgia Press, 1995.

Seabrook, William B. *The Magic Island.* New York: Harcourt, Brace, 1929.

Seeman, Erik R. *Death in the New World: Cross-Cultural Encounters, 1492–1800.* Philadelphia: University of Pennsylvania Press, 2010.

Seibert, Gerhard. *Camaradas, clientes e compadres: Colonialismo, socialismo e democratização em São Tome e Príncipe.* Lisbon: Vega, 2002.

———. "Creolization and Creole Communities in the Portuguese Atlantic: São Tomé, Cape Verde, the Rivers of Guinea and Central Africa in Comparison." In *Brokers of Change: Atlantic Commerce and Cultures in Precolonial Western Africa,* edited by Toby Green, 29–51. Oxford: Oxford University Press, 2012.

———. "Performing Arts of São Tomé and Príncipe." In *African Folklore: An Encyclopedia,* edited by Philip M. Peek and Kwesi Yankah, 680–87. New York: Routledge, 2004.

Selka, Stephen. "Black Catholicism in Brazil." *Journal of Africana Religions* 2, no. 2 (2014): 287–95.

Semedo, José Maria, and Maria R. Turano. *Cabo Verde: O ciclo ritual das festividades da tabanca.* Praia: Speel-Edições, 1997.

Senna, Manuel Roiz Lucas de. *Dissertação sobre as ilhas de Cabo Verde: 1818.* Edited by António Carreira. Lisbon: Mem-Martins, 1987.

Sensbach, Jon F. *Rebecca's Revival: Creating Black Christianity in the Atlantic World.* Cambridge, MA: Harvard University Press, 2005.

———. "Religion and the Early South in an Age of Atlantic Empire." *Journal of Southern History* 73, no. 3 (August 2007): 631–42.

———. "'The Singing of the Mississippi': The River and Religions of the Black Atlantic." In *Gods of the Mississippi,* edited by Michael Pasquier, 17–35. Bloomington: Indiana University Press, 2013.

Serrão, Joel, and A. H. de Oliveira Marques. *Nova história da expansão Portuguesa.* 11 vols. Lisbon: Editorial Stampa, 2005.

Serrão, José Vicente, ed. *Em nome do Espírito Santo: História de um culto.* Lisbon: Torre do Tombo, 2004.

Sesay, Chernoh M., Jr. "Emancipation and the Social Origins of Black Freemasonry, 1775–1800." In *All Men Free and Brethren: Essays on the History of African American Freemasonry,* edited by Peter P. Hinks and Stephen Kantrowitz, 21–39. Ithaca, NY: Cornell University Press, 2013.

Sharpe, John. "Proposals for Erecting a School, Library and Chapel at New York." In *Collections of the New-York Historical Society for the Year 1880,* 341–63. New York: Trow & Smith, 1880.

Shaw, Jenny. *Everyday Life in the Early English Caribbean: Irish, Africans, and the Construction of Difference*. Athens: University of Georgia Press, 2013.

Shell, Robert C.-H. "Civic Status and Slavery from Dordt to the Trek." *Kronos* 19 (November 1992): 28–63.

Skidmore-Hess, Cathy. "Njinga of Matamba and the Politics of Catholicism." In *Women and Religion in the Atlantic Age, 1550–1900*, edited by Emily Clark and Mary Laven, 123–42. Farnham: Ashgate, 2013.

Slenes, Robert W. "Saint Anthony at the Crossroads in Kongo and Brazil: 'Creolization' and Identity Politics in the Black South Atlantic, ca 1700/1850." In *Africa, Brazil and the Construction of Trans-Atlantic Black Identities*, edited by Livio Sansone, Elisée Soumonni, and Boubacar Barry, 209–58. Trenton, NJ: Africa World Press, 2008.

Smith, James McCune. *Introduction to a Memorial Discourse, by Rev. Henry Highland Garnet*. Philadelphia: Joseph M. Wilson, 1865.

Smith, Mark M., ed., *Stono: Documenting and Interpreting a Southern Slave Revolt*. Columbia: University of South Carolina Press, 2005.

Smith, Michael P. *Mardi Gras Indians*. Gretna, LA: Pelican, 1994.

———. *Spirit World: Pattern in the Expressive Folk Culture of Afro-American New Orleans*. New Orleans: New Orleans Urban Folklife Society, 1984.

Smith, Ronald R. "Arroz Colorao: Los Congos of Panama." In *Music and Black Ethnicity: The Caribbean and South America*, edited by Gerard H. Béhague, 239–66. New Brunswick, NJ: Transaction, 1992.

Smith, William. *A New Voyage to Guinea*. London: Frank Cass, 1967.

Soares, Mariza de Carvalho. *Devotos da cor: Identidade étnica, religiosidade e escravidão no Rio de Janeiro, século XVIII*. Rio de Janeiro: Civilização brasileira, 2000.

Sobel, Mechal. *Trabelin' On: The Slave Journey to an Afro-Baptist Faith*. Westport, CT: Greenwood Press, 1979.

Sojo, Juan Pablo. *Estudios del folklore venezolano*. Caracas: Biblioteca de Autores y Temas Mirandinos, 1986.

Southern, Eileen. *The Music of Black Americans: A History*. New York: W. W. Norton, 1997.

Souza, Marina de Mello e. *Além do visível: Poder, Catolicismo e Comércio no Congo e em Angola (séculos XVI e XVII)*. São Paulo: Edusp, 2018.

———. "Kongo King Festivals in Brazil: From Kings of Nations to Kings of Kongo." *African Studies Quarterly* 15, no. 3 (June 2015): 39–45.

———. "Reis do Congo no Brasil. Séculos XVIII e XIX." *Revista de História* 152, no. 1 (2005): 79–98.

Splendiani, Anna Maria, and Tulio Aristizábal, eds. *Proceso de beatificación y canonización de San Pedro Claver. Edición de 1696*. Bogotá: CEJA, 2002.

Sponsler, Claire. *Ritual Imports: Performing Medieval Drama in America.* Ithaca, NY: Cornell University Press, 2004.

Stein, Stanley. *Vassouras: A Brazilian Coffee County, 1850–1900.* Princeton, NJ: Princeton University Press, 1985.

Stevenson, W. B. *Historical and Descriptive Narrative of Twenty Years' Residence in South America: Containing Travels in Arauco, Chile, Peru and Columbia,* 3 vols. London: Hurst, 1825–29.

Stokes, Isaac N. P., ed. *The Iconography of Manhattan Island, 1498–1909.* 6 vols. New York: Robert H. Dodd, 1922.

Strathern, Alan. "Catholic Missions and Local Rulers in Sub-Saharan Africa." In *A Companion to Early Modern Catholic Global Missions,* edited by Ronnie Po-chia Hsia, 151–78. Leiden: Brill, 2018.

Streefkerk, C. "Godsdienstige gebruiken en opvattingen." In *Cultureel mozaïek van de Nederlandse Antillen, varianten en constanten,* edited by René A. Römer, 43–55. Zutphen: Walburg Pers, 1977.

Stuart, Isaac William. *Hartford in the Olden Time; Its First Thirty Years, by Scæva.* Edited by W. M. B. Hartley. Hartford, CT: F. A. Brown, 1853.

Stuckey, Sterling. *Going through the Storm: The Influence of African American Art in History.* Oxford: Oxford University Press, 1994.

———. *Slave Culture: Nationalist Theory and the Foundations of Black America.* New York: Oxford University Press, 1988.

Sublette, Ned. *The World That Made New Orleans: From Spanish Silver to Congo Square.* Chicago: Lawrence Hill Books, 2008.

Swan, Robert J. *New Amsterdam Gehenna: Segregated Death in New York City, 1630–1801.* Brooklyn, NY: Noir Verite Press, 2006.

Sweet, James H. "African Identity and Slave Resistance in the Portuguese Atlantic." In *The Atlantic World and Virginia, 1550–1624,* edited by Peter C. Mancall, 225–50. Chapel Hill: University of North Carolina Press, 2007.

———. *Recreating Africa: Culture, Kinship, and Religion in the African-Portuguese World, 1441–1770.* Chapel Hill: University of North Carolina Press, 2003.

Sypher, Francis J., ed. *Liber A: 1628–1700 of the Collegiate Churches of New York.* Grand Rapids, MI: William B. Eerdmans, 2009.

Tachard, Guy. "Tachard's First Voyage." In *Early French Callers at the Cape,* edited by E. Strangman, 95–122. Cape Town: Juta, 1936.

Tallant, Robert. *Mardi Gras.* Garden City, NY: Doubleday, 1948.

Tardieu, Jean-Pierre. *Los negros y la iglesia en el Perú, siglos XVI-XVII.* 2 vols. Quito: CCA, 1997.

———. *Resistencia de los Negros en la Venezuela colonial. Representaciones y planteamientos semiológicos.* Madrid: Iberoamericana, 2013.

Tate, Adam L. *Catholics' Lost Cause: South Carolina Catholics and the American South, 1820–1861.* Notre Dame: University of Notre Dame Press, 2018.

Tavares, Manuel de Jesus. *Aspectos evolutivos da música cabo-verdiana.* Praia: INCV, 2005.

Teensma, B. N., and Niels Erik Hyldgaard Nielsen, eds. *Seventeen Letters by Vincent Joachim Soler, Protestant Minister in the Service of the West Indies Company, Written in Recife, Brazil, Between 1636 and 1643.* Rio de Janeiro: Index, 1999.

Teenstra, Marten Douwes. *De landbouw in de kolonie Suriname.* 2 vols. Groningen: H. Eekhoff, 1835.

Telles, Baltasar. *Crônica da Companhia de Jesus em Portugal.* 2 vols. Lisbon: Paulo Craesbeeck, 1645–47.

Tertre, Jean-Baptiste Du. *Histoire générale des Antilles habitées par les françois.* 4 vols. Paris: Thomas Iolly, 1667–1671.

———. *Histoire générale des Isles de Christophe, de la Guadeloupe, de la Martinique et autres dans l'Amérique.* Paris: Langlois, 1654.

Thomas, Charles W. *Adventures and Observations on the West Coast of Africa, and its Islands.* New York: Derby and Jackson, 1860.

Thomas, Robert Murray. *Roots of Haiti's Vodou-Christian Faith: African and Catholic Origins.* Santa Barbara, CA: Praeger, 2014.

Thompson, Robert Farris. *The Four Moments of the Sun: Kongo Art in Two Worlds.* Washington: National Gallery of Art, 1981.

Thornton, John K. *Africa and Africans in the Making of the Atlantic World, 1400–1800.* Cambridge: Cambridge University Press, 1998.

———. "African Dimensions of the Stono Rebellion." *American Historical Review* 96 (1991): 1101–13.

———. "The African Experience of the '20 and Odd Negroes' Arriving in Virginia in 1619." *William and Mary Quarterly* 55, no. 3 (July 1998): 421–34.

———. "Afro-Christian Syncretism in the Kingdom of Kongo." *Journal of African History* 54, no. 1 (2013): 53–77.

———. "Central African Names and African-American Naming Patterns." *William and Mary Quarterly* 50, no. 4 (October 1993): 727–42.

———. "The Development of an African Catholic Church in the Kingdom of Kongo, 1491–1750." *Journal of African History* 25, no. 2 (1984): 147–67.

———. "'I Am the Subject of the King of Kongo': African Political Ideology and the Haitian Revolution." *Journal of World History* 4, no. 2 (1993): 181–214.

———. "The Kingdom of Kongo." In *Kongo: Power and Majesty*, edited by Alisa Lagamma, 87–118. New York: Metropolitan Museum of Art, 2015.

———. *The Kingdom of Kongo: Civil War and Transition 1641–1718.* Madison: University of Wisconsin Press, 1983.

―――. "The Kingdom of Kongo and Palo Mayombe: Reflections on an African-American Religion." *Slavery & Abolition* 37, no. 1 (2016): 1–22.

―――. *The Kongolese Saint Anthony: Dona Beatriz Kimpa Vita and the Antonian Movement, 1684–1706.* Cambridge: Cambridge University Press, 1998.

―――. "Mbanza Kongo/São Salvador: Kongo's Holy City." In *Africa's Urban Past,* edited by David M. Anderson and Richard Rathbone, 67–84. Oxford: James Currey, 2000.

―――. "On the Trail of Voodoo: African Christianity in Africa and the Americas." *The Americas* 44, no. 3 (January 1988): 261–78.

―――. "Portuguese-African Relations, 1500–1750." In *Encompassing the Globe: Portugal and the World in the Sixteenth and Seventeenth Centuries,* edited by Jay A. Levenson, 57–63. Washington, DC: Smithsonian Institution, 2007.

―――. "The Portuguese in Africa." In *Portuguese Oceanic Expansion, 1400–1800,* edited by Francisco Bethencourt and Diogo Ramada Curto, 138–60. Cambridge: Cambridge University Press, 2007.

―――. "Rural People, the Church in Kongo and the Afroamerican Diaspora (1491–1750)." *Transkontinentale Beziehungen in der Geschichte des Außereuropäischen Christentums,* edited by Klaus Koschorke, 33–44. Wiesbaden: Harrassowitz, 2002.

Tinhorão, José Ramos. *Os Negros em Portugal: Uma presença silenciosa.* Lisbon: Caminho, 1988.

Todd, John M. *African Mission: A Historical Study of the Society of African Missions Whose Priests Have Worked on the Coast of West Africa and Inland, in Liberia, the Ivory Coast, Ghana, Togoland, Dahomey and Nigeria, and in Egypt, since 1856.* London: Burns & Oates, 1962.

Towne, Laura M. *Letters and Diary of Laura M. Towne: Written from the Sea Islands of South Carolina, 1862–1884.* Edited by Rupert Sargent Holland. Cambridge: Riverside Press, 1912.

Trajano Filho, Wilson. "As cores nas tabancas: Sobre bandeiras e seus usos." In *Travessias Antropológicas: Estudos em Contextos Africanos,* edited by Wilson Trajano Filho, 339–66. Brasília: ABA Publicações, 2012.

―――. "Os cortejos das tabancas: Dois modelos da ordem." In *As festas e os dias: Ritos e sociabilidades festivas,* edited by Maria Laura Viveiros de Castro Cavalcanti and José Reginaldo Santos Gonçalves, 37–73. Rio de Janeiro: Contra Capa, 2009.

Trigoso, Sebastião Francisco de Mendo, ed. *Viagem de Lisboa à ilha de São Tomé escrita por um piloto português.* Lisbon: Portugalia Editora, n.d.

Troconis de Veracoechea, Ermila, ed. *Documentos para el estudio de los esclavos negros en Venezuela.* Caracas: Academia Nacional de la Historia, 1969.

Truth, Sojourner. *Narrative of Sojourner Truth*. Edited by Margaret Washington. New York: Vintage Books, 1993.

Tuckey, James Hingston. *Narrative of an Expedition to Explore the River Zaire, Usually Called the Congo, in South Africa, in 1816*. New York, W. B. Gilley, 1818.

Turner, Mary. *Slaves and Missionaries: The Disintegration of Jamaican Slave Society, 1787–1834*. Urbana: University of Illinois Press, 1982.

Turpin, Thomas D. "May and New River Mission, S.C. Con., to the Blacks." *Christian Advocate and Journal* 8–9 (October 25, 1833), 34.

Udemans, Godefridus. *'T geestelyk roer van 't coopmansschip*. Dordt: Francois Boels, 1640.

Updike, Wilkins. *History of the Episcopal Church in Narragansett, Rhode Island*. New York: Henry M. Onderdonk, 1847.

Vainfas, Renaldo, ed. *Dicionário do Brasil colonial: 1500–1808*. Rio de Janeiro: Objetiva, 2000.

Valdez, Francisco Travassos. *Six Years of a Traveller's Life in Western Africa*. 2 vols. London: Hurst and Blackett, 1861.

Van den Broecke, Pieter. *Journal of Voyages to Cape Verde, Guinea and Angola (1605–1612)*. Translated by J. D. La Fleur. London: Hakluyt Society, 2000.

Vasconcelos, Basílio de, ed. *Itinerário do Dr. Jerónimo Münzer*. Coimbra: Imprensa da Universidade, 1931.

Venema, Janny, ed. *Deacons' Accounts 1652–1674 Beverwijck/Albany*. Rockport, ME: Picton Press, 1998.

Vernooij, Joop. *De regenboog is in ons huis: De kleurrijke geschiedenis van de r.k. kerk in Suriname*. Nijmegen: Valkhof Pers, 2012.

Very, Francis George. *The Spanish Corpus Christi Procession: A Literary and Folkloric Study*. Valencia: Moderna, 1962.

Vicente, João. "Quatro séculos de vida cristã em Cacheu." In *Mansas, escravos, grumetes e gentio: Cacheu na encruzilhada de civilizações*, edited by Carlos Lopes, 99–133. Lisbon: Imprensa Nacional-Casa da Moeda, 1993.

Vidal, Cécile. *Caribbean New Orleans: Empire, Race and the Making of a Slave Society*. Chapel Hill: University of North Carolina Press, 2019.

Vide, Rafael Castello de. "Viagem e Missão no Congo (1780–1788)." In Academia de Ciências, Lisbon, Série Vermelha de Manuscritos, manuscript no. 396. Edited by Arlindo Correia. http://arlindo-correia.com/161007.html.

Vide, Rafael de Castello de, André de Couto Godinho, and João Gualberto de Miranda. "Relação da viagem que fizeram os padres missionários, desde a cidade de Loanda, d'onde sahiram a 2 de Agosto de 1780, até à presença do Rei do Congo, onde chegaram a 30 de Junho de 1781." *Anais do Conselho Ultramarino*, 2 Parte Não Oficial (1859): 62–80.

Vila Vilar, Enriquete. *Hispano-América y el comercio de esclavos: Los asientos portugueses.* Sevilla: CSIC, 1977.

Vilar, Hermínia Vasconcelos. *A vivência da morte no Portugal medieval: A Estre-
madura portuguesa (1300 a 1500).* Redondo: Patrimónia, 1995.

Villault, Nicolas, Sieur de Bellefond. *Relation des costes d'Afrique, appellées Guinée.* Paris: Denys Theirry, 1669.

Vincent, Bernard. "Les confréries de noirs dans la Péninsule Ibérique (XV–XVIII
siècles)." In *Religiosidad y costumbres populares en Iberoamérica*, edited by
David González Cruz, 17–28. Huelva: Universidad de Huelva, 2000.

Vincent de Paul, Saint. *Correspondence, entretiens, documents.* Edited by Pierre
Coste. 14 vols. Paris: Librairie Lecoffre, J. Cabalda, 1920–25.

Viterbo, Sousa. *Artes e artistas em Portugal: Contribuições para a historia das artes
e industrias portuguezas.* Lisbon, Livraria Ferreira, 1920.

Voorhoeve, Jan. "Historical and Linguistic Evidence in Favour of the Relexifica-
tion Theory in the Formation of Creoles." *Language in Society* 2, no. 1 (April
1973): 133–45.

Vos, Jelmer. "Kongo Cosmopolitans in the Nineteenth Century." In *The Kongo
Kingdom: The Origins, Dynamics and Cosmopolitan Culture of an African
Polity*, edited by Koen Bostoen and Inge Brinkman, 235–53. Cambridge:
Cambridge University Press, 2018.

———. *Kongo in the Age of Empire, 1860–1913: The Breakdown of a Moral
Order.* Madison: University of Wisconsin Press, 2015.

Waddell, Hope Masterton. *Twenty-Nine Years in the West Indies and Central Africa: A Review of Missionary Work and Adventure, 1829–1858.* London: T.
Nelson and Sons, 1863.

Wade, Melvin. "'Shining in Borrowed Plumage': Affirmation of Community in
the Black Coronation Festivals of New England (c. 1750–c. 1850)." *Western
Folklore* 40, no. 3 (1981): 211–31.

Wade, Richard C. *Slavery in the Cities: The South 1820–1860.* New York: Oxford
University Press, 1964.

Walker, Sheila S. "Congo Kings, Queen Nzinga, Dancing Devils and Catholic
Saints African/African Syncretism in the Americas." In *Héritage de la mu-
sique africaine dans les Amériques et les Caraïbes*, edited by Alpha Noël Ma-
longa and Mukala Kadima-Nzuji, 124–32. Paris: L'Harmattan, 2005.

Walker, Tamara J. "The Queen of los Congos: Slavery, Gender, and Confraternity Life in Late-Colonial Lima, Peru." *Journal of Family History* 40, no. 3
(2015): 305–22.

Walker, Timothy D. *Doctors, Folk Medicine and the Inquisition: The Repression of
Magical Healing in Portugal during the Enlightenment.* Leiden: Brill, 2005.

Wannyn, Robert L. *L'Art ancien du métal au Bas-Congo*. Champles: Éd. du Vieux Planquesaule, 1961.

Ward-Price, Henry Lewis. *Dark Subjects*. London: Jarrolds, 1939.

Warner-Lewis, Maureen. *Central Africa in the Caribbean: Transcending Time, Transforming Cultures*. Barbados: University of the West Indies Press, 2003.

Warren, Wendy. *New England Bound: Slavery and Colonization in Early America*. New York: Liveright, 2016.

Wartemberg, J. Sylvanus. *Sao Jorge d'El Mina, Premier West African European Settlement: Its Traditions and Customs*. Ilfracombe: Stockwell, 1951.

Washington, Margaret. "Community Regulation and Cultural Specialization in Gullah Folk Religion." In *African-American Christianity: Essays in History*, edited by Paul E. Johnson, 47–79. Berkeley: University of California Press, 1994.

———. *Sojourner Truth's America*. Urbana: University of Illinois Press, 2009.

Wätjen, Hermann. *Das holländisches Kolonialreich in Brasilien*. The Hague: M. Nijhoff, 1921.

Watson, John F. "Notitia of Incidents at New Orleans in 1804 and 1805." *American Pioneer* vol. 2, no. 1 (January 1843), 227–37, and no. 5 (May 1843): 233–36.

Weed, Thurlow. *Letters from Europe and the West Indies, 1843–1862*. Albany, NY: Weed, Parsons, 1866.

Wells, A. F., and D. Wells. *Friendly Societies in the West Indies*. London: Her Majesty's Stationary Office, 1953.

Westergaard, Waldemar. *The Danish West Indies under Company Rule (1671–1754)*. New York: MacMillan Company, 1917.

Wheat, David. *Atlantic Africa and the Spanish Caribbean, 1570–1640*. Chapel Hill: University of North Carolina Press, 2016.

———. "My Friend Nicolas Mongoula: Africans, Indians, and Cultural Exchange in Eighteenth-Century Mobile." In *Coastal Encounters: The Transformation of the Gulf South in the Eighteenth Century*, edited by Richmond F. Brown, 117–31. Lincoln: University of Nebraska Press, 2007.

Whipple, Henry B. *Bishop's Whipple's Southern Diary, 1843–1844*. Minneapolis: University of Minnesota Press, 1937.

White, Shane. "'It Was a Proud Day': African Americans, Festivals, and Parades in the North, 1741–1834." *Journal of American History* 81, no. 1 (1994): 13–50.

———. "Pinkster in Albany, 1803: A Contemporary Description." *New York History* 70, no. 2 (1989): 191–99.

White, Shane, and Graham White. *Stylin': African American Expressive Culture from Its Beginnings to the Zoot Suit*. Ithaca, NY: Cornell University Press, 1998.

Whitten, Norman Earl. *Black Frontiersmen: Afro-Hispanic Culture of Ecuador and Colombia*. Prospect Heights, IL: Waveland, 1974.

Wiesinger, Evelyn. "Acteurs et échanges linguistiques dans les premiers temps en Guyane française coloniale: Contribution à l'étude de la genèse du créole guyanais." *Creolica* (May 22, 2013). http://www.creolica.net/article-80.html.

Williams-Myers, Albert James. *Long Hammering: Essays on the Forging of an African American Presence in the Hudson Valley to the Early Twentieth Century.* Trenton, NJ: Africa World Press, 1994.

Wiltgen, Ralph M. *Gold Coast Mission History, 1471–1880.* Techny, IL: Divine Word, 1956.

Winston, Anne. "Tracing the Origins of the Rosary: German Vernacular Texts." *Speculum: A Journal of Medieval Studies* 68, no. 3 (July 1993): 619–36.

Winston-Allen, Anne. *Stories of the Rose: The Making of the Rosary in the Middle Ages.* University Park: Pennsylvania State University Press, 1997.

Winthrop, John. *Winthrop's Journal: "History of New England," 1630–1649.* Edited by James Kendall Hosmer. 2 vols. New York: Barnes & Noble, 1959.

Wittwer, Norman C. *The Faithful and the Bold: The Story of the First Service of the Zion Evangelical Lutheran Church, Oldwick, New Jersey.* Oldwick, NJ: Zion Evangelical Lutheran Church, 1984.

Wolbers, Julien. *Geschiedenis van Suriname.* Amsterdam: H. De Hoogh, 1861.

Wood, Betty. *Slavery in Colonial Georgia, 1730–1775.* Athens: University of Georgia Press, 1984.

Wood, Peter H. *Black Majority: Negroes in Colonial South Carolina from 1670 through the Stono Rebellion.* New York: Knopf, 1974.

Woods, James M. *A History of the Catholic Church in the American South, 1513–1900.* Gainesville: University Press of Florida, 2011.

Woofter, T. J., Jr. *Black Yeomanry: Life on St. Helena Island.* New York: Henry Holt, 1930.

Wright, Irene A. "Dispatches of Spanish Officials Bearing on the Free Negro Settlement of Gracia Real de Santa Teresa de Mose, Florida." *Journal of Negro History* 9, no. 2 (April 1924): 144–95.

Writers' Program Georgia, eds. *Drums and Shadows: Survival Studies among the Georgia Coastal Negroes.* Athens: University of Georgia Press, 1940.

Writers' Program Virginia, eds. *The Negro in Virginia.* Winston-Salem, NC: J. F. Blair, 1994.

Young, Jason R. *Rituals of Resistance: African Atlantic Religion in Kongo and the Lowcountry South in the Era of Slavery.* Baton Rouge: Louisiana State University Press, 2007.

Zucchelli, Antonio. *Relazioni del viaggio e missione di Congo nell'Etiopia inferiore occidentale.* Venice: Bartolomeo Giavarina, 1712.

Zuluar, Alba. *Os homens de Deus: Um estudo dos santos e das festas no catolicismo popular.* Rio de Janeiro: Zahar Editores, 1983.

INDEX

Afonso I, king of Kongo, 32, 62–66, 69–71, 99, 101

All Saints' Day, 21, 29, 54

All Souls' Day, 21, 47, 54–55, 63, 73, 75, 79

amulets, 7, 17, 45, 76, 111, 131, 184–85

Andrade, João Vieira de, 14–15, 45–46, 48

angels, 21, 24, 49, 62–64, 73, 100, 104, 111, 199

Anglican Church, 146, 177–81. *See also* missionaries

Angola
    Caribbean slavery from, 107–8, 121, 130–31
    Catholicism in, 30, 67, 69, 81–85, 91, 101–2, 120, 148
    fraternities in and from, 32, 83–85, 96, 166, 171
    Iberian slavery from, 32
    Latin American slavery from, 60, 94, 121
    music, dance, and performance in and from, 32, 96, 169, 184
    Ndongo kingdom, 29, 81–82
    North American slavery from, 4, 35, 121, 137–39, 145–48, 150, 169, 171, 184, 194–95, 250n.170
    Portuguese colony, 29, 66–69, 77, 81–85, 177

Azores, 30, 40, 130

Bamba, 71–72, 79

banners. *See* flags

baptism
    colonialism and, 25, 37–38, 43, 51, 56, 62–65, 69, 109, 120, 129, 151
    of the enslaved in Protestant churches, 141–46, 179, 181, 195
    and identity, 26, 35–36, 57, 112, 115, 129, 132, 163, 176, 180–81, 199
    and manumission, 40, 42, 109, 121, 114, 144–46, 148, 165, 176, 178–82
    performed by laymen, 52, 93, 100, 103, 117–18, 120, 130, 186
    rituals for, 45, 58, 75, 111, 186
    See also catechization; funerals; saints

Baptist churches, 10, 69, 81, 122–23, 136, 149, 177, 186, 189, 193, 196–201, 207, 210. *See also* Black evangelicalism; missionaries

Barbados, 2, 119–20, 124

Bastian, Adolf, 81, 136

Berlin, Ira, 5, 153, 162–63, 177, 182

Bible, 3, 24, 57, 122, 204

Bight of Benin. *See* Lower Guinea

Black evangelicalism
    Catholic elements in, 157, 176–77, 180–81, 183, 186–92, 199
    importance of fraternities to, 10–11, 186–87, 189–91, 193–94, 197, 200–203
    indigenous African elements in, 162, 181–82, 187–92
    in Latin America, 106
    as a pathway to freedom, 175–76, 178–81, 195
    See also Baptist churches; catechization; Methodist churches

Black militias, 140, 174, 180

Bonomi, Patricia, 165, 183

bozales, 40, 42–43, 55, 112, 118, 218n.34

Braga, Teófilo, 46, 48–49

Brásio, António, 7

Brazil
    Catholicism in, 16, 36, 60, 69, 90–92, 94, 101–2, 154, 209
    Dutch Brazil, 67, 108, 121, 130, 137, 139–40, 142–44, 174, 176–77
    fraternities in, 16, 31, 95–100, 102, 105, 166
    music, dance, and performance in, 62, 99, 100, 102–4, 134, 156, 172, 188
    slavery in, 55, 60, 67, 86, 129–30

Brenneker, Paul, 112

Brooks, George, 7, 45, 55

brotherhoods. *See* fraternities

Brown, Ras Michael, 177, 194, 199

burials. *See* funerals

Cabrera, Lydia, 89, 99, 184

Cacheu, 37–38, 41–42, 53–54

Caltanissetta, Luca da, 68, 72, 76

Cape Colony, 36, 143, 176

Cape Verde Islands
    Caribbean slavery from, 107–10, 129–31
    Catholicism in, 6, 40–50, 104, 153–54
    fraternities in, 14–15, 47–50
    Iberian slavery from, 25
    Latin American slavery from, 42–43, 91
    music, dance, and performance in and from, 14, 44–50, 190, 193
    North American slavery from, 4, 35, 121, 138, 164, 193

Capuchins. *See* Order of Friars Minor Capuchin

carnival, 24, 85, 105, 154–55, 158, 170

Carvalho, Henrique Augusto Dias de, 54–55

catechisms, 74, 134, 144

catechization
    in preparation of baptism, 39, 42, 77, 79, 82–83, 90–92, 120, 127, 129
    by Catholic missionaries, 26–27, 44, 74, 77, 91–92, 104

by laypeople
—assisting Catholic missionaries, 64, 70–71, 73–74, 83, 90–91, 110, 129, 152
—assisting Protestant missionaries, 117, 182, 196
—operating autonomously as Catholics, 44–45, 50, 80, 92–94, 102, 111–13, 117–18, 123, 127, 132–34, 188
—operating autonomously as Protestants, 182, 199–200
See also missionaries
Catholic Church
bias against Afro-Atlantic Catholics, 14–15, 50, 77, 93–94, 105, 114, 126, 130, 132, 152–53, 157
bias against Protestants, 38, 119–20, 149, 176
concerns about the (slave) trade in Catholics, 31, 38, 120, 128
involvement in colonization, 50–51, 61–65, 68, 82, 85–86, 95, 151
involvement in the slave trade, 25, 28, 31, 38, 43, 67, 85, 120, 128–30, 147
lay resistance to orthodoxy in, 15–16, 39, 50, 61, 87, 114
See also missionaries; papacy; Propaganda Fide; Vatican
Catron, John, 122, 192, 194, 200
cemeteries, 46, 65, 153–54, 180, 189, 207
chaplets, 36, 51, 77, 79, 127
charity, 19–20, 29–30, 201
charms. *See* amulets
Christmas, 23–24, 57, 73, 123
Colombia, 37, 39, 62, 90, 94

confession, 20–21, 44, 53, 60, 69, 71, 74, 91, 133, 205
confraternities. *See* fraternities
congadas, 62, 100, 134
Congregation of the Holy Spirit, 50, 80, 133. *See also* missionaries
Corpus Christi, 17–18, 2324, 33, 44, 73, 97, 132, 155–56
Creel, Margaret Washington, 196–98
creolization. *See* syncretism
cross
as devotional object, 24, 57–59, 63, 73, 80–81, 133, 162, 205
Holy Cross fraternity and festivities, 47, 49–50
as identity marker, 2–3, 53, 65, 75, 94, 101, 103, 116, 131, 184
sign, 45, 80, 103, 129, 131, 188
See also Order of Christ
crucifix, 2, 52–53, 56–57, 59, 76, 79–81, 83, 124, 133, 164, 186, 205–6
Cuba, 89, 96–99, 102, 105, 110, 149, 173–74, 205
Curaçao, 2, 106–15, 137, 143–44, 177

dance
as an expression of faith, 17–18, 22–24, 44, 54, 87, 93, 102–5, 111, 155, 186–88, 192
in fraternities, 32–34, 49–50, 84–85, 104, 186
as indigenous African heritage, 26, 61–62, 64, 69, 99–100, 119, 123–25, 134, 169–70, 172, 184, 186–88, 193
repudiation of, 8, 18–19, 33, 60, 84, 96, 105, 157, 191–92
See also drama; funerals; processions

Danish Virgin Islands, 116–19, 163, 174, 180, 199. *See also* Moravian Church
Dapper, Olfert, 56–57, 77
Davis, Cyprian, 10–11, 164, 201
devil, 23–24, 50, 69, 97, 100, 105, 156
Dicomano, Raimondo da, 3, 75
Dominican Order, 27, 29, 52, 112, 129–30. *See also* missionaries
Dominican Republic, 94–95, 103–4, 106
Douglass, Frederick, 175
drama, 24, 54, 61–62, 85, 100, 104
Dutch Reformed Church, 2, 58, 67, 107, 109, 114–15, 137, 141–45, 166–67, 175–84. *See also* missionaries
Dutch West India Company, 35–36, 42, 58, 67–68, 101, 106–16, 137–45, 174. *See also* Netherlands, the

Easter, 23, 48, 54
Elmina, 56–59
epiphany, 24, 97, 99, 104, 110, 135, 155–56
ex-votos. *See* vows

flags, 20, 23, 27, 32, 49–50, 62, 80, 98, 103, 112, 126, 134–35, 161, 166, 171, 185, 188, 193, 198, 234n.104. *See also* processions
Florida, 148–49, 173–74, 191, 194–95, 199
França, António Pinto da, 13
France
    Catholicism, 68, 126–29, 134, 151, 156–57, 180
    colonialism, 52, 126–36, 150–59

language, 129, 131, 133, 136, 150, 164
slave trade, 150
See also Huguenots
Franciscan Order, 23, 29–30, 51, 69, 92, 115, 130. *See also* missionaries
Franco, António, 171–72
fraternities
    in Africa, 14, 47–49, 54, 58, 60–62, 70–74, 83–85, 161–62, 188
    in Asia, 13, 113
    in the Caribbean, 110–12, 118–19, 122–25, 128, 131, 135
    in Iberia, 14–15, 19–23, 27–34
    king celebrations, 14, 23, 30, 32, 119, 123–26, 132, 135, 166–73, 184, 190, 193, 202
    in Latin America, 16, 95–105, 156, 173, 186
    in North America, 10–11, 153, 155, 158, 166–75, 185–95, 198–202, 210
    as secret societies, 77, 198–99, 201–2
    See also cross; dance; flags; funerals; music; prayers; processions; saints; Virgin Mary
Frijhoff, Willem, 181, 184
Fromont, Cécile, 7–8, 70, 77, 99
funerals
    of children, 21, 104, 198–99
    dance during, 21, 46, 84, 118
    music during, 21, 46–47, 104, 161, 198
    organized by fraternities, 16, 20–21, 29, 31, 47, 49, 61, 95, 97, 103–4, 112, 118, 124–25, 128, 135, 151, 153–54, 158, 161–62, 189, 198, 201

rituals of, 18, 44–47, 46, 75, 81, 124, 135, 153–54, 168, 178, 189–90
of souls, 21, 61, 129
of the unbaptized, 25, 65, 95, 112, 118, 165

Gallo, Bernardo da, 72, 77, 79
Garcia II, King of Kongo, 67, 176
Georgia, 192–202, 250n.170
Gerbner, Katharine, 179–80, 195
Giggie, John M., 11, 190, 201
Gillard, John, 10, 152, 201
Gold Coast. *See* Lower Guinea
Grace, Charles Manuel, 193
Great Britain
    colonialism, 42, 52, 119–28, 145–49
    language, 1, 115, 136, 150, 180
    slave trade, 38, 43
    See also Anglican Church

Haiti, 132–34, 150, 152, 164, 172–73
Hastings, Adrian, 79, 87, 177
Heywood, Linda M., 4, 75, 82, 96, 174, 177
Hodges, Graham Russell, 166, 171, 183, 249n.119
Holy Spirit, 20, 23, 71, 104, 185–87
Hoornaert, Eduardo, 16, 101, 105
Horta, José da Silva, 51, 76
Huguenots, 59, 129, 181, 195

indigenous African religions, 6–8, 28, 45, 52–53, 56, 65, 67, 70, 75–76, 84, 87–88, 90, 112, 132, 148
Inquisition, 59, 76, 92
Irish, 2, 119–22, 147, 157, 185–86

Islam, 5, 7, 18, 23–24, 38, 41, 51–52, 62–64, 85, 100, 209
Iyanaga, Michael, 104, 188

Jamaica, 122–24, 186
Jesuits. *See* Society of Jesus
Jews, 3, 23, 40–41, 107–8, 111, 142
João II, King of Portugal, 39, 56, 205

Kikongo, 74–75, 80, 100, 151, 190, 197
Kimbundu, 83, 91
Kongo
    Caribbean slavery from, 116–18, 121–22, 124–25, 127, 130–36
    Catholicism among enslaved people from, 3–5, 8, 36, 88–91, 101–3, 111, 116–18, 120, 125, 127, 130, 132, 134, 148, 180, 186–87, 194
    Catholicism in, 62–82, 86–88, 101, 111, 120, 176, 190, 199, 206
    fraternities in and from, 31–32, 71–74, 96–100, 103–6, 118, 124, 166
    Iberian and European slavery from, 32, 64, 180
    kingdom of, 32, 36, 62–81, 85, 120, 135–36, 161–62, 176–77, 184, 190, 204–6
    Latin American slavery from, 89–92, 95, 121, 205
    music, dance, and performance in and from, 32, 61–62, 64, 85, 97, 100–101, 104, 134, 161–62, 173, 204–5
    North American slavery from, 3–4, 35, 121, 138, 148, 150–52, 184–87, 194–97, 202
Kristons, 51–54, 112–13

ladinos, 26, 40, 42–43, 55, 91–92, 94, 97, 137, 140, 174, 179–80, 218n.34

Laing, Annette, 162–63

Landers, Jane, 148–49, 173–74

Lent, 22, 44, 48, 53, 73, 84, 111, 156, 158

Louisiana, 4, 150–59, 162, 169–71, 173, 189

Lower Guinea, 55–62, 92, 134, 150

MacGaffey, Wyatt, 76, 78

Madeira, 40, 131, 138, 195

Manuel I, King of Portugal, 20–21, 25, 38, 64

Mardi Gras Indians, 158–59

Maroons, 92–95, 103, 124, 149

Marques, A. H. de Oliveira, 16–19

Martins, Ignácio, 26–27

Maryland, 147, 163–64, 201, 207

masonry, 126, 171–73, 201, 207

mass, 14, 29, 33, 48–50, 52–53, 71–72, 79, 93–94, 104, 117, 126–27, 133, 152, 155, 186, 201

Merolla da Sorrento, Girolamo, 36, 76, 90, 101, 120, 190

mestres, 45, 50, 71, 73–74, 80, 102

Methodist churches, 149, 187, 189–91, 196–97, 200, 202, 210. *See also* Black evangelicalism; missionaries

Mexico, 94, 96, 145

Miller, Joseph C., 4–5, 88

missionaries
  Anglicans, 145, 181–83, 195–96
  Baptists, 122, 149, 177
  Capuchins, 3, 22, 36, 51, 60, 67–69, 71–77, 81–82, 103, 120, 128, 134–35, 151, 180

Carmelites, 70

Dominicans, 52, 112, 130

Dutch Reformed, 142–45, 177

Franciscans, 51, 69, 115

Jesuits, 25–26, 36–39, 42–43, 51, 53–54, 66, 71, 74, 77–78, 82, 84, 90–91, 94–95, 102, 127, 129, 131–32, 149, 180

laypeople, 43–45, 50, 70–71, 73–74, 80, 83, 90–92, 102, 110–13, 117–18, 123, 127, 129, 131–33, 152, 182, 196

Methodists, 149, 191, 196

Moravians, 115–18, 174, 180, 182

Spiritans, 50, 80, 133

Monteiro, Félix, 46, 104, 153

Moors. *See* Islam

Moravian Church, 115–19, 122, 178–80, 182. *See also* missionaries

music
  bells, 23, 80–81, 203–6
  as an expression of faith, 8, 17–21, 24, 29, 43, 50, 54, 73, 79, 81, 102–5, 111, 127, 133, 149, 157, 164, 182, 186–88, 190, 206
  hand clapping, 104, 187–88, 190
  indigenous African, 26, 32–34, 49–50, 54, 61–62, 64, 69, 73, 99–100, 119, 123–25, 134, 169–70, 172, 184, 186–88, 193
  marching bands, 20, 49, 61, 87, 103, 125–26, 164, 166–75, 193
  percussion instruments, 14, 23, 32–33, 46, 48–50, 54, 98, 101–2, 103–4, 111, 125, 148, 157, 161, 166, 168, 175, 187–88, 190, 193

played by fraternities, 20–21, 29, 33, 49, 73, 84, 97, 100, 125–26, 128, 166, 171, 175, 186, 190, 193

Portuguese and Luso-African, 17–18, 21–24, 32–33, 50, 54–55, 62, 65, 84–85, 96, 100–101, 185, 204–5

song, 8, 17–18, 19–21, 24, 29, 33, 46–47, 49–50, 54, 73, 79–81, 100, 103–5, 111, 114, 121, 123, 127–28, 133–34, 149, 153, 182, 186–88, 190, 193, 198, 201

string instruments, 23, 32, 191, 193

woodwind and brass instruments, 14, 32–33, 44, 48–49, 84, 161, 188, 193

See also dance; funerals

Native Americans, 106–7, 109, 130, 140, 142–43, 149–50, 173, 180, 194

Neau, Elias, 145, 181

Netherlands, the
language, 106, 143, 180, 202
slave trade, 2–3, 107–9, 121, 130, 137–38, 145, 176
See also Dutch Reformed Church; Dutch West India Company

New England, 147, 164, 166–68, 171–72, 175, 178

New Jersey, 182, 207

New Netherland, 3–4, 35–36, 108, 115, 121, 137–45, 147, 166–67, 176–81, 184

New York, 1–2, 161–64, 168–69, 171–72, 182–86, 189–90, 202–3, 207

Njinga, Queen of Ndongo and Matamba, 82

oaths, 3, 19, 71–72, 191, 211n.11

Oldendorp, Christian Georg Andreas, 117–18, 165, 174, 180

Order of Christ, 2–3, 6, 38, 40, 62, 66, 69, 81, 136, 162, 211n.11

Order of Friars Minor Capuchin, 3, 22, 31, 36, 51–52, 60, 67–77, 81–82, 103, 120, 128, 134–35, 151, 180. *See also* missionaries

Ortiz Fernández, Fernando, 99, 173

Our Lady. *See* Virgin Mary

padroado, 38–39, 65–67, 90

Panama, 62, 92, 100

papacy, 25, 31, 38, 43, 64–67, 69, 78, 120

parades. *See* processions

Pavia, Andrea da, 73, 103

Peabody, Sue, 127, 131

Pennsylvania, 163, 171, 178, 189, 207

Pentecost, 20, 23, 104, 168–69, 183–86, 188, 202

Pereira, Daniel, 41, 43

Peru, 42, 91–92, 95, 97, 153

Philipp II, King of Spain, 23, 29

Phillippo, James M., 122–24, 165

Pinkster. *See* Pentecost

piracy. *See* privateering

Ponte, Mark, 176, 178, 181, 240n.249

Portugal
Catholicism in, 6–7, 14–25, 35–36, 38–39, 43–44, 56, 79, 86, 131, 153, 216n.66
colonialism, 6–7, 14, 38–43, 50–51, 55–58, 61–69, 81–82, 85–86, 108, 204–5
fraternities, 13–16, 19–23, 27–33, 173

Portugal (*cont.*)
  language, 13, 26, 38, 40–41, 43,
    49, 51, 55–57, 59, 64–65, 68,
    71, 80, 87, 89, 106–7, 113–15,
    124, 130–31, 136–37, 139–40,
    143, 148, 163–64, 179,
    240n.249
  music, dance, and performance in
    and from, 17–18, 21–24, 32–33,
    50, 54–55, 62, 65, 84–85, 96,
    101, 185, 204–5
  slavery, 25–29, 31, 40, 43
  See also Order of Christ; *padroado*
prayers
  Ave Maria, 20, 53, 60, 69, 73, 94,
    111, 149
  by fraternities, 13, 27–29, 49, 74,
    95, 118, 123, 155, 188, 198, 201
  during funerals, 21–22, 47, 55, 73,
    84, 153, 155, 198, 205
  Holy Rosary, 20, 25, 28–29, 47,
    52, 57, 65, 69, 72, 79, 90, 94,
    100, 104, 112, 126, 154, 180,
    190, 201
  loas, 20, 73, 104, 134
  novenas, 47, 50, 104, 111, 133
  Our Father, 20, 50, 53, 60, 94,
    155, 158, 203
  rituals of, 2, 17–18, 20–22, 44–47,
    49–50, 56–58, 72–73, 77, 79–81,
    91, 94, 102–4, 111–14, 118, 120,
    123, 127, 129, 148, 152, 154–55,
    164, 186, 188, 192, 196, 203
  Salve Regina, 50, 73, 104
  songs as, 20, 22, 47, 49, 104–5,
    111, 182
  velaciones, 102, 104
preaching, 26, 33, 59, 68, 74, 85,
  92–93, 118, 133, 182, 187, 190,
  192, 198, 200, 208

privateering, 42, 108, 121, 130, 137,
  139, 145, 181
processions
  with flags, 20, 23, 27, 32, 49, 80,
    84, 98, 103, 161, 171, 185, 193,
    198, 234n.104
  during funerals, 18, 21–22, 46–47,
    73, 103, 118, 135, 153, 155, 161
  with music and dance, 21, 32–34,
    49–50, 61, 84–85, 87, 100,
    103–5, 123, 125–26, 156,
    158–59, 161, 164, 166–75, 186,
    190, 193
  organized by fraternities, 13–15,
    20–21, 23, 29, 31–32, 48–50,
    58, 61, 72–73, 84, 95, 97–99,
    104–5, 110, 126, 167–76,
    183–85, 190, 234n.104
  rituals of, 17, 21–24, 26–27, 33,
    44, 54, 57, 59, 63, 68, 73,
    79–81, 84, 102–3, 127, 133,
    151–52, 155–56, 158, 169
Propaganda Fide, 31, 58, 66–67, 120
Protestantism
  bias against Afro-Atlantic Catholics,
    51, 57, 77–78, 114, 122–23,
    152, 157, 165, 200
  bias against Catholicism, 2, 53,
    57–60, 109, 113–14, 122,
    142–44, 176, 181, 183–84, 194,
    196, 209
  conversion of Afro-Atlantic
    Catholics, 117, 122, 142,
    176–80, 183, 194, 196–99,
    202–3
  See also baptism; Black
    evangelicalism; Catechization;
    missionaries
purgatory, 20–22, 47, 73, 79, 84,
  103–4, 123–24, 155, 166, 192

Raboteau, Albert, 39, 200, 208
racism, 7, 28, 33–34, 130, 157, 169, 182, 200
Ramos, Arthur, 99, 101
Roboredo, Manuel, 70, 74
Rome. *See* Vatican
rosary
  as devotional object, 20, 28, 50, 52, 57, 59, 65, 79, 87–88, 100–101, 111, 154
  prayer, 25, 28–29, 47, 52, 57, 69, 72, 79, 90, 94, 104, 112, 126, 180, 188, 190, 201
  See also Virgin Mary
Rožmitál, Zdeněk Lev of, 21, 153

Saint-Domingue. *See* Haiti
Saint Kitts, 122, 126–27
saints
  devotion of, 15, 18–22, 32, 44, 46, 48–50, 53, 57, 62, 64, 72, 76, 80–81, 83, 87, 104, 111, 126, 131, 134, 158, 187–88, 196, 206
  in fraternities, 20, 24, 29, 32, 49, 58, 60, 101, 112, 126, 128, 185
Saint Amarus, 84
Saint Anthony, 22, 30, 32, 44, 53, 58–59, 71–72, 77, 80, 84, 86, 102–3, 111, 114, 134, 154
Saint Antonio da Noto of Caltagirone, 30, 216n.66
Saint Barbara, 152
Saint Benedict, 29–30, 102, 216n.66
Saint Blaise, 44
Saint Dominic, 126
Saint Francis, 72, 80, 84
Saint George, 33
Saint Gonçalo, 17, 86

Saint James the Greater, 29, 63, 86, 101, 134, 161
Saint John the Baptist, 22–23, 44, 48, 50, 84, 103, 111–12, 155, 201
Saint Joseph, 83–84, 119, 154, 158, 201
Saint Lucia/Lucy, 84, 112, 154
Saint Luke, 85
Saint Mary Magdalene, 84, 123
Saint Peter, 112
Saint Roch, 154
Saint Rose of Lima, 128
Saint Stephen, 23
  See also Virgin Mary; vows
Sandoval, Alonso de, 37, 39, 42, 55, 90, 95
São Tomé, and Príncipe, 4, 6, 35, 55–62, 65, 96–97, 138, 180, 187–88
Sarmento, Alfredo de, 3, 79–80
Savona, Cherubino de, 68, 71
Saxon, Andrew, 1–4, 163, 209
Saxon, Lyle, 154–56, 170
Seeman, Erik, 161–62
self-flagellation, 72–73, 156
seminaries, 39, 43, 45, 48–49, 59, 66
Senegambia. *See* Upper Guinea
Sensbach, Jon F., 117–18, 174
sermons. *See* preaching
slavery
  accommodation to, 30–31, 40, 92, 140, 167, 169, 174–75, 178–80
  African nations, 26–27, 32–33, 92, 95, 97–99, 103, 111, 113, 124–25, 130, 150–51, 158
  charter generations, 3–6, 36, 106–15, 121–22, 126–27, 129, 136–40, 145–47, 161–66, 176, 183, 209–10

slavery (*cont.*)
  escaping from, 1–2, 92–95,
    109, 103, 116, 124, 127,
    148–49, 163–64, 182,
    194–95, 203
  manumission, 28–29, 31, 40, 42,
    60, 96, 121, 131, 140, 144–46,
    148, 163, 174–75, 178–79,
    195, 203
  resistance against, 37, 96, 116, 122,
    125, 148, 150, 164, 168, 185,
    194, 209
  slave trade, 3–5, 25, 37–38, 40–43,
    52, 55, 60, 65, 67, 88, 108–9,
    120, 143, 194–95
  See also baptism; Catholic
  Church
Sobel, Mechal, 136–37, 141, 152–53,
  189
Society for the Propagation of
  the Gospel. *See* Anglican
  Church
Society of Jesus, 25–27, 32, 37, 43,
  66, 82–83, 91, 95, 110, 131,
  147, 180. *See also* missionaries
souls
  rituals for the deceased's soul,
    20–22, 46–47, 54–55, 59, 61,
    71, 73–76, 79, 84, 103, 118,
    152, 155, 201, 205
  tormented, 20–22, 47, 111
  See also funerals
South Carolina, 4, 148–49, 162–63,
  187, 189, 191–202, 209,
  250n.170
Souza, Marina de Mello e, 90, 101,
  173, 209
Soyo, 62, 65, 68, 72–73, 80, 96,
  120–21, 206

Spain
  colonialism, 4, 60, 93–94, 109,
    148–50, 194–95
  granting freedom to Catholic
    escapees, 109–10, 116, 127, 148,
    194–95
  language, 43, 74, 92, 100, 140–41,
    163, 240n.249
  slavery, 31, 40, 43
Spanish Negroes, 2, 124, 164
Spiritual churches, 157–58
Stuckey, Sterling, 168, 187
Stuyvesant, Petrus, 108–9, 137, 144,
  147
superstition, 16, 19–20, 22, 45, 52, 59,
  67, 72, 76–78, 82, 84, 87, 200
Suriname, 115–16, 182
Sweet, James, 147, 178
swords, 3, 24, 57, 64, 66, 80, 85,
  99–100, 134, 166–68, 170–71,
  173
syncretism
  in communities, 13, 40–43, 51–55,
    83, 140
  in languages, 41, 55, 106, 113,
    140–41
  in performances, 45. 61–62,
    84–85, 100–101, 124, 184
  in religions, 18–19, 32–33, 45–50,
    56–59, 61, 75–79, 92–94, 134,
    200

tabancas, 49–50, 153, 193
Tertre, Jean-Baptiste Du, 129–31
theater. *See* drama
Thornton, John K., 4, 6, 36, 38, 70,
  75–76, 78, 82, 88, 92, 145, 148,
  172, 174, 177
Truth, Sojourner, 202–3

Unity of Brethren. *See* Moravian
   Church
Upper Guinea, 25, 37–38, 40–41,
   50–55, 94–95, 107, 110,
   112–13, 150–51, 205

van Cortlandt, Jacob, 1–3
van Geel, Joris, 67, 72
Vatican, 25, 31, 64–67, 78, 120
Venezuela, 2, 92–93, 103, 105, 107,
   109–10, 188
Viaticum, 20–21, 103–4, 122–24,
   155
Vieira, António, 43, 94–95
Virgin Mary
   devotion to, 17, 21, 24–25, 27,
      32, 45, 57–59, 63, 69, 74,
      79–80, 83, 88, 91, 118–19,
      133–35, 148–49, 154, 176,
      199, 202, 206
   Our Lady Mediatrix of All Graces,
      53
   Our Lady of Atalaya, 33
   Our Lady of Carmel, 72
   Our Lady of Guadalupe, 29
   Our Lady of Light, 53
   Our Lady of Mercy, 20, 96–97
   Our Lady of Muxima, 83
   Our Lady of Nazareth, 68, 84
   Our Lady of Peñafrancia, 62

Our Lady of Pinda, 206
Our Lady of the Candles, 53
Our Lady of the Cape, 84
Our Lady of the Immaculate
   Conception, 71, 85
Our Lady of the Kings, 153
Our Lady of the Rosary
   —devotion to, 25, 28–29, 33,
      53, 73, 90, 101, 104 (*see also*
      prayers)
   —fraternities dedicated to, 13–14,
      27–30, 32, 47–48, 60–61,
      71–72, 82, 84, 95–98, 102, 131,
      176
Our Lady of Victory, 65
Saint Mary of the Snows, 32
Virginia, 138, 145–46, 164, 168,
   171, 179, 189–90
Vives, Juan Baptist, 66–67
Vodou, 133–34, 154–55
vows, 18, 21, 24, 32, 62, 87–88,
   102–3, 154, 166, 188, 192

Warri, 56–57
Whitefield, George, 183, 195–96

Young, Jason, 194, 199

Zulu Social Aid and Pleasure Club,
   158, 169–71

JEROEN DEWULF

is director of the Center for Portuguese Studies and professor
in the Department of German and Dutch Studies
at the University of California, Berkeley.
He is the author of a number of books,
including *The Pinkster King and the King of Kongo:
The Forgotten History of America's Dutch-Owned Slaves*
and *From the Kingdom of Kongo to Congo Square:
Kongo Dances and the Origins of the Mardi Gras Indians.*

CPSIA information can be obtained
at www.ICGtesting.com
Printed in the USA
LVHW081332130722
723393LV00004B/72